The Solar System

The Solar System

Volume 1
Antimatter – Infrared Astronomy
1-384

edited by
Roger Smith

SALEM PRESS, INC.
Pasadena, California   Englewood Cliffs, New Jersey

Original essays appeared in the following sets, edited by FRANK N. MAGILL: *Magill's Survey of Science: Space Exploration Series* (1989); *Magill's Survey of Science: Earth Science Series* (1990); *Magill's Survey of Science: Physical Science Series* (1992); new material has been added.

∞ The paper used in these volumes conforms to the American National Standard for Permanence of Paper for Printed Library Materials, Z39.48-1984.

Library of Congress Cataloging-in-Publication Data

The solar system / edited by Roger Smith
    p.   cm. — (Magill's choice)
Includes bibliographical references and index.
ISBN 0-89356-959-3 (set : alk. paper). — ISBN 0-89356-960-7 (v. 1 : alk. paper). — ISBN 0-89356-961-5 (v. 2 : alk. paper) ISBN 0-89356-962-3 (v. 3 : alk. paper)
1. Solar system. 2. Space astronomy I. Smith, Roger, 1953-   . II. Series.
QB501.S625   1998
523.2—dc21   97-51552
                                                                         CIP

First Printing

PRINTED IN THE UNITED STATES OF AMERICA

Contents

Publisher's Note

Since the early 1990's, advances in our knowledge of the solar system—from the astonishing images returned by the Hubble Space Telescope to the detailed close-ups of the Martian landscape transmitted by Sojourner during the Mars Pathfinder mission—have reinvigorated our interest in the solar system. *Magill's Choice: The Solar System* presents, in one three-volume source, the essential information about our solar system and the universal and cosmological forces that drive it. Here students and general readers will find the fundamental facts: about the planets, moons, comets, asteroids, Sun, and other bodies that form the solar system; about phenomena both familiar (eclipses and auroras) and invisible (the greenhouse effect, solar wind, magnetic fields); and about the methodologies—from telescopes to radio astronomy—that scientists use to investigate it.

Because our solar system literally does not exist in a vacuum, the editors have chosen to include coverage of topics that reach beyond our solar system yet cannot be separated from it: Stellar and galactic phenomena, cosmological theories, and techniques such as neutrino astronomy therefore are included here. Students may have wondered: How did our solar system, and our planet, form? What is the "big bang," and how do scientists explain the beginnings of the universe? Will it end? Are black holes real? Do planets outside our solar system exist? Could life have existed on Mars or the moons of Jupiter? The best scientific answers to those and other questions are summarized here in language that the general reader can understand.

Magill's Choice: The Solar System combines articles from three previously published Salem reference works in the Magill's Survey of Science series: the *Space Exploration Series* (1989), the *Earth Science Series* (1990), and the *Physical Science Series* (1992). From these publications, 131 of the most essential essays on both solar system and deep-space astronomy have been gathered, arranged alphabetically from "Antimatter" and "Asteroids" through "White Dwarf Stars" and "X-ray and Gamma-ray Astronomy." An additional nine essays, commissioned expressly for this publication, round out the contents list and bring it up to date: "Brown Dwarf Stars," "Eclipses," "Europa" (Jupiter's moon), "Extra-Solar Planets" (approximately a dozen have been detected so far), "Extraterrestrial Life in the Solar System" (exobiology), "Gravitational Lensing and Einstein Rings," "Nemesis and Planet X," "Quantum Cosmology," and "Telescopes: Space-Based" (with emphasis on the Hubble Space Telescope).

All essays have been written by experts and academicians in the field, and each essay is signed. The articles follow the familiar Magill format, dividing the discussion into sections for easy access to the information: Top matter lists the topic and its primary field or fields of study. The text of the 3,000- to 3,500-word essay then presents an "Overview" that defines the topic and its importance; following this primary information is a section identifying "Applications," "Methods of Study," or "Knowledge Gained," depending on the nature of the topic under discussion. The "Basic Bibliography" presents recommended resources for study. In addition, to each essay the editors have added a "Current Bibliography" which offers a select listing of publications appearing in the previous decade. Black-and-white photographs illustrate the text, and line drawings help to elucidate scientific concepts.

Several reference tools appear at the end of Volume 3. Terms central to the study of the solar system and the related disciplines of planetology, astronomy, and cosmology are defined in the Glossary. There follows a Categorized List of Essays, which places each article in all appropriate fields of study, from Astrophysics through Telescopes and Observational Techniques; the list allows users of this work to locate all articles significantly related to these arenas of study. Finally, a comprehensive Subject Index, listing pages containing significant discussion of personages, concepts, and methodologies, completes the volume.

The editors wish to thank Editor Roger Smith, who reviewed the essays, assisted in bringing them up to date, and identified new topics for inclusion. We also wish to thank the experts and academicians who contributed essays, often on highly technical topics, prepared with students and general readers in mind. A list of their names and academic affiliations begins on the following page.

List of Contributors

Stephen R. Addison
University of Central Arkansas

Arthur L. Alt
College of Great Falls

Michael S. Ameigh
St. Bonaventure University

Victor R. Baker
University of Arizona

Iona C. Baldridge
Lubbock Christian University

Thomas W. Becker
Webster University

Reta Beebe
New Mexico State University

Timothy C. Beers
Michigan State University

John L. Berkley
State University of New York College at Fredonia

Gary S. Blanpied
University of South Carolina

Larry M. Browning
South Dakota State University

Michael L. Broyles
Collin County Community College

David S. Brumbaugh
Northern Arizona University

Dennis Chamberland
Science Writer

D. K. Chowdhury
Indiana University and Purdue University at Fort Wayne

John H. Corbet
Memphis State University

Tom R. Dennis
Mount Holyoke College

Bruce D. Dod
Mercer University

Dave Dooling
D2 Associates

Steven I. Dutch
University of Wisconsin—Green Bay

John J. Dykla
Loyola University of Chicago

Dale C. Ferguson
Baldwin-Wallace College

David G. Fisher
Lycoming College

Richard R. Fisher
National Center for Atmospheric Research

Gerald J. Fishman
*National Aeronautics and Space Administration
Marshall Space Flight Center*

Dennis R. Flentge
Cedarville College

George J. Flynn
State University of New York College at Plattsburgh

John W. Foster
Illinois State University

Donald R. Franceschetti
Memphis State University

Roberto Garza
San Antonio College

Karl Giberson
Eastern Nazarene College

David Godfrey
National Optical Astronomy Observatory

Gregory A. Good
West Virginia University

Noreen A. Grice
Bentley College

Robert M. Hawthorne, Jr.
Independent Scholar

Paul A. Heckert
Western Carolina University

Paul Hodge
University of Washington

David Wason Hollar, Jr.
Rockingham Community College

Earl G. Hoover
Science Writer

Hugh S. Hudson
University of California, San Diego

Brian Jones
Science Writer

Richard C. Jones
Texas A&M University

Pamela R. Justice
Collin County Community College

Karen N. Kähler
Independent Scholar

Henry Emil Kandrup
Syracuse University

Christopher Keating
Independent Scholar

John P. Kenny
Bradley University

Firman D. King
University of South Florida

Richard S. Knapp
Belhaven College

Joel S. Levine
National Aeronautics and Space Administration Langley Research Center

James C. LoPresto
Edinboro University of Pennsylvania

George E. McCluskey, Jr.
Lehigh University

Linda McDonald
North Park University

Michael L. McKinney
University of Tennessee, Knoxville

V. L. Madhyastha
Fairleigh Dickinson University

David W. Maguire
C. S. Mott Community College

F. Curtis Michel
Rice University

Theresa A. Nagy
Pennsylvania State University

Divonna Ogier
Oregon Museum of Science and Industry

Steven C. Okulewicz
City University of New York, Hunter College

Satya Pal
New York Institute of Technology

Michael D. Papagiannis
Boston University

George R. Plitnik
Frostburg State University

Howard L. Poss
Temple University

Gregory J. Retallack
University of Oregon

Clark G. Reynolds
College of Charleston

Mike D. Reynolds
University of North Florida
NASA Teacher-in-Space Program

J. A. Rial
University of North Carolina at Chapel Hill

David M. Schlom
California State University, Chico

Stephen J. Shulik
Clarion University of Pennsylvania

R. Baird Shuman
University of Illinois at Urbana-Champaign

Paul P. Sipiera
William Rainey Harper College

Roger Smith
Willamette University

Joseph L. Spradley
Wheaton College, Illinois

Peter Culley Stine
Bloomsburg University of Pennsylvania

Peter J. Walsh
Fairleigh Dickinson University

Randii R. Wessen
Astronautics Unlimited

James L. Whitford-Stark
Sul Ross State University

J. Wayne Wooten
Pensacola Junior College

Clifton K. Yearley
State University of New York at Buffalo

Ivan L. Zabilka
Independent Scholar

The Solar System

Antimatter

Antimatter is a general name for a quantity of mass that is similar in many respects to ordinary matter. When antimatter is brought into contact with ordinary matter, however, the two annihilate each other, leaving only energy. On the microscopic level, antimatter refers to antiatoms made up of antiparticles. Each type of particle has a corresponding antiparticle. When a particle interacts with its antiparticle, both are annihilated, leaving only energy or other particle-antiparticle pairs. Particle–antiparticle pairs may be created from electromagnetic radiation.

Overview

Scientists believe that the universe is made almost exclusively of matter, rather than antimatter. This is a difficult assumption to test. A local mixture is not possible, but a galaxy made up of antimatter would differ in no observable way from one made of matter. If there were a rough balance of regions dominated by either matter or antimatter, occasional encounters would be expected. The interstellar dust and gas made up of matter would interact with the boundary of an antimatter region, resulting in annihilation reactions with the emission of high-energy photons (gamma rays). Observational limits on such photons are very low. Searches for antiparticles among the high-energy cosmic rays that penetrate the Earth's atmosphere are consistent with no incident antimatter; however, in 1997 a satellite observatory detected antimatter gushing from the center of the Milky Way. Antiparticles are produced in the interactions between these high-energy cosmic rays and the nuclei in the Earth's atmosphere. Despite this lack of antimatter in the present universe, there are theoretical reasons why the current excess of matter need not characterize the initial state of the universe. The fact that matter and antimatter are equivalent in almost every respect makes it appealing to assume that the early universe was formed of equal amounts of both. Thus, very early in the first second after the big bang, something is speculated to have happened to change the balance between particles and antiparticles. To understand the conditions in the early universe, one must turn to the study of elementary particles.

Using the duality of properties between waves and particles, everything in the universe can be described in terms of particles with quantum mechanical properties. One such property of all particles is called spin. One way of picturing spin is to imagine the particles as analogous to tops spinning about an axis, but this is misleading, since they cannot have a well-defined axis about which to spin. What spin does is to define what particles look like when they are viewed from different directions. Spin 0 looks the same from every direction, while other values require one to turn the particle through a certain angle in order to see a symmetric image. All particles can be divided into two groups, those of $\frac{1}{2}$ spin, which make up all of the matter that is observed in the universe, and those of spin 0, 1, and 2, which give rise to the forces between matter particles. All $\frac{1}{2}$ spin particles, which are called fermions, obey the Pauli exclusion principle. The spin 0, 1, and 2 particles are called bosons, and it is the exchange of virtual bosons that gives rise to the interaction between the fermions.

In 1928, Paul Adrien Maurice Dirac formulated the first theory that was consistent with the principles of quantum mechanics and with Albert Einstein's special theory of relativity. It explains mathematically why the electron had $\frac{1}{2}$ spin and predicted that the electron should have a partner, the antielectron or positron. The existence of the positron was confirmed in 1932. Even though Dirac's equation strictly applies only to fundamental $\frac{1}{2}$ spin particles, one finds that for every charged fermion and charged boson, there exists an antiparticle that has the same mass and spin as the particle. The electric charge and magnetic moment of the particle and the antiparticle are equal in magnitude but opposite in sign. The magnetic dipole moment can be thought of crudely as arising from small balls of electric charge spinning about an axis, acting like the classical array of a loop of current. The classical current loop gives rise to a magnetic field like that of a permanent magnet, and of a magnitude proportional to the current times the area of the loop. The fact that the neutrally charged neutron has a nonzero dipole moment is one indication that it is not a fundamental particle, but is instead made up of a combination of positively and negatively charged particles of zero net charge. A neutron and an antineutron with parallel spins have equal and opposite magnetic moments. If they have no magnetic or electric moment, particles may be self-conjugate (their own antiparticle), like the photon or the neutral pion (π^0), or they may have distinct antiparticles, like the neutrino (v). The intrinsic parity, the property of whether the particle is unaffected (even) or is reversed (odd), as viewed in a mirror, is the same for antibosons, but is the opposite for antifermions. Particle-antiparticle symmetry is not limited to individual particles, but because of the identity of the forces, it extends to nuclei, atoms, and perhaps worlds. Physicists have produced the nuclei of antideuterium and antitritium and the antihydrogen atom.

Individual bosons may appear or disappear, but fermions are generated or annihilated in particle-antiparticle pairs. This observation is included in the theory by requiring the conservation of baryons (protons, neutrons, antiprotons, antineutrons, and so on) and the conservation of leptons (electrons, muons, taus, and the different neutrinos).

The process of producing matter from electromagnetic radiation is best understood in terms of the quantum-mechanical picture of light. Two massless photons collide and disappear, putting all their energy and momentum into the production of two or more material particles. There is a threshold energy above which this process can happen. The pair of photons must have energy that is more than twice the rest mass energy of the particles (greater than $2mc^2$). Momentum must also be conserved in the process. Given enough energy, it is always possible to create any kind of particle–antiparticle pair in collisions of photons.

Matter and Antimatter

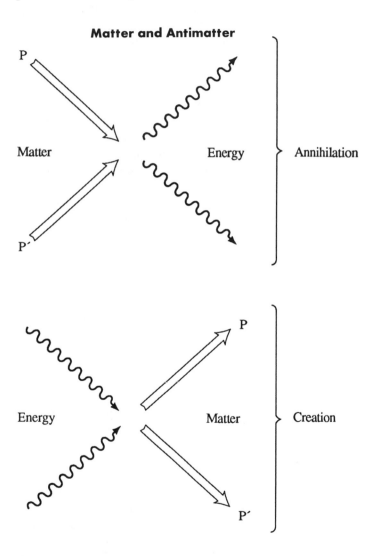

An elementary particle (P) and an antiparticle (P') may collide, annihilating each other and releasing energy (wavy arrows). The reverse may also occur, creating matter. Such collisions are relatively rare at the present stage of the universe's evolution.

Annihilation of a pair occurs in a variety of ways. For electron-positron pairs, the annihilation is mostly electromagnetic, and two photons are emitted. In the case of nucleon-antinucleon pairs, pi-mesons (π) are the most frequent product, along with some strange mesons. Electromagnetic annihilation into an electron-positron pair or two photons is rare.

The baryons are not fundamental particles, but are made up of fractionally charged quarks. The four of interest here are made from a combination of the quarks called "up" (u) and "down" (d) and their antiparticles ($\bar{u}, \bar{d}$). If the charge of the electron is denoted by $-e$, then the up quark has a charge of $+\frac{2}{3}e$, the down-quark has $-\frac{1}{3}e$, the antiup has $-\frac{2}{3}e$, and the antidown has $+\frac{1}{3}e$. The proton is composed of u u d, the neutron of u d d, the antiproton of $\bar{u}\,\bar{u}\,\bar{d}$, and the antineutron of $\bar{u}\,\bar{d}\,\bar{d}$.

The imbalance between matter and antimatter that is seen today is theorized to have happened shortly after the big bang. At one-millionth (10^{-6}) of a second, photons had enough energy to create nucleon-antinucleon pairs, $\bar{p}p$ or $\bar{n}n$. These processes are expected to yield exactly equal amounts of matter and antimatter. The difference started earlier, at a much higher temperature, when photons produced quark-antiquark pairs. At a time before 10^{-30} seconds, the balance was upset by forces that violated the conservation of charge symmetry and parity symmetry. These violating forces caused decay rates that favor particles over antiparticles. This is the era associated with the grand unified theories (GUTs). If this is indeed the case, then after 10^{-6} seconds, when the temperature of the radiation field was too low for the photons to have the threshold energy required to produce nucleon-antinucleon pairs, the antimatter would have annihilated with an equal quantity of matter. This was accomplished in the first second. At 10^{-6} seconds, there was a rough balance between photons and baryons. Today, there is one baryon per 1 billion photons. At 10^{-6} seconds, the excess of baryons to antibaryons would only have had to be this one part in 1 billion, and in this theory it is this difference that remains today.

Applications

The interaction of antimatter with matter continues to be an important subject in nuclear and particle physics. The fact that an antiproton has a negative charge makes it act like a heavy electron in atomic orbit. As it enters the field of an atom, it is captured in an excited bound state and then undergoes a series of transitions toward the atomic ground state. With each transition, a photon of increasing energy is released, the highest of which is in the X-ray region of the electromagnetic spectrum. When the atomic orbit of the antiproton overlaps the atomic nucleus, it is annihilated. In atomic hydrogen, this usually takes place at the lowest or first excited energy level. For heavier atomic nuclei, the annihilation takes place at higher atomic energy levels. From the observed X rays, one can measure aspects of the antinucleon-nucleon interaction other than the annihilation process.

Nuclear physicists also study the interaction of antiprotons of velocities between 20 and 90 percent of the speed of light with atomic nuclei. Topics of interest include elastic scattering, hyperon pair production (baryons that contain a strange quark), and annihilation into the many meson channels, including searches for exotic meson states in the annihilation debris. In annihilation reactions, one measures the interior regions of the nucleons that contain quarks. In scattering, one can learn about the virtual pion clouds that form the outer part of the nucleon. Some aspects of low-energy proton-antiproton annihilation seem to be well explained by a statistical thermodynamical description and may serve as small-scale versions of the quark-gluon plasma that existed shortly after the big bang.

Improvements in techniques for the collection of antiprotons in "magnetic bottles" have led to many new experiments with low-energy antiprotons. The most difficult experiment is the measurement of the gravitational attraction of the antiproton by the Earth. This experiment requires antiprotons that are much "colder" (slower) than the molecules that make up the air.

High-energy physicists use particle-antiparticle annihilation reactions in their search for new fundamental particles and other tests of the standard model. At collider-accelerator facilities, the charged particles are accelerated and kept in a closed orbit by steering magnetic fields, while the oppositely charged antiparticles are accelerated and steered into the same orbit in the opposite direction. The head-on collisions lead to annihilations that leave a large amount of concentrated energy that can be converted into new massive particles or into the fundamental particles that make up the nucleon. Experimental evidence for quarks and their exchange bosons, the gluons, are found in "jets" that follow high-energy electron-positron annihilations. These reactions are similar to the reactions that must have occurred after the big bang. The electron and positron annihilate and produce a quark-antiquark pair that leaves the interaction region back to back. The nature of the quarks does not allow them to be free from each other, so they in turn undergo a process called "hadronization," in which they produce other quark-antiquark pairs that re-form, creating both baryons and mesons. Each group of hadrons is called a jet. The sum of the linear momentum of all the particles in the jet is equal to the momentum of the original quark. Three-jet events have also been observed. These correspond to the creation of a quark-antiquark pair that interacts through the exchange of a gluon, which also undergoes hadronization, forming a jet of its own.

In 1983, the intermediate vector bosons (W^+, W^-, Z^0) of the weak interaction were discovered. International teams of scientists, one of which was led by Carlo Rubbia, used the antiproton-proton collider at CERN (European Laboratory for Particle Physics) in Switzerland. The experiment was made possible by a new technique of stochastic cooling developed by Simon van der Meer. Rubbia and van der Meer received the Nobel Prize in Physics in 1984. In these experiments, antiprotons are created in high-energy collisions with a metal target and are steered magnetically into a storage ring. On the average, one relatively low-energy antiproton is produced for every million high-energy protons that pass through the target. In 1983, it took about twenty-four hours to collect enough antiprotons in the storage ring. The antiprotons that are produced have a range of velocities. If this range is not somehow reduced, they will be lost long before twenty-four hours pass. The range can be reduced by either electron cooling or stochastic cooling.

Electron cooling is accomplished by passing a well-focused electron beam with a very small range of velocities beside the beam of particles that must be cooled. The electrons acquire some of the unwanted components of velocity and reduce the range of velocity of the beam. The stochastic technique developed by van der Meer uses feedback of the measurement of the unwanted components of velocity on one side of the orbit in the storage ring to a correction device across the diameter of the ring.

Context

The idea of genesis from the big bang came out of the observation of the Doppler shift of light from other galaxies. In 1929, Edwin Powell Hubble announced that the amount of the redshift for galaxies increases roughly in proportion to their distances. It appears that the universe is undergoing an explosion in which every galaxy is rushing away from every other galaxy, which is consistent with the idea of a common origin.

In 1965, radio astronomers Arno A. Penzias and Robert W. Wilson used the Bell Telephone Laboratory's 6-meter horn antenna to measure the radio noise coming from this galaxy. What they found instead was a diffuse background of electromagnetic radiation that was left over from a time shortly after the beginning of the universe. This background has an equivalent temperature of about 3 Kelvins and is consistent with a model of dense high-temperature photons that lose temperature as the universe expands. The observation of the amount of hydrogen in the universe is consistent with this model. The lack of antimatter in the universe and details about the early time after the big bang cannot be explained without the aid of the advances in particle physics that came out in the late 1960's. These advances include the quark model of hadrons, the unification of the theory of the electromagnetic and the weak interaction, and the grand unified theories and symmetry. These theories include the observed violations of charge symmetry and parity symmetry that are necessary to explain the lack of antimatter in the universe.

Techniques for producing, collecting, and trapping antiparticles continue to improve. The uses of low-energy positrons, antimuons, and antiprotons are increasing. Physicists can now detect the two photons that are released after positron annihilation in crystals, and they can determine the magnitude of the electric fields in crystals. Antimuons, which are positively charged and thus do not form bound states with atoms, are used to map out the magnetic fields in solids. Since there are no muons in ordinary matter, the antimuons move through the material for long distances. This technique of muon spin rotation and relaxation (μSR) is well established. Materials science studies of perovskites, which have relatively high superconductivity transition temperatures, have included μSR to probe the magnetic behavior of these superconductors. The list of things that can be done with bottled antiprotons is long. One idea under study is antihydrogen propulsion, a new form of space propulsion in which milligrams of antihydrogen are used to heat tons of reaction fluid to high temperatures. Improvements are needed in the generation efficiency of antiprotons, methods for converting antiprotons to antihydrogen, and techniques for cooling, trapping, long-term storage, and effective utilization of milligram quantities of antihydrogen.

Gary S. Blanpied

Basic Bibliography

Alfvén, Hannes. *Worlds: Antimatter in Cosmology.* Translated by Rudy Feichtner. San Francisco: W. H. Freeman, 1966. This book is not consistent with the present theories of antimatter, but it was read by many present-day physicists when they were students. It is still an enjoyable book, but some of the speculations should not be taken too seriously.

Carrigan, Richard A., Jr., and W. Peter Trower, eds. *Particles and Forces at the Heart of Matter: Readings from Scientific American Magazine.* New York: W. H. Freeman, 1990. Includes twelve articles with added postscripts and notes.

Carrigan, Richard A., Jr., and W. Peter Trower, eds. *Particle Physics in the Cosmos: Readings from Scientific American Magazine.* New York: W. H. Freeman, 1989. Interesting articles from *Scientific American.*

Cline, David B., ed. *Low Energy Antimatter: Proceedings of the Workshop on the Design of a Low Energy Antimatter Facility Held at the University of Wisconsin-Madison, October, 1985.* Singapore: World Scientific, 1986. Results of a conference of technical talks combined with speculations on future uses of antiprotons in science and technology.

Davies, Paul. *The Cosmic Blueprint: New Discoveries in Nature's Creative Ability to Order the Universe.* New York: Orion Productions, 1988. The author of *God and the New Physics* and *Superforce* advances an argument for the existence of a predestined universal plan. He discusses brain research, biological evolution, computers, and astrophysics. He argues that all matter and energy have the ability to self-organize according to common principles.

Hawking, Stephen W. *A Brief History of Time: From the Big Bang to Black Holes.* New York: Bantam, 1988. Hawking is one of the great minds of this century, and his first popular work explores the limits of knowledge of astrophysics and the nature of time and the universe. His research into black holes offers insights into the beginning of time.

Schramm, David N. "The Early Universe and High-Energy Physics." *Physics Today* 36, no. 4 (1983): 27. A good overview of a cosmologist's view of antimatter in the universe.

Weinberg, Steven. *The First Three Minutes: A Modern View of the Origin of the Universe.* New York: Basic Books, 1977. Still a wonderful book, this was the first great popular work to combine cosmology and particle physics. In the preface, Weinberg says he has written this book for the reader who is willing to puzzle through some detailed arguments but is not familiar with mathematics or physics.

Current Bibliography

Forward, Robert L. *Twenty-first Century Space Propulsion Study.* Edwards Air Force Base, Calif.: Astronautics Laboratory, 1990.
Nieto, Michael Martin. *The Arguments Against Antigravity and the Gravitational Acceleration of Antimatter.* Physics Reports 205. Amsterdam: North-Holland, 1991.
Taubes, Gary. "The Antimatter Mission." *Discover* 17, no. 4 (April, 1996): 72-80.
Tyson, Neil de Grasse. "Antimatter Matters." *Natural History* 105, no. 5 (May, 1996): 72-75.

Cross-References

The Big Bang, 32; Cosmology, 97; General Relativity, 302; Quantum Cosmology, 767.

Asteroids

Asteroids are the numerous small bodies in orbit around the Sun, primarily between Mars and Jupiter. They provide important clues to the nature and earliest history of the solar system, including the effect of their collisions on the surfaces of planets and moons.

Overview

Although the discovery of the first asteroid was accidental, it was not completely unexpected. In 1766, the German astronomer Johann Titius (1729-1796) found that the positions of the planets could be approximated very closely by a simple empirical rule: Add 4 to each number in the sequence 0, 3, 6, 12, 24, 48 . . . and divide the sum by 10 to obtain the planetary distances from the Sun in astronomical units (the distance from the Earth to the Sun is 1 AU), with the exception of the fifth entry, where an apparent gap occurs at 2.8 AUs. This rule was publicized by Johann Bode (1747-1826) and led to a search for a missing planet in the gap between Mars, at 1.5 AUs and Jupiter, at 5.2 AUs. On January 1, 1801, the Sicilian astronomer-monk Giuseppe Piazzi (1746-1826) accidentally discovered a moving object during a routine star survey. He named it Ceres, for the patron goddess of Sicily. Soon its orbit was calculated by Carl Friedrich Gauss (1777-1855) and, at 2.77 AUs, was found to conform closely to the Titius-Bode rule.

Since Ceres seemed to be too small to be a planet, the search continued, and in March of 1802, the German astronomer Heinrich Olbers (1758-1840) found a second small body at the same predicted distance. He named it Pallas. In 1803, Olbers proposed that meteorites come from an exploded planet near 2.8 AUs. This possibility led to a continuing search that resulted in the discovery of Juno in 1804 and Vesta in 1807, the latter by Olbers again. It took some time until a fifth small body was discovered in 1845, but by 1890, the total had reached three hundred. These bodies came to be called "asteroids," for their faint, starlike images. In 1891, the German astronomer Max Wolf (1863-1932) began using a long-exposure camera to detect asteroids, and over the next few years, some five hundred were revealed by their photographic trails. By 1984, the three thousandth asteroid had been numbered in the official catalog of the Institute of Theoretical Astronomy in Leningrad, after its orbit had been calculated and confirmed. Asteroids are usually referred to by number and name, such as 3 Juno or 1,000 Piazzia.

About one hundred newly numbered asteroids are cataloged each year, and recent sky surveys indicate as many as 500,000 asteroids large enough to appear on telescopic photographs.

Most asteroids are found in the asteroid belt, which extends from 2.1 to 3.4 AUs, about half are between 2.75 and 2.85 AUs. Asteroids revolve around the Sun in the same direction as the planets but tend to have more elongated orbits. Their orbits are inclined up to 30 degrees from planetary orbits, but they are more regular than comet orbits. The smallest asteroids are a few kilometers wide; the largest, 1 Ceres, about 1,000 kilometers wide. In 1867, the American astronomer Daniel Kirkwood (1814-1895) discovered gaps in the asteroid belt where relatively few asteroids are found. These so-called Kirkwood gaps occur where the asteroid orbits have periods that are simple fractions of the twelve-year period of giant Jupiter, resulting in their being affected by repeated gravitational forces called resonances. Such depletions occur, for example, at about 3.3 AUs (where the periods have a six-year, 1:2 resonance with Jupiter) and 2.5 AUs (a four-year, 1:3 resonance); other resonances, however, act to stabilize certain asteroids, such as the Hilda group at 4 AUs (2:3 resonance), which is named for 153 Hilda.

Some asteroids have orbits departing greatly from the main belt. In 1772, the French mathematician Joseph Lagrange (1736-1813) showed that points in Jupiter's orbit 60 degrees ahead of and behind the planet are gravitationally stable (1:1 resonance). In 1906, Max Wolf discovered the first so-called Trojan asteroid, 588 Achilles, at the Lagrange point 60 degrees ahead of Jupiter. Subsequent discoveries have revealed several hundred Trojan asteroids. Those ahead of Jupiter are named for Greek heroes, and those behind are named for Trojan heroes; there is one Greek spy (617 Patroclus asteroid) in the Trojan camp, and one Trojan spy (624 Hektor) in the Greek camp. Hektor is the largest known Trojan asteroid and the most elongated of the larger asteroids, at about 150 by 300 kilometers. At least two objects have orbits that extend beyond Jupiter: 944 Hidalgo, which may be a burnt-out comet nucleus, and 2060 Chiron, whose orbit extends beyond Saturn.

Some asteroids depart from the main belt over only part of their orbit. They include the Mars-crossing Amor group, with elongated orbits that carry them inside Mars' orbit but outside Earth's orbit, and the Earth-crossing Apollo group, which cross inside Earth's orbit. (The groups were named for their first examples, discovered in 1932.) Estimates indicate about thirteen hundred Apollos ranging in size from 0.4 to 10 kilometers with an estimated average Earth-collision rate of about one in 250,000 years. The closest known approaches were Hermes, in 1937, at about 780,000 kilometers, and 1566 Icarus, in 1968, at about 6 million kilometers. Smaller Apollos may be an important source of meteorites, and 100-meter objects capable of making a 1-kilometer crater strike Earth about every two thousand years. Aten-type asteroids are Earth-crossers with elliptical orbits smaller than Earth's. Some asteroids appear to be grouped in families that may be the fragments resulting from an earlier collision between asteroids.

The properties of asteroids are mostly determined by remote-sensing techniques used to study their reflected light and other radiation characteristics. More than five hundred asteroids have been studied by remote sensing, which has indicated compositions similar to those of meteorites. Comparison with reflected light from meteorites suggests several classes. The rare E-type asteroids have the highest albedo (23 to 45 percent reflection). They appear to be related to enstatite (a magnesium silicate mineral) chondrites and are concentrated near the inner edge of the main belt. About 10 percent of asteroids are S-type; they have relatively high albedos (7 to 23 percent) and are reddish in color. They appear to be related to stony chondrites, are found in the inner to central regions of the main belt, and they generally range in size from 100 to 200 kilometers. The largest S-type is 3 Juno, at about 250 kilometers, but much smaller Apollo asteroids are also in this category. A few asteroids in the middle belt are classified as M-type, since their reflected light (7 to 20 percent) shows evidence of large amounts of nickel-iron metals on their surface, like iron or stony-iron meteorites.

About three-quarters of all asteroids are C-type, with relatively low albedos (2 to 7 percent) and grayish colors similar to that of the Moon. They are found in the outer belt and among the Trojans, and they resemble the rare carbonaceous chondrite meteorites, containing water-bearing silicate and carbon-based minerals along with some organic compounds (about 1 percent). The largest asteroid, 1 Ceres, is in this category, and there is some evidence that it has a mixture of ice and carbonaceous minerals on its surface. Dark reddish, D-type asteroids are found in the same regions and have similar albedos. About 10 percent of asteroids remain unclassified and are designated as U-type. In general, asteroids with low-temperature volatile materials lie farther from the Sun, whereas those in the inner part of the main belt are richer in high-temperature minerals and show little evidence of volatile water and carbon compounds.

Many asteroids exhibit periodic variations in brightness that suggest irregular shapes and rotation. Their measured rotational periods range from about three to thirty hours. There is some evidence that S-type asteroids rotate faster than C-type asteroids but slower than M-type asteroids. Large asteroids (greater than 120 kilometers) rotate more slowly with increasing size, but small asteroids rotate more slowly with decreasing size, suggesting that large asteroids may be primordial bodies while smaller ones may be fragments produced by collisions. Calculations show that rotation rates longer than two hours produce centrifugal forces weaker than gravity, which indicates that loose debris can exist on the surface of even the fastest known rotating asteroid, the Apollo object 1566 Icarus, which has a 2.25-hour rotation rate. Studies of the polarization of light reflected from asteroids indicate that many do have dusty surfaces, and computer models suggest the possibility that larger asteroids have a deep layer of dust and rock fragments, or regolith, similar to that on the surface of the Moon. Those with diameters larger than 100 kilometers are believed to have undergone a process of differentiation in which heavier metals sank to the core, leaving a stony surface of lighter materials that was later pulverized by collisions to form a layer of dust.

Asteroid elongations can be estimated from the change in brightness, which can vary by a factor of three or more. Kilometer-scale asteroids have been observed with lengths up to six times greater than their width. Main-belt asteroids tend to be less elongated than Mars-crossers of the same size, perhaps because of more erosion from collisions in the belt. Asteroids larger than about 400 kilometers tend to be more nearly spherical, since their gravitational pressures exceed the strength of their rocky materials, causing deformation and plastic flow into a more symmetric shape. An asteroid's size occasionally can be determined quite accurately by timing its passage in front of a star. In a few cases, the light from such stars has been obscured more than once, suggesting that asteroids with satellites may exist. Some evidence indicates that the unusual Trojan asteroid 624 Hektor (150 by 300 kilometers) may be a dumbbell-shaped double asteroid.

The distribution of asteroid sizes and masses supports the idea that many have undergone a process of fragmentation. Typical velocities of encounter

Five of the Largest Asteroids Shown Relative to the Western U.S.

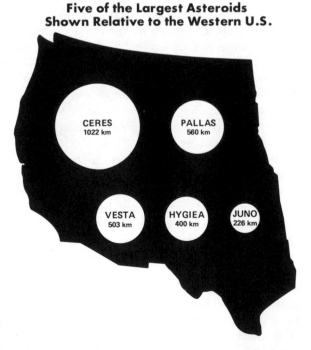

Source: Richard O. Fimmel, James Van Allen, Eric Burgess. *Pioneer: First to Jupiter, Saturn, and Beyond.* NASA SP-446. Washington, D.C.: National Aeronautics and Space Administration, 1980, p. 33.

of about 5 kilometers per second in the main belt are quite adequate to fragment most asteroids. Ceres contains nearly half the mass of all the asteroids, but it is more than three times smaller than the Moon and about fifty times less massive. About 80 percent of the total mass of all asteroids is contained in the four largest ones, and only about ten are larger than 300 kilometers. Studies suggest that the main belt was several times more massive in the past but that in the process of fragmentation, the smallest dust particles were removed by radiation pressure from the Sun.

Methods of Study

The Galileo space probe passed near enough to two asteroids to photograph them directly. For the most part, however, indirect methods of remote sensing must be used to determine their properties by studying the reflected light and other radiation that comes from their surfaces. These methods include photometry, infrared radiometry, colorimetry, spectroscopy, polarimetry, and radar detection. They can be augmented by comparative studies with meteorites, whose composition and structure can be analyzed by direct methods in the laboratory. Such methods include chemical, spectroscopic, and microscopic analysis, and processes of fragmentation can be studied by producing high-speed collisions between comparable materials in the laboratory. Such comparative studies must recognize various differences between meteorites and asteroids. The masses of only the three largest asteroids have been determined from their gravitational effects on other bodies; their densities are between 2.3 and 3.3 grams per cubic centimeter.

Photometry is the study of how light is scattered by various surfaces. The varying brightness of reflected sunlight from asteroids can be measured by photoelectric observations to determine their rotation periods and approximate shapes. One test of this method was made in 1931, when the Amor asteroid 433 Eros came close enough (23 million kilometers) for scientists to observe the tumbling motion of this elongated object (7 by 19 by 30 kilometers) and to confirm its 5.3-hour rotation. The size of an asteroid can be estimated from its brightness together with its distance, orbital position, and albedo. The albedo is important, since a bright, small object may reflect as much light as a dark, large object. Since a dark object absorbs more heat than a light object, albedos can be determined by comparing reflected light with thermal radiation measured by infrared radiometry. Photometric measurements also give information on surface textures. Colorimetry involves measuring the range of wavelengths in the reflected light to determine surface colors. Most asteroids are either fairly bright, reddish objects (with albedos of up to 23 percent) composed largely of silicate-type materials or grayish objects, at least as dark as the Moon (11 percent albedo), composed of carbonaceous materials.

Spectroscopy is the analysis of the spectrum of light and can be used to infer the composition of many asteroids. Optical and infrared reflectance spectra exhibit absorption bands at characteristic frequencies for given material. Asteroids' surface composition is determined by comparing their spectra with the spectra of light reflected from meteorites of known composition. Examples of this method applied to U-type asteroids include the identification of pyroxene (a silicate mineral) in the infrared spectrum of Apollo asteroid 1685 Toro and the matching of the surface of Vesta with a basaltic achondrite that resembles lava. Most asteroids appear to have unmelted surfaces with little or no evidence of lava eruptions. About two-thirds of the Trojans are D-type asteroids with no known meteorite counterparts because of their distance from Earth. Their spectra have been matched with the spectra of coal-tar residues, suggesting possible organic compounds.

Polarimetry uses measurements of the alignment of the vibrations of the reflected sunlight and its variation with direction to estimate albedos. Polarization measurements have also been interpreted as evidence for dust-covered surfaces, but they leave uncertainty about the depth of the dust layer. Radar observations of Eros during a close approach to Earth in 1975 were made at a wavelength of 3.8 centimeters and indicated that the surface must be rough on a scale of centimeters. Since optical polarimetry suggests that Eros is dusty, the radar results imply that the dust must be too thin to smooth rock outcrops of more than a few centimeters. Radar measurements also provide independent estimates of the size of Eros, confirming photometric estimates of its dimensions.

The best method to study asteroids would be by means of a space probe. When Pioneers 10 and 11 passed through the asteroid belt, scientists found that it has no more dust than any other part of the solar system. The Galileo probe encountered Gaspra in 1991 and Ida in 1993, both S-type asteroids. The probe determined the masses, sizes, and shapes.

Context

Asteroids usually cannot be seen with the unaided eye, but they provide important clues for understanding planet formation, and they can have major effects on the Earth and its history. At one time, it was assumed that the asteroid belt was formed by the breakup of a planet between Mars and Jupiter; however, the combined mass in the belt is much less than that of any planet (only 0.04 percent Earth's mass), and the observed differences in the composition of asteroids at different locations in the belt make it unlikely that they all came from the same planet-sized object. It now appears that asteroids are original debris that was left over after planet formation and that has undergone complex processes such as collisions, fragmentation, and heating. Apparently, the strong tidal forces caused by Jupiter's large mass prevented small bodies between it and Mars from combining to form a single planet in their region.

It appears, therefore, that asteroids are among the oldest objects in the solar system, left over from the time immediately before complete planet formation. Studies of these objects should provide clues to the structure and composition of the primitive solar nebula. The different types of asteroid

Asteroid Ida and its moon. *(National Aeronautics and Space Administration)*

found in different regions of space seem to support the theory of planetesimal origin through a sequence of condensation from a nebular disk around
the Sun. Asteroids farther from the Sun, beyond the main belt, may have
contained more ice; those that formed closer, within the belt, may have been
primarily stony or stony-iron materials. Some of these planetesimal precursors of asteroids were probably perturbed during close passes by neighboring planets into elongated Apollo-like orbits that cross Earth's orbit. Other
objects on similar orbits may have been comets that remained in the inner
solar system long enough to lose their volatile ices by evaporation. Processes
of collision and fragmentation among these objects provide direct evidence
about the earliest forms of matter.

Special interest in Apollo asteroids arises from their potential for Earth
collisions. Objects as small as 100 meters hit Earth about once every two
thousand years, and the 30 percent that fall on land can produce 1-kilometer
craters. Such impacts would devastate much wider areas by their shock
waves, and dust thrown into the upper atmosphere could have marked
effects on climate. Growing evidence suggests that asteroid collisions in the
past might have contributed to major extinctions of species, such as the
dinosaurs, and perhaps even caused reversals of Earth's magnetism. Thin
layers of iridium, often found in meteorites, have been identified in Earth's
crust at layers corresponding to such extinctions. Satellite photography has
revealed about one hundred apparent impact craters on Earth with diame-

ters up to 140 kilometers. It is likely that many more succumbed to processes of erosion. Knowledge of Apollo orbits might make it possible to avoid such collisions in the future.

Asteroids also offer the possibility of recovering resources with great economic potential. Some contain great quantities of nickel-iron alloys and other scarce elements; others may yield water, hydrogen, and other materials useful for space construction. Estimates of the economic value of a kilometer-sized asteroid reach as high as several trillion dollars. A well-designed approach to space mining might someday help to take pressure off Earth's ecosystem by providing an alternative to dwindling resources, and space-borne manufacturing centers might alleviate pollution on Earth.

Joseph L. Spradley

Basic Bibliography

Baugher, Joseph F. *The Space-Age Solar System.* New York: John Wiley & Sons, 1988. This book is an excellent and highly readable introduction to the solar system, with an emphasis on exploration and results from interplanetary spacecraft. An eight-page chapter on asteroids provides a good overview, supplemented by chapters on comets, meteorites, and species extinctions. A ten-page bibliography provides about five hundred references on planetary studies. The style of the book is suitable for high school and college-level readers.

Chapman, Clark R. *The Inner Planets.* New York: Charles Scribner's Sons, 1977. This book concentrates on the rocky inner planets; it includes a chapter on asteroids. The author is a leading expert on asteroids and planetary cratering. The book is written in an informal style with much anecdotal material about researchers in the field. Suitable for the general reader.

Delsemme, A. H., ed. *Comets, Asteroids, Meteorites.* Toledo, Ohio: University of Toledo, 1977. This book is the result of an international colloquium on the interrelations, evolution, and origins of comets, asteroids, and meteorites. It contains about seventy-five articles, including eighteen specifically on asteroids by leading experts. Although the text is quite technical, much of it can be read by college students interested in detailed information and a firsthand account of research results.

Gehrels, T., ed. *Asteroids.* Tucson: University of Arizona Press, 1979. The most authoritative and comprehensive book on asteroids available in English. It contains about fifty articles on every aspect of asteroid research, including extensive references to original research papers. Most articles are technical, but the first seventy-five pages provide a readable introductory survey. Tabulations in the last section provide data of various kinds on all asteroids that have been studied.

Hartmann, William K. *Moons and Planets.* Belmont, Calif.: Wadsworth, 1983. A college-level textbook on planetary astronomy by one of the leading authorities in the field. The chapter on asteroids is one of the best summaries at the introductory level. It has excellent charts, diagrams, and reproductions of the author's original paintings of imaginary space scenes. Additional material relating to asteroids is included in chapters on comets, meteorites, planetary evolution, and cratering. An appendix on planetary data includes some asteroid data for comparison, and an extensive bibliography includes about seventy entries on asteroids.

Veverka, Joseph. *Planetary Geology in the 1980s.* NASA SP-830-I. Washington, D.C.: National Aeronautics and Space Administration, 1985. This book is a summary of a report compiled by the Planetary Geology Working Group of NASA. It contains introductory chapters on planetary geology, a chapter on the geology of small bodies, and a chapter on remote sensing. The book concludes with recommendations for future research and some three hundred references on planetary geology. It is suitable for general readers with scientific interests.

Current Bibliography

Barnes-Svarney, Patricia L. *Asteroid: Earth Destroyer or New Frontier?* New York: Plenum Press, 1996.

Edberg, Stephen J., and David H. Levy. *Observing Comets, Asteroids, Meteors, and the Zodiacal Light.* New York: Cambridge University Press, 1994.

Editors of Time-Life Books. *Comets, Asteroids and Meteorites.* Alexandria, Va.: Time-Life Books, 1990.

Kowal, Charles T. *Asteroids: Their Nature and Utilization.* 2d ed. New York: Wiley, 1996.

Lewis, John S. *Rain of Iron and Ice: The Very Real Threat of Comet and Asteroid Bombardment.* Reading, Mass.: Addison-Wesley, 1996.

Cross-References

Astroblemes, 18; Meteorites: Achondrites, 539; Meteorites: Carbonaceous Chondrites, 548; Meteorites: Chondrites, 556; Meteorites: Nickel-Irons, 563; Meteorites: Stony Irons, 569; Meteors and Meteor Showers, 576.

Astroblemes

Space Age discoveries about the surface character of other terrestrial planets have led to the realization that the Earth must have been heavily scarred by impacts with planetesimals in the past. Erosion processes and plate tectonics have obliterated most of the ancient craters, but new interest in the phenomenon and evidence that major impacts may have had a significant role in shaping the course of evolution have spurred a search for astroblemes, circular surface features considered to have been large impact craters.

Overview

Impact cratering is one of the most fundamental geologic processes in the solar system. Craters are found on the surfaces of all the solid planets and satellites thus far investigated by spacecraft. Mercury and the Moon, bodies whose ancient surfaces have not been reworked by subsequent geologic processes, preserve a vivid record of the role that impact cratering has played in the past. It is inconceivable that the Earth somehow escaped the bombardment that caused such widespread scarring, or that it does not continue to be a target for planetesimals still roaming the solar system.

As recently as a quarter-century ago, only a handful of sites on the Earth were accepted to be of impact origin. Recently the number of confirmed astroblemes was well in excess of one hundred and increasing at the rate of several per year. In addition, there are many "probable" and "possible" impact features under study. Nevertheless, an enormous discrepancy exists between the number of identified or suspected impact sites on the Earth and the number that might be expected.

It is assumed that the flux of incoming bodies is the same for the Earth as it is for the Moon. Making allowances for the fact that the Earth is the largest "target" of any of the terrestrial planets and that two-thirds of its surface is covered by water, planetologists calculate that the land areas of the Earth should have been scarred by at least fifteen hundred craters of 10 kilometers or more in diameter. In actuality, only about half of the known astroblemes are in this size range. On a global scale, 99 percent of the predicted large impact craters seem to be missing. This statistic is not a valid indicator of the impact history of the Earth, however, because, although the impact phenomenon is a geographic process, the probability for discovering impact sites is strongly modified by the geologic stability of various regions of the Earth and by the intensity of the search programs in those areas. Roughly one-half of all the confirmed astroblemes have been found in Canada, which constitutes only 1 percent of the Earth's surface. In part, this is owing to the stability of the Precambrian rock of the Canadian Shield, but it also reflects a diligent research effort by Canada's Department of Energy, Mines, and Resources. In general, the number of large impact sites found in the well-explored areas of the Earth agrees with the accepted rate of crater formation on the other terrestrial planets in the past two billion years.

The obvious difference between the surface appearances of the Earth and Moon is explained not by any difference in the rate at which impact craters have formed, but in the rate at which they are destroyed. Most of the numerous craters on the Moon are more than 3.9 billion years old, while the Earth's oldest surviving astroblemes were formed less than 2 billion years ago. Studies have shown that erosion effectively removes all traces of a 100-meter (diameter) crater in only a few thousand years, and that a 1-kilometer-wide crater, such as the well-known Barringer Meteor Crater in Arizona, will disappear within a million years. Only craters with diameters greater than 100 kilometers can be expected to leave any trace after a billion years of erosion. This explains not only the absence of widespread cratering on the landscape but also the fact that, among the astroblemes known to exist, medium and large scars are more common than small ones.

Significant craters can be produced only by objects having masses of hundreds of thousands to billions of tons. The Barringer Crater, 1.2 kilometers wide and 200 meters deep, is believed to have been formed by a one-million-ton planetesimal that was perhaps 50 meters in diameter. A 27-kilometer-wide astrobleme known as Ries Crater in West Germany required an impacting body greater than 1 kilometer in diameter with a mass in excess of 1 billion tons. Planetesimals as large as these two examples are not characteristic of the vagrant meteors that wander through the solar system and occasionally streak into the Earth's skies as shooting stars.

Most of the past impacts on the Earth and the Moon appear to be attributable to a family of asteroids known as the Apollo-Amor group (after two specific members of the family). Members of this group are in orbits that graze the Earth's orbit and become subject to orbital perturbations that lead them across the Earth's path periodically. It is estimated that the average Apollo-Amor object intersects the Earth's orbit once every five thousand years, although usually the planet is at some other point on its orbit when this happens. The probability of a collision between the Earth and any given Apollo-Amor object is small, but several studies have shown that this family contains between 750 and 1,000 asteroids larger than 1 kilometer in diameter. Statistical analysis suggests that such monsters must collide with the Earth an average of once every 600,000 years.

The number of Apollo-Amor objects of a given size seems to follow an inverse-square relationship, leading scientists to believe that there are some 100,000 members of the family of at least 100 meters in diameter. Collisions with bodies of this size can be expected once every twenty-five centuries, although two out of every three of these bodies probably strike the ocean. The inverse-square relationship also suggests that there may have been at least a few members of the group as big as 100 kilometers in diameter, and the surface of the Moon bears testimony to long-ago impacts with objects of that size. None of the Apollo-Amor asteroids known today is close to this big, so it may be that all of those in this size range have already impacted and no longer pose a threat.

Impact events involve tremendous transfers of energy from the incoming planetesimal to the Earth's surface. A projectile's energy of motion increases only linearly with its mass but as the square of its velocity, so surprisingly large craters result from relatively small bodies traveling at hypervelocities. Depending on the directions of motion of the Earth and of the planetesimal, impacts on the planet may involve relative velocities as high as 50 kilometers per second. At velocities surpassing 4 kilometers per second, the energy of the shock wave created by the impact is far greater than the strength of molecular adhesion for either the planetesimal or the Earth, so that on impact the planetesimal acquires the properties of a highly compressed gas and explodes with a force equivalent to a similar mass of blasting powder.

The shock wave from this explosion intensely compresses the target material and causes it to be severely deformed, melted, or even vaporized. (In all but the smaller impacts, the entire projectile is also vaporized.) The shock wave swiftly expands in a radial fashion, pulverizing the target material and intensely altering the nature of the target rock by extreme and almost instantaneous heat and pressure. This is immediately followed by decompression and what is called a rarefaction wave that restores the ambient pressure. The rarefaction wave moves only over free surfaces, so it travels outward over the ground surface and into the atmosphere above the impact and becomes the excavating force that lifts vast quantities of the pulverized target material upward and outward to create the crater cavity.

The rarefaction wave excavates a hole whose depth is one-third of its diameter and whose profile follows a parabolic curve, but this depression is short-lived and is therefore called the transient cavity. After the passage of the rarefaction wave, a large amount of pulverized target material from the walls of the transient cavity slumps inward under gravity, and some of the ejecta lofted straight up into the atmosphere falls back into the excavation. Together, these sources contribute to a lens-shaped region of breccia that fills the true crater's floor and leaves a shallower, flat-floored apparent crater as the visible scar of the impact. Apparent craters generally exhibit a depth of only one-tenth to one-twentieth of their diameters. Meanwhile, the rarefaction wave carries ejecta particles outward over the surrounding landscape, where they fall to the Earth as a blanket of regolith that is distinguishable from the local target rock by the effects of shock metamorphism.

Methods of Study

Impact phenomena are rare enough on the human time scale that no crater-forming events are known to have occurred in recorded history.

Owing to this passage of time, and to the fact that most existing astroblemes have been severely altered by erosion, impact cratering has been studied by the unique modifications that a powerful impact shock makes in the rocks and minerals at the site, by the deformation and structural damage to buried strata, and by the presence of certain rare elements and minerals in the sediments surrounding suspected impact sites.

Much attention has been given to the effects of the shock wave on terrestrial rocks, since shock metamorphism is considered to be the most enduring and positive identifier of ancient astroblemes. Shock metamorphism differs from endogenic metamorphism by the scales of pressure and temperature involved and by the very short duration of the exposure to those pressures and temperatures. Endogenic metamorphism usually involves pressures of less than 1 gigapascal (100,000 atmospheres) and temperatures not greater than 1,000 degrees Celsius. The pressures involved in shock metamorphism are exponentially greater, reaching several hundred gigapascals for an instant in the vicinity of the impact. Rock exposed to pressures in excess of 80 gigapascals and temperatures of several thousand degrees Celsius is immediately vaporized. Lesser pressures and temperatures at increased distances from the point of impact produce signs of melting, thermal decomposition, phase transitions, and plastic deformation.

Pockets of melt glass up to several meters thick are commonly found in the breccia within the crater, indicating that pressures there reached 45-60 gigapascals. Coesite and its denser relative, stishovite, are forms of quartz that occur naturally only at impact sites. Shatter cones, conically shaped crystals created at pressures of from 2 to 25 gigapascals, are another prominent feature of shock metamorphism and are particularly well developed in fine-grained isotropic rock. Microscopic examination of impact-shocked porous rock reveals that quartz grains are deformed so as to fill the pores and interlock like the pieces of a jigsaw puzzle. Even at a considerable distance from the impact point, quartz grains tend to be elongated in the direction of the shock wave's passage.

Theories concerning cratering dynamics can also be tested by analogy to some of the craters produced by the detonation of nuclear devices. This latter technique has adequately explained the morphology of the smaller astroblemes, those with diameters that do not exceed 2-4 kilometers. Larger impact events involve additional dynamics that are not mimicked by nuclear devices thus far tested. Astroblemes greater than 2 kilometers in diameter in sedimentary rock or 4 kilometers in diameter in crystalline rock display a pronounced central uplift owing to an intense vertical displacement of the strata under the center of the impact. An additional feature distinguishing complex craters is that their depths are always a much smaller fraction of their diameters than is the case with simple craters.

Photographic imaging of the Earth from space has revealed some young and well-preserved astroblemes in remote and poorly explored areas of the Earth, such as the Sahara Desert. More important has been the satellite's ability to reveal structures that still preserve a faint but distinct circularity when seen from orbit, although at ground level they are so eroded that their circularity has escaped detection. One of the largest astroblemes yet discovered was found from Landsat satellite images in this way. New imaging technologies, including advanced radar and sonar mapping, promise to extend the capabilities of space surveillance and remote sensing in recognizing possible impact sites.

Context

The degree to which the Earth is in danger of being struck by a massive planetesimal began to be appreciated about the middle of the twentieth century. In 1980, a team led by Nobel physicist Luis Alvarez announced dramatic evidence suggesting that an asteroid impact that occurred 65 million years ago created such planetary trauma that it might explain a mysterious massive extinction of life-forms known to have occurred on the Earth at that time. At several sites around the world, the researchers had discovered that the sediments at the boundary layer between the Cretaceous and Tertiary periods contained up to one hundred times the normal abundance of the metal iridium, which is rare in the crustal rocks of the Earth but 1,000 to 10,000 times more abundant in the makeup of many asteroids. This Cretaceous-Tertiary boundary layer is coincident with the point at which fully 70 percent of the life-forms then existing on the Earth, including the dinosaurs, became extinct. Further study has also revealed that this same sediment layer is rich in shock-metamorphosed quartz grains, known only to occur naturally from impact explosions.

Debate continues as to whether an asteroid impact was the primary cause of the mass extinctions at the close of the Cretaceous period or merely a contributing factor, but there is general agreement that a colossal impact occurred at that time. The volume of material represented in the boundary sediments suggests that the planetesimal was perhaps 10 kilometers in diameter and would have created a crater of as much as 200 kilometers in width. An astrobleme in the Gulf of Mexico near Belize, called the Chicxulub crater, closely fulfills these criteria. Many scientists accept it as the impact site for the K-T (German for Cretaceous-Tertiary) event, although the precise scenario is not known. Meanwhile, several other iridium spikes (abnormally high concentrations of the metal) have been found in the sedimentary beds coinciding with other recognized mass extinctions.

Three related discoveries suggest the possibility that impact cratering may not be an entirely random process, so far as its distribution through time is concerned. Paleontologists David Raup and J. John Sepkoski, Jr. have shown evidence based on a rigorous analysis of the marine fossil record that mass extinctions appear to occur with regularity every 26 million years. Independently, the team of Walter Alvarez (also a member of the team that discovered the K-T iridium anomaly) and Richard Muller have discovered evidence that the ages of the major known terrestrial astroblemes seem to be periodically distributed at intervals of roughly 28 million years. For some time, researchers have sought a mechanism that could account for the numerous polarity reversals in the Earth's magnetic field over geologic history, and some have suggested that major impact events may be the cause. Several studies have reported an apparent fine-scale periodicity in the Earth's magnetic field reversals with a cycle of 30 million years. Although the intervals are not in perfect agreement, they are very close, considering the difficulty of precisely dating extinctions and the exact ages of astroblemes.

These discoveries suggest that there may be an as yet undiscovered member of the solar system which moves in such a way as periodically to disrupt the Oort Cloud, the cloud of comets believed to exist on the fringes of the solar system, causing a barrage of planetesimals to descend upon the inner planets. Although the existence and location of such a body remain speculative and controversial, it has been characterized as a dwarf companion star of the Sun and is called Nemesis.

Richard S. Knapp

Basic Bibliography

Grieve, Richard A. F. "Terrestrial Impact Structures." *Annual Review of Earth and Planetary Science* 15 (1987): 245-270. A thorough summary of what is known about the cratering process on the Earth, written by a leading authority on the subject. It is intended for the scientific reader, but its illustrations, extensive bibliography, and the introductory and summary sections of the text are of value even to those who are not familiar with the concepts and terminology in the body of the article.

Hartmann, William K. "Cratering in the Solar System." *Scientific American* 236 (January, 1977): 84-99. A comprehensive explanation of the role attributed to impact cratering in shaping the surfaces of all of the terrestrial planets. The author explains the basis for estimating the frequency of impacts for various sizes of planetesimals and the logic behind using crater counts to estimate the ages of planetary surfaces. The article also explains the theory that the first half-billion years of solar system history involved an extremely heavy bombardment of all the inner planets.

Kerr, Richard A. "When Disaster Rains Down from the Sky." *Science* 206 (November 16, 1979): 803-804. Written in descriptive terms easily comprehended by laypersons, this article summarizes research by several investigators attempting to compute the frequency with which the Earth is struck by crater-forming bodies. It places particular emphasis on the Apollo asteroid group and examines suggestions that the Apollo family is supplied with new planetesimals by the decay of former comets.

Morrison, David, and Tobias Owen. *The Planetary System*. Reading, Mass.: Addison-Wesley, 1987. With this single source, the subject of impact cratering can be studied in its broader context, as a major surface-shaping phenomenon throughout the solar system. Written as an introductory textbook for a descriptive undergraduate course in planetary science, it is readable, well illustrated, and up to date.

Muller, Richard. *Nemesis: The Death Star.* New York: Weidenfeld & Nicolson, 1988. Despite its tabloid title, this is an excellent discussion of the chain of discoveries leading to the Nemesis theory by the Berkeley physicist who developed it. Organized in two parts, the first recaps the evidence for a major impact at the K-T boundary, and the second tells how further research led Muller to postulate the existence of Nemesis. The book is intended for lay readers and gives insight into how the scientific discovery process works, as well as explaining the theory.

Murray, Bruce, Michael C. Malin, and Ronald Greeley. *Earthlike Planets.* San Francisco: W. H. Freeman, 1981. Although terrestrial impact craters are not specifically discussed, the impact mechanics that produce craters are presented here in terms that are suitable for general readers. It is also an excellent discussion of cratering as a ubiquitous aspect of the surfaces of all the inner planets.

Raup, David M. *The Nemesis Affair.* New York: W. W. Norton, 1986. The author is a significant figure in the field of paleontology and has done leading research on the apparent periodicity of extinctions and magnetic reversals. His narrative is a fascinating personal account of the ideas and the individuals who led the scientific community from extreme skepticism to general acceptance that impact "catastrophism" may have played a major role in the Earth's evolution and its life-forms.

Wetherill, George W. "Apollo Objects." *Scientific American* 240 (March, 1979): 54-65. A clearly written explanation of the role that the family of near-Earth asteroids is believed to have in causing impact cratering on the Earth, the Moon, Mars, and Venus. The discussion contains good information on the problems of determining the number of Apollo asteroids and the frequency with which the Earth and other terrestrial planets are hit.

Current Bibliography

Consolmagno, Guy. *Worlds Apart: A Textbook in Planetary Sciences.* Englewood Cliffs, N.J.: Prentice-Hall, 1994.

Elder, John. *The Structure of the Planets.* Orlando: Academic Press, 1987.

Encrenaz, Therese. *The Solar System.* 2d ed. New York: Springer, 1995.

Hartmann, William K. *Moons and Planets.* 3d ed. Belmont, Calif.: Wadsworth, 1993.

Teisseyre, R., J. Leliwa-Kopystynski, and B. Lang, eds. *Evolution of the Earth and Other Planetary Bodies.* New York: Elsevier, 1992.

Cross-References

Asteroids, 9; Meteorites: Achondrites, 539; Meteorites: Carbonaceous Chondrites, 548; Meteorites: Chondrites, 556; Meteorites: Nickel-Irons, 563; Meteorites: Stony Irons, 569; Meteors and Meteor Showers, 576.

Auroras

Auroras, the northern and southern lights, are caused by geomagnetic activity taking place in the Earth's atmosphere. By understanding auroras, scientists can gauge the effects of solar activities on the Earth's environment.

Overview

"Aurora" is a general term for the light produced by charged particles interacting with the upper reaches of the Earth's atmosphere. The term "aurora borealis" specifically refers to the northern dawn, or northern lights; "aurora australis" refers to the southern lights. The aurora appears in an oval girdling the Earth's geomagnetic poles, where the field lines are perpendicular to the surface. In this region, the Earth is not shielded from the space environment as it is at lower latitudes (where the field lines are almost parallel to the surface); thus, electrons and ions moving along magnetic field lines can strike the atmosphere directly. Normally, the auroral oval is located about 23 degrees from the north magnetic pole and 18 degrees from the south magnetic pole. Because the north magnetic pole is located in Greenland, the oval is offset toward Canada and away from Europe. Generally, the auroras appear at altitudes between 100 and 120 kilometers high, in sheets 1 to 10 kilometers thick and several thousand kilometers long.

The auroral oval is a product of the Earth's magnetic field and is driven by the Sun's output of charged particles. The oval can be enlarged as far north or south as 20 degrees latitude; its normal range is around 55-60 degrees. These variations in range and intensity have been correlated with sunspots, showing that solar activity is the engine that drives the aurora and other geomagnetic disturbances. Additionally, scientists usually describe auroral activity in terms of local time relative to the Sun rather than the geographic point over which it occurs. Thus, the Earth can be considered to be rotating beneath the auroral events (even though the shape of the oval remains skewed). The first indication that the aurora might be linked to solar activity came in 1859, when Richard Carrington observed an especially powerful solar flare in white light. A few hours later, he observed a strong auroral display and suspected that the two might be linked.

Auroras are caused by electron precipitation: Electrons "rain" on the upper atmosphere from this field-aligned current. The analogy is limited, as rain falls at random, while electrons moving in a magnetic field do so in a

A view of Earth showing an aurora. *(National Aeronautics and Space Administration)*

helix wrapped around a field line, somewhat like the rifling of a gun barrel. The helix of electrons trapped in the Earth's magnetic field will become more pronounced as they approach the poles, until finally their direction is reversed (at the "mirror point") and they are reflected back to the opposite pole. Motion back and forth is quite normal.

If the electrons are accelerated into the ionosphere, they encounter oxygen atoms (from molecules dissociated by sunlight) and nitrogen molecules. These collisions will release *Bremsstrahlung* (braking) X rays, which are absorbed by the atmosphere or radiated into space. The oxygen is ionized (and an electron freed) and radiates light when it is neutralized by a free electron. Nitrogen either is excited and radiates when it returns to the "ground" state or is dissociated and excited.

The aurora has been compared to a television picture tube: The face of the tube has been relatively simple to understand, but the circuitry that drives the display remains elusive. As the atmosphere fades gradually into space, starting at about 60 kilometers above the surface of the Earth, it forms an electrified layer called the ionosphere, where oxygen and nitrogen molecules are dissociated by sunlight. Because many of these free atoms and molecules are also ionized by sunlight, electric fields and currents move freely, although the net electrical charge is zero.

The structure of the aurora varies widely. Three major forms have been discerned: quiet (or homogeneous) arcs, rayed arcs, and diffuse patches. Homogeneous arcs appear as "curtains" or bands across the sky. They sometimes will occur as pairs or (rarely) sets of parallel arcs and have also been described as resembling ribbons of light. The lower edge of the arc will be sharply defined as it reaches a certain density level in the atmosphere, but the upper edge usually simply fades into space. Pulsating arcs vary in brightness, as energy is pumped in at different rates. Also in the category of quiet arcs are diffuse luminous surfaces, which are like clouds and have no defined structure; they may also appear as a pulsating surface. Finally, the weakest homogeneous display is a feeble glow, which actually is the upper level of an auroral display just beyond the horizon.

Auroras with rays appear as shafts of light, usually in bundles. A rayed arc is similar to a homogeneous arc but comprises rays rather than evenly distributed light. The formation and dissipation of individual rays may produce the illusion that rays are moving along the length of a curtain. Among rayed arcs, the "drapery" most resembles a curtain and is most active in shape and color changes. If the viewer is directly below the zenith of an auroral event, then it appears as a corona, with parallel rays appearing to radiate from a central point. Drapery displays are often followed by flaming auroras that move toward the zenith.

A controversial aspect of auroras is whether they produce any sound. Many observers, from antiquity, have reported "hearing" the aurora; however, sensitive sound-recording equipment has yet to capture this sound. This leaves open the question whether the sound is a psychological perception, an electrostatic discharge, or some other phenomenon.

The colors of the aurora—pink, red, green, and blue-green—are distinct and correspond with specific chemistry rather than being a continuous spectrum typical of a uniformly hot body (such as the Sun). Major emissions come from atomic oxygen (at 557.7 and 630 nanometers wavelength) and molecular nitrogen (391.4, 470, 650, and 680 nanometers). These emissions come from distinct altitudes. The green oxygen line (557.7 nanometers), which peaks at 100 kilometers altitude, is caused by an energy state that decays in 0.7 second. The red oxygen line (630 nanometers), which peaks at about 300 kilometers, comes from an energy state that decays in 200 seconds. While oxygen is energized to this level at lower altitudes, its energy will be lost to collisions with other gases long before it can decay naturally. From such comparisons, geophysicists were able to deduce some of the vertical structure of the atmosphere. X rays and ultraviolet light are also emitted but cannot be detected from the ground. The Dynamics Explorer 1 satellite has recorded the aurora at 130 nanometers in hundreds of images taken several Earth radii above the North Pole.

The brightness of the aurora can vary widely. Four levels of international brightness coefficients are assigned, ranging from IBC I, which is comparable to the brightness of the Milky Way, to IBC IV, which equals the illumination received from a full moon. Auroras usually are eighty times brighter in atomic oxygen than in ionized nitrogen molecules, indicating their origins higher in the atmosphere. Doppler shifting is commonly recorded in the spectra around 656.3 nanometers (hydrogen-alpha), indicating the motion of protons that are neutralized and reionized as they accelerate up or down the field lines. It is theorized that, as with many natural effects, only a small fraction (about 0.5 percent) of the energy that goes into the auroras actually produces light. The remainder goes into radio waves, ultraviolet rays, and X rays, and into heating the upper atmosphere.

Single images from the Dynamics Explorer satellite have confirmed the indication by ground-based camera chains that the aurora is uneven in density and brightness. One image for example, shows that the auroras thin almost to extinction on the dayside but expand to several hundred kilometers in thickness between about 10:00 P.M. and 2:00 A.M. local time. "Theta" auroras have been recorded in which a straight auroral line crosses the oval in the center, giving the appearance of the Greek letter θ. This phenomenon may be caused by the splitting of the tail of the plasma sheet (which extends well into the tail of the magnetosphere) or by the solar wind's magnetic field when it has a direction opposite the Earth's.

Imagery by the spin-scan auroral imagers aboard the Dynamics Explorer 1 satellite showed that auroral substorms start at midnight, local time, and expand around the oval. Observations of hundreds of substorms showed that they have the same generalized structure but that no two are alike. The satellite imager also showed expansions and contractions in the aurora in response to changes in the interplanetary magnetic field and in the solar wind. As the solar wind—which is simply a plasma—meets the Earth's magnetosphere, a shock wave is formed, and the wind is diverted around the Earth. This diversion compresses the Earth's magnetic field on the sunward side, while it extends like a comet's tail on the nightside. When the field of the solar wind is oriented toward the south, its field lines reconnect with the field lines of the Earth and allow protons (free hydrogen nuclei) and electrons to enter the magnetosphere (they are normally blocked when the field is oriented to the north).

Auroral activity is strongly driven by the solar wind. If the magnetic field of the wind points north—aligned with the Earth's magnetic field—then the auroral oval is relatively small, and its glow is hard to see. When the solar wind's magnetic field reverses direction, a substorm occurs. The oval starts to brighten within an hour, and bright curtains form within it. At its peak, the oval will be thinned toward the noon side and quite thick and active on the midnight side. As the storm subsides, about four hours after the field reversed (actually, as it starts to revert to normal), the aurora dims and curtains form. Finally, a large, diffuse glow covering the pole may be left as the field becomes stronger in the northward direction.

The flow of the solar wind past the magnetosphere generates massive electrical currents, which flow mostly from one side of the magnetosphere to the other. Some of the currents, however, connect down the Earth's magnetic field, into and through the auroral oval. Because an electric current is caused by the flow of charged particles (electrons in this case), in the process, electrons are brought directly into the ionosphere around the poles. The primary currents enter around the morning side and exit around the evening side. Secondary currents flow in the opposite direction. Changes in the electrical potential of the magnetosphere, as when it is pumped up by particles arriving in the solar wind, will force the electrons through the mirror point; they are then accelerated deeper into the ionosphere. This auroral potential structure, as it is called, is thin but extends around the auroral oval for thousands of kilometers, even to the point of closing on itself.

Electrojets also form in the auroras at low altitudes from an effect known as "E-cross-B drift" (written $E \times B$). At high altitudes, electrons and protons flow freely because there is a low gas density and no net current change. At lower altitudes, around 100 kilometers, the protons are slowed by collisions with atoms and molecules, but the electrons continue to move unopposed. The result is a pair of electrojets, eastward (evening) and westward (morning), which flow toward midnight, then cross the polar cap toward noon. These electrojets heat the ionosphere, especially during active solar periods, when the aurora is more intense.

This $E \times B$ drift in the auroral ovals appears to be a major source of plasma for the magnetosphere. It appears that the ions (which are positively charged) are accelerated upward along the same magnetic field lines where electrons (negatively charged) precipitate. Hydrogen, helium, oxygen, and nitrogen make up this ion flow. Each has the same total energy, so their paths vary according to mass. The net effect is that of an ion fountain blowing upward from the auroras then spread by a wind across the poles.

A little-known subset of the aurora is the sub-auroral red (SAR) arcs, which appear at the midlatitudes; the magnetic field lines on which they occur are different from those on which auroras appear. SAR arcs always emit at 660 nanometers (from oxygen atoms) and are dim and uncommon. Modern instrumentation has shown that the SAR arcs are a separate phenomenon from the polar auroras. These arcs may be caused by cold electrons in the plasmasphere interacting with plasma waves or with energetic ions. SAR arcs are believed to originate at approximately 19,000-26,000 kilometers altitude during especially strong geomagnetic storms, although the arcs themselves appear at altitudes around 400 kilometers as the energy from the storm leaks or is forced downward.

The aurora also appears in the radio spectrum. Studies in the twentieth century showed that the aurora could be sounded by radar at certain frequencies. Satellites in the 1970's started recording bursts of energy in the low end of the AM radio spectrum. This radiation is called auroral kilometric radiation (AKR), because its wavelength is up to 3 kilometers, reflected outward by the ionosphere. Such bursts can release 100 million to 1,000 million watts at a time, making them far more powerful than conventional broadcasts by humans. The bursts originate in a region of the sky about 6,400-18,000 kilometers high, in the evening sector of the auroral oval. Because the radiation is polarized, it is likely that AKR is caused directly by electrons spiraling along magnetic field lines in a natural mimic of free-electron lasers in the laboratory.

Methods of Study

The space age owes its birth in some measure to the aurora, for it was the desire to study the earth-space interface around the globe at high altitude that resulted in the launching of the first satellites, during the International Geophysical Year in 1957-1958. Until then, ground-based photography and instrumentation were almost the only methods of studying the aurora (aircraft and rockets played a lesser role). Ground-based instrumentation in the 1940's and 1950's confirmed that auroras were linked to the geomagnetic field, for studies showed that the aurora occurred in a circle around the north magnetic pole. Photography of the aurora has always been difficult because the display is dynamic, sometimes changing from second to second. Not until the 1950's were electronic devices available to analyze the entire auroral spectrum visible from the ground.

Satellites in the 1970's and 1980's have expanded the array of instruments available to investigators. While field and particle instrumentation has been used to analyze gases and plasmas, imaging instruments have been equally revealing. Notable cameras of various sorts have been carried by Dynamics Explorer 1, the U.S. Air Force HiLat (high latitude) satellite, and the Swedish Viking satellite. In addition, some imaging was performed by polar-orbit weather satellites, but with lesser spectral and spatial resolution. The Skylab crews observed some auroral activity. The Spacelab 3 crew in 1985 photographed the aurora from above the atmosphere. Combining images taken a few seconds apart allowed formation of stereo pairs so that the structure could be studied better. In other experiments, small electron guns have been carried into space aboard rockets and spacecraft to fire electrons back at the atmosphere in an attempt to generate artificial auroras.

A key finding by the satellites was that auroras are often more active on the dayside of the Earth, although sunlight and sky completely overwhelm it, and that large quantities of radiation are generated in the ultraviolet. This radiation is not seen at the Earth's surface, because the atmosphere absorbs the light.

Context

Auroras are the most visible manifestation of the interaction between the Earth and space. The study of plasmas has been enhanced by observations made of them. A clear understanding of the aurora will provide a means of diagnosing activities in the magnetosphere and the effects of solar activities on the terrestrial environment.

Auroras also serve as a means to study stars and planets. The same basic physics takes place in stars' atmospheres as in the auroras and the magnetosphere of Earth, although the energies and chemistries may be vastly different. Thus, the terrestrial aurora can serve as a vast laboratory for testing theories. Planets with magnetic fields also have auroral activity. Much of Jupiter's radio noise is caused by auroral kilometric radiation, and the

Einstein Observatory recorded X rays that apparently came from *Bremsstrahlung* radiation in the Jovian atmosphere. The Voyager 1 spacecraft observed a 29,000-kilometer-long aurora on the nightside of Jupiter, plus lightning pulses in and above the clouds coincident with the auroral activity.

Dave Dooling

Basic Bibliography

Akasofu, Syun-Ichi. "The Dynamic Aurora." *Scientific American* 260 (May, 1989). A detailed, college-level treatment of the current understanding of auroras, written by the physicist who is generally accepted as the world expert.

Delobeau, Francis. *The Environment of the Earth.* New York: Springer-Verlag, 1971. A technical description of the terrestrial environment, written as a reference for space scientists. Although the work is dated by subsequent discoveries, its description of auroral chemistry is still valid.

Dooling, Dave. "Satellite Data Alters View on Earth-Space Environment." *Spaceflight* (July, 1987). An article focusing on the exploration of the magnetosphere by the Dynamics Explorer satellites, with details on auroral imaging and radiation.

Eather, Robert H. *Majestic Lights: The Aurora in Science.* Washington, D.C.: American Geophysical Union, 1980. A well-illustrated, informative booklet describing auroras through history and their modern scientific interpretation. Written for general audiences.

Petrie, William. *Keoeeit: The Story of the Aurora Borealis.* Oxford: Pergamon Press, 1963. Highly detailed description of the history of auroras (largely from the Canadian and Eskimo point of view) and of the structure of auroral displays. Also tells much of the ground-based exploration of the aurora.

Current Bibliography

Bone, Neil. *The Aurora: Sun-Earth Interactions.* 2d ed. New York: John Wiley, 1996.

Savage, Candace Sherk. *Aurora: The Mysterious Northern Lights.* San Francisco: Sierra Club Books, 1994.

Cross References

The Big Bang

The big bang theory describes the creation of the universe in a way that unifies cosmology and elementary particle physics: Starting from an infinitesimal point of pure energy about 15 billion years ago, it began expanding to form all space, matter, and radiation.

Overview

The big bang theory of the origin of the universe was introduced to explain the idea of an expanding universe. Sir Isaac Newton's law of universal gravitation led him to suggest that a static universe with a finite distribution of stars would collapse, but that an infinite universe could be stable. In 1917, Albert Einstein used his general theory of relativity to show that a universe may exist in which all positions of a curved space are equivalent, with no boundary or center of gravity. Such a universe, however, whether finite or infinite, appeared to be unstable. Therefore, Einstein added an arbitrary cosmological constant to his field equations to represent a repulsion that would balance gravitational attraction on a cosmic scale and thus permit a static universe. In 1922, the Soviet mathematician Alexander Alexandrovich Friedmann showed that Einstein's equations allowed for the changing spatial curvature of an expanding universe without the need for a cosmological constant.

Evidence for an expanding universe was first published by Vesto Melvin Slipher at Lowell Observatory in 1917, after he had observed a shift of spectrum lines in photographs of spiral nebulas toward the longer wavelengths of red light. Such a redshift could be interpreted as a stretching of the wavelength of light from a rapidly receding source. In 1924, Edwin Powell Hubble demonstrated that the spiral nebulas were distant galaxies of stars far beyond the Milky Way. In 1929, Hubble showed that their redshifts were consistent with receding velocities proportional to their distances. Such a recession of the galaxies corresponded to the kind of universal expansion predicted by Friedmann's dynamic universe.

Even before the publication of Hubble's law for the expansion rate of the universe, it was predicted by the Belgian astronomer Georges Lemaître. Unaware of Friedmann's earlier work, he obtained solutions of Einstein's equations for an expanding universe in 1927 and recognized a cosmic connection to the radial velocities of the galaxies. Lemaître was the first to suggest a big bang model for the origin of the universe. Extrapolating backward in time, he realized that the galaxies would come together at the same time in the distant past, thus pointing to a unique beginning of the universe. He envisioned all the matter and space of the universe compressed into a "primeval atom." An enormous explosion would initiate the expansion of curved space and its fragmented matter, which would then form the receding galaxies so that at any later time the fastest galaxies would be at the greatest distances, as was soon shown by Hubble.

Starting in 1935, Friedmann's student George Gamow proposed the idea that the early dense stages of the universe were hot enough to produce thermonuclear reactions that could synthesize the elements by nuclear fusion. By 1946, he suggested that the primordial substance consisted of neutrons at a temperature of about 10 billion degrees, which decayed during the early stages of expansion to form protons and electrons. Successive captures of neutrons would then lead to the formation of the elements. Gamow worked out the details of this nucleosynthesis of the elements with Ralph A. Alpher. When they published their results in 1948, they persuaded Hans Albrecht Bethe, who first described nuclear fusion in stars, to add his name to the paper to make the list of authors "Alpher, Bethe, Gamow" as a pun on the first three letters of the Greek alphabet. Thus was born the alpha-beta-gamma theory for the origin of the universe.

In their theory, Gamow and his colleagues worked out a detailed account of the big bang model from Lemaître's hypothesis that the universe began in an intensely hot compressed fireball from which it began to expand. They were able to show that the nucleosynthesis of helium would match its observed cosmic abundance relative to hydrogen in the universe, and they described the subsequent expansion and formation of the galaxies. In 1948, Alpher and Robert C. Herman published a further analysis of the early universe that led to the prediction of a cosmic background radiation left over as a kind of fossil relic from the prestellar stages of the universe. Because of the expansion and the corresponding redshift of this radiation, they predicted that it would have cooled to a very low temperature of only about 5 degrees above absolute zero at the present time.

The accidental discovery of the cosmic background radiation by Arno A. Penzias and Robert W. Wilson in 1965 led to renewed interest in the big bang theory. They found uniform radiation with no directional variations, corresponding to about 3.5 Kelvins at a wavelength of 7.3 centimeters in the microwave spectrum. This radiation was soon identified by Robert H. Dicke and his colleagues at Princeton University as the residual temperature from the primeval fireball predicted by Gamow's theory. Subsequent measurements have revealed a temperature of 2.74 Kelvins over a microwave spectrum of intensities that fits precisely the shape predicted from thermal equilibrium between matter and radiation in the early stages of the universe. The shape of this radiation spectrum would have been retained forever in the subsequent expansion and cooling of the primeval radiation.

After 1965, a number of physicists began to work out the details of the "standard model" of the big bang theory in the light of more recent elementary particle theories, such as the 1964 quark theory. Extrapolation of the equations that describe the expansion of the universe back some 15 billion years to the beginning of time results in a mathematical singularity of infinite density and temperature. The first particles and antiparticles that would have materialized from energy according to ideas about mass-energy equivalence ($E = mc^2$) and pair creation are not well understood, although unified field theories are beginning to suggest their possible properties. At very high temperatures, particles move so fast that they escape any attraction caused by nuclear or electromagnetic forces, but as they cooled they would interact to produce new forms of matter, leading to an era dominated by quarks. After about a trillionth of a second (10^{-12} seconds), the known laws of physics begin to account for the particles that would exist at the expansion temperature of about 10 million billion degrees (10^{16} Kelvins). By this time, all observable space would occupy less than a cubic millimeter, filled with quarks, leptons (electrons, neutrinos, and the like), photons, and their antiparticles at energies too high for quarks to combine into more familiar particles.

The quark era ended after about a millisecond (10^{-3} seconds) of cosmic expansion to about 300 kilometers of observable space and temperatures of about 1,000 billion degrees (10^{12} Kelvins). This was cool enough for quarks to combine and form protons and neutrons, but too high for protons and neutrons to combine into atomic nuclei. As this particle era began, there was a slight excess of particles over antiparticles of about one part in a billion. Mutual annihilation of protons, neutrons, and their antiparticles into photons produced a brilliant fireball of radiation, eliminating most antiparticles and leaving a surplus of about 1 billion photons to each proton and neutron in a sea of leptons. During this particle era, protons transmuted into neutrons and vice versa by interacting with neutrinos (neutral massless particles), but were kept equal in number by thermal equilibrium until the temperature fell to about 100 billion degrees (10^{11} Kelvins). Below this temperature, there was not enough energy to produce the slightly heavier neutron, so protons began to exceed neutrons in a sequence that determined precisely their relative availability in the early universe.

The lepton era began after about one second, when the temperature had dropped to 10 billion degrees (10^{10} Kelvins) and the observable universe was about the size of the Earth's orbit around the Sun. Neutrinos now had insufficient energy to interact with other particles and began to behave independently of other particles. At about 5 billion degrees and five seconds of expansion, the temperature dropped below the threshold for producing electrons and positrons (antielectrons), so they began to annihilate faster than they could be re-created out of radiation, and the universe rapidly became dominated by photons. Soon, all positrons and all but one electron out of a billion disappeared.

After three minutes and forty-six seconds, when the temperature was only below 1 billion degrees (10^9 Kelvins), the universe was cool enough for colliding protons and neutrons to hold together and form deuterium nuclei (heavy hydrogen ions). In rapid succession, deuterium nuclei then collided with protons and neutrons to form helium nuclei, and soon almost all the remaining neutrons combined to form helium. When this nucleosynthesis

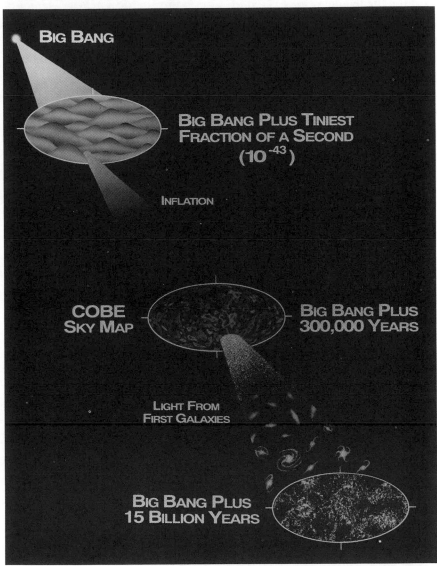

An artist's conception of the expansion of the universe, starting with the big bang. The first oval represents the universe just after the big bang. The second shows a Cosmic Background Explorer (COBE) Differential Microwave Radiometer sky map from one year of observations and represents the universe less than half a million years after the big bang. At this time stars and galaxies could begin to form. The third oval represents today's universe. *(National Aeronautics and Space Administration)*

began, the neutron-proton ratio had dropped to about 13 percent neutrons. Since half of all nuclear particles were then bound into helium (two neutrons and two protons), the matter of the universe should now be about 26 percent helium by weight. Most of the rest of the matter should be hydrogen because the temperature was too low at that time to form heavier elements. The cosmic abundance of helium in the universe matches this predicted amount within the limits of current measurements (22 to 28 percent). The heavier elements eventually formed at higher temperatures inside stars.

At the end of this primeval nucleosynthesis stage, the energy of particle-antiparticle annihilation had given photons a temperature about 40 percent higher than neutrinos. One electron remained for each free or bound proton (in hydrogen and helium nuclei), but the universe was much too hot for electrons to bind with nuclei to form atoms. During this radiation-dominated era (energy density greater than matter density) the universe expanded for about 700,000 years before it was cool enough to produce stable atoms. When this happened, the lack of free electrons made the universe transparent to radiation.

The decoupling of matter and radiation occurred at about 3,000 Kelvins and allowed atoms to begin to form into galaxies and stars. As the matter-dominated era began, the universe continued to expand and cooled the primeval radiation until it reached the 3 Kelvins temperature of the present cosmic background radiation discovered in 1965. It was this measured temperature that made it possible to calculate the cosmological helium production and establish the standard model of the big bang theory back to within less than a billionth of a second after the creation of the universe.

Applications

The successful predictions and applications of the big bang theory led to more successes, but also raised new problems. The cosmological interpretation of the galactic redshift not only supported the predictions of an expanding universe from general relativity but also it shed new light on the most distant objects with the largest redshifts. It was recognized that these objects were being seen as they were billions of years ago in early stages of galactic development. Thus, highly energetic sources like quasars (quasi-stellar radio sources) could be most likely identified as infant galaxies.

The microwave background radiation was found to be uniform in all directions within a hundredth of a Kelvin, making it possible to measure the velocity of the Earth's motion relative to this radiation from the slight decrease in its wavelength in the direction of motion. The measured radiation temperatures made it possible to calculate the cosmic abundances of light elements, including about 26 percent helium, 74 percent hydrogen, a thousandth of a percent deuterium, and a millionth of a percent lithium, all within the observational uncertainties. Since no other source for deuterium production is known, it provides impressive evidence for the big bang theory back to the first second.

Nevertheless, these very successes raised problems that led to adjustments in the theory. The uniformity of cosmic radiation implies thermal equilibrium in the early universe, even though various regions of the expanding universe moved apart faster than the speed of light. This "horizon problem" arises since thermal equilibrium requires radiation to carry temperature information to all regions. One attempt to avoid this problem was developed by Alan Guth in the early 1980's. He suggested a very early period of rapid expansion at an exponential rate instead of the decreasing rate observed at the present time because of gravity. Such an "inflationary" expansion would have smoothed out any initial irregularities in the universe, much like blowing up a wrinkled balloon, so that the uniformity of the background radiation could have evolved from many different nonuniform initial states. Yet, uniformity also raises a "galaxy problem" concerning the formation of stars and galaxies, which would seem to require sustained density fluctuations in the early universe that would begin the action of gravity to produce galaxies. Fortunately, inflationary models do allow for the possibility that early microscopic quantum fluctuations required by Werner Heisenberg's uncertainty principle would be amplified by inflation-like blemishes in the rubber fabric of an expanding balloon.

Conditions in the earliest stages of the big bang have become a kind of laboratory to unite cosmologists and elementary particle physicists in the light of recent discoveries and theories relating to the unification of the fundamental forces in nature. The discovery of the W and Z particles in 1983 by Carlo Rubbia and Simon van der Meer confirmed the electroweak theory that predicted unification of the electromagnetic force and the weak force of radioactivity at high temperatures (about 10^{15} Kelvins). The quark theory predicts a weakening of the strong nuclear force at even higher temperatures, suggesting the possibility of a grand unification of forces at a high enough temperature. Although particle accelerators do not begin to reach these grand unification energies and temperatures, it might be possible to test such a theory with astronomical evidence.

These ideas in particle physics suggest a complete symmetry of forces at the earliest intelligible instant allowed by quantum theory (10^{-43} seconds) when the temperature (10^{32} Kelvins) would be high enough to equalize the strengths of their interactions. This grand unification era would last until the time (10^{-35} seconds) when the temperature is low enough (10^{27} Kelvins) for the strong nuclear force to become distinct. The grand unified theory predicts a very massive X-particle to mediate quark-lepton transmutations at high enough energies for pair-creation of X-particles and antiparticles. At the end of the grand unification era, X-particles would begin to decay slightly faster than their antiparticles in order to produce slightly more quarks and leptons than antiquarks and antileptons. This kind of asymmetric decay has been observed in some light particles (K mesons) and could explain the "antimatter problem" of why the universe now contains virtually no antimatter and only about one proton for every billion photons. If the

X-particle exists, it would also make the proton slightly unstable.

A possible result of the decoupling of the strong nuclear force is a release of energy that might account for a sudden inflationary expansion of the universe. Inflation would also prevent the formation of magnetic monopoles predicted by grand unification theories, solving the problem of why such particles are not now observed. After the separation of the strong force, the W and Z particles would maintain the symmetry of electromagnetic and weak interactions. This electroweak era would end after ten trillionths of a second (10^{-11} seconds) when the temperature had cooled to a million billion degrees (10^{15} Kelvins). Then W and Z particles could no longer be produced, so radioactivity and electromagnetism would become distinct forces. After another millisecond, the quark era would end with the formation of protons and neutrons as described in the standard model of the big bang theory.

Context

Several competing theories have attempted to avoid the creation implications of the big bang theory, but none have been able to offer a successful alternative. Mention has already been made of Einstein's preference for a static universe and his attempt to introduce an arbitrary cosmological constant to balance gravitational attraction. When it was later shown that his equations without this constant were compatible with the observed expansion of the universe, Einstein is reported by Gamow to have remarked that the cosmological constant was the greatest blunder of his life. It is ironic that the inflationary model—introduced to resolve problems in the big bang theory—requires a repulsive force that must have the same form as the cosmological constant during the brief instant of inflation.

The most serious attempt to defeat the big bang theory was the steady state theory of the universe, introduced in 1948 by Hermann Bondi, Thomas Gold, and Fred Hoyle. This theory did not require an origin of the universe in time, but assumed the continuous creation of matter throughout space at a rate that keeps the mean density of the universe constant at all times as the universe expands. Creation would occur so gradually that it could not be observed until atoms began to form stars. Such a steady state universe would be infinite and eternal. Ironically, it required the Christian idea of creation *ex nihilo* (from nothing) to avoid the nearly biblical big bang idea of a unique creation in the remote past.

Although the steady state theory provided the main competition for the big bang theory during the 1950's, it did not stand the test of time. Since stars and galaxies would form throughout space from the continuous creation of atoms, young and old galaxies should be found together in space. Yet, this is contrary to the evidence that quasars (young galaxies) are only observed at great distances. The steady state theory was virtually abandoned after the 1965 discovery of the cosmic background radiation, the predicted fossil remnant of the big bang fireball. Even Hoyle, chief spokesman for the steady state theory, helped work out the details of the standard model of the big bang theory in 1967.

One other attempt to avoid a finite age for the universe is the idea of an oscillating universe. If the density of matter in the universe is large enough eventually to reverse its expansion by gravitational attraction, it would collapse toward a "big crunch." The oscillating universe theory proposes that another big bang might follow the big crunch, giving rise to a series of such oscillations between successive big bangs indefinitely in the past and future. Nevertheless, this is really not a theory, since there is no known mechanism to produce another big bang. Other theories predict that if a crunch occurs, the universe will collapse into a universal black hole. Furthermore, if oscillations could occur, each cycle would increase the ratio of photons to nuclear particles (and increase the associated entropy) as the universe expands and contracts. Although this ratio is large, it is not infinite, so the universe must have had only a finite number of cycles and thus a finite origin.

Joseph L. Spradley

Basic Bibliography

Barrow, John D., and Joseph Silk. *The Left Hand of Creation*. New York: Basic Books, 1983. This is a readable account of the origin and evolution of the expanding universe by two astronomy teachers with a good grasp of cosmology. Discusses many theories and problems associated with the big bang model, and includes a good glossary of astrophysical terms and an index.

Hawking, Stephen W. *A Brief History of Time: From the Big Bang to Black Holes*. New York: Bantam Books, 1988. A very popular and readable account of the development of cosmology and the big bang theory. Includes a helpful glossary and an index.

Jastrow, Robert. *God and the Astronomers*. New York: Warner Books, 1978. A brief but interesting history of the discovery of the expanding universe and development of the big bang theory. Contains many historical photographs of the originators of the theory and supplements on its theological implications.

Lang, Kenneth R., and Owen Gingerich, eds. *A Source Book in Astronomy and Astrophysics, 1900-1975*. Cambridge, Mass.: Harvard University Press, 1979. This volume contains many of the original articles that established the ideas of the expanding universe and the big bang theory, with good introductory sections for each. Authors include Einstein, Hubble, Friedmann, Lemaître, and Gamow. Some articles are technical, but much can be understood by the general reader.

Silk, Joseph. *The Big Bang: The Creation and Evolution of the Universe*. San Francisco: W. H. Freeman, 1980. A good introduction to the standard model of the big bang theory, although it was written before the introduction of inflationary theories. Includes a good glossary, index, and a thirty-five-page section on mathematical details.

Trefil, James S. *The Moment of Creation: Big Bang Physics from Before the First Millisecond to the Present Universe.* New York: Charles Scribner's Sons, 1983. A good introduction to the big bang theory. Includes a discussion of grand unification and inflationary theories.

Weinberg, Steven. *The First Three Minutes.* New York: Bantam Books, 1977. An excellent introduction to the details of the standard model of the big bang by a leading theoretical physicist and Nobel laureate. It includes a helpful mathematical supplement, books for further reading, a glossary, and an index.

Current Bibliography

Coles, Peter, and Francesco Lucchin. *Cosmology: The Origin and Evolution of Cosmic Structure.* New York: John Wiley, 1995.

Fraser, Gordon, Egil Lillestol, and Inge Sellevag. *The Search for Infinity: Solving the Mysteries of the Universe.* Introduction by Stephen Hawking. New York: Facts on File, 1995.

Hawking, Stephen. *Hawking on the Big Bang and Black Holes.* Advanced Series in Astrophysics and Cosmology 8. River Edge, N.J.: World Scientific, 1993.

Loore, Camiel W. H. de, and C. Doom. *Structure and Evolution of Single and Binary Stars.* Astrophysics and Space Science Library 179. Boston: Kluwer, 1992.

Milone, E. F., and J.-C. Mermilliod, eds. *The Origins, Evolution, and Destinies of Binary Stars in Clusters: An International Symposium Held at the University of Calgary, 18-23 June 1995.* Astronomical Society of the Pacific Conference Series 90. San Francisco: Astronomical Society of the Pacific, 1996.

Schramm, David N. *The Big Bang and Other Explosions in Nuclear and Particle Astrophysics.* River Edge, N.J.: World Scientific, 1996.

Shafter, Allen W., ed. *Interacting Binary Stars: A Symposium Held in Conjunction with the 105th Meeting of the Astronomical Society of the Pacific, San Diego State University, 13-15 July 1993.* Astronomical Society of the Pacific Conference Series 56. San Francisco: Astronomical Society of the Pacific, 1994.

Terrell, Dirk, Jaydeep Mukherjee, and R. E. Wilson. *Binary Stars: A Pictorial Atlas.* Foreword by Slavek M. Rucinski. Malabar, Fla.: Krieger, 1992.

Wijers, Ralph A. M. J., Melvyn B. Davies, and Christopher A. Tout, eds. *Evolutionary Processes in Binary Stars.* NATO ASI Series. Series C, Mathematical and Physical Sciences 477. Boston: Kluwer, 1996.

Cross-References

Antimatter, 1; Black Holes, 48; Cosmology, 97; General Relativity, 302; Quantum Cosmology, 767; Stellar Evolution, 942; The Universe: Evolution, 999; The Universe: Expansion, 1007.

Binary Stars

Two stars that are gravitationally bound to each other are known as a binary star system. Observationally, there are subclasses of binary stars, which are defined by the physical properties of the binary star system under study. These classes will be discussed in detail below.

Overview

Used as an adjective, the word "binary" is defined in Webster's dictionary as "compounded or consisting of or marked by two things or parts." When this adjective is used to modify the noun "stars," it has a more specific definition as utilized by astronomers. As one looks at the three-dimensional sky, the eye transforms the image onto a two-dimensional space. Astronomers differentiate between two stars that appear very close together and those that are physically connected through the force of gravitational attraction. Ptolemy used the term "double star" to define the former case and Sir William Herschel in 1802 was the first to use the term "binary star" in his paper "On the Construction of the Universe." Herschel's definition is consistent with the latter case and is quite specific as to the physical conditions on the two stars defined as binary stars. Herschel thus called a "real" double star a binary star.

Some double stars are known as "fixed," which means that the component members have not moved with respect to each other since they were first discovered. One of the most famous "fixed" doubles is the beautiful (the primary star is yellow gold and the secondary star is blue) double star in the constellation Cygnus known as Albireio (the nose of the swan), which was first discovered by Friedrich Georg Wilhelm von Struve in 1832. Most double stars, however, have moved with respect to each other since their discovery. The parameter that astronomers use to define the location of the secondary component relative to the primary component is the position angle, as shown in the figure.

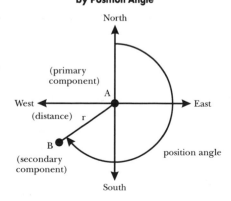

Binary Star Pair and Their Relative Orientation by Position Angle

Since the binary star system contains more than one object, one must differentiate the component members. With binary stars, the star of the system that appears to be the brightest (apparent magnitude—how bright the star appears as seen from Earth) is designated as the A component. The next brightest is the B component, and so on in the case of dimmer members of a system. For example, the bright star Sirius in the constellation Canis Major is a known binary star. Thus, the brightest component is known as Sirius A and its fainter, physical companion is known as Sirius B.

Double stars are either optical doubles or visual binaries. The former category are only a result of the viewing direction and are thus considered impostors. The best-known system is the optical double Alcor and Mizar in the handle of the Big Dipper (Ursa Major), but Mizar itself is a visual binary. Visual binaries are two stars that orbit each other. The time it takes two stars to orbit each other varies considerably. Typically, the time it takes for visual binaries to orbit each other (known as the orbital period) will range from a few years to tens of thousands of years. For other classes of binary stars, the orbital period is much shorter. Visual binaries are those that can be separated with the naked eye. By simple deduction, they are separated by reasonably large distances but are still gravitationally bound to each other, which results in a closed orbit of the binary star system.

As stars move around each other, at times the total light from the system is reduced as one star blocks (eclipses) all or part of the light from the other component. As a result, the total light from the binary star varies as a function of time and thus eclipsing binary star systems are a subset of the class of stars known as variables. The most interesting group of binary stars are those known as spectroscopic binaries. These systems are such that even with the most powerful optical telescope on Earth, the component members of the binary star system cannot be resolved. Astronomers study the spectra (the dispersed light from an object by wavelength) of such systems that determines the nature of the component members. Minute blueshifts and redshifts in the spectra of the system occur as the component member star alternately approaches and recedes relative to observers on Earth.

In 1955, the binary-star astronomer Zdenek Kopal classified close binaries in three groups: detached, semi-detached, and contact. The closer together that component members are, the shorter the orbital period. Thus, the contact binaries have the shortest periods. Traditionally, the two subclasses of contact binaries are the A-type and the W-type systems. In 1981, a third, B-type, subclass was proposed by astronomer Stefan W. Mochnacki based on the work of Leon B. Lucy and Robert W. Wilson. The W-type systems are by far the most numerous of all the eclipsing variable stars. As the stars revolve, the W-type systems are those where the more massive component blocks the smaller, less massive component that is the brighter star of the pair. The prototype of this subclass is the system W Ursa Major. Most of these systems have orbital periods in the six- to twelve-hour range. The stars that make up these systems are older stars with spectral types late F and G. The total mass of these systems is small, with values typically only 0.8 to 3 solar masses. (The mass of the Sun is used as a reference unit of mass for other stars.)

The A-type systems typically have component members with spectral type A (but sometimes B). The fact that they normally are A-type stars is the source of the name. In these systems, the deepest eclipse (the largest

Close Binary System

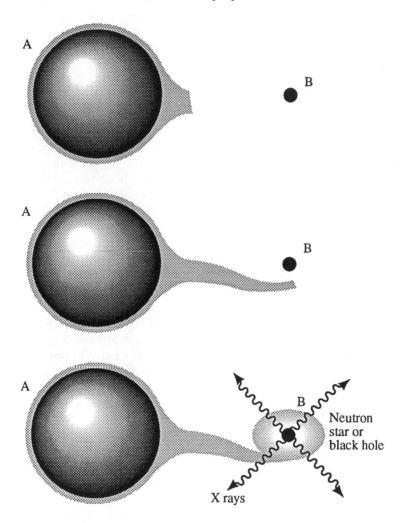

In a close binary system, gas from the larger and less massive star of the pair (A) is pulled toward the smaller and more massive star (B) by gravity; if B is a neutron star or a black hole, the resulting friction causes an emission of X rays, which can be detected on Earth by X-ray telescopes.

decrease in the total light from the system) occurs when the less massive star is in front and blocking the light of the more massive and brighter star. The stars that are members of these systems are younger and hotter than those stars in the W-type systems. The total mass of the systems is larger than the W-type systems, with total masses at 4 to 5 solar masses.

Applications

Stars are typically measured for a specific parameter. For example, an astronomer may wish to measure how bright the stars are in a given range of wavelengths. This collection of measurements would then be a photometric catalog. Another observer may wish to determine the distance to a given set of nearby stars. This list would then be a parallax catalog. The majority of binary stars are the result of spectral classification catalogs.

The majority of measured stars in the sky are other than single stars. Gravitational forces are in evidence for the double and multiple-star systems. Binary stars are the most common type followed by single stars. Triple-star systems are quite unusual, and the Castorian system (to the unaided eye, the star known as Castor in the constellation Gemini) is even more unusual. Each of the members of this triple-star system is a spectroscopic binary star system. Thus, the Castorian system is really a six-star system. The Castor A binary star system has an orbital period of 9.2 days, the Castor B system has an orbital period of 2.9 days, and the Castor C system has an orbital period of 0.8 days. The measurements of this fascinating system began in 1826 by Struve. The orbital period of the Castor A-Castor B systems around each other is in the range of 340 to 477 years. There is much error involved when only a small portion of the orbit (the path defined by one object gravitationally bound to another) has been measured and with varying degrees of precision over the years since the initial observations in 1826. The situation is worse for the orbital period of the Castor C system around the quadruple members of Castor A plus Castor B: The revolution period must be on the order of 25,000 years.

Sirius, the brightest star in the sky other than the Sun, has intrigued observers for almost two centuries. Early observations by Friedrich Wilhelm Bessel in 1834 showed some variability in the motion of the star. Since Sirius is so bright, it became an observational challenge to try to detect the "unseen" companion that was causing the variability in the motion of Sirius. In addition, since the primary component is so bright, it became difficult to determine accurately the spectral class of the secondary component. As observing methods and equipment became more sophisticated, it has been determined that Sirius B is one of the most famous examples of a class of stars known as white dwarfs.

Context

The history of observational astronomy is flush with examples of the discovery of the prototype of a new class of object. Astronomers are now searching for other examples of such objects. In the seventeenth century, the Italian astronomer Giambattista Riccioli discovered the first double star in the constellation Ursa Major. Mizar was the first double star measured on the photographic plates taken by G. P. Bond at the Harvard College Observatory in 1857. One of the members of Mizar was determined to be another class of binary star by Edward Charles Pickering in 1889. The early history of binary stars is full of chance encounters with this class of object found often while looking for another object. It was not until Edmond Halley's discovery in 1718 that some of the brighter stars were in motion that caused a major interest in the field of astrometry (the branch of astronomy that deals with the precise measurement of positions of stars). Astrometry was one of the newest areas of astronomy because the technology required for precise measurement lagged the requirement for such technology.

The commonly recognized "fathers of double-star astronomy" are Christian Mayer and Herschel. In 1779, Mayer first speculated that there were small suns revolving around larger suns. These speculations were based on observations at Mannheim (a city in southwest Germany near the French border) in 1777 and 1778. His work contains the first known catalog of double stars ever published. This first catalog is a tabular listing of eighty entries. Included in this list of eighty double stars is Castor, one of the most famous stars in the constellation Gemini.

Herschel started his study of the planets and stars in May of 1773, but it was not until 1779 that he initiated a systematic search for the class of objects known as double stars. In all, Herschel prepared three lists of double stars that he observed with his own telescopes (probably the finest at the time). In 1782, he presented his first list to the Royal Society, which contained 269 double stars, 227 of which had not been noticed previously. In 1784, Herschel presented his second list with 434 additional objects. Both of these lists included a position for the major component, a position angle and a measured estimate of the angular separation of the two components. Herschel's third and final list was published in 1821 (about a year prior to his death) and included a final list of 145 pairs but without the detailed measurements of the first two lists.

The position angle as defined today is different from that used by Herschel in his early lists of double stars. It is important to remember that this parameter is one that typically changes (except for the "fixed" binaries) as a function of time. The changes vary with the orbital period of the binary system, the distance of the system to Earth, and the orientation of the orbital plane in the sky. Since a circle by definition has 360 degrees, a complete orbit will result in a 360-degree change in the position angle. Nevertheless, the orbits of binary star systems are typically ellipses, thus a change in the position angle of 180 degrees does not mean half of the orbital period. For example, the position angle of Sirius B in 1990 is 2 degrees (almost due north of Sirius A) and 182 degrees in 1998 (almost due south of Sirius A), yet the orbital period of the system is 49.94 years. Thus, Sirius B uses only about eight years to change its position angle by 180 degrees and requires the remaining forty-two years of its orbital period to change the remaining 180 degrees. Thus, Sirius B has changed its position angle by 180 degrees in only about one-sixth of the orbital period. Several graphically presented orbits of bright double-star systems have been published. The generation of these plots requires a basic knowledge of celestial mechanics and projection geometry.

Binaries are extremely useful systems for astronomers since their motions obey the well-understood laws of motion. In addition, a temporal study of these systems provides clues as to how these systems are changing or evolving, which in turn is important for the study of stellar evolution. The Thermal Relaxation Oscillation (TRO) model of Lucy, created independently also by Brian P. Flannery, is such that W-type contact binary star systems are unevolved even though the physical parameters that define the system's orbit may vary with time. In fact, this type of system appears to oscillate between a state of marginal contact and a state of no contact. The W-type contact binary star systems are ten to thirty times more common than all other eclipsing variables combined. A model that is to describe contact binaries must first deal with these systems effectively. Lucy also proposed that the A-type systems are in full contact and in equilibrium. Some evidence exists that stars in A-type systems evolved into a contact situation, which supports the TRO model. The problem is that the TRO model predicts that there should be broken contact systems, but there is no known system that satisfies that condition unambiguously.

Another major theoretical model was developed by Frank Shu, Stephen Lubow, and Lawrence Anderson and is called the contact discontinuity model (DSC). The basic tenet of this model is that binary star systems formed in contact and they are also in equilibrium. The end of the life of a contact system, as predicted by the DSC model, is that the fate of the systems is cataclysmic in nature. The shortest known orbital period of any binary star is eleven minutes. If this discovery holds, the system would provide direct proof of a collision between two stars.

Theresa A. Nagy

Basic Bibliography

Aitken, Robert G. *The Binary Stars.* Reprint. New York: Dover, 1964. A basic textbook on binary stars. Provides a good historical outline for the subject, but many of the analysis methods are now obsolete as used in modern astronomical computations.

Croswell, Ken. "Contact Binaries: Stars That Touch." *Astronomy* 10 (December, 1982): 66-70. A very readable discussion of contact binary stars and the major theories that define their role in stellar evolution.

Goldstein, Alan. "Split a Star in Two." *Astronomy* 17 (December, 1989): 88-91. A short discussion of observational techniques for observing five close double stars. The graphical presentation of the orbits for these systems is very useful and enlightening.

Harrington, Phil. "The Ten Best Double Stars." *Astronomy* 17 (July, 1989): 78. A discussion of double stars for the general reader.

"How Many Stars Are Binary?" *Sky and Telescope* 74 (July, 1987): 8. Discusses binary stars. For a wide audience.

MacRobert, Alan. "Observing Double Stars." *Sky and Telescope* 68 (November, 1984): 417. For the amateur astronomist. Discusses double stars.

Current Bibliography

Boss, Alan P. "Companions to Young Stars." *Scientific American* 273, no. 4 (October, 1995): 134-140.

Piran, Tsvi. "Binary Neutron Stars." *Scientific American* 272, no. 5 (May, 1995): 52-60.

Van den Heuvel, Edward P. J., and Jan van Paradijs. "X-Ray Binaries." *Scientific American* 269, no. 5 (November, 1993): 64-72.

Cross-References

Cosmology, 97; Galactic Structures, 279; Galaxies and Galactic Clusters, 287; Globular Clusters, 310; Quantum Cosmology, 767; Stellar Evolution, 942; The Universe: Evolution, 999; The Universe: Structure, 1015.

Black Holes

Black holes, objects so dense that not even light can escape, are a remarkable prediction of general relativity, believed responsible for such diverse phenomena as X-ray binaries, quasars, and active galaxies.

Overview

One obvious characterization of the gravity of Earth or any other object is its escape velocity: How fast would something have to be launched from its surface to overcome gravity and escape far away into space? For Earth, this escape velocity is only about 11.2 kilometers per second. If the mass of Earth were unchanged but it were shrunk somehow to a smaller radius, however, its escape velocity would increase. Indeed, according to the "ordinary" laws of physics, dating back to Sir Isaac Newton in the seventeenth century, it should be possible, at least in principle, to compact Earth, or any other object, to such a small size that its escape velocity would be greater than the velocity of light, approximately 300,000 kilometers per second. Light generated on the surface of this object would be unable to escape, so that, to a distant observer, the object would be completely invisible. It would have become a "black hole."

The possibility of such black holes, first noted by the amateur British astronomer John Michell in 1783, takes on a special significance in view of the fact that, according to Albert Einstein's theory of relativity, nothing can travel faster than the velocity of light. The obvious question, therefore, is whether black holes are consistent with relativity. According to Einstein's vision—very different from Newton's—gravity is viewed as a "warping" of space and time, rather than a force like electricity; nevertheless, one is led once again to the possibility of black holes. There can exist objects so dense that nothing—not even light—can ever escape.

To say that black holes can exist in principle, however, does not imply that they do exist; indeed, the size of a black hole, known as its Schwarzschild radius, seems almost absurdly small. To convert Earth into a black hole, one would have to compact it down to a radius of about one centimeter; the Schwarzschild radius of the much more massive Sun would be about three kilometers. What could cause such dense configurations?

It seems unlikely that an object with the mass of Earth could ever be compacted into a black hole, yet very large stars with much stronger gravitational fields are expected to end their lives as black holes. To understand

A view of the nucleus of Whirlpool Galaxy, thought to contain a central black hole. *(Nino Panagia and National Aeronautics and Space Administration)*

why this is so requires a digression into the theory of how stars work. Basically, a star such as the Sun is a large, nearly spherical mass of very hot gas bound together by gravity; if it were not so very hot, it could not exist in anything like the form that we see. Gravity is working very hard to shrink a star, or any other object, to a small size, and it is only the enormous pressure provided by the extremely hot gas that lets the star resist gravity and remain as large as it is. This pressure relies, however, on the fact that the gas is so hot—the core of the Sun, for example, has a temperature of about 15 million degrees Celsius—and this in turn requires a continuous source of energy. If something deep in the Sun were not continuously heating it up, the Sun would cool off and begin to contract in only a few million years. Because the Earth is 330,000 times less massive than the Sun, it can exist as a cool, largely solid entity, but this is impossible for an object as massive as a star.

What keeps the Sun from cooling off, and what will let it survive as an ordinary star for a total lifetime of about ten billion years, is the nuclear fusion of hydrogen into helium. Eventually, however, the Sun, like every other star, will have exhausted the supply of hydrogen in its core. Without a source to heat up the core, the pressure will decrease and gravity will force its insides to contract. This contraction may be halted temporarily by the fusion of helium into still heavier elements, such as carbon and silicon, but eventually, unless something else happens, the core of the star will be converted into iron, the ultimate nuclear ash. After this happens, no nuclear reactions can extract any additional energy.

If the star has a mass of less than 1.4 times the mass of the Sun (the Chandrasekhar limit), the contraction will be halted long before this stage by so-called electron degeneracy pressure, and the star will end up as a white dwarf with a radius of about ten thousand kilometers. If instead its mass exceeds the Chandrasekhar limit, but is still less than four or five times that of the Sun, the star will contract still further until neutron degeneracy pressure sets in, and the star will end up as a neutron star with a radius of only ten to twenty kilometers. Finally, if its mass is still larger, there is no known source of pressure in the universe which could prevent it from shrinking smaller than its Schwarzschild radius. The burnt-out corpse of a star with a mass greater than about four or five times that of the Sun must end up as a black hole.

Because it is invisible, there is very little about a black hole which can be probed from the outside. One can in principle determine its mass, for example by measuring how long it takes for a rocket or a bit of debris to orbit around it. Similarly, if the black hole was formed from a rotating object, it will have a net spin, or "angular momentum," which distorts the fabric of space and time around it and will alter the orbits of anything nearby. Finally, if the black hole contains some net electric charge, that would be felt by any charged particles which happened to be nearby. These, however, are its only external manifestations. The so-called no-hair theorem proves that, to any observer outside, the black hole is characterized completely by its mass, its electric charge, and its angular momentum.

Short of stumbling upon one accidentally, then, how could one ever detect such an invisible object? The answer is that one must watch for interactions with any nearby matter. If a black hole is surrounded by some gas, its gravity will suck that gas toward it; as that gas is sucked toward the black hole, it can be heated to the point at which it emits an enormous amount of radiation, extending from radio waves to X rays, which one can try to detect. Moreover, even if the radiation is too weak to detect, there is the simple fact that the presence of a black hole, like that of any other source of gravity, should distort the distribution of any nearby matter.

The first observational evidence for black holes was provided in 1971 by the Uhuru satellite (Explorer 42, or SAS-1). Launched on December 12, 1970, to look for X-ray sources in the sky, Uhuru detected 339 such objects before its transmitter and batteries failed in 1973. Among these objects were several so-called X-ray binaries, consisting of a large red giant star and a tiny "something else" emitting X rays, which orbit about each other.

Red giants are swollen stars (with a radius of up to one hundred times that of the sun) which, having already depleted the hydrogen in their cores, are releasing their outer layers in an active stellar wind at a rate of up to one solar mass in a million years. If such a red giant is an isolated object, this gas will simply be ejected into interstellar space, but if the giant is in a binary system of stars, some of this ejecta will fall onto the companion object. If this companion is an ordinary star, this mass transfer is not particularly dramatic, but if instead the companion is a neutron star or a black hole, the consequences are spectacular. Because the binary system is rotating, the gas will spiral toward the companion in an "accretion disk," rather than falling in directly; as it spirals inward, a small cloud of gas will generate an enormous amount of radiation—largely in the form of X rays—via friction with other clouds of gas. Indeed, a very modest rate of matter infall, one solar mass per ten trillion years, will generate more energy than does the Sun today with all of its nuclear fusion.

It is generally believed that all known X-ray binaries consist of a red giant and a tiny neutron star or black hole. The only question is whether, for some given system, the tiny object is really a black hole. The easiest way to prove that it is a black hole is to show that its mass is greater than five times that of the Sun, so that it could not be a neutron star. For many systems, this

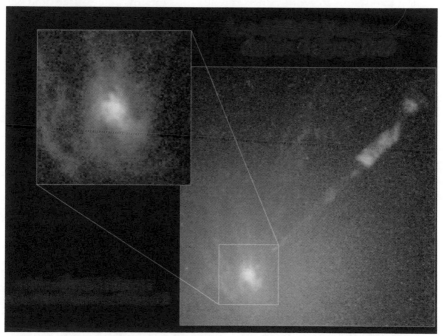

An image of a spiral-shaped disk of hot gas in the core of galaxy M87. The disk is spinning so rapidly that it is thought to contain a massive black hole at its hub. *(National Aeronautics and Space Administration)*

companion object clearly is a neutron star; for many others it is very hard to be sure. For at least one X-ray binary, namely Cygnus X-1 (so named as the first X-ray source discovered in the constellation Cygnus), there is very nearly conclusive evidence that the companion is a black hole. By studying the red giant in the system, which is about thirty times as massive as the Sun, and how it orbits its tiny companion, one can prove that this companion must have a mass at least six times that of the Sun, definitely too massive to be a neutron star.

Toward the end of the 1970's, astronomers discovered that other, much larger black holes may also exist. For example, the very center of the galaxy M87 contains many more stars than one would normally expect, moving about at unusually high velocities, a phenomenon that it seems one could explain only by postulating the presence of a black hole with a mass about five billion times that of the Sun—that is, roughly one percent of the mass of the Milky Way galaxy. Subsequently, astronomers also found indications that the very center of the Milky Way may contain a black hole with a mass about three million times that of the Sun. The center of the Galaxy, located in the constellation Sagittarius, seems to be emitting copious amounts of radiation of all sorts—including X rays, infrared, and radio waves—of a form consistent with the inflow of matter into a black hole. Moreover, just as for M87, the stars in the center of the galaxy are moving with high velocities in a fashion that seems to require the presence of some invisible source of mass.

Knowledge Gained

The discovery of black holes, first in X-ray binaries and later in the centers of galaxies, quickly led scientists to recognize that the theory of relativity, viewed originally as belonging to the most esoteric and arcane realms of theoretical physics, is actually of direct relevance in "real" astronomy. The most important fact was simply that black holes can provide a natural explanation for the generation of huge amounts of radiation. If a small black hole accreting gas at a rate of one solar mass every ten trillion years can generate more energy than the Sun, what would happen if a giant black hole such as that in M87 were to capture matter at a significantly more substantial rate? Indeed, it was recognized quickly that if such a supermassive black hole were to accrete only three solar masses of material each year—a paltry amount compared with the total mass of several hundred billion solar masses in our galaxy—it would emit more than five trillion times as much energy as does the Sun, much more than the total energy output of the Milky Way.

This sort of energy production might have seemed absurd were it not for the fact that, starting in the middle of the 1960's, astronomers had been discovering new objects called quasars (or quasistellar objects), some of which do apparently emit such enormous amounts of energy. First recognized as distinct entities in 1963, quasars are the most distant objects which have ever been observed, detected by their radio signals at distances where even entire galaxies are too faint to be seen, so far away that it has taken light from them many billions of years to reach Earth. Before the discovery of black holes, astronomers were at a total loss to account for such an enormous output of energy; indeed, there was a concerted effort to prove that quasars are actually much closer to the Earth than believed, so that they would not have to be emitting so very much energy. With the discovery of black holes in X-ray binaries and then of much larger black holes elsewhere, however, there has emerged a growing consensus that the energy from quasars could, and most likely should, be explained by the fall of matter into a supermassive black hole.

How such large black holes came into being is the subject of intense debate, involving both detailed theoretical arguments and computer simulations, but there is virtually no doubt that they must be there. Nothing else could explain the generation of such enormous quantities of energy.

Context

Perhaps the most important and lasting consequence of the discovery of black holes was the change that it wrought in the psychology of astronomy. Before the late 1960's, theoretical astronomy was in many respects a conservative discipline, concerned more with the implications of well-established ideas from physics and chemistry than with blazing new paths of its own. By 1970, white dwarfs, first explained by Subrahmanyan Chandrasekhar in 1931, were well-known and generally accepted objects, but neutron stars, only slightly less bizarre than black holes, had only been discovered two years earlier in the form of pulsars by Jocelyn Bell, a young graduate student in England. Only a very few scientists, such as Chandrasekhar and, especially, John Wheeler, seemed able to appreciate fully the potential significance of black holes. Even Einstein had doubted that they could exist.

All of this was to change. Spurred on in large part by the discovery of black holes, John Wheeler and Kip Thorne and their students in the United States and Yakob Zeldovich and his students in the Soviet Union rapidly worked out the details of how a black hole should interact with its environment and, in so doing, gave birth to the discipline of relativistic astrophysics, the application of Einstein's relativity to theoretical astronomy. Motivated originally by Wheeler's insistence that black holes must arise from the deaths of large stars, and by Thorne's conviction that black holes and relativity must somehow be relevant in explaining quasars, the discipline of relativistic astrophysics matured and expanded rapidly. By the middle of the 1970's, attention had focused on the possibility of large, but not supermassive, black holes in the centers of globular clusters, the oldest concentrations of stars in our galaxy. By the early 1980's, with the discovery of a possible black hole in the galaxy M87, it had become a matter of nearly universal consensus that quasars could contain supermassive black holes that might explain their enormous energy outputs.

In the mid-1960's, an astronomer who speculated on the possible implications of black holes was considered at least slightly eccentric. By the middle of the 1980's, an astronomer who did not allow for such black holes would have been considered behind the times. It had by then become accepted practice to speculate on the role of black holes in almost everything in astronomy, from quasars and X-ray binaries and globular clusters even to the earliest stages in the history of the universe. As an outgrowth of this increased sense of freedom, theoretical astrophysics came to play an increasingly important role in the evolution of theoretical physics.

Henry Emil Kandrup

Basic Bibliography

Asimov, Isaac. *The Collapsing Universe.* New York: Walker Publishing Co., 1977. A book dealing with other issues as well, it contains a twenty-page chapter on black holes that is very readable for even the most uninitiated.

Geroch, Robert. *General Relativity from A to B.* Chicago: University of Chicago Press, 1978. An elegant, readable account of what general relativity is all about, including a careful discussion of what a black hole really is, rather than how it behaves. Containing no equations, it still requires some intellectual sophistication, making it most appropriate for high school and college levels.

Greenstein, George. *Frozen Star.* New York: Freundlich Books, 1983. Communicates beautifully the flavor of what actually happened when black holes and neutron stars were first discovered—for example, the story behind Bell's discovery of pulsars in 1968 and the launching of the Uhuru satellite in 1970. Remarkably accurate technically, though accessible to a general audience, it is based on interviews with some of the leading authorities on black hole physics.

Hawking, Stephen W. "The Quantum Mechanics of Black Holes." *Scientific American* 231 (January, 1977): 34-40. The best discussion of a subject not touched on in this article at all, namely how black hole physics, and more generally relativity, can be combined with quantum mechanics, the other major thread of twentieth century physics. Accessible to anyone who has heard of the so-called Uncertainty Principle, for example, by reading F. Capra's *The Tao of Physics* (New York: Bantam Books, 1977).

Kaufmann, William J. *The Cosmic Frontiers of General Relativity.* Boston: Little, Brown and Co., 1977. The most challenging book in this bibliography, but also the most instructive. Although it contains no equations, it is difficult reading and is recommended only for the dedicated. It has been used in the past to supplement introductory courses in astronomy for college freshmen.

Sullivan, Walter. *Black Holes.* New York: Anchor Press, 1979. One of the better nontechnical books, it covers a broad range of material yet requires only a minimal amount of mathematical sophistication. This book is especially useful because it ties black hole physics to the larger issue of cosmology—theories regarding the nature of the universe itself. Accessible to a general audience.

Thorne, Kip S. "The Search for Black Holes." *Scientific American* 228 (December, 1974): 19, 32-43. An early discussion of the evidence that the X-ray binary system Cygnus X-1 contains a black hole, it is still probably the best discussion available for the layman. Requires some sophistication to appreciate fully, but motivated readers should find it accessible.

Current Bibliography

Begelman, Mitchell C., and Martin Rees. *Gravity's Fatal Attraction: Black Holes in the Universe.* New York: Scientific American Library, 1996.

D'Eath, P. D. *Black Holes: Gravitational Interactions.* New York: Oxford University Press, 1996.

Ferguson, Kitty. *Prisons of Light: Black Holes.* New York: Cambridge University Press, 1996.

Moss, Ian G. *Quantum Theory, Black Holes, and Inflation.* New York: Wiley, 1996.

Pickover, Clifford A. *Black Holes: A Traveler's Guide.* New York: Wiley, 1996.

Cross-References

The Big Bang, 32; Cosmology, 97; Galactic Structures, 279; General Relativity, 302; Quantum Cosmology, 767; Stellar Evolution, 942; The Universe: Evolution, 999; The Universe: Structure, 1015.

Brown Dwarf Stars

Between the class of large planets such as Jupiter, which produce no heat or light, and the small but true red dwarf stars, where nuclear reactions sustain radiation, stars exist whose mass is almost great enough to have initiated nuclear reactions but which are now just radiating the heat that nearly ignited them. Such stars, the first of which was unequivocally identified only in 1995, are known as brown dwarfs.

Overview

Brown dwarfs are defined as stars of very low luminosity, perhaps 10^{-6} times that of the Sun. Despite their catchy name, brown dwarfs are a very dim red. Their surface temperature is 1,000 Kelvins (degrees absolute) or less, accounting for their low luminosity. In contrast, the Sun—by no means a very hot star—has a surface temperature of about 6,000 Kelvins. The mass of typical brown dwarfs is about 5 to 8 percent that of the Sun. When the mass of low-luminosity stars is about one-half that of the Sun, their color and temperature is such that they are red dwarfs. If their mass is about 1 percent that of the Sun's, they have no luminosity at all and are simply very large planets like Jupiter, whose mass is about one-tenth of one percent that of the Sun.

Brown dwarfs were given their name in 1975 by astronomer Jill Tarter. In subsequent years other astronomers predicted their appearance and physical properties, postulating that the universe contained many of them, because their near relatives, the red dwarfs, were so abundant. Astronomers reasoned that since red dwarfs constitute about 80 percent of nearby, visible stars, brown dwarfs should be equally abundant, if not more so, assuming that there is continuity in the mass or size of star-like objects in the universe. They even suggested that brown dwarfs might account for the "missing" mass in the universe, a view since abandoned, for it is unknown how the aggregate mass of brown dwarfs—once discovered—will look.

Methods of Study

Tarter's speculation touched off a search for brown dwarfs by many of the world's major observatories. The problems in identifying such stars—or more properly, substellar bodies—were formidable. Brown dwarfs emit very weak radiation. Thus, only powerful telescopes and long photographic exposure times reveal them. Furthermore, their radiation fades very rapidly (in astronomical time). Some virtually burn out in less than one hundred million years, while none appear to reach a billion. In contrast, the universe is about one hundred billion years old. Thus, brown dwarfs are likely to be found only in star formations that are a hundred million to less than a billion years old (for example, the Pleiades). By the late twentieth century not many such formations had been precisely dated, and of those that had been, many were too far away for clear observation. Search programs thus targeted young, nearby star formations.

Other equally vexing problems were easier to solve technologically. Many of the readily observable brown dwarfs were companion bodies to stars of much greater magnitude. That is, they weakly rotated around stars of normal brightness (as planet and sun) or the star and brown dwarf both orbited around a common center of gravity. The luminosity of such stars, which was often many times greater that that of their brown dwarfs, interfered with observation. Fortunately, effective masking techniques were available, making reasonably delicate and precise observations possible.

Another problem had also been partially solved in advance. It had been discovered that the radiation indicating the presence of cool bodies such as brown dwarfs lay in that part of the electromagnetic spectrum known as the near-infrared—in a range of wavelengths of about 0.5 to 2.5 microns. The major compounds to be identified were water (H_2O) and methane (CH_4); in both the bond between the hydrogen atoms and the central oxygen or carbon atom absorbs energy in a narrow band within the near-infrared. Identification of these bands confirmed that these compounds, which can survive only on relatively cool bodies, were probably associated with brown dwarfs. The Earth's atmosphere contains enough water vapor to interfere seriously with the water spectrum, even when observations are made with high-altitude telescopes. Methane, however, is present in small enough concentrations so that its interference can be regarded as background absorption and corrected for. More recent measurements by the Hubble space telescope have confirmed the methane identifications in Earth's atmosphere.

The spectral evidence that clinched the case was provided by the element lithium. The isotope lithium-7 can undergo nuclear reaction when bombarded with a proton; its nucleus splits and two atoms of helium-4 (normal helium) are formed. This happens, however, at the temperatures only found in regular stars, even those as small as the red dwarfs. Stars thus show no spectral absorption at 0.67 microns, the characteristic absorption rate of lithium, because they long ago "burned up" all their lithium. A brown dwarf is cool enough for lithium to be consumed very slowly, if at all. If its spectrum is determined before its lithium is gone and its general radiation has disappeared (another reason for choosing young star formations for observation), any lithium present is regarded as proof that the body in question is a brown dwarf. Oxides of vanadium and titanium— additional elemental signatures—give partial confirmation of brown-dwarf status, but as some cool red stars can retain traces of these elements, such evidence is not airtight. Only lithium clearly identifies bodies as brown dwarfs.

Models of a Lithium Atom

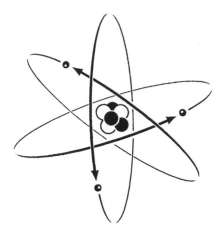

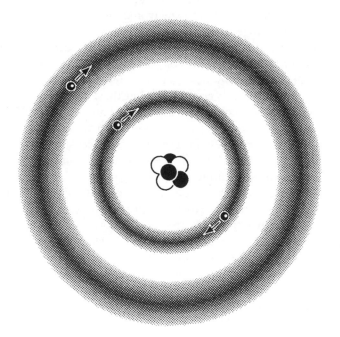

Models of a lithium atom: simple (top) and shell (bottom). The high temperature of regular stars causes lithium to undergo nuclear reaction and be "burned up." Brown dwarf stars, however, are cool enough for lithium to be consumed very slowly, if at all. Thus, the presence of lithium clearly identifies bodies as brown dwarf stars.

The first starlike bodies to be identified as brown dwarfs were Teide-1 in the Pleiades and Gliese 229B, associated with the true star Gliese 229, which was found near the constellation *Canis major* (the Big Dog). Gliese 229B is apparently part of a binary star system. Since Gliese 229's distance from the Earth was accurately known, the brown dwarf's distance could also be ascertained: about 19 light-years. Teide-1 is much farther away (about 400 light-years) and harder to observe. Although Teide-1 was discussed in the research literature before Gliese 229, it had to await final confirmation while the existence of Gliese 229B became fully established.

In 1995 Gliese 229B was the subject of two papers: one published in *Science*, which provided methane spectral evidence, and the other in *Nature*, which provided lithium data. Because the methane spectrum was so strong, Gliese 229B was considered to be surrounded by a thick methane atmosphere, like Jupiter. The lithium spectrum was the final piece of evidence, confirming that Gliese 229B was a brown dwarf. Its mass was not immediately determined, because star and planet masses are calculated on the basis of orbital paths, which can be established only by continuous observation over months or even years.

Context

The Identification of Teide-1 and Gliese 229B as brown dwarfs was of major scientific importance. Although the subsequent identification of other similar bodies substantiated the initial findings, Teide-1 and Gliese 229B had already established that brown dwarfs exist. To understand the importance of this fact, it is necessary to review our understanding of star formation.

Matter is not evenly distributed throughout the universe. Hydrogen atoms account for more than 90 percent of the matter between the stars. Additionally, there are lesser amounts of helium; some elements of low-atomic number like carbon, nitrogen, and oxygen; and traces of higher elements including the iron-cobalt-nickel triad. This mix is thin in some places and dense in others. (Density is relative: While 10^{22} hydrogen molecules per cubic centimeter are present at the Earth's surface, there are only one or two dissociated atoms per cubic centimeter in interstellar space.) Denser patches of interstellar atoms are the breeding grounds for new stars. Such accumulations can separate themselves from their surroundings by rotational motion. Over millions of years their atoms draw in toward the center of rotation as a result of gravitational attraction. This shrinkage causes an increase in temperature, the result of the atoms' close-range attraction and their kinetic energy. When the cloud of atoms has shrunk to about 1 percent of its original volume, the temperature is so high that nuclear reactions begin, with hydrogen fusing into helium. This reaction produces much more heat than the kinetic energy of gravity-stressed atoms, and if enough matter is present, the nuclear fusion reaction becomes self-sustaining, causing the birth of a star.

In ordinary chemistry even the most energetic reactions—fires, vaporizations, explosions—involve only a few of the outermost electrons outside the atomic nucleus. The nucleus itself is never affected by chemical processes, no matter how violent or high-temperature. Why, then, does high temperature initiate nuclear reactions in space? Chemical reaction temperatures are rarely greater than 5,000 or 6,000 Kelvins, but the interior temperatures of stars or protostars (matter becoming stars) can range from hundreds of thousands to millions of Kelvins, depending on the quantity of matter present. Two effects promote nuclear reactions: First, the nuclei themselves become destabilized and thus reactive; and second, the protective electron shells are stripped away, causing the nuclei to approach each other and react. The equivalent of this heat energy on Earth is the small but intense field used to initiate hydrogen fusion in the laboratory. Energy and hydrogen must be supplied continuously for reactions to take place, both of which are readily available in protostars. The size of developing stars is also a factor in causing nuclear reactions. Even red dwarfs form from clouds of matter as large as our entire solar system. Small amounts of matter will fail to produce the heat and hydrogen necessary for self-sustaining reactions, while increasingly larger amounts will produce increasingly brighter stars.

Masses of matter ranging from about 10 to 50 percent of the Sun's mass produce red dwarf stars. As mass increases, nuclear reactions can generate more and more heat, affecting the color of stars. While our Sun is yellow, stars fifty or sixty times more massive are white or even bluish-white. At the other end of the range of stellar masses are the heavy planets like Jupiter—stars that never made it. Below its surface, Jupiter has the necessary hydrogen and helium to be a star, but it lacks the mass that would have generated enough heat to start and sustain a nuclear reaction. Theory suggests that between the failed stars like Jupiter and the weak but successful red dwarfs, a class of stars may exist that almost made it—stars that generated substantial heat when their matter coalesced and perhaps "burned" deuterium (heavy hydrogen) and other light elements until these elements were exhausted. Such a class of stars—the brown dwarfs—might possess enough residual heat to be detectable by telescopes.

The brown-dwarf piece in the jigsaw puzzle of star-formation was of vital importance for astronomy. If no brown dwarfs had been discovered or if brown-dwarf candidates had proved to be altogether different astronomical bodies, the logical structure of star formation might have to be fundamentally altered or even abandoned. However, brown dwarfs were successfully identified, and more and more of them are being discovered all the time. Collectively they fill the last gap in theory; star formation is now reasonably clearly understood.

Robert M. Hawthorne, Jr.

Basic Bibliography

Boss, Alan P. "Extrasolar Planets." *Physics Today* 49 (September, 1996): 32-38. This article discusses large planets, brown dwarfs, and small stars and has a short but fine bibliography.

Henry, Todd J. "Brown Dwarfs Revealed—At Last!" *Sky and Telescope* 91 (April, 1996): 24-28. A clear, nonprofessional discussion of the problems of brown-dwarf identification, with information about Gliese 229B and Teide 1.

Marley, M. S., et al. "Atmospheric, Evolutionary, and Spectral Models of the Brown Dwarf Gliese 229 B." *Science* 272 (June 28, 1996): 1919-1921. A fairly technical article, but it provides the actual data upon which the identification of Gliese 229B is based.

Nakajima, T., et al. "Discovery of a Cool Brown Dwarf." *Nature* 378 (November 30, 1995): 463-465. Data on such aspects of Gliese 229B as mass, temperature, and luminosity and a demonstration that this brown dwarf is as far from Earth as its parent star. A technical article.

Rosenthal, Edward D., Mark A. Gurwell, and Paul T. P. Ho. "Efficient Detection of Brown Dwarfs Using Methane-Band Imaging." *Nature* 384 (November 21, 1996): 243-244. Methane data following on Nakajima's article.

Stephens, Sally. "Needles in the Cosmic Haystack." *Astronomy* 23 (September, 1995): 50-55. A good, nontechnical, state-of-the-art discussion on brown dwarfs that appeared just prior to the first identifications.

Tyson, Neil de Grasse. "When a Star Is Not Born." *Natural History* 105 (March, 1996): 62-63. A popular discussion of brown dwarfs and their formation, this article touches on the theoretical question of whether brown dwarfs fit into existing star-formation mechanisms.

Current Bibliography

Chaisson, Eric, and Steve McMillan. *Astronomy Today.* 2d ed. Upper Saddle River, N.J.: Prentice-Hall, 1997. One of a very small number of introductory texts that discusses particular brown dwarfs.

Kulkarni, S. R. "Brown Dwarfs: A Possible Missing Link Between Stars and Planets." *Science* 276 (May 30, 1997): 1350-1354. A somewhat technical, but very informative article. This and the eight that follow (through page 1391) are presented under the collective title "Stellar Birth and Death." A good overall look at the topic.

Martin, Eduardo L., Rafael Rebolo, and Maria Rosa Zapatero-Osorio. "The Discovery of Brown Dwarfs." *American Scientist* 85 (November-December, 1997): 522-529. The most complete and general discussion of brown dwarfs, by the people who identified Teide-1. It contains a good bibliography, with leading citations of technical literature.

Mayor, Michel, and Disier Queloz. "Swiss Find 10 New Brown Dwarfs." *Astronomy* 25 (February, 1997): 24-29. Part of the rush of discovery that followed Teide-1 and Gliese 229B.

_____. "Many Brown Dwarfs Being Found by Lithium Signature." *Sky and Telescope* 93 (February, 1997): 17-23. More recent discoveries, as in the preceding citation.

Cross-References

Cosmology, 97; Galactic Structures, 279; Stellar Evolution, 942; The Universe: Evolution, 999; The Universe: Structure, 1015.

Cepheid Variables

A star whose brightness changes over time is called a variable star. Among the periodic variables, the most significant are the Cepheid variables, for they have provided a key to the distance scale of the universe.

Overview

For more than three centuries, stars have been known to vary in brightness. In the late 1600's, the bright star Algol (Beta Persei, commonly called "the ghost") was explained successfully as an eclipsing two-star (binary) system. In the last two hundred years, tens of thousands of variable stars of different types have been discovered, both in the Milky Way and in other galaxies. Variables that do not have a name already assigned such as Polaris, Betelgeuse, or Delta Cephei are labeled starting with R to Z followed by the possessive of the constellation name; for example, R Coronae Borealis. Then the letters RR, RS, through ZZ are used. Finally, AA through QZ, omitting J are used. This system allows for 334 variables in each constellation. After that, V335, V336, and so on are used.

Several categories of variable stars exist. The broadest classification is into extrinsic and intrinsic variables. The extrinsic variables change brightness because of circumstances external to the star, while intrinsic variables change because of internal physical changes. Most extrinsic variables are eclipsing star systems whose orbital plane is close enough to astronomers' line of sight for the stars to pass in front of one another.

There is a wide variety of intrinsic variables. They may be exploding stars, such as novas and supernovas whose brightness increases many magnitudes; for example, Nova Aquilae 1918 increased eight magnitudes, or fifteen thousand times in brightness. Others vary irregularly, some erratically, some irregularly cyclical, some semiregularly. Still other variables are periodic. Among these are two main types: those that display multiple periodicities, such as the Beta Canis Majoris stars and the Delta Scuti stars; and those that are regularly periodic, such as the RR Lyrae (periods of less than a day), the Cepheids with periods from one to forty-five days, and the long-period variables with periods above fifty days.

The Cepheids, named after Delta Cephei, which was discovered in 1784, are yellow supergiant stars and the most useful of the variable stars. They have attracted extensive astronomical attention because of their contribution to distance measurement. For the more than six hundred Cepheids

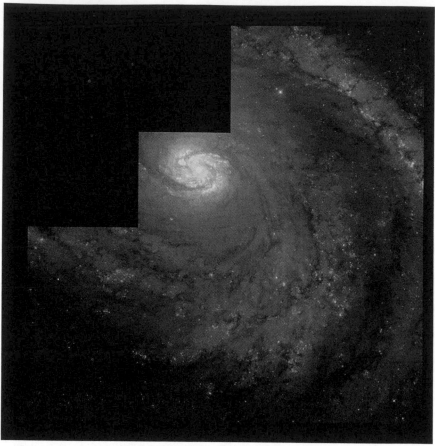

Spiral galaxy M100 with cepheid variables embedded in its spiral arms. *(J. Trauger, Jet Propulsion Laboratory, and National Aeronautics and Space Administration)*

discovered within the Milky Way, the periods cluster at seven days, with very few having periods shorter than three days or longer than thirty days. The central tendency varies from galaxy to galaxy in a fashion related to the evolutionary history of the galaxy.

When brightness is plotted against time, a "light-curve" is produced. If the period is more than a few hours, the light-curve has to be pieced together from observations over many nights or with observations from different observatories, a difficult and tedious process. The light-curves of all Cepheids are not the same, although most of them brighten more rapidly than they fade. Each has a characteristic shape with bumps in the curve, a sort of unique fingerprint for each star. Further, the shape of the curve is related to the length of the period of variation. This is true of Cepheids from other galaxies as well as the Milky Way, an indication that they are the same wherever they occur. Although Cepheids vary from one another, each is extremely regular, with the length of the period constant to one part in a million.

When Cepheids change brightness, they also change in color and in character of their spectrum. As expected, when brightest they have the highest surface temperature and are blue in color. As the Cepheid approaches its brightest level, the lines in its spectrum move toward the violet end, indicating that the surface of the star is moving toward Earth; that is, it achieves maximum radial velocity where radial velocity is motion along the line of sight. As the star approaches its minimum brightness, the spectrum is displaced toward the red end of the spectrum, indicating that the surface is moving away from Earth. The implication of these motions is that the change in brightness is related indirectly to physical vibration or pulsation of the star. The brightness is related directly to changes that take place in the surface temperature of the star at the same time as the pulsations. An average Cepheid is estimated to change radius by 7 to 8 percent during a pulsation cycle and changes about one magnitude in brightness during a cycle.

Accumulating intensive studies of Cepheids have established that the period of a star that pulsates as a result of gravitational controls will depend in an inversely proportional way upon its density. The period-luminosity relationship, however, flows more from the relationship between mass and luminosity, which holds for all stars, rather than from pulsation theory. Most notable is that Cepheid-type pulsation occurs only with stars in a fairly narrow band of temperatures related to spectral classes F and G. There is, similarly, a limited range in luminosities from about −1.5 to −6.

The pulsations are associated with a layer of ionized hydrogen and helium below the surface of the star. As the star pulsates, the gases alternately ionize and recombine, alternately impeding and permitting the outward flow of radiation. The reason for the limited temperature range for the variables is that a higher temperature results in this layer being too near the surface of the star to be effective. If it is too cool, the layer is too deep in the star and is essentially smothered and ineffectual. In stable stars, the outward pressure of radiation matches the inward pressure of gravity. Cepheids oscillate around this equilibrium point. While these features alone would make Cepheids fascinating objects for study, the most striking feature of all is that the longer the period, the brighter or more luminous the star, on an absolute scale. This was the discovery that allowed the Cepheids to be used as a measuring rod for the scale of the universe and made them very significant in the development of twentieth century astronomy.

Applications

Cepheids would have been just another astronomical phenomenon of interest had it not been for their role in establishing the scale of distance in the universe. At the beginning of the twentieth century, the most reliable means of establishing distance was through triangulation, or measurement of parallax. This method used the orbit of Earth as a baseline, and while that distance is great, on the cosmic scale it is minute. As a consequence, stars could be measured out to only a few hundred years. Therefore, the search was under way for alternative means of establishing the distance of stars. Several statistical methods based upon brightness, color, and other measures were attempted with varying degrees of success.

The major breakthrough came in 1912 when Henrietta Swan Leavitt was working at Harvard's southern astronomical station at Arequipa, Peru. She had been surveying the Magellanic Clouds, two small galaxies satellite to the Milky Way. Leavitt had already discovered thousands of Cepheid variables in these clouds. One evening before beginning her measurements, she drew up a list of twenty-five of the variables according to their brightness. She noticed immediately that they were also arranged according to period. The brighter the star, the longer the period. By that simple task, she had discovered the period-luminosity relationship. She recognized the significance of this discovery and realized that if the distance of even one Cepheid could be known reliably, it could provide a means of determining the distance of almost any Cepheid whose light-curve could be traced anywhere in the universe.

The difficulty was establishing such an absolute scale. Ejnar Hertzsprung made the first attempt to calibrate the Cepheids by a study of the brightest ones, which occur primarily in the spiral arms of the Milky Way. By statistical means, he calculated a mean luminosity for a particular period and estimated the luminosity. His result, which was far too dim, was still startling, for it made the Cepheids very bright stars. The most luminous had an absolute magnitude of −4, about four thousand times as bright as the Sun. Following Hertzsprung and improvements made by Harlow Shapley, initial estimates of Cepheid distances were made, and systems of stars including the Magellanic Clouds that contained Cepheids were measured. The next step was the identification by Shapley and others of Cepheids in open clusters of stars within the Milky Way. The color-magnitude array was matched with the main sequence stars on the Hertzsprung-Russell diagram for clusters, which was then calibrated by the nearby Hyades cluster, whose distance was known geometrically. As a consequence, when Cepheids were discovered in more distant clusters, there was a means of establishing their distance and getting their luminosity from that. The result was that the Cepheids were found to be even brighter than Hertzsprung had estimated.

The actual use of Cepheids for distance measurement is not as simple. They were visible in only about thirty of the closest galaxies. Three significant complications arise from several factors: First, the relationship between period and luminosity is not a neat line. In the real world, the stars are dispersed about that line, most within a half magnitude of the line. This dispersion means that distance to any galaxy is only poorly known if based upon one or even a few Cepheids. The more Cepheids available, the more accurate the statistical estimate of the distance. Second, the dispersion is related to the location of the Cepheid in the evolutionary sequence of stars. As this factor has become more clearly understood, compensation has allowed the refinement of the measurement of the distance of particular galaxies of interest. A third complication stems from the fact that in more distant galaxies only the very brightest Cepheids can be observed. Adjustments for this distortion have also been made.

By 1925, Hertzsprung and Shapley's calibration of the Cepheids allowed Edwin Powell Hubble to estimate the distance of the Magellanic Clouds and the Andromeda galaxy (M31). By 1929, the calibration of the Cepheids enabled Hubble to discover the redshift distance (actually, velocity of recession) relationship.

Additional adjustments in the distance scale were necessary from further study of the variable stars. In 1944, Henry Mineur found that the variables with periods shorter than one day (now called the RR Lyrae variables) were about one magnitude fainter than the classical Cepheids, a fact that immediately explained why they were not found as expected in the Magellanic Clouds. They were too dim to be seen by the equipment available at that time. Another major adjustment in the distance scale came with the discovery by Walter Baade in 1944 of two populations of stars, which resulted in more than doubling the distance of the galaxies. The significance for the study of Cepheids is that two types of Cepheids were also discovered: the classical Cepheids belong to population I, and the RR Lyrae (short period) and cluster Cepheids belong to population II. The cluster Cepheids are found primarily in the center of the galaxy or in the globular clusters that form a spherical halo around the center of the galaxy. The prototypical stars (eight of them) were discovered in omicron Centauri. These eight protostars had periods in the day-and-a-half to fifty-eight-day range. Their light-curve, luminosity, and color differed from the classical Cepheids, and they had a luminosity about a magnitude and a half dimmer than the classical Cepheids, which led to erroneous distances for all star clusters and galaxies that were based upon their use. These stars occur both in and out of globular clusters, but they do occur far from the galactic plane, while the classical Cepheids all lie near the galactic plane and tend toward the galactic center. Baade's adjustment was confirmed with the discovery of the nineteenth magnitude RR Lyrae stars in the Magellanic Clouds, which led to more than doubling of the distance of the Clouds, as well as the rest of the galactic distance scale.

For more remote galaxies where variables cannot be observed, the amount of shift toward the red end of the spectrum for the galaxy as a whole is used to estimate the distance. Nevertheless, even this method depends upon the calibration for the near galaxies given by the Cepheids. Cepheids have therefore proven the most valuable tool in the effort to measure galactic distances. In addition to measurements involving distance, they are useful also in any studies aided by the need for bright stars. Thus, they have been used extensively for studies of the size, structure, and galactic rotation of the Milky Way, for their radial velocities do confirm the rotation, although the bright O and B stars actually give somewhat better confirmation. They have been prominent also in studies of stellar evolution. It would be difficult to overestimate the progress that modern astronomy has made as a consequence of improved understanding of the nature and functions of the Cepheid variable stars.

Context

The study of Cepheid variables has been prominent in twentieth century astronomy. In the three major divisions of astronomy (planetary, galactic, and extragalactic), the study of Cepheids is primarily within galactic studies. They were prominent, however, in initially establishing the distance of exterior galaxies and remain a necessary link in calibrating the redshift to velocity of recession relationship.

The most active period of study of Cepheids was from 1910 through the 1960's. Since then, telescopes and detectors in space have led to dramatic new discoveries that overshadow Earth-based study of Cepheids. Individual research efforts continue, tending to refine what was previously known about the Cepheids. The Cepheids and other variable stars have become more prominent in later years for their usefulness in studies of stellar evolution than as distance indicators.

Unless some striking new phenomena involving Cepheids are discovered, they have enjoyed their time of most intense study and greatest usefulness. Further investigations of them will tend to be sporadic and relatively undramatic, primarily reserved for the pages of the technical journals in physics and astronomy. Their potential for collapse into black holes and other facets of their evolution will remain the primary focus of stellar studies relating to them.

Cepheids remain a wavering beacon of brightness that has aided in unlocking the scale of distances in the universe. They have also given humankind a more accurate picture of humanity's place in space and the grandeur of the universe. The study of variables contributed to the unlocking of the distance scale so that the expanding universe could be discovered. Variables are indirect contributors to the development of the generally accepted big bang theory of the origin of the cosmos. Credit must be given to the pioneering astronomers who devoted much time to the study of Cepheids and other variable stars in the early part of this century.

Ivan L. Zabilka

Basic Bibliography

Campbell, Leon, and Luigi Jacchia. *The Story of Variable Stars.* Philadelphia: Blackstone, 1941. An older popular explanation of the theory and observations of variable stars. While a clear presentation, it has the disadvantage of preceding the discovery of the two populations of stars and the resolution of problems with the distance scale.

Cox, Arthur N., Warren M. Sparks, and S. G. Starrfield, eds. *Stellar Pulsation.* New York: Springer-Verlag, 1987. Based on the proceedings of a conference held as a memorial to John P. Cox at the Los Alamos National Laboratory, New Mexico, from August 11 to 15, 1986. While very technical, the introductions and conclusions provide helpful insights. About a fourth of the papers directly relate to Cepheids. Bibliography.

Glasby, John S. *Variable Stars.* Cambridge, Mass.: Harvard University Press, 1969. A popular account that is complete and easy to read. The information is reliable and not too technical. Accessible to the general reader, it gives an adequate account of the importance of Cepheid variables to modern astronomy.

Hoffmeister, Cuno. *Variable Stars.* Translated by Storm Dunlop. Berlin: Springer-Verlag, 1985. Technical, but a comprehensive survey revised by Gerold Richter and Wolfgang Wenzel. Considers the theory and use of all types of variables. Appropriate for the interested general reader who is willing to skip over some of the more difficult mathematics for the valuable descriptive portions.

Leavitt, Henrietta S. "Discovery of the Period-Magnitude Relation." In *Source Book in Astronomy, 1900-1950,* edited by Harlow Shapley. Cambridge, Mass.: Harvard University Press, 1960. A short discussion of the original discovery of the relationship between the period of a variable and its absolute brightness. The missing piece in this description is the frustration Leavitt endured when her supervisors did not allow her to develop the concept, but rather moved into the field and essentially claimed it for their own.

Payne-Gaposchkin, Cecilia, and Katherine Haramundanis. *Introduction to Astronomy.* 2d ed. Englewood Cliffs, N.J.: Prentice-Hall, 1970. While somewhat dated, this remains the clearest and most comprehensive explanation of the types and significance of the variable stars in a general astronomy textbook.

Current Bibliography

Percy, John R., Janet Akyuz Mattei, and Christiaan Sterken, eds. *Variable Star Research: An International Perspective: Proceedings of the First European Meeting of the American Association of Variable Star Observers: International Cooperation and Coordination in Variable Star Research.* New York: Cambridge University Press, 1992.

Scovil, Charles E. *The AAVSO Variable Star Atlas.* 2d ed. Cambridge, Mass.: American Association of Variable Star Observers, 1990.

Cross-References

Cosmology, 97; Galactic Structures, 279; Stellar Evolution, 942; The Universe: Evolution, 999; The Universe: Structure, 1015.

Comets

A comet is a small body composed mostly of frozen ices but typically embedded with solids. Comets orbit the Sun in highly elliptical orbits. The Oort Cloud is a vast cloud of cometary bodies that extends billions of kilometers out from the Sun.

Overview

Comets are familiar to nearly everyone as striking starlike objects with long tails stretching across a wide band of the sky. The most famous comet, Halley's comet, makes its return to the night skies every seventy-five years. The word "comet" is derived from a Greek word meaning "long haired." Comets were greatly feared before the twentieth century as bad omens. Since then, they have been identified and cataloged as objects that come from deep space. Most of them occupy orbits that carry them far outside the solar system. Many comets make only a single approach to the Sun and never return again, while others exist in stable, but highly elliptical orbits that allow them to return after an extended period of time, such as Halley's comet.

In 1986, the European space probe Giotto passed about 600 kilometers from Comet Halley as it made its close approach to the Sun. The probe verified existing theories that comets are made up of ices covered by black dust or soil. The spacecraft confirmed a theory that had been advanced prior to the reconnaissance that described comets as "dirty snowballs." Using data taken by the spacecraft, scientists determined that the dust is composed of carbon, hydrogen, oxygen, and nitrogen. Other metals have also been discovered in comets, such as iron, calcium, nickel, potassium, copper, and silicon. Halley's comet was one of the darkest objects ever seen in the solar system; it was basically flat black.

Comets are composed of a mixture of ices and dust. As a comet approaches the Sun, it absorbs the Sun's energy and warms up. The main body of the comet is called the nucleus. As the nucleus warms, the ices beneath the comet's soil evaporate. Because the comet has no atmosphere, the evaporated substance (also called a volatile) escapes into the vacuum of space as a gaseous envelope that surrounds the comet called the "coma." As the coma grows, it forms a plume of vapor that carries away some of the comet's surface dust as well. This mixture of evaporated volatile and dust is carried away from the comet by the solar wind, is ionized by high-energy particles, and creates the spectacular tail of the comet. The comet's tail, glowing in the solar wind, can stream behind the comet for millions of kilometers. The nucleus of the comet consists of mostly volatile ices and dust. The ice is nearly all water ice, but there is also evidence of ices composed of carbon dioxide and methane. More elementary compounds of nitrogen, oxygen, and carbon monoxide may exist as volatile ices.

Comets are typically small bodies. Halley's comet is a potato-shaped object, 14 by 17 kilometers. The largest known comet is Chiron, which is estimated to be approximately 200 kilometers in diameter. Comets are thought to have formed as the solar system evolved. The material of which comets are composed was constructed by accretion at the outer edge of the disk of material that ultimately became the Sun and planets. Because the comet material was fashioned at the outer edge of the solar system, the Sun did not evaporate the volatiles in the cometary material. At the same time, the giant planets of the solar system formed at what would become the outer orbits of the solar system. These massive planets encountered the newly formed comets, and the comets that were not engulfed by the giant planets were, over the first billion years, catapulted into interstellar space by the planets' massive gravitational fields. Not all comets met that fate, however. Some were gently nudged into stable orbits closer to the Sun. Others were flung into the inner solar system and impacted the inner planets. (There is some speculation that Earth's oceans came from cometary ices.)

What remained after billions of years of planetary encounters was an extraordinarily large cloud of comets extending outward from orbits beyond Pluto in all directions. A virtual spherical-shaped cloud of comets surrounds the Sun at a distance from 1,000 up to 100,000 astronomical units. This cloud, which may contain as many as 2 trillion comets of all shapes and sizes,

Hale-Bopp comet. *(National Aeronautics and Space Administration)*

is called the Oort Cloud, named for the Dutch astronomer Jan Hendrik Oort, who first proposed its existence in 1950. The spherical-shaped Oort Cloud is not the only source of comets in the solar system. There is a disk-shaped source of comets that extends from about 35 to 40 astronomical units out from the Sun to about 1,000 astronomical units. This Kuiper belt was named for the astronomer Gerard Peter Kuiper, who theorized its possible existence in 1951. The disk-shaped Kuiper belt blends with the spherical Oort Cloud at about 1,000 astronomical units.

The Oort Cloud is the source for long-period comets, with orbital periods of greater than two hundred years. The Kuiper belt is most likely the primary source for short-period comets, with orbital periods of less than two hundred years, such as Halley's comet. Comets have definite lives, unlike planets. Each time a comet streaks in toward the Sun, the volatile gases that stream off the comet and form the beautiful cometary tail also deplete the comet's mass. The comet melts away with each pass toward the Sun. When Halley's comet streamed past the Sun in 1986, the Giotto spacecraft measured a loss of 40 tons of mass per second from the comet. If the supply of comets were not steadily replenished from deep space, they would have all been lost long ago.

The Sun is one among billions of stars in the Milky Way galaxy. In the relatively near region of the galaxy, there are hundreds of local stars, which are all rotating around the galaxy and are moving relative to one another. Because the stars are so far apart on the average, the chance of one star colliding with another is practically nonexistent. Yet, the possibility of a local star passing near to or through the Oort Cloud, which extends up to 100,000 astronomical units away from the Sun, is very high over millions of years. It is estimated that since the solar system formed, about five thousand stars have passed within 100,000 astronomical units from the Sun. If an object as massive as another star passed close to the Oort Cloud, it could easily cause enough gravitational perturbations to send comets in toward the Sun.

Comets may appear from any part of the sky. Since the Oort Cloud is sphere-shaped, long-period comets can appear to streak in to the Sun from any point in space. Short-period comets, originating from the Kuiper belt, always appear to emanate from a band along the ecliptic plane (the plane that contains the planetary orbits). After careful study of where comets actually originate, an analysis was made of their orbits. It has been discovered that there are areas of the sky that are more rich in comets than others and other areas of the sky that appear to be practically devoid of comets. Four different theories have been advanced to explain the source of these newly appearing comets. The first theory postulates that the passage of stars in or near the Oort Cloud may so affect the gravitational balance of comets that they are sent falling toward the Sun. The second theory involves brown dwarfs, which are massive objects—about thirty times the mass of Jupiter—that are not quite planets and not quite stars. Yet, they do not have enough mass to create the conditions for thermonuclear ignition at their core, which would initiate the process of stellar formation. They radiate

Comet West over Table Mountain in California, 1976. This visitor from beyond Pluto will not return for over 500,000 years. *(Jet Propulsion Laboratory)*

nearly all infrared energy and cannot be easily seen from Earth. Current estimates approximate the number of brown dwarfs near the Sun to be sixty times greater than that of ordinary stars. A brown dwarf should pass through the Oort Cloud every 7 million years. Such an object would travel very slowly with respect to the Sun and would gravitationally release large swarms of comets into the solar system. These two stellar mechanisms (the action of either a passing star or brown dwarf) are estimated to have been the source of about one-third of the observed comets.

According to the third theory, huge molecular clouds in interstellar space, much more massive than a single star, may pass at very large distances (tens of light-years), and may still cause a release of comets through gentle perturbations of their orbits. The final theory for the source of newly appearing comets is galactic tidal action. Each galaxy has a gravitational field, which causes an attraction toward the midplane of the galaxy of all bodies (comets and stars). As these bodies orbit the galaxy, they are gravitationally influenced by one another. The galactic tide is the difference between the galactic forces acting on the Sun and the comet. Because the force of the galactic tide is very specific with respect to direction, it cannot act toward the poles of the Sun or toward the equator. Observations of cometary tracks confirm that comets from deep space do not seem to approach the Sun from these segments of the celestial sphere. This mechanism appears to explain the approach of the majority of all long-period comets entering the solar system from the Oort Cloud.

Applications

The study of comets involves detailed knowledge of the composition of the outer regions of the solar system and the space between the last planet and 100,000 astronomical units outward. Cometary study also seeks to understand complex gravitational interactions between bodies separated by wide distances and even gravitational interactions between tiny comets and the entire galaxy. Astronomers want to learn more about the makeup of comets, their behavior when approaching the Sun, and something of the makeup and evolution of the early solar system.

New comets approaching the Sun for the first time have been held in deep freeze in the Oort Cloud and are thought to be composed of primordial material of the newly forming solar system. They have been tied up in the Oort Cloud for billions of years at temperatures slightly above absolute zero. As they approach the Sun, their internal gases begin to stream away. A detailed study of an approaching comet may tell cosmologists about the composition of the early solar system. Comets and their approach have also hinted at the existence of the elusive brown dwarfs, thought to be one of the most common bodies of interstellar space. Because they are so dim, they are all but invisible from Earth. On the other hand, because brown dwarfs are thought to be so plentiful, the study of comets and their orbits may give the first real clues to the former's reality and abundance.

In the early 1980's the existence of galactic tidal action was merely speculation. Since then, careful study of cometary orbits and approaches has favorably supported the theory of galactic tides. In the close approach of Halley's comet by unmanned spacecraft in 1986, a wealth of information was recovered on the shape, behavior, and composition of comets. The existence of the Oort Cloud and the concept of gravitational interactions by passing objects in space have led to the theory of periodic comet showers. Such comet showers, separated by periods of tens of millions of years, may be responsible for mass extinctions on Earth. There is wide speculation that Earth was struck by one or more comets 70 million years ago, which wiped out the dinosaurs. Some scientists have speculated that this extinction was the result of a shower of comets from the Oort Cloud, sent on their close approach to the Sun by a passing star or brown dwarf through the Oort Cloud.

Context

Humankind has always looked to the heavens in awe and wonder, and sometimes in fear. Perhaps no other astronomical phenomenon except a total solar eclipse has historically evoked as much fear as comets. When the specter of fear is removed, however, they emerge as strikingly beautiful objects in the sky. It was once believed that if Earth passed through the tail of a comet, its inhabitants would die; this theory has been discredited. Comets are messengers from a time long past. Most are chunks of dirty ice, locked away in the Oort Cloud for billions of years.

Comets have been used to judge vast distances, evaluate the composition of the solar system as it was being born, and even test the idea that the gravity of the entire galaxy can make a difference to the smallest of objects in space. Comets have been used as yardsticks to evaluate what may be the most common type of star in the galaxy—the brown dwarf—which ironically is one that may never be seen. Comets have been called dirty snowballs. Halley's comet was so black that it was the darkest object ever seen in space. Yet, from these dirty specks of ice, cosmologists have witnessed some of the most spectacular light shows. Ultimately, comets may also generate clues to some of the most fundamental secrets about the solar system and planets. From these tiny messengers, cosmologists may unlock and examine pristine elements from creation itself.

Dennis Chamberland

Basic Bibliography

Benningfield, Damond. "Where Do Comets Come From?" *Astronomy* 18 (September, 1990): 28-36. A fine summary of comets, superbly illustrated and written for the general public. Addresses the question of the Oort Cloud and Kuiper belt in detailed, scaled illustrations. Discusses possible linkage to the extinction of the dinosaurs and the latest satellite discoveries.

Brandt, John C., and Robert D. Chapman. *Introduction to Comets.* New York: Cambridge University Press, 1986. A semitechnical discussion of comets, their origin, structure, and manifestation in the solar system. Illustrated and readable by those with some background in astronomy. Contains detailed tables and charts pertaining to comets, positions, and orbits.

Cornell, James, and Alan P. Lightman. *Revealing the Universe.* Cambridge, Mass.: MIT Press, 1982. Discusses in some detail specific areas of observational and theoretical astronomy. A discussion of comets is included, specifically with respect to their structure and composition and the solar system itself. Somewhat technical; best approached by those with a scientific background. Illustrated.

Delsemme, Armand. "Whence Come Comets?" *Sky and Telescope* 70 (March, 1989): 260-264. This article, written by one of the best-known comet researchers, is a concise, detailed review of the modern theories about comet origins. An explicit description of the various theories of comet replenishment and the forces that may be at work from brown dwarfs and close passes by nearby stars. Illustrated. For a wide audience.

Harwit, Martin. *Cosmic Discovery.* New York: Basic Books, 1981. A good work for understanding the place of comets in the history of astronomy. A fascinating expedition through the history and foundation of astronomy. Illustrated. For interested readers.

Sagan, Carl, and Ann Druyan. *Comet.* New York: Random House, 1985. This coffee table book is a fine work of art, written by the most popular astronomer in the United States. Filled with beautiful color and historical black-and-white photographs and illustrations. For general audiences.

Current Bibliography

Levy, David H. *The Quest for Comets: An Explosive Trail of Beauty and Danger.* New York: Plenum Press, 1994.

Schaaf, Fred. *Comet of the Century: From Halley to Hale-Bopp.* New York: Copernicus, 1997.

Thomas, Paul J., Christopher F. Chyba, and Christopher P. McKay, eds. *Comets and the Origin and Evolution of Life.* New York: Springer, 1997.

Verschuur, Gerrit L. *Impact!: The Threat of Comets and Asteroids.* New York: Oxford University Press, 1996.

Cross-References

Asteroids, 9; Halley's Comet, 347; Meteors and Meteor Showers, 576.

Coordinate Systems

There are several astronomical coordinate systems that are in common usage. In each system, the position of an object in the sky, or on the celestial sphere, is denoted by two angles: the reference plane and a reference direction.

Overview

An astronomical coordinate system is a way for locating the position of an object in the sky, or on the celestial sphere, as denoted by two angles. There are several astronomical coordinate systems, and each system uses the measurement of two angles: the reference plane, which contains the observer, and the reference direction, which is the direction from the observer to some arbitrary point lying in the reference plane. The intersection of the plane and the celestial sphere is a great circle defining the equator of the coordinate system. The celestial poles, each 90 degrees from the equator, are imaginary points around which the celestial sphere appears to rotate; they are the poles of the coordinate system. Great circles passing through these poles intersect the equator of the system at right angles.

One of the two angular coordinates of each coordinate system is measured from the equator of the system to the object along the great circle passing through it and the poles. Angles on one side of the equator are considered positive; those on the opposite side are negative. The other angular coordinate is measured along the equator from the reference direction to the intersection of the equator, with the great circle passing through the object and the poles.

In addition to a reference plane and reference direction, each system uses a "latitude" coordinate with a range as well as a "longitude" coordinate with a range. The range of the latitude for four commonly used systems is from 0 to 90 degrees, with positive degrees located north of the equator and negative toward the south. On the other hand, the longitude coordinates are measured to the east and range from 0 to 360 degrees, or, equivalently, from 0 to 24 hours. The latitude and longitude of each system can be compared with the terrestrial latitude and longitude. On Earth, the plane of the equator is the fundamental plane and the Earth's equator is the equator of the system. The North and South terrestrial poles are the poles of the system. One coordinate—the latitude—is either positive (north) or negative (south) of the equator. Longitude is measured along the equator to the intersection of the equator and the Greenwich meridian. Terrestrial longitude is either east or west, depending upon whichever is less. On the other hand, the corresponding coordinate in the celestial system is generally in one direction to the east, from 0 to 360 degrees, or 0 to 24 hours.

Four astronomical coordinate systems are commonly used: horizon, equator, ecliptic, and galactic. The horizon system has as its reference plane the horizon plane, which is a great circle on the celestial sphere 90 degrees from the zenith. Its reference direction is the north point and its latitude coordinate is defined by its altitude (h) being positive toward the zenith and negative toward the nadir. Its range is plus or minus 90 degrees. The longitude coordinate has its azimuth (A) measured to the east along the horizon from the north point; its range is 0 to 360 degrees. The equator system uses the plane of the celestial equator as its reference plane, with the reference direction the vernal equinox. The latitude coordinate has a declination that is positive toward the north celestial pole and negative toward the south celestial pole with a range of 0 to 90 degrees. The longitude coordinate has a right ascension measured to the east along the celestial equator from the vernal equinox and has a range of 0 to 24 hours.

In the ecliptic system, the reference plane is the plane of the Earth's orbit, which is ecliptic, and its reference direction is the vernal equinox. The latitude is the celestial latitude toward the north ecliptic pole and is positive; toward the south ecliptic pole, the latitude is negative and the range is 0 to 90 degrees. The longitude coordinate is the celestial longitude measured to the east along the ecliptic from the vernal equinox, and it has a range from 0 to 360 degrees. The fourth coordinate system is the galactic system, which has a reference plane that is the mean plane of the Milky Way with a direction to the galactic center. The latitude coordinate is the north galactic pole, which is positive, and toward the south galactic pole, it is negative. Its range is plus or minus 90 degrees. The longitude is the galactic longitude measured along the galactic equator to the east from the galactic center and with a range of 0 to 360 degrees.

The coordinates of the stars are not completely fixed, since the phenomenon of precession alters the frame of reference. Precession is the slow circular motion of the Earth's axis in space. The proper motion of the stars themselves slowly causes the coordinates to change, as do other slight influences. Star positions are updated periodically to allow for these changes. At present, most star catalogs and charts use the positions of the stars in 1950 as a basis for comparison. Astronomical atlases often give formulas for working out up-to-date coordinates from those of the standard reference. The three motions of the Earth can be illustrated by likening the Earth to a spinning top placed on the edge of a merry-go-round. The top's spinning represents the rotation of the Earth on its axis, and the top's motion around the center of the merry-go-round represents the revolution of the Earth around the Sun. This top is not spinning upright; its axis of rotation is tipped from the perpendicular to the floor of the merry-go-round, with the result that the axis of rotation itself rotates around the

78

perpendicular (as all tops do, especially as their spinning slows down). This motion is precession.

The positions of the celestial poles and celestial equator do not remain fixed on the celestial sphere. They wander in a predictable way as a result of precession. The celestial poles, for example, describe a circle on the celestial sphere, which repeats itself every 25,800 years. Because of precession, the equinoxes are wandering westward so that gradually the seasons are changing. The vernal equinox, now in Pisces (March 21), occurs about a month earlier than it did two thousand years ago, when it was in Aries. Polaris will eventually cease to be the pole star. At the time of the building of the Great Pyramid in Egypt, more than forty-five hundred years ago, Thuban in Draco was the pole star. The builders lined up the pyramid's main passages with the star. In about ten thousand years, Vega in Lyra will be the pole star. Understanding precession is important to the coordinate system, since its effect must be allowed in accurate observational astronomy. It is the main factor in the periodic updating of star positions in star catalogs and almanacs.

Applications

An application of the coordinate system is shown by star maps, which show the position of the stars on the celestial sphere. Like all maps, these maps slightly distort what they represent, since they show a curved surface on flat paper. The maps are crisscrossed with a reference grid, which shows the equatorial coordinates of right ascension and declination. The coordinates relate to epoch 1950.

The sky is divided into six equatorial segments and northern and southern circumpolar regions. Stars are included down to the fourth magnitude of brightness. Many of the best-known stars are named. Others accompanying the maps are identified by Greek letters according to the Bayer system, which classifies the stars in a constellation in order of their brightness. Magnitude can be apparent, which is brightness of a body as it appears to an observer on Earth, or absolute, which is the brightness it would appear from a distance of 32.6 light-years. A light-year is the distance light travels in a year. Also included on the maps are the brighter star clusters, galactic nebulas, and external galaxies. They are identified by their Messier (M) numbers or by their *New General Catalogue* (NGC) numbers. Star brightness is measured on a scale based on stars visible to the naked eye. On this scale, brightness is divided into six categories of brightness, denoted as first, second, third, fourth, fifth, and sixth magnitude. The brightest stars in the sky are of the first magnitude (mag 1); those just visible are of the sixth magnitude (mag 6). A first magnitude star is 2.5 times brighter than one of the second magnitude, which is 2.5 times brighter than one of the third magnitude, until the comparison of a mag 1 star, which is one hundred times brighter than a mag 6 star. A typical star from each of the equatorial segments and the northern and southern circumpolar regions is identified by its right ascension range, which is shown in the following table:

Star Map Number	Right Ascension Range	Star Name
1	Northern circumpolar	Ursa Major, the Great Bear
2	22 hours - 2 hours	Pegasus, the Flying Horse
3	2 hours - 6 hours	Orion, the Mighty Hunter
4	6 hours - 10 hours	Canis Major, the Great Dog
5	10 hours - 14 hours	Centaurus, the Centaur
6	14 hours - 18 hours	Scorpius, the Scorpion
7	18 hours - 22 hours	Cygnus, the Swan
8	Southern circumpolar	Crux, the Southern Cross

Since hour circles are to stars in the sky what meridians are to cities on Earth, the hour circle must rise and set with the stars. The hour circle chosen as the reference is the one that passes through the vernal equinox. A star's position with reference to this prime hour circle is given as right ascension and is measured only to the east in hours instead of in degrees (24 hours equals 360 degrees). An important distinction between solar and sidereal time is that stars set four minutes earlier each day according to solar time, therefore, the clocks set to "sidereal time" (star time) must run four minutes faster each day. The solar day begins at midnight when a point in the sky exactly opposite the Sun crosses the meridian of a given locality (or in actual practice crosses the midpoint of a time zone). The sidereal "day" begins when the vernal equinox crosses the meridian of a particular locality (time zones are not being used or are not of any use in this case).

The vertical axis is declination and is measured in number of degrees north (+) or south (–) of the celestial equator; as a result, the celestial equator has 0 degrees declination, the north celestial pole is positive 90 degrees, and the south celestial pole has a declination of negative 90 degrees. The scale of right of ascension is fixed arbitrarily by assuming a particular line to be zero. The zero point, which is zero hour, is the vernal equinox. The equinoxes are the two points where the celestial equator crosses the ecliptic, which is the path the Sun follows across the sky in the course of the year. The vernal equinox is one of these points that the Sun crosses on its way north each year; the other point is the autumnal equinox.

To find a star's celestial coordinates, one can measure the number of hours around the celestial equator to its hour circle and the number of degrees north or south of the celestial equator to its declination. A star's right ascension is equal to the length of time that elapses after the vernal equinox crosses the meridian until the star crosses the same meridian. The interval is measured in sidereal time. The stars are essentially fixed in the sky, therefore, their right ascension and declination do not change measurably over short periods of time. The Sun, Moon, and planets, though, wander through the sky with respect to the stars; their right ascension and declination change during the course of a year. An example of how a star's location is described by its coordinates is shown in the Messier Catalog description for the Crab nebula:

Magnitude	NGC	Right ascension		Declination	
		Hours	Minutes	Degrees	Minutes
1	1952	05	34.5	+22	01

One of the brightest stars in the sky is Sirius; it is identified by its coordinates, as follows:

Rank	Star	Constellation	Magnitude	Right ascension		Declination	
				Hours	Minutes	Degrees	Minutes
1	Sirius	Canis Major	−1.46	06	45	−16	43

Context

The earliest references to measurements and locations of stars stem from Hellenistic astronomy. The strength of Hellenistic culture was caused to a great extent by the merging of Greek and Asian elements. In astronomy, there is an abundance of observed facts and Greek independence of thought, combined with theoretical power of abstraction. An acquaintance with Babylonian methods and instruments stimulated Greek scholars to become observers of stars. In the hands of the Greeks, the Babylonian results for the periods and irregularities became the basis of geometrical constructions and led to conceptions of spatial world structure.

The center of world commerce and science around 300 to 30 B.C. was Alexandria, the capital of Egypt. The Macedonian kings, the Ptolemies, founded a kind of academy of science. Although the extent and regularity of the observations did not compare with the work of the Babylonian priests, the Greeks did use unknown instruments to locate stars. Euclid mentioned a diopter in his astronomical work. This instrument did not have a graduated circle but merely fixed two opposite points of the horizon. Ptolemy, between 296 and 272 B.C. gives distances to the equator—that is, declinations of a number of stars—as well as differences of longitude measured in degrees and subdivisions, indicating that instruments existed with a graduated circle.

The development of the astronomical coordinate system was important for several reasons; however, the most important was that it allowed for the accurate development of a calendar, which was essential for agriculture and navigation. As a result, the length of the year could be fixed, months and days could be intercalated, and the change of the solstices and equinoxes could be established. The establishment of the coordinate system was important to humankind for practical and theoretical purposes, since a precise calendar led to more accuracy in weather prediction and planting schedules. Many of the uncertainties of navigation could be predicted, and with a better understanding, commerce was able to expand to newer trade areas. Many of the contemporary writers had a great understanding of astronomy and used this understanding to enlighten readers in prose and poetry. In addition, the fixing of the stars by coordinate systems led to the astrologic predictions, almanacs with the positions of planets computed ahead.

The role of coordinate systems in the future is for detailed mapping of galaxies and charting manned and unmanned space exploration.

Earl G. Hoover

Basic Bibliography

Abel, George O. *Exploration of the Universe.* 3d ed. New York: Holt, Rinehart and Winston, 1975. An excellent introductory reference book. Mathematics has been kept to a minimum. Contains an extensive bibliography for each chapter and a useful glossary. Geared for the undergraduate college student.

Bergamini, David. *The Universe.* New York: Time-Life Books, 1969. A popular series written in an informative style that is easy to read and understand. Well illustrated, with photographs, drawings, graphs, and tables. There is a limited bibliography. Of particular interest are the first few chapters covering myths and conceptions. An ideal reference for the high school student.

Menzel, Donald H., and Jay M. Pasachoff. *Field Guide to the Stars and Planets.* 2d ed. Boston: Houghton Mifflin, 1983. An excellent handy reference. Suitable for all high school upper-level students, college students, and the hobbyist. Useful tables give star names and coordinates. In addition, one chapter has an easy-to-read discussion on coordinates, time, and calendars. Highly recommended.

Moche, Dinah L. *Astronomy: A Self-Teaching Guide.* 3d ed. New York: John Wiley & Sons, 1987. A self-instructional text designed so that students with no formal astronomy background can easily learn basic principles and concepts. The material in each chapter is presented in short, numbered sections. The chapter on understanding the starry night is especially recommended for its coverage of the coordinate systems. An excellent book for the upper-level high school and lower-level college student.

Pannekoek, A. *A History of Astronomy.* London: Barnes & Noble Books, 1969. As the title denotes, it is a history and as such is written in a nonscientific format. Should appeal to the college-level student and interested general reader. Of special interest are the early chapters covering the Babylonians, Assyrians, and Chaldean contributions. A good general history; recommended.

Roth, G. D. *Astronomy: A Handbook.* Translated by Arthur Beer. New York: Springer-Verlag, 1975. A college-level text. Presents a wide range of applied astronomy. Divided into theory and practice. The appendix includes the Greek alphabet, astronomical abbreviations and symbols, signs of the zodiac and symbols for the planets, classification of variable stars, double stars, star clusters and nebulas, and the Messier catalog of 1784. Also contains an excellent bibliography of several hundred references.

Stoy, R. H. *Everyman's Astronomy.* New York: St. Martin's Press, 1974. Designed to provide the well-informed reader with a compact and reliable guide to astronomy. Of special interest are the star charts given at the end of chapter 1. Compact and well written.

Current Bibliography

Boucher, C., ed. *Earth Rotation and Coordinate Reference Frames.* International Association of Geodesy Symposia 105. New York: Springer-Verlag, 1990.

Kovalevsky, Jean. *Modern Astrometry.* New York: Springer, 1995.

Lankford, John, ed. *History of Astronomy: An Encyclopedia.* Garland Encyclopedias in the History of Science 1. New York: Garland, 1997.

Maran, Stephen P., ed. *The Astronomy and Astrophysics Encyclopedia.* Foreword by Carl Sagan. New York: Van Nostrand Reinhold, 1992.

Cross-References

Optical Astronomy, 653; Optical Telescopes, 661; Telescopes: Ground-Based, 967; Telescopes: Space-Based, 976.

Cosmic Microwave Background Radiation

Cosmic microwave background radiation is widely interpreted as the remnant of radiation produced when the universe was very hot and dense—a state very different from the present one. Although this background radiation was discovered through ground-based observations, many aspects of the phenomenon are best studied with instruments carried above Earth's atmosphere by spacecraft.

Overview

The discovery of cosmic microwave background radiation in 1964 was one of the most important events of all time—in the same class as such epoch-making discoveries as the proof (in the 1600's) that Earth is one of the planets and, like them, moves around the Sun in an elliptical orbit; Sir Isaac Newton's discovery (in 1687) of the law of universal gravitation; and Edwin Hubble's 1929 discovery of the expansion of the universe. All these events have in common that each, in its time, revolutionized man's concept of the structure of the universe.

Despite its vast importance to cosmology, however, cosmic microwave background radiation is not very well known to the public. It surrounds all living things—which are immersed in it, like embryos in amniotic fluid—but it cannot be seen, felt, heard, smelled, or photographed. It is a very elusive phenomenon.

Its commonly accepted name, "cosmic microwave background radiation," is a very straightforward description of the phenomenon. Still, none of those words is plain English—even "background" is used here in a special sense. The analysis of each of these terms in turn, beginning at the end, will clarify the nature of the phenomenon.

"Radiation" is shorthand for "electromagnetic radiation," the all-inclusive name for light, radio waves, infrared rays, ultraviolet light, X rays, and gamma rays. The term goes back to 1872, when a brilliant Scottish physicist, James Clerk Maxwell, discovered that all known phenomena of electricity and magnetism could be described by a single mathematical theory. Maxwell postulated the existence of two kinds of field, the electrical field and the magnetic field, and his theory described the properties and interactions of these two fields. Maxwell's theory explained all the known laboratory phenomena—the results of experiments with coils of wire, batteries, and the like—with accuracy and elegance. Furthermore, it predicted a previously unknown and unsuspected phenomenon: the existence of electromagnetic waves which could propagate through empty space with the speed of light.

Maxwell's prediction was first verified by Heinrich Hertz, who in the process also invented the radio transmitter and the radio receiver. Subsequent work has shown that it is no coincidence that the velocity of Maxwell's waves is the same as that of light. Because of the electrical nature of matter (electrons and protons), atoms and molecules are capable of transmitting and receiving electromagnetic waves, and often do so. When one "sees" sunlight, electromagnetic radiation has been produced by atom-sized "transmitters" in the Sun, has traveled through interplanetary space for about eight minutes at the speed of light, and has finally been detected by the molecular "receivers" in one's retina.

If ordinary light and radio waves are so similar—if they are both examples of electromagnetic radiation—then how do they differ? Maxwell's theory answers in terms of wavelength, or, equivalently, frequency. If a small pebble is dropped into calm water, circular ripples travel away from the disturbance. The distance between successive wave crests is called the wavelength, and the number of waves that pass a given spot in a given interval of time is called the frequency.

According to the theory, it is possible for an electromagnetic wave to have any wavelength whatsoever. The wavelength is determined by the process that generates the wave. By analogy, a large stone will generate pond ripples of longer wavelength than will a small pebble. All wavelengths, however, travel at the same velocity, the speed of light. The product of the frequency and the wavelength is always equal to the velocity. Thus, the longer the wavelength of electromagnetic waves, the lower will be the frequency.

In terms of wavelength it is very simple to describe the difference between radio waves and light waves. Light waves have short wavelengths (between about 4×10^{-7} and 7×10^{-7} meter) and correspondingly high frequencies (between 7.5×10^{14} and 4.3×10^{14} hertz). Radio waves, on the other hand, have long wavelengths (longer than about 1×10^{-3} meter) and correspondingly low frequencies (lower than 3×10^{11} hertz). The radio waves used in radio and television broadcasting have frequencies ranging from about 0.5 to about 800 megahertz; corresponding wavelengths range from 600 meters to 37.5 centimeters.

Traditionally, the shortest radio wavelengths—ranging from 1 millimeter to 30 centimeters—have been called microwaves. These are shorter wavelengths (and higher frequencies) than have been used in broadcasting, but many astronomical objects—for example, the hydrogen in interstellar space, radio galaxies, and quasars—radiate in this range of frequencies. It is also in this range—at the short-wavelength, high-frequency end of the microwave range—that cosmic microwave background radiation (CMBR) is detected.

One form of background radiation is familiar to everyone: the light of the daytime sky. It is sunlight—its ultimate source is the Sun—but because of scattering by molecules in Earth's atmosphere, it seems to come more or less uniformly from all over the sky. Similarly, CMBR comes uniformly from all over the sky. It is this uniformity that sets CMBR apart from most things astronomers observe in the sky. Starlight, for example, is not at all uniformly distributed in the night sky: It is concentrated into discrete sources, which themselves are concentrated in a broad band, the Milky Way, that encircles the sky. One of the most important features of CMBR is that it appears to be absolutely uniform on a small scale: That is, despite many intensive observational programs, no one has been able to detect any small-scale differentiation within it.

On the largest scale, astronomers have managed to detect a very small deviation from absolute uniformity: CMBR seems to be slightly more intense in one direction and correspondingly dimmer in the opposite direction. This kind of nonuniformity is reasonable, given Earth's complicated motion: Earth orbits the Sun, which itself orbits the center of the Galaxy, and the Galaxy and its neighbor M31 (the Andromeda Galaxy) are orbiting each other. The observed microwave background radiation does not arise from individual objects within the universe—stars or galaxies—but from the universe itself. Furthermore, it is thought that CMBR was produced long ago, when the universe was in a totally different state. If these assumptions are correct (and most astronomers and physicists believe that they are), then this phenomenon offers important clues regarding the history and structure of the universe.

As early as 1948, Ralph A. Alpher and Robert Herman, who was at that time a student and collaborator of George Gamow, demonstrated by numerical calculations that the hot big bang theory of Gamow and Alpher had a remarkable implication: The universe of today should be filled with a microwave background radiation. In the 1950's, however, radio astronomy was in its infancy, and it would not have been readily possible for anyone to test the prediction of Alpher and Herman. Furthermore, Gamow and his collaborators were perhaps not taken as seriously as they deserved; not only was there no immediate effort to observe the hypothesized CMBR, but indeed the prediction attracted little notice and was soon forgotten.

By the 1960's, however, there had been a decade of furious competition between advocates of the big bang theory and of the steady state theory, and mainstream scientists were beginning to realize that observational cosmology deserved to be taken seriously. Furthermore, Albert Einstein's general theory of relativity was beginning to be accepted, providing a theoretical basis in which cosmological observations could be considered.

In this context, Robert H. Dicke at Princeton University was conducting active experimental and theoretical investigations in cosmology. In the early

1960's, while investigating the possibility of an oscillating universe, he and his coworkers independently rediscovered Alpher and Herman's long-forgotten idea concerning the possibility of a CMBR. By then, radio technology had progressed greatly, and it was no longer unrealistic to think of detecting it. They therefore built a small radio telescope on a rooftop on Princeton's campus to determine if indeed the universe at the present time is filled with microwave radiation, and if so, to measure its temperature.

Around the same time, Arno A. Penzias and Robert W. Wilson, at Bell Laboratories, were conducting engineering studies with a radio telescope sensitive to very short microwaves. They made the (to them) completely unexpected and inexplicable discovery that no matter where they might point their antenna, it detected a signal. It was only when the groups at Princeton and Bell came into contact that the mystery was solved: Penzias and Wilson were detecting CMBR.

Soon thereafter, the Princeton group confirmed the discovery with their apparatus, operating at a somewhat shorter wavelength. Observations at both wavelengths gave approximately the same temperature, 3 Kelvins, thus greatly strengthening confidence that the observed microwave background radiation was indeed cosmic. In 1992 the Cosmic Background Explorer (COBE) mapped tiny variations in CMBR.

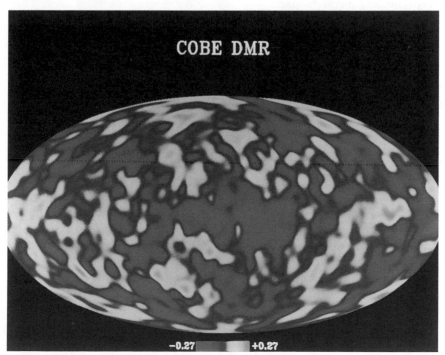

A microwave map of the whole sky showing one year of data collected by the Cosmic Background Explorer (COBE) Differential Microwave Radiometer. *(National Aeronautics and Space Administration)*

Knowledge Gained

Since the discovery of CMBR, it has been studied by many scientists, using a wide variety of techniques.

One line of effort has concerned the spectrum, or wavelength curve: Does the observed MBR have the same wavelength curve as is predicted by the simple big bang theory? This is a surprisingly difficult question to answer. Even subtle differences between the observed and predicted spectrum might be sufficient to devastate the big bang interpretation; unfortunately, the precise comparison of the intensity of radiation at different wavelengths is one of the most technically difficult tasks of the astronomer. In the case of background radiation, this difficulty is compounded by the fact that many objects—equipment as well as astronomical sources—may radiate at the same wavelengths. By the late 1980's, the observed spectrum had conformed closely to the predictions of the theory, yet findings regarding the shortest wavelengths were proving a bit troublesome.

Another line of inquiry concerns the uniformity of the background. On the largest scale, it has been found that the observed radiation is very slightly warmer over half the sky than over the other half. This fact is not interpreted as posing a difficulty for the big bang theory, but as indicating that the Milky Way is moving through space.

Despite much meticulous work by many different astronomers using many different radio telescopes all over the world, it has not been possible to detect small-scale fluctuations. This is contrary to the expectations of many theorists, who had expected that the formation of galaxies and galaxy clusters billions of years ago (but after the formation of the CMBR itself) would modify the background radiation slightly, giving it a very subtle "mottled" character.

Context

One of the oldest and most puzzling questions concerns the nature of time and the history of the universe. The Judaic tradition, for example, posits a definite time of creation, while the Buddhist tradition imagines an endless cycling. These same issues have arisen in the scientific study of the universe. Einstein imagined that the universe must be in a static state, which was found to be contrary to observation. Once the cosmic expansion was discovered, this position had to be abandoned and was replaced by two alternative hypotheses, commonly called the steady state theory and the big bang theory.

Because the existence of CMBR is predicted by the big bang theory, and because its observed properties seem to fit the theory so precisely, the discovery of CMBR has been interpreted by many as "proving" that theory. It is probably wiser to bear in mind, however, the point of view attributed to the philosopher Karl Popper: Scientific theories cannot be proved, but only disproved. From this point of view, the big bang theory has been remarkably successful in passing the many tests to which it has already been subjected, but scientists are still busy devising many ingenious challenges for the theory.

One danger currently facing the big bang theory is the possibility that the CMBR is too smooth. It is thought that the process of galaxy formation should have modified and distorted the CMBR more than is observed to be the case. In addition, the spectrum of the CMBR has not yet been studied in detail at all relevant wavelengths, and there is the possibility that problems may arise from that area. Thus, it is premature to conclude that CMBR definitely "proves" that we live in an evolving universe. The issue is still definitely a live one, and worthy of further investigation.

Tom R. Dennis

Basic Bibliography

Chaisson, Eric. *Universe: An Evolutionary Approach to Astronomy.* Englewood Cliffs, N.J.: Prentice-Hall, 1988. A prize-winning expositor's textbook of descriptive astronomy, which includes several chapters relating to the big bang theory.

Harrison, Edward R. *Cosmology: The Science of the Universe.* New York: Cambridge University Press, 1981. A comprehensive descriptive account of all aspects of cosmology. It is noteworthy for the many sidelights it covers. More accessible to the general reader than Weinberg's work (below).

Silk, Joseph. *The Big Bang: The Creation and Evolution of the Universe.* New York: W. H. Freeman Co., 1980. A college-level text for the nonspecialist. At about the same level as Weinberg's work (see below), but with much more detail and with a broader range of topics.

Weinberg. Stephen. *The First Three Minutes: A Modern View of the Origin of the Universe.* New York: Basic Books, 1977. A true classic of exposition, by a Nobel laureate physicist. Describes the big bang theory and the discovery of the CMBR, and gives an account of events as they may have occurred in the first three minutes of the universe. Accessible to the general reader, but most will find it difficult.

Current Bibliography

Cronin, James W., Thomas K. Gaisser, and Simon P. Swordy. "Cosmic Rays at the Energy Frontier." *Scientific American* 276, no. 1 (January, 1997): 44-50.

Lakhovsky, G. *The Secret of Life Cosmic Rays and Radiations and Radiations of Living Beings and Electro-Magnetic Waves.* New York: Gordon Press, 1991.

Shapiro, Maurice M., ed. *Composition and Origin of Cosmic Rays.* Norwell: Kluwer, 1983.

Cross-References

Cosmic Rays, 91; Cosmology, 97; Gamma-ray Bursts, 296; Infrared Astronomy, 378; New Astronomy, 621; Novas, Bursters, and X-ray Sources, 628; Quantum Cosmology, 767; Thermonuclear Reactions in Stars, 983; Ultraviolet Astronomy, 991; X-ray and Gamma-ray Astronomy, 1068.

Cosmic Rays

The high-energy cosmic rays are samples of material from outside the solar system. The elemental and isotopic compositions of the cosmic rays constrain the models for element production in a variety of astrophysical sources.

Overview

The cosmic rays are charged particles, electrons, and positively charged ions ranging from protons to the heaviest elements, which arrive at Earth from space. About 98 percent of the cosmic rays are positively charged nuclei, with most of the remainder being negatively charged electrons. Although some of the lowest-energy cosmic rays are particles emitted by Earth's sun, most of the cosmic rays are too energetic to be confined to the solar system and are samples of material from other parts of the galaxy. Because the cosmic rays are charged particles, their paths from the sources to Earth are bent by the magnetic fields in the galaxy. As a result, traditional astronomy in which electromagnetic radiation intercepted by a detector, such as a telescope, is traced back in a straight line to its source is not possible with the cosmic rays. Nevertheless, the cosmic rays provide important clues to the processes that occur in stars, supernova, and other astrophysical sources.

Measurement of the composition of the cosmic rays permits comparison to the composition of the Earth, the lunar samples returned by the Apollo missions, the meteorites, and the Sun. This allows the processes by which elements are produced within stars to be examined and compared to theoretical models for nucleosynthesis.

The nucleus of each element has a unique charge, so the methods of determining the composition of the cosmic rays require a measurement of the charge of each individual cosmic-ray particle. Generally, these techniques require two independent measurements. The first measurement might determine the rate at which the cosmic ray loses energy in traversing the detector. This rate of energy loss is proportional to the square of the ratio of the charge to velocity of the particle. A second measurement might then determine the velocity, or some other property that depends on velocity in a different manner than the rate of energy loss. From these two measurements, the charge can be determined.

A number of innovative charge measurement techniques have been developed. These detectors can be divided into three general categories: recording detectors, such as photographic emulsions; visual detectors, such as cloud chambers; and electronic detectors, such as Geiger-Müller counters.

In the late 1940's, groups of cosmic-ray investigators at the University of Minnesota and the University of Rochester employed photographic emulsions carried to high altitudes, frequently above 27,000 meters, by balloons to determine the charge and energy of the cosmic rays. These high altitudes were required because collisions between incoming cosmic rays and air molecules can cause the cosmic rays to fragment into several lighter nuclei, thus altering their composition. At high altitudes, the probability of such a collision is low; therefore, the balloon detectors measure the primary composition (that is, the true composition) of the particles in space. These early experiments demonstrated that of the nuclei in the cosmic rays, about 87 percent are hydrogen, or protons; 12 percent are helium; and the remaining 1 percent are nuclei heavier than helium. It is the composition of these heavier nuclei that contain the clues to the nucleosynthetic processes.

Following the initial discovery of heavy nuclei among the cosmic rays, the emphasis in cosmic-ray research shifted to the determination of the charge spectrum, or relative abundances, of each element. The early experiments made use of the magnetic field of the Earth as a velocity selector. The paths of charged particles are bent when they encounter a magnetic field, so only particles exceeding a given cutoff energy can penetrate through a region of given magnetic field intensity. The magnetic field of the Earth is so strong near the equator that only particles with velocities very close to the speed of light can penetrate. Thus, for cosmic rays detected near the equator, the magnetic cutoff identifies the velocity to be approximately the speed of light. A single measurement of the rate of energy loss for these particles provides a measurement of their charge.

These early experiments indicated the difficulty of detection of the heavy nuclei among the cosmic rays. A 1-square-meter detector placed in space, above the Earth's atmosphere and outside the Earth's magnetic field, would register several hundred nonsolar protons per second and about one-seventh that number of helium nuclei. Yet, only one or two nuclei heavier than carbon would be measured every second, and the detector would register a single iron nucleus every fifteen seconds. To observe a single lead nucleus would require several months of detector operation. Cosmic-ray astrophysicists recognized that large detectors with long exposure times would be required to determine accurately the composition of the heavy cosmic rays.

In 1956, Frank McDonald, a physicist at Iowa State University, developed a combination of two electronic detectors—a scintillation counter and a Cherenkov counter—to determine the charge and velocity of the cosmic rays. This combination of detectors provided good measurements of the elemental abundances for elements up to iron. The elements heavier than iron were so rare that their identification required a new technique. In the mid-1960's, Robert Fleischer, Buford Price, and Robert Walker, researchers at the General Electric Research and Development Center, found that the trails of ionizing particles were recorded in certain types of plastics and that these trails could be revealed later by etching the plastic in an appropriate chemical agent. They demonstrated that if the rate at which the trail was etching as well as the total etchable length were both measured, the charge and energy of the particle could be determined. Balloon flights with these plastic detectors provided information on the composition of the heavier elements in the cosmic rays.

In the 1970's, cosmic-ray researchers employed orbiting Earth satellites to increase the duration of their measurements. Large plastic detectors were flown for several months on the U.S. Skylab space station. The IMP-7 and IMP-8 satellites, launched in 1972 and 1973, respectively, provided good measurements on the isotopic composition of the lighter cosmic rays. In 1978, the third High Energy Astronomical Observatory (HEAO-3) carrying a 6-square-meter electronic detector, provided high-quality measurements of the abundances of nuclei up to the element bismuth.

Applications

Astrophysicists generally believe that the only elements present in the early universe were hydrogen, helium, and perhaps small amounts of lithium, beryllium, and boron. Most of the elements now present were produced by nuclear reactions in stars, in stellar explosions, or by other astrophysical mechanisms in a process called nucleosynthesis. Theoretical calculations show that the elemental and isotopic abundances produced depend on the particular conditions of the nucleosynthetic event. Thus, the abundances of the elements and isotopes of material from outside Earth's solar system might be different from those of solar system material, and those differences would provide clues to the differing nucleosynthetic conditions at those sites. This comparison requires a knowledge of the cosmic-ray composition at the source.

The composition of the cosmic rays can be altered during their journey through space to Earth. Radioactive decay will remove those radioactive elements with short half-lives, compared to the time it took for the cosmic rays to reach Earth. Collisions between the cosmic rays and interstellar gas atoms will cause fragmentation of some of the cosmic rays.

Measurements of the cosmic-ray composition provide clues to the "age" of the cosmic rays, that is, the duration of their journey through space. The light nuclei, lithium, beryllium, and boron, are much more abundant in the cosmic rays than in solar system materials. These excess light nuclei are believed to have been produced by spallation, or collisional fragmentation with interstellar gas atoms. Since the abundance of interstellar gas atoms is known from other astronomical measurements, the amount of excess light elements provides a measure of the duration of the cosmic-ray journey. Astrophysicists indicate that the cosmic rays presently arriving at Earth began their journey about 10 million years ago. Since the solar system formed about 4.5 billion years ago, the cosmic rays may be sampling a much younger type of material than the solar system.

Once the age of the cosmic rays is known, the abundances of the heavier elements detected at Earth can be corrected back to the source by removing the spallation contribution. Generally, the elemental composition of the cosmic rays is similar to that of the solar system, but the differences provide clues to differences in the nucleosynthetic processes.

The largest difference in the heavy element composition is for the isotope neon 22, which is four times more abundant relative to the other neon isotopes in the cosmic rays than in solar system matter. Isotopic measurements also show excesses of magnesium 25, magnesium 26, silicon 29, and silicon 30 in the cosmic rays when compared to solar system matter. These latter discrepancies could be explained if the cosmic ray sources were stars with initial abundances of carbon, nitrogen, and oxygen about twice that seen in Earth's sun. Nevertheless, even this alteration of the stellar composition cannot explain the unusually high neon-22 abundance.

The abundances of the heavier elements may provide clues to the site of the production of cosmic rays. Astrophysicists have identified several different nucleosynthetic processes. The two major ones both proceed by the addition of neutrons to light target nuclei. In the "*s*-process," the time between successive neutron capture events is long enough that the new nucleus can be transformed (beta decay) to a stable nucleus before the next capture. This process occurs in the interior of stars. In the "*r*-process," neutron capture proceeds so rapidly that beta decay is not possible between individual capture events, leading to the production of more neutron-rich elements. This process is believed to occur in explosive processes such as supernova. Only the *r*-process can produce elements heavier than bismuth.

Since astrophysicists have suggested that supernova are a likely source of the cosmic rays, they would be expected to contain the *r*-process elemental and isotopic abundance signatures. The presence of elements heavier than bismuth in the cosmic rays would suggest an *r*-process origin. Thus far, the experimental results are ambiguous. Rare events, possibly attributable to elements heavier than bismuth, were reported from balloon flights carrying photographic emulsions and plastic detectors; however, the HEAO-3 detected no such events. Because of the scarcity of these heavy elements, longer duration, large area cosmic-ray detectors will be required to resolve the question.

Elemental and isotopic measurements on the cosmic rays indicate that their sources differ in significant ways from the source of solar system material. Because of these differences, more precise measurements of the elemental and isotopic compositions of the heavier elements are required for detailed comparisons to the nucleosynthetic models.

Context

The formulation of a detailed model of the nucleosynthesis of the heavy elements by Geoffrey Burbidge, Margaret Burbidge, William A. Fowler, and Fred Hoyle in 1957 provided predictions of the elemental and isotopic

Fred Hoyle, who investigated the nature of cosmic rays together with Geoffrey Burbidge, Margaret Burbidge, and William A. Fowler. *(Archive Photos/Express Newspapers)*

abundances expected from the r-process and s-process. This information, coupled with the discovery of heavy elements in the cosmic rays in the late 1940's, suggested comparison of the cosmic-ray composition with the predictions of the nucleosynthetic models. Rapid advances in electronic detectors in the 1950's made such comparisons possible, but the limited flight duration of high-altitude balloons restricted the number of elements that could be measured because of the low abundance of heavy elements. The use of Earth satellites in the 1970's significantly increased the duration of cosmic-ray composition experiments. Nevertheless, even these long-duration satellite experiments were inadequate to answer the question of the abundance of heavy elements in the cosmic rays.

The development of high-resolution electronic detectors, permitting high-quality determinations of the isotopic composition, showed significant differences between the neon, magnesium, and silicon isotopic abundances in the cosmic rays and solar system matter. Advances in the modeling of the nuclear processes in stellar interiors allowed astrophysicists to calculate that most of these discrepancies were consistent with nucleosynthesis in a star with carbon, nitrogen, and oxygen abundances approximately double that of Earth. Long duration, large area cosmic-ray detectors, possibly on a space station, will be required to determine the abundances of elements heavier than bismuth, allowing direct comparison of the cosmic-ray composition with that expected for r-process nucleosynthesis in supernova, which are suggested as the cosmic-ray source.

George J. Flynn

Basic Bibliography

Friedlander, Michael W. *Cosmic Rays.* Cambridge, Mass.: Harvard University Press, 1989. Well-illustrated account of the history of cosmic-ray astronomy. Deals with methods of detection, elemental and isotopic composition, and implications for the cosmic-ray sources.

Ginzburg, V. L., and S. I. Syrovatskii. *The Origin of Cosmic Rays.* New York: Macmillan, 1964. A technical account of cosmic-ray astrophysics. Includes a good discussion of how the light element abundances provide an age for the cosmic rays. Suitable for college physics students.

Pomerantz, Martin A. *Cosmic Rays.* New York: Van Nostrand Reinhold, 1971. Suitable for readers with only an introductory physics background. Describes cosmic-ray interaction with matter and how these interactions are used to detect and determine the properties of the cosmic rays. Well illustrated.

Rossi, Bruno. *Cosmic Rays.* New York: McGraw-Hill, 1964. A firsthand account by one of the pioneers of cosmic-ray physics. Describes how cosmic rays are detected and discusses ideas about their origins.

Wefel, John P. "Matter from Outside Our Solar System—New Insights. Part 1: The Astrophysical Framework." *The Physics Teacher* 20 (April, 1982): 222-229.

Wefel, John P. "Matter from Outside Our Solar System—New Insights. Part 2: Experimental Measurements and Interpretation." *The Physics Teacher* 20 (May, 1982): 289-297. Discusses the history of cosmic-ray physics, the mechanisms of nucleosynthesis, the construction of cosmic-ray detectors, and the implications of the composition on the sources. Well illustrated. Suitable for high school science students.

Current Bibliography

Cronin, James W., Thomas K. Gaisser, and Simon P. Swordy. "Cosmic Rays at the Energy Frontier." *Scientific American* 276, no. 1 (January, 1997): 44-50.

Lakhovsky, G. *The Secret of Life: Cosmic Rays and Radiations and Radiations of Living Beings and Electro-Magnetic Waves.* New York: Gordon Press, 1991.

Shapiro, Maurice M., ed. *Composition and Origin of Cosmic Rays.* Norwell: Kluwer, 1983.

Cross-References

Cosmic Microwave Background Radiation, 84; Cosmology, 97; Gamma-ray Bursts, 296; Infrared Astronomy, 378; New Astronomy, 621; Novas, Bursters, and X-ray Sources, 628; Quantum Cosmology, 767; Thermonuclear Reactions in Stars, 983; Ultraviolet Astronomy, 991; X-ray and Gamma-ray Astronomy, 1068.

Cosmology

Cosmology is the astronomical study of the large-scale structure of the universe, including the distribution of billions of galaxies, galactic clusters, and quasars throughout space and time. It also encompasses the evolution of stars, planetary systems, matter, and life throughout the universe.

Overview

Cosmology is the study of the universe. Originally, cosmology was a branch of philosophy devoted to understanding the nature of reality and the origin and structure of everything that exists. With the growth of astronomy and astrophysics during the nineteenth and twentieth centuries, cosmology rapidly became a major province of astronomical research. Today, cosmological theories are detailed mathematical models of the universe that incorporate astronomical and astrophysical data. Still, modern cosmology retains some philosophical qualities.

Modern cosmology is the scientific study of the large-scale structure of the universe. It is concerned with the nature of objects within the universe, such as galaxies, quasars, and black holes. It is related to the evolution of physical processes within the universe, including the births, lives, and deaths of stars; the thermonuclear reactions within stars; the chemical composition of stellar and interstellar matter; the development of planetary systems around stars; and the origin and evolution of life. Cosmology embraces many fields of science, including physics, chemistry, biology, mathematics, geology, and philosophy. Cosmogony, a branch of cosmology, deals with the origin and evolution of the universe. Cosmologists use physical laws to derive models of the early universe to within one second of its beginning. They also extrapolate events into the distant future.

The predominant cosmological theory describing the origin of the universe is the big bang theory, which was first proposed by the Belgian astronomer Georges Lemaître in the 1920's and which was popularized by the Soviet-American physicist George Gamow in the 1940's. The big bang theory maintains that all the energy and matter of the universe was released from a single infinitely massive point in space, known as a singularity (that is, black hole). This very hot early universe expanded isotropically (that is, in all directions). Within the first few seconds of the cosmic expansion from the big bang, the temperature dropped below 1 billion Kelvins so that a small fraction of the energy became matter, such as electrons, protons, and neutrons. This matter coalesced to form the lighter elements hydrogen, helium, and lithium. After approximately 100,000 years, the temperature had fallen below 3,000 Kelvins; below this temperature, hydrogen and helium could produce the necessary pressures and temperatures of nucleosynthesis, the production of heavier elements within the thermonuclear furnaces of stars.

The present temperature of the universe is approximately 2.76 Kelvins, a value predicted by Gamow and later verified in 1964 by Arno A. Penzias and Robert W. Wilson of Bell Telephone Laboratories. About 100,000 years after the big bang, stars formed from the gravitational clumping of hydrogen and helium. This clumping produced intense pressures and temperatures, which caused fusion reactions to start. The fusion reactions of stars combine smaller elements, such as hydrogen, into larger, heavier elements (from helium to iron) and release energy.

Furthermore, many stars became gravitationally attracted to form large, flattened disk-shaped structures called galaxies. The first galaxies are believed to have formed approximately 100 million years after the big bang. A typical galaxy is a rotating mass of several hundred billion stars, each rotation requiring perhaps 100 to 200 million years to complete. The central region of a galaxy is a very dense spherical mass of older population II stars. The outer, flattened regions of a galaxy are less dense and contain younger population I stars that form from the surrounding interstellar hydrogen gas.

It is estimated that the universe contains approximately 1 trillion galaxies, each of which contains hundreds of billions of stars. Earth's star, the Sun, is but one of approximately 400 billion stars composing the Milky Way galaxy, which is but one of a trillion galaxies composing the universe. Galaxies come in a variety of shapes, usually variations upon elliptical or spiral patterns. The Milky Way galaxy, with its 400 billion stars, is immense; it is approximately 150,000 light years in diameter. A light year is nearly 10 trillion kilometers, or the distance traveled by a photon of light energy in one year. Therefore, the Milky Way galaxy is approximately 1,500,000 trillion kilometers in diameter. Earth's sun is located in a spiral galactic arm about 300,000 light years, or 320,000 trillion kilometers, from the galactic center. The nearest large galaxy to the Milky Way is the Andromeda galaxy (Messier 31), which is located approximately 1 million light years from Earth.

Galaxies are gravitationally attracted to one another to form galactic clusters, which are gravitationally attracted to other galactic clusters to produce superclusters. The Milky Way is a member of the local galactic group, which also includes the Small and Large Magellanic Clouds and the massive Andromeda galaxy. Furthermore, the local group is only one of many galactic clusters that compose the Virgo local supercluster, a gravitationally bound accumulation of several hundred galaxies, the most massive of which is Messier 87, a galaxy located in the constellation Virgo that may contain as many as 100 trillion stars. The Virgo local supercluster is being pulled toward an even more massive cluster of galaxies (as yet unidentified)

A Hubble Space Telescope view of star-birth clouds in Eagle Nebula, constructed from three separate images taken in the light of emission from different types of atoms. *(Jeff Hester, Paul Scowen, and National Aeronautics and Space Administration)*

called the great attractor. One can see that the universe is very ordered, with gravity reigning supreme. Atoms fuse to form stars, stars attract to form galaxies, galaxies attract to form clusters, and galactic clusters attract to form superclusters, and so on. Galaxies appear to be evenly distributed in all directions throughout the universe. This viewpoint has given rise to the cosmological principle, which maintains that the universe is homogeneous in all directions.

Since galaxies formed approximately 100,000 years after the big bang, they have evolved for about 10 to 20 billion years, which is the estimated age of the universe based upon the half-life decay rates of certain long-lived radioactive isotopes (for example, thorium 232). Stars have evolved considerably over this same time span. Massive stars have lifetimes as short as 10 million years, during which they consume their nuclear fuel (that is, progressively heavier elements from hydrogen to iron). After about 10 million years, these massive stars collapse, ricocheting matter and energy outward in a tremendous catastrophe called a supernova. After the supernova explosion, the contracted remains of the former star form an incredibly dense rotating object, either a supermassive neutron star or an infinitely massive black hole, from which nothing can escape. Less massive stars such as Earth's sun (its estimated age is 5 billion years) may last up to 10 billion years, going through successive stages of expansion and contraction, eventually ending up as cool burnt-out relics such as white and brown dwarf stars.

Since the initial big bang, the universe has been expanding isotropically. Over the past 10 to 20 billion years, galaxies have been moving farther and farther apart, much like several dots on a balloon that is being inflated. For an observer located at any point in space, all objects appear to be moving away. Thus, the universe is inflationary; it is expanding. From physics, the Doppler effect (shift) maintains that an object moving away from an observer will emit radiation of lower frequency and longer wavelength; based upon the visible light spectrum (red, orange, yellow, green, blue, indigo, violet), an object moving away from an observer appears to be red. Therefore, receding objects are redshifted. Similarly, an object moving toward an observer will emit radiation of higher frequency and shorter wavelength, much like the high pitch of a train whistle as the train is approaching. Based upon the visible light spectrum, such an approaching object exhibits a blueshifted spectrum. More than 90 percent of observable galaxies are redshifted; that is, they are moving away from Earth and from one another as the universe continues to expand.

Redshift and Blueshift

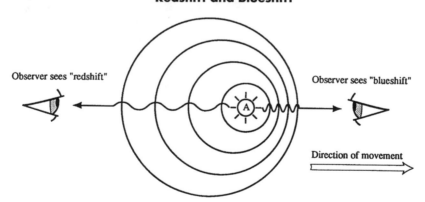

A moving source of radiation (A) will seem to a stationary observer to be emitting radiation of longer or shorter wavelengths, depending on whether that observer is in front of or behind the emitting object. If the object is a star or galaxy emitting light, the radiation will shift to the lower-wavelength (red) end of the spectrum in relation to the cosmic background radiation; hence the name redshift. The opposite (blueshift) occurs if the observer is in front of the emitter. The redshift is evidence that the universe is expanding after the big bang.

The recessional velocity of a galaxy can be calculated based upon the degree of the galaxy's redshift. Galaxies located very far away have high redshifts. Nearby galaxies have very low redshifts. The preponderance of cosmic redshifts over blueshifts is one major verification of the inflationary universe theory proposed by the astronomer Edwin Powell Hubble in 1929. To date, quasars have the highest redshifts of any objects yet observed in the universe. It is believed that quasars are the most distant and oldest objects identified in the universe. The most distant quasar yet detected has a redshift recessional velocity of 4.73, which places it between 10 and 15 billion light years distant and old. It should be emphasized that for every cosmic object that is viewed, one is looking backward in time. The more distant the object, the older it is and the longer travel time is required for light and other radiations emitted from that object to reach the viewer. For example, Earth's sun is a star located approximately 150 million kilometers from Earth. At the speed of light (about 300,000 kilometers per second), light requires more than eight minutes to reach Earth. Therefore, when humans see the Sun, it is seen as it was eight minutes ago. Similarly, the nearest star other than the Sun, Alpha Centauri, is 4.3 light years distant; humans see it as it appeared 4.3 years ago.

The distant quasars represent an epoch in the history of the universe preceding the existence of galaxies. Their composition or physical properties are not known. They are tremendously powerful radiation emitters, releasing visible light, radio waves, X rays, and the like. They represent the first stages of thermonucleosynthesis in the universe, or they may represent vestiges of the big bang itself.

As of the early 1990's, cosmologists have a fairly accurate picture of the early universe back to 10^{-34} seconds following the big bang. This understanding of the early universe is based upon Albert Einstein's theory of general relativity and upon the four principal forces that hold the universe together: the strong, weak, gravitational, and electromagnetic forces. Earlier than 10^{-34} seconds, these forces break down. The major obstacle to big bang cosmology is the development of the grand unified theory (GUT), which will unite these four forces into a single force at times earlier than 10^{-34} seconds following the big bang. A number of GUTs have been proposed, one of the more promising theories being a controversial concept called the "superstring theory."

While cosmologists are interested in the universe's past, they also are interested in the future of the universe. Given an inflationary (that is, expanding) universe, three possible futures are predicted: a hyperbolic, or open, universe that continues to expand forever to infinity, where matter eventually disintegrates and/or is absorbed by black holes; a flat universe that slowly expands; or a closed universe whose mass is great enough to slow the expansion, eventually leading to contraction and ending in a big crash. As of 1990, astronomers have not detected enough mass to support a closed universe. Some cosmologists have proposed a missing mass, unseen matter that lies in the huge voids of interstellar space between stars. Even with the proposed missing mass added, the universe may be flat.

Applications

The value of cosmology lies in understanding the structure and organization of the universe, where it came from, and how it will develop in the future. At the same time, cosmology gives astronomers vital information about the evolution of the Sun, solar system, and galaxy, and about humans' place in the universe as a living species. Cosmology also helps astronomers test the laws of physics on a grand universal scale.

The principal instruments for visualizing the universe are optical, radio, X-ray, and neutrino telescopes. Optical telescopes detect the light emission from stars, galaxies, and quasars. Huge radio telescopes can detect faint natural radio emissions from the same objects. X-ray telescopes must be launched above the Earth's atmosphere to detect X-ray emissions from objects such as quasars and suspected black holes (for example, Cygnus X-1). Neutrino telescopes are located deep underground in mine shafts to filter out "noise"; they consist of enormous tanks of perchloroethylene (a colorless nonflammable liquid), with computerized detectors to monitor the passage of neutrinos through the perchloroethylene. It is believed that neutrinos are massless elementary particles that travel at the speed of light, which theorctically were released from the big bang explosion and which have been released from supernovas (for example, Supernova 1987A). Radio astronomers analyze the data from these instruments with the assistance of supercomputers to obtain information concerning the organization of galaxies in time and space, plus the nature and evolution of stars, galaxies, and quasars. Theoretical physicists and cosmologists, such as Stephen Hawking of the University of Cambridge, England, and Igor Novikov of the U.S.S.R. Space Research Institute in Moscow, have applied the laws and theories of mathematics and physics to the prediction and explanation of various processes that occur in the universe. Besides the need for a grand unified theory to link the four fundamental forces of the universe, additional problems confronting theoretical cosmology are the fate of the universe (the "missing mass" problem), supraluminal (faster than light) quasar velocities, the existence of black holes, and the matter/anti-matter asymmetry in the universe.

If the universe is not very massive, it will continue to expand forever, either quickly (open universe) or slowly (flat universe). For either the open or flat universe scenarios, all matter will disintegrate within several trillion years, leaving a universe containing nothing but energy. Experiments are under way to detect the rate of decay of protons to verify their theoretically predicted decay rate. If the universe is very massive, the gravitational attraction of everything in the universe eventually will slow the universe's expansion to a standstill, followed by a contraction phase in which everything pulls together into a black hole after about 50 billion years. Only 10 percent of the needed mass to produce such a closed universe appears to exist. Astronomers are searching for the appropriately termed "missing mass," which may lie in invisible interstellar hydrogen gas, in numerous black holes scattered across the cosmos, or in previously presumed massless particles (such as neutrinos). Most cosmological theories support a closed universe.

Quasars are presumed to be the oldest and most distant objects detected in the universe. Nevertheless, several astronomers, most notably Halton C. Arp of the Max Planck Institute for Radio Astronomy in Bonn, Germany, argue that quasars may be ejections of matter from galactic nuclei. Arp bases his hypothesis upon statistical correlations of certain quasars with certain galaxies and upon the fact that these quasars appear to have supraluminal velocities with greatly exaggerated redshifts. He argues that the Doppler redshifts may be in error because matter supposedly cannot exceed the speed of light. Nevertheless, many astronomers disagree with Arp's controversial hypothesis. The supraluminal velocities of quasars can be explained by a position effect based upon the quasar location relative to the associated galaxy and observer over time.

Black holes are extremely massive objects from whose gravitational attraction nothing can escape, although they are believed to be emitters of X rays. They should be produced during the catastrophic collapse of massive stars (supernovas). The Milky Way may contain millions of black holes, although there is no absolute evidence of their existence. There is some evidence of black holes at the centers of the Milky Way galaxy and the Andromeda galaxy, as well as in certain star systems, such as Cygnus X-1.

Another major problem in cosmology is the fact that the amount of matter in the universe greatly exceeds the amount of antimatter. Theoretically, equal amounts of both should have been created during the big bang. Yet, equal amounts of matter and antimatter would annihilate each other, leaving nothing. Various theories have been and continue to be developed to address the matter/antimatter asymmetry problem and other cosmological uncertainties.

Context

Cosmologists wish to understand the nature of the cosmos, its composition, its fate, and humans' place within it. Although it started as a branch of philosophy, cosmology has become an integral component of astronomy and astrophysics. It has shifted from being primarily a speculative, qualitative science to being primarily an exact, quantitative science. Several assumptions in cosmology remain philosophical in scope, one being the concept that the universe is isotropic and homogeneous. Astronomers have viewed less than 1 percent of the universe; it is assumed that the rest of the universe is the same.

Quantitatively, big bang cosmology rests upon several important measurements: Doppler redshifts, the 2.76 Kelvins microwave background temperature of the universe discovered by Penzias and Wilson, radioactive isotope decay rates, and the physical behavior of millions of cataloged galaxies. Doppler redshifts show that the universe is expanding with most galaxies moving away from one another. The 2.76-Kelvin microwave background temperature was predicted by theory and verified by experiment. The universe is approximately 10 to 20 billion years old, based upon radioactive isotope decay. Astronomers have mapped several million galaxies.

The future of the universe will be either infinite expansion forever, with the decay of all matter into pure energy after many trillions of years (open or flat universe) or eventual collapse into a big crash in approximately 30 billion years (closed universe). Cosmologists speculate whether or not Earth's universe is the only universe, whether or not there are many dimensions to the known universe that have yet to be discovered, and how the four principal forces can be unified to explain events that occurred less than one second after the big bang. Cosmologists also speculate upon the existence of life throughout the universe.

A number of cosmologists are exobiologists, who speculate upon the existence of intelligent life throughout the universe. Many of these cosmologists support the anthropic principle, which maintains that conditions in the universe will favor the inevitable evolution of life and intelligent life. Astronomers such as Frank Drake of the University of California at Santa Cruz and the late Carl Sagan of Cornell University have pursued the Search for Extraterrestrial Intelligence. They use radio telescopes to attempt to detect intelligent radio signals from extraterrestrial civilizations. Numerous searches are under way at various observatories throughout the world. Since humans are part of the universe, several cosmologists have appropriately observed that "we are the universe contemplating itself."

David Wason Hollar, Jr.

Basic Bibliography

Arp, Halton. *Quasars, Redshifts, and Controversies.* Berkeley, Calif.: Interstellar Media, 1987. A prominent astronomer's summary of his own research data that contradict several basic cosmological assumptions. Arp proposes that quasars are ejecta from galaxies and that the Doppler cosmic redshift measurement scale is in error. Discusses the sociology and politics of American science.

Bartusiak, Marcia. *Thursday's Universe.* New York: Times Books, 1986. A thorough survey of major twentieth century breakthroughs and theories in astronomy, astrophysics, and cosmology. Discusses the development of major cosmological principles and the people behind these ideas. Big bang cosmology is described clearly from very early stages of the universe to the distant future universe.

Guth, Alan H., and Paul J. Steinhardt. "The Inflationary Universe." *Scientific American* 250 (May, 1984): 116-129. This general review article is an excellent presentation of big bang cosmology. The authors present a new theory in which the universe undergoes rapid inflation during the early seconds of the big bang. This theory is compared to the standard inflationary universe model; possible futures for the universe are described.

Hawking, Stephen W. *A Brief History of Time.* New York: Bantam Books, 1988. This enormously popular bestseller is a clear, outstanding discussion of cosmology. Hawking describes the evolution of the universe, grand unified theories, and black holes.

Kippenhahn, Rudolf. *Light from the Depths of Time.* New York: Springer-Verlag, 1987. An exciting description of cosmology and the universe. Kippenhahn, an astrophysicist, describes the history of cosmological thought in the twentieth century. Describes the evolution of the universe and basic cosmological principles using humorous fictional characters.

Novikov, Igor. *Black Holes and the Universe.* Cambridge, England: Cambridge University Press, 1990. A brief, clear presentation of big bang cosmology and black holes. Novikov, a leading Soviet theoretical physicist and cosmologist, describes the predicted properties of black holes and the role they should play in the evolution of the universe.

Seielstad, George A. *At the Heart of the Web: The Inevitable Genesis of Intelligent Life.* Boston, Mass.: Harcourt Brace Jovanovich, 1989. An excellent survey of cosmological thought. Seielstad describes the order and evolution of the universe while stressing the anthropic principle and the need for cosmic awareness.

Silk, Joseph. *The Big Bang.* Rev. ed. New York: W. H. Freeman, 1989. A comprehensive, readable discussion of cosmological views on the origin and evolution of the universe. The properties and evolution of stars, black holes, galaxies, and quasars are described.

Tully, R. Brent, and J. Richard Fisher. *Nearby Galaxies Atlas.* New York: Cambridge University Press, 1987. This reference atlas for serious astronomers, written by two leading radio astronomers, provides important information for hundreds of carefully cataloged galaxies. Galaxy shapes, cluster and supercluster locations, and redshift/blueshift velocities are provided for each galaxy.

Zeilik, Michael, and Elske van Panhuys Smith. *Introductory Astronomy and Astrophysics.* 2d ed. Philadelphia: Saunders College Publishing, 1987. This very readable, information-packed book can serve either as an introductory college textbook or as a reference guide for astronomers. Every major aspect of astronomy, astrophysics, and cosmology is covered in intricate detail. Excellent photographs and data tables make this book a valuable asset.

Current Bibliography

Barrow, John D. *The Origin of the Universe.* New York: BasicBooks, 1994.

Bernstein, Jeremy. *An Introduction to Cosmology.* Englewood Cliffs, N.J.: Prentice-Hall, 1995.

Lachieze-Rey, Marc. *Cosmology: A First Course.* Translated by John Simmons. New York: Cambridge University Press, 1995.

Smolin, Lee. *The Life of the Cosmos.* New York: Oxford University Press, 1997.

Cross-References

The Big Bang, 32; Galactic Structures, 279; Galaxies and Galactic Clusters, 287; General Relativity, 302; New Astronomy, 621; Quantum Cosmology, 767; Stellar Evolution, 942; The Universe: Evolution, 999; The Universe: Expansion, 1007; The Universe: Structure, 1015.

Earth-Sun Relations

The relationship between the Earth and the Sun controls life on this planet. Earth's "heat budget" is a result of many factors, including the effects of the atmosphere and of the oceans, but the phenomena of Earth rotation and revolution are primary. Earth motions also produce observable periodic changes in apparent Sun paths, perhaps most visible in the directions of sunrise and sunset.

Overview

Earth-Sun relations are the dominant controls of life on Earth. The Sun is a star, and its radiation warms the Earth and supplies the energy that supports life on the planet. Earth-Sun relations are the phenomena that determine the amount, duration, and distribution of solar radiation that is received by Earth. The Earth motions of rotation and revolution cause day and night and the seasons, which serve to distribute solar radiation over the Earth. Earth's atmosphere and oceans influence the reflection, absorption, and distribution of solar energy. The result of these interacting phenomena is an Earth heat budget that is hospitable and constant. Earth motions also result in a pattern of periodic changes that are observable in the apparent paths of the Sun.

The Sun radiates energy from every part of its spherical surface. Earth, 150 million kilometers away, receives a minute portion of the star's radiation, no more than one two-hundred billionth, and yet Earth cannot tolerate full exposure to even that amount of radiation. The greatest amount of solar radiation is, in effect, wasted as far as Earth is concerned, radiating outward in all directions. That small amount of the Sun's energy that strikes Earth is Earth's energizer. It sustains life on Earth and drives the weather systems and the oceans' circulations. Solar radiation from the past has been preserved in the form of fossil fuels—coal, petroleum, and natural gas.

Perhaps the most remarkable aspects of Earth—remarkable because they are rare in the universe—are the moderate temperatures of Earth and the constancy of those temperatures. The adjectives "hot" and "cold" are frequently used in describing the weather. In relation to the temperatures that are found in the solar system, Earth is always moderate, and the words "hot" and "cold" better describe the other planets. The mean temperature of Earth is about 15 degrees Celsius; the absolute extremes recorded anywhere on Earth are 58 degrees in North Africa and –89 degrees in Antarctica. Few inhabitants of Earth will ever experience a temperature range of much over

55 degrees in a lifetime. Compare those temperatures with those of Earth's near neighbor, the Moon, where temperatures range from 127 to –173 degrees. Earth's sister planet Venus has a surface temperature of about 480 degrees. The outer planets of the solar system experience a permanent deep freeze, below –200 degrees. All the planets' temperatures are extreme in comparison with Earth's.

The most convincing proof of the moderate nature of Earth's temperature is the presence of the world's oceans. Water in the liquid state is extremely fragile and will exist only in a narrow temperature band, 0-100 degrees at Earth's atmospheric pressure. Water must be rare indeed in the universe; it is probably nonexistent elsewhere in the solar system, with the possible exception of trace amounts on Mars. Yet, Earth has 71 percent of its surface covered with this rare and fragile substance. Almost 98 percent of Earth's water is in the liquid state. The polar ice caps contain 2 percent, and a minute portion is water vapor in the atmosphere at any time.

The factors that cause Earth to experience such a moderate and unchanging temperature are complex and interrelated. The Sun is the source of the energy. Yet being the right distance from the Sun cannot be the sole cause of Earth's moderate temperature; witness the Moon. Rather, the explanation has to do with Earth's atmosphere, the oceans, and—in particular—Earth-Sun relations, determined by rotation and revolution. The atmosphere protects Earth during both daylight and darkness. During daylight, the atmosphere blocks excessive amounts of short-wave solar radiation from reaching the surface. During darkness, the atmosphere retards the escape of long-wave infrared heat energy back into space and thus prevents excessive overnight cooling. The result is a moderation of temperatures. The oceans, also, have a pronounced effect on the heat budget of Earth. Water has the highest specific heat of any common substance. More heat is needed to raise the temperature of water than to raise the temperature of other materials. Summers and daylight periods are kept cooler by the water's ability to absorb great amounts of solar energy without the water's temperature being raised significantly. During winter and during darkness, on the other hand, the water slowly gives up large amounts of heat without significant cooling of the water. Thus, the oceans act as a huge temperature buffer and, similar to the atmosphere, add a moderating effect to temperature extremes.

Even more significant in controlling the temperature of Earth, however, are Earth's rotation and revolution. Rotation is Earth's turning on its axis (counterclockwise, if one's vantage point were above the North Pole). Rotation causes places on Earth to be alternately turned toward and away from the Sun. The effect is to prevent Earth from overheating or overcooling. If one side of the Earth were continuously exposed to the Sun, the illuminated side would heat to hundreds of degrees, and the dark side would cool hundreds of degrees. The rotation of Mercury is such that a given point on the planet's surface is exposed to the Sun for eighty-eight Earth days and then is on the dark side for eighty-eight days. The resultant temperature extremes range from about 450 to –170 degrees Celsius. The other planets have various rates of rotation. If the rate of Earth rotation, once in twenty-four hours, were different, Earth's heat budget would be different. A slower rotation would result in greater extremes of daily temperatures.

One complete revolution, or orbit, of Earth around the Sun defines the time unit of one year. During a single revolution, Earth rotates on its axis $365\frac{1}{4}$ times; therefore, there are 365 days in a year, with an extra day every fourth year—leap year. Earth orbits the Sun in an elliptical path, or an ellipse, and the ellipse lies in a plane referred to as the plane of the ecliptic. The Sun is located at one of the two foci of the ellipse; thus, Earth is nearer to the Sun at one position in the orbit than at any other position. That position occurs on or about January 3 and is called perihelion, meaning "near the Sun." The Earth-Sun distance at perihelion is about 147,000,000 kilometers. At the opposite position on the elliptical orbit, called aphelion, on or about July 4, Earth is farthest from the Sun, 152,000,000 kilometers away.

This variation in Earth's distance from the Sun does alter the amount of solar radiation that is received by Earth, but it is not the cause of the seasons. Perihelion, when Earth is nearest to the Sun and seemingly when Earth would be the warmest, occurs during winter in the Northern Hemisphere, and aphelion occurs during the Northern Hemisphere's summer. The distance variations are out of phase with the Northern Hemisphere's seasons, then, but in phase with seasons in the Southern Hemisphere. In both cases, they modify the seasons but do not cause them. The cause of the seasons is the fact that Earth's axis of rotation is tilted 23.5 degrees from the vertical to the plane of the ecliptic. The figure shows how the axis is tilted. The tilt remains constant year-round in reference to space and the plane of the ecliptic, but because Earth revolves around the Sun, the axis in the Northern Hemisphere alternately tilts toward and away from the Sun. When the North Pole is tilted away from the Sun, the Southern Hemisphere receives more solar radiation than does the Northern Hemisphere. At the position in orbit where the northern tip of the axis is tilted directly away from the Sun, the Sun is directly overhead at the Tropic of Capricorn (23.5 degrees south latitude), and the circle of illumination is tangent to the Arctic Circle (66.5 degrees north latitude). This position in orbit is referred to as the December solstice and occurs on December 21 or 22. For the Northern Hemisphere, it is the "winter solstice," but it is the "summer solstice" for the Southern Hemisphere. Six months later, when the northern tip of the axis is tilted directly toward the Sun, the Northern Hemisphere in turn receives more solar radiation than does the Southern Hemisphere. This position in orbit, known as the June solstice, occurs on June 21 or 22. At this time, the Sun is directly overhead at the Tropic of Cancer (23.5 degrees north latitude), and the entire area north of the Arctic Circle is experiencing continuous daylight. Approximately halfway in the orbit between the two solstices occur the two equinoxes. The March equinox, occuring on March 20 or 21, is the vernal or spring equinox for the Northern Hemisphere, but it is the autumnal or fall equinox for the Southern Hemisphere. The September equinox, September 22 or 23, is the fall equinox for the Northern Hemisphere but the spring equinox for the Southern Hemisphere. On the two equinoxes, the Sun is directly overhead at the equator (0 degrees latitude), and the circle of illumination passes through both poles and bisects the parallels of all latitudes. Both hemispheres receive equal solar radiation on the equinoxes, but in March the Sun is moving northward, whereas in September it is moving southward. It is on these two dates only that daylight and darkness are equal. It is also only on these dates that the Sun rises due east and sets due west.

Earth in Orbit Around the Sun

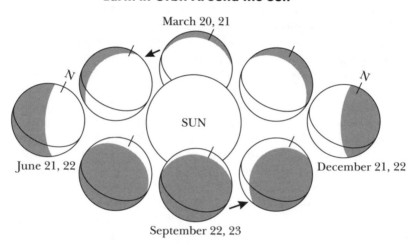

Between March and September, when the Sun's vertical rays are north of the equator, sunrise is north of east and sunset is north of west. This is true for all locations that would experience sunrise and sunset on a particular date, both Northern and Southern Hemisphere locations. (The places that would not experience sunrise and sunset are those areas near the poles that would be experiencing either continuous daylight or continuous darkness on that date.) Sunrise would be farthest north of east on the June solstice, and sunset would be farthest north of west on that same day. After the June solstice, sunrise and sunset both migrate daily southward, being due east and due west on the September equinox. Between September and March, sunrise is south of east and sunset is south of west for all places that experience sunrise and sunset on a particular date, for both hemispheres. Sunrise is farthest south of east and sunset farthest south of west on the December solstice, after which they both begin a northward migration to repeat the pattern.

Methods of Study

Astronomers and astrophysicists study the Sun as they do any other star—that is, as having a life cycle that will eventually end in its death some 5 billion years hence, when it begins to exhaust its hydrogen fuel. Earth scientists, however, investigate the Earth-Sun system as though the Sun were everlasting, which, from the perspective of Earth-Sun relations, it is. Earth scientists are concerned principally with the effects of Earth's rotation and revolution on the amount of solar energy Earth receives as well as with the effects of the atmosphere and of the ocean. Changes in the Earth are considered more likely to alter Earth's heat budget than are changes in the Sun. Nevertheless, Earth scientists are interested in the study of such solar phenomena as sunspots, prominences, and flares in order to ascertain whether they have any effects on Earth's weather and climate patterns. The cycles of solar phenomena are compared to the records of tree growth rings. These solar phenomena are detected and photographed by filtering solar radiation so that light of a particular wavelength (color) can be viewed. Spectacular solar prominences have been captured on film.

Modern technology enables precise measurements over time of rotation and revolution in reference to the stars. Telescopic photography and the principle of parallax enable scientists to record Earth's position in space over time with great precision. Friction caused by tidal action, in turn caused by the Moon's gravity, may have caused an eons-long slowdown in rotation. Perhaps, over time, precise measurements will shed light on such matters. It has been determined that there are wobbles and gyrations in Earth's axis tilt. At present, the axis orientation is slowly moving away from the star Polaris and toward Vega. It is hypothesized that the ellipticity of the orbit undergoes cyclic changes. The positions in orbit where the solstices and equinoxes occur have been ascertained to be slowly changing. A changing relationship between the solstices and perihelion will doubtless alter the distribution of solar radiation between the hemispheres. The analysis of orbit changes offers a possible explanation for the ice ages.

Several areas of research relate to possible Earth-Sun relations in the past. Fossils, sedimentation rates, and extinction of species offer insight into heat budgets that prevailed on Earth in former eras. Hypotheses of the causes of the ice ages make reference to such factors as changes in solar output, changes in Earth output, changes in Earth's atmospheric makeup, a reconfiguration of ocean currents, and even the presence of volcanic dust. Satellite images of the oceans, on the various wavelengths of the electromagnetic spectrum, are analyzed to detect any slight temperature changes over time that may portend changes in Earth's environment. Sensitive instruments measure and record the intensity of sunlight in such areas as Antarctica. Satellite imagery also is providing an accurate record-base for areas of snow cover in polar regions. If Earth's heat budget should change, the areas and duration of snow cover will be among the earliest evidences to be detected.

Intense research continues on changes in the composition of the atmosphere and their possible effects on the heat budget. One conclusion seems clear: Earth's heat budget is a product of many factors in Earth-Sun relations, not all of which are fully understood, and any changes in the budget are likely to be detrimental.

Context

Life on Earth is profoundly dependent upon the relationship between Earth and the Sun. Fortunately, the Sun is a long-lived and constant radiating star. Yet, it would blister Earth if Earth were exposed to it continuously. Rotation and revolution make Earth a rotisserie, slowly turning so as to expose all sides for a more even heat. The lengths of daylight and darkness and the changes of the seasons are phenomena that are beyond human control. It is to be hoped that they will not change, because life on Earth can tolerate very little change.

While humans cannot alter basic Earth-Sun relations, they apparently can have effects on other factors in Earth's heat budget. The atmosphere protects Earth from overheating by day and from overcooling at night. Earth's "greenhouse effect" is a result of the atmosphere's ability to trap solar radiation as heat during the day and retard its escape back into space at night, when the Sun is not above the horizon. A critical constituent gas that is responsible for the greenhouse effect is carbon dioxide. There is concern that a global warming resulting from an enhanced greenhouse effect may be under way because of additional carbon dioxide being added to the atmosphere through the burning of fossil fuels. This effect is exacerbated by deforestation. Another concern regarding changes in the atmosphere is that man-made pollutants, principally chlorofluorocarbons, may be depleting the gas ozone in the upper atmosphere. A reduction of ozone would allow greater amounts of harmful ultraviolet radiation to penetrate to Earth's surface.

The temperature of Earth is at a fine balance between the input of radiation from the Sun and the absorption of that solar radiation and subsequent reradiation of heat energy from Earth back into space. Life on the planet is dependent on this solar energy and the moderate, constant temperature that results. Changes could possibly occur in Earth's rotation, revolution, or axis tilt. Any such changes would be catastrophic. If any changes in Earth's heat budget occur, however, it is more likely that they will be as a result of changes in the atmosphere brought about by human actions.

John H. Corbet

Basic Bibliography

Ahrens, C. Donald. *Meteorology Today.* St. Paul, Minn.: West, 1982. This introductory college-level text on meteorology presents a thorough treatment of weather phenomena and explains the seasons and the effects of solar energy on the atmosphere. Written for students with little background in science or mathematics. Includes many illustrations.

Gabler, Robert E., Robert J. Sager, Sheila M. Brazier, and D. L. Wise. *Essentials of Physical Geography*. 3d ed. New York: Saunders College Publishing, 1987. A general introductory-level text on physical geography. Covers rotation, revolution, solar energy, and the elements of weather and climate. Well illustrated. For the general reader.

Harrison, Lucia Carolyn. *Sun, Earth, Time, and Man*. Chicago: Rand McNally, 1960. This book is considered the classic reference for Earth-Sun relations. Although dated, it is an excellent source of information and offers a remarkably extensive coverage of Earth-Sun relations. Most useful to the student who already has a working knowledge of Earth-Sun relations and wants to investigate further.

Jones, B. W., and Milton Keynes. *The Solar System*. Elmsford, N.Y.: Pergamon Press, 1984. A thorough discussion of the entire solar system from the life cycle of a star to the minor members of the system, including comets and meteoroids. Provides highly detailed information on each of the planets and its satellites. Contains some highly technical data, but they are presented in a lucid manner.

Oberlander, Theodore M., and Robert A. Muller. *Essentials of Physical Geography Today*. 2d ed. New York: Random House, 1987. A general introductory text on physical geography, the book includes explanations of Earth-Sun relations and the energy balance of Earth, atmosphere, and ocean systems. Well illustrated with maps and diagrams.

Pasachoff, Jay M. *Astronomy Now*. Philadelphia: W. B. Saunders, 1978. An introductory text in astronomy for students with no background in mathematics or physics. Well illustrated, it covers the planets, the solar system, and the galaxies. The portion on the structure and nature of the Sun is helpful.

Scott, Ralph C. *Physical Geography*. New York: John Wiley & Sons, 1988. A general introductory-level text on physical geography. Earth-Sun relations are presented within an introduction to the study of Earth's weather and climates. Clearly written and well illustrated. Recommended as an initial source.

Strahler, Arthur N., and Alan H. Strahler. *Modern Physical Geography*. 3d ed. New York: John Wiley & Sons, 1987. In this general college-level text on physical geography, Earth-Sun relations are discussed within the context of the study of weather and climate. Diagrams are well employed to explain Earth's orbit, rotation, revolution, and axis tilt. Easy to read.

Tarbuck, Edward J., and Frederick K. Lutgens. *Earth Science*. 5th ed. Columbus, Ohio: Merrill, 1988. Several chapters in this introductory text deal with the solar system. The nature of solar activity and the Earth's motions are explained. Well illustrated and highly accessible.

Current Bibliography

Ahrens, C. Donald. *Meteorology Today: An Introduction to Weather, Climate, and the Environment.* 5th ed. Minneapolis, Minn.: West, 1994.

Hidore, John J. *Climatology: An Atmospheric Science.* New York: Macmillan, 1993.

Holton, James R. *An Introduction to Dynamic Meteorology.* 3d ed. San Diego: Academic Press, 1992.

Lutgens, Frederick K. *The Atmosphere: An Introduction to Meteorology.* 6th ed. Englewood Cliffs, N.J.: Prentice-Hall, 1995.

Cross-References

Earth's Atmospheric Evolution, 130; Earth's Origins, 213; Earth's Rotation, 220; Eclipses, 241; The Greenhouse Effect, 338; Planetary Orbits, 711; Planetary Orbits: Couplings and Resonances, 718; Planetary Rotation, 725.

Earth System Science

Scientists have developed a method, called Earth system science, that views the planet as a dynamic, unified system of simultaneous, interacting forces. It is hoped that promotion of Earth system science can help to stem and even reverse much of the ecological and environmental damage caused by humans.

Overview

A new viewpoint of the Earth as a set of interacting forces all in motion at the same time has come to replace the traditional series of separate Earth science disciplines studied in isolation. This new and promising viewpoint came about as a result of a growing recognition of the interactive nature of Earth's forces exerting an influence upon one another, as opposed to the idea that the forces act independently. The result of these developing ideas and viewpoint is an entirely new approach to Earth studies. Scientific concepts of a static and quiet Earth were replaced by the realization that the planet is a constantly moving and dramatic entity of plate tectonic activity, volcanism, mountain building, earthquakes, severe storms, dynamic oceans, and changing climatic patterns and atmospheric conditions. Scientists view the Earth as a unified whole, and instead of concentrating attention on one component at a time, they adopt a "systems approach" that uses total global observation methods together with numerical modeling.

The Earth systems science approach was first detailed by an Earth System Science Committee (ESSC) appointed by the Advisory Council of the National Aeronautics and Space Administration (NASA). In 1986, the committee completed a three-year study of research opportunities in Earth science and recommended that an integrated, global Earth observation and information system be adopted and in full operation by the mid-1990's. The committee's *Overview Report* was released June 26 of the same year. Requests for the findings of the committee from the National Oceanic and Atmospheric Administration (NOAA) and the National Science Foundation (NSF), along with other federal agencies, have drawn the three top agencies—NASA, NOAA, NSF—into a scientific alliance. The committee's report outlined immediate needs in several wide-reaching areas: scientific understanding of the entire Earth as a system of interacting components; the ability to predict both natural and human-induced changes in the Earth system; strong, coordinated research and observational programs in NASA, NOAA, and NSF as the core of a major United States effort; long-term measurements, from space and from Earth's surface, to describe changes as they occur and as a basis for numerical modeling; modeling, research, and analysis programs to explain the functioning of individual Earth system processes and their interactions; a sequence of specialized space research missions of a global approach, including the Upper Atmosphere Research Satellite (UARS), the joint United States/France Ocean Topography Experiment (TOPEX/POSEIDON), and the Geopotential Research Mission (GRM); and an earth-observing system using polar-orbiting platforms planned as part of the U.S. Space Station complex combining NOAA and NASA instrumentation.

The Earth system science approach utilizes new technologies in global observations, space science applications, computer innovations, and quantitative modeling. These new tools of advanced technology allow scientists to probe and learn about the interactions responsible for Earth evolution and global change. In the quest for practical means to improve the quality of human life, recent advances in technologies for weather prediction, agriculture, and forestry and for navigation and ocean-resource management will accompany a still better understanding of the Earth system. Examples of research made possible by new tools are the opportunity to include the effects of global atmospheric motions into models of ocean circulation, the study of volcanic activity as a link between convection in the Earth's mantle and worldwide atmospheric properties, and the tracing of the global carbon cycle through the many transformations of carbon biological organisms, atmospheric chemical reactions, and the weathering of Earth's solid surface and soils.

Beginning in the 1970's and 1980's, there was a growing realization among scientists that human activities have brought about significant processes of global change that are altering the evolution of the Earth at a surprising pace. Widespread concern for the destructive consequences of careless human behavior has prompted several special studies by the sixteen members of the Earth System Science Committee (ESSC), the International Council of Scientific Unions, and the Committee for an International Geosphere-Biosphere Program of the U.S. National Academy of Sciences.

The goal of Earth system science is to obtain a scientific understanding of the entire Earth system on a global scale by describing how its component parts and their interactions have evolved, how they function, and how they may be expected to continue to evolve on all time scales. This evolution is influenced by human activities—the depletion of the Earth's energy and mineral resources and the alteration of atmospheric chemical composition—that sometimes are easily identified. It is the overall long-range consequences of these human actions that are difficult to understand; the changes do not occur fast enough for immediate recognition and, indeed, often take decades to evolve fully. The challenge to Earth system science, which provides a definite research focus, is to develop the capability to predict those changes that will occur in the twenty-first century, both naturally and in response to human activity. In meeting this challenge, a vigorous program is being undertaken that includes concepts of global observations, information systems built to process global data, existing numerical models which already are contributing to a detailed understanding of individual Earth components and interactions, and the need for interdisciplinary research support and interagency cooperation.

Observations from space, the best vantage point from which to obtain the detailed, global data required to discriminate among worldwide processes operating on both long and short time scales, are essential to the future study of the Earth as a system. Rapid variations in atmospheric and ocean properties, global effects of volcanic eruptions, ocean circulations, and motions of the Earth's crustal plates are examples of such processes. The Space Science Board of the National Academy of Sciences recommended orbital observation as a major method of global study; the Earth System Science Committee accepted the recommendations and expanded on them. Of particular value are NASA and NOAA satellites already on station in orbit, such as the Laser Geodynamics Satellites, which employ laser ranging to measure motions and deformations of Earth's crustal plates. Weather satellites already have supplied a sizable fund of data about the atmosphere and oceans as well as enabled a good start on numerical modeling of weather variations. The committee commented especially on the high value of currently operating programs that permit a coordinated sequence of studies of specific Earth system processes, such as the Earth Radiation Budget Experiment (1984), the Laser Geodynamics Satellites (1976 and 1983), the Navy Remote Ocean Sensing System (1985), and the Upper Atmosphere Research Satellite (1982).

In order to implement the full measure of the Earth system science concept, an advanced information system is needed to process global data and allow analysis, interpretation, and quantitative modeling. Also required is the implementation of new observing programs such as the ocean color imager, scanning radar altimeter for surface topography, and an atmospheric carbon-monoxide monitor. Thus, a vigorous program of instrument development will have to be prepared for satellite experiments, and ground-level measurements to complement, validate, and interpret global observations from space must be devised. In addition to a vigorous program implementation schedule, the development of new management policies and mechanisms are required to encourage cooperation among agencies around the globe in order to ensure the coordination necessary for a truly worldwide study of the Earth. International cooperation is essential to the success of Earth system science. A number of major international research programs are already operating, such as the World Climate Research Program, sponsored by the International Council of Scientific Unions, and the World Meteorological Organization. To accomplish these many programs and objectives, the Earth System Science Committee recommends two specific areas in which the three major United States agencies—NASA,

NOAA, and NSF—must work closely together. The first is to establish and develop the advanced information system required by Earth system science as a cooperative venture, especially to create the necessary management structures, and the second is close cooperation in programs of basic research.

Methods of Study

Methods to be used by scientists in the study of Earth system science are very new and highly advanced. As the study continues, modifications in these advanced methods will introduce even more sophisticated qualitative and quantitative tools because of the fast pace of technological innovation.

The most significant tool for global observation is the discerning satellite that can precisely measure large areas of the Earth at one time. Meteorological satellites to gather data about temperature, weather patterns and forces, and atmospheric changes and ingredients and to monitor variations of climate and storm systems can add an enormous amount of data to the growing fund of global observations. The satellites are placed in geosynchronous orbit at an altitude of 35,000 kilometers so they can continuously monitor the same region of the Earth over long periods of time. The satellite orbits at a speed relative to the speed of the Earth's rotation so that they remain over the same spot on the Earth's surface. Earth observation satellites, working in the infrared band of the spectrum, allow scientists to gather imagery and information about volcanic action, earthquakes, geological formations, mineral resources, and geographic changes to provide still another perspective of the Earth. Orbiting the Earth from pole to pole many times a day, they are able to make a record of large sections of the Earth in a twenty-four-hour period. Earth observation satellites also carry instruments that measure temperatures, record cloud cover, and monitor catastrophic changes. Other satellites measure ocean dynamics such as the temperature of large sections of seas and oceans, wave action, ocean water content, and relationships between water and the land it touches. Special instruments monitor ice conditions and snowfall at sea and watch over changes in polar regions.

Manned spacecraft, carrying astronaut-photographers, are important to provide a platform for getting pictures of discrete regions. The spacecraft also carry radar-imaging devices to measure precise distances and relationships between land features. Continual advances in films and camera optics allow astronauts to gather high-quality pictures and even allow special night photography. The international space station has, as one of its most important objectives, the function of a permanently orbiting platform on which both humans and unattended instruments can work over long periods of time to monitor Earth activities and topography. The space station will be able to contribute large amounts of data because it can function both as information gatherer and processor using advanced onboard automated equipment such as specialized computers.

Although much of the Earth system science instrumentation will be spaceborne, much of it also will have to be ground-based where measurements and important kinds of data are being gathered on-site. Earth activities such as volcanoes, earthquakes, hurricanes, tornadoes, and thunderstorms, for example, must be measured on the ground to determine their effects on other Earth surface processes. Ground data then can be compared and synthesized with data gathered from space to offer a broader view.

One of the most valuable of tools is the computer for the receipt, storage, retrieval, analysis, and supply of large quantities of information. Ground-based and spaceborne computers will be able to work in conjunction with each other for the interaction, comparison, and large-scale analysis of data, which can be networked to any place on Earth by means of telephone lines and data-relay satellites. Advanced computers, such as the super computer, aid in processing a truly enormous amount of data from large periods of historic time, thus speeding up the process of analysis. The computers are especially useful in creating theoretical models of various kinds of processes. By feeding weather data from the past hundred years into a computer, for example, scientists can begin to construct long-term models of weather patterns and global changes in climate and rainfall or drought. Soon to be added are innovative artificial intelligence systems that assist in the processing, analysis, and further use of billions of pieces of separate data. A new study method in use is the creation and management of a global information system into which is fed data from countries all over the world; all nations can retrieve data for their own research as well as input data to add to the ongoing process of worldwide data analysis.

Context

It is imperative that citizens of the twenty-first century understand the forces and processes that are causing global changes because, individually and collectively, they are major contributors to those changes. Human contributions—mostly destructive—include continued clear-cutting of vast forest areas, thus inviting massive deforestation (destruction of forests); removal of protective trees and underbrush from areas adjacent to desert areas, thus encouraging rampant desertification (the spread of desert conditions); and intense pollution of the atmosphere and waterways by carbon monoxide exhaust, massive oil spills, and the use of cosmetic aerosol sprays, thus producing chlorofluorocarbon that attacks and destroys the atmosphere. Over time, these acts have slowly depleted Earth's natural resources and violently upset the fragile balance of nature worldwide. When left alone, the Earth and its processes follow a natural course of events designed to ensure its own perpetual existence. Human intervention, however, has triggered cataclysmic events that, if not stopped, will cause irreversible damage in the long term and that threaten to bring about the eventual destruction of the planet.

Two of these events—the greenhouse effect and the ozone layer depletion—are already in the beginning stages. The natural balance of atmosphere-ocean-land has been seriously upset. The warming of the planet by trapped solar radiation is raising Earth's temperature and is hindering the normal cooling actions of wind, water, and climate. The effect on planets, animals, and humans is being felt already. If continued, the whole process will raise the overall temperature, melt the polar caps, and cause a corresponding rise in ocean levels, which will flood present landmasses. The current destruction of the ozone layer of the atmosphere by chlorofluorocarbons has been carefully studied and documented. If the ozone layer continues to decay, it will fail to block normal amounts of solar radiation, and the temperature rise described as the greenhouse effect will continue to escalate and become a permanent destructive force.

The new methodology of Earth system science offers the human species a chance to prevent this disaster, both in the study of Earth from a more integrated perspective and in the raising of public awareness of the human practices that are destroying the planet. Nothing less than a sustained worldwide effort is required.

Thomas W. Becker

Basic Bibliography

Earth System Science Committee. *An Integrated Global Earth Observation and Information System to Be in Full Operation by the Mid-1990's.* Boulder, Colo.: University Corporation for Atmospheric Research, 1986. This thirty-page information brief is a statement containing an explanation of the entire concept of Earth system science, written by the key people who created the method. A very basic presentation of the subject written in terse and brief language. A highly usable and understandable text on which the reader can rely as one of the starting points for comprehending the entire concept. Copies of the brief may be obtained from the Earth System Sciences Committee, University Corporation for Atmospheric Research, P.O. Box 3000, Boulder, Colorado 80307, or from the Public Affairs offices of the National Aeronautics and Space Administration (NASA), the National Oceanic and Atmospheric Administration (NOAA), and the National Science Foundation (NSF).

Houghton, Richard A., and G. Woodwell. "Global Climatic Change." *Scientific American* 260 (April, 1989): 36-44. Two long-acknowledged experts have teamed up to present yet more disturbing evidence of the rapid global warming trend. Their creation of warming and atmospheric models fit very well with Earth system science concepts. Sounding once again the global alarm for major changes in human activities that are accelerating the warming trend, the authors clearly present a picture of the Earth's future unless massive and costly preventive programs are undertaken immediately. The text is well written and logically presented, and the graphic illustrations are a perfect complement to the evidence. Appropriate for the high school student and the layperson.

Matthews, Samuel W. "This Changing Earth." *National Geographic* 143 (January, 1973): 1-37. This beautifully illustrated text about the forces which sculpt and change the Earth is most likely one of the earliest articles to describe the Earth's dynamic processes in a language that the public can readily understand. The subjects of tectonic plate science and continental drift theory are clearly and precisely treated. In addition, the author takes the reader on a historic tour of the development of these modern processes, recalling pioneering scientists and the reception each received as a theorist. Superb diagrams and supportive photography.

National Aeronautics and Space Administration Advisory Council. *Earth System Science Overview.* Washington, D.C.: Government Printing Office, 1986. This exquisite, full-color booklet is the basic document for approaching the subject of Earth system science. Created by the Earth System Sciences Committee of the NASA Advisory Council, the fifty-page document details in easy-to-understand text all the intricate natural mechanisms at work on the planet. Far more important, the booklet describes and pictures the entire Earth system science concept and outlines in depth how the new tools and methods will be brought together to focus on a global data-gathering and archiving information system through international cooperative efforts. The illustrations are excellent examples of highly professional photography and artwork. Written for the high school student and the layperson.

_____. *Planetary Exploration Through Year 2000.* Washington, D.C.: Government Printing Office, 1983. The immediate value of this comprehensive and detailed full-color booklet created by the Solar System Exploration Committee of the NASA Advisory Council is its use to explain how the Earth and its moon fit into the overall solar system. The book shows how continued exploration of the solar system has brought an enormous amount of new data to the field of comparative planetology. The illustrations from NASA files are superb, but the text might prove to be a struggle for the high school student, mainly because of its detail and its heavy focus on technology. Nevertheless, it is still well worth the effort.

National Geographic Society. "Can Man Save This Fragile Earth?" *National Geographic* 174 (December, 1988). This chilling and timely "report" on the health and wealth of planet Earth—commanding a special issue of the magazine—is the result of a symposium sponsored by the National Geographic Society in January, 1988. In 175 pages of thought-provoking text and magnificent illustration, the authors of the nine articles lead the reader through numerous examples of the major destructive forces now at work on our planet, calling for sober assessments of processes and their renewals. Earth system science is described in various perspectives. The reading level is appropriate for the high school student.

"Planet of the Year: Endangered Earth." *Time* 133 (January 2, 1989). This special issue is the result of a major international conference held at Time, Incorporated, in November, 1988, which centered its attention on the plight of the planet. World-renowned experts from many nations, including the Soviet Union, met and discussed the processes that threaten to destroy the Earth. Terse text, startling photographs, and urgent recommendations make for a fast-moving narrative of what some scientists regard as "desperation science" in order to stop the already-advancing processes. Text is suitable for junior high school to adult readers.

Current Bibliography

Asrar, Ghassem. *EOS: Science Strategy for the Earth Observing System*. New York: American Institute of Physics, 1994.

Nierenberg, William A., ed. *Encyclopedia of Earth System Science*. San Diego, Calif.: Academic Press, 1992.

Skinner, Brian J. *The Blue Planet: An Introduction to Earth System Science*. New York: John Wiley, 1995.

Cross-References

Earth-Sun Relations, 107; Earth's Atmospheric Evolution, 130; Earth's Composition, 139; Earth's Magnetic Field at Present, 192; The Greenhouse Effect, 338.

Earth's Age

Determining the age of the Earth is one of the great achievements of science. Until the eighteenth century, all geological phenomena were believed to have been produced by historical catastrophes such as great floods and earthquakes. The new geology showed that the Earth was billions of years old, rather than thousands as many had previously believed, and that the Earth had the form it did because of slow uniform processes rather than catastrophes.

Overview

In the middle of the seventeenth century Joseph Barber Lightfoot of the prestigious University of Cambridge in England penned the following words: "Heaven and earth, center and circumference, were made in the same instant of time, and clouds full of water, and man was created by the Trinity on the 26th of October 4004 B.C. at 9 o'clock in the morning." At the time that Lightfoot wrote those words, this statement expressed the most informed opinion on the age of the earth—namely, that it could be calculated by adding up the ages of the people recorded in the Old Testament and assuming that Adam and Eve were created at about the same time as was the Earth. This was the method that most scientists—including Nicolaus Copernicus, Johannes Kepler, and Sir Isaac Newton—used to date the Earth, and much effort was expended analyzing the first few books of the Old Testament "scientifically."

A little over a century later, a Scottish geologist named James Hutton suggested that there was a better way to determine the past history of the Earth than by poring over biblical genealogies. Hutton believed that processes currently operating in nature could be extrapolated back in time to shed light on the historical development of the Earth. This idea—that historical processes are essentially the same as present processes—is called uniformitarianism. In 1785, he presented his new views on geology in a paper entitled "Theory of the Earth: Or, An Investigation of the Laws Observable in the Composition, Dissolution, and Restoration of Land upon the Globe." Uniformitarianism became the foundation of the newly developing science of historical geology. Charles Lyell, who was born in the year of Hutton's death, extended these new ideas and laid the foundation for what was to become a powerful new science. The major argument was over the age of the Earth. Was it really billions of years old, as suggested by new discoveries and theories, or was it only a few thousand years old, as everyone had previously believed? The materials from which the Earth is constructed are certainly very old. Many of the atoms in the Earth date from the beginning of the universe, 15 to 20 billion years ago. The establishment of criteria by which the age of anything will be determined is guided by the need for that age to be a meaningful physical quantity. The conventional definition of age for a person (number of years since birth) is meaningful; the number of years since the origin of the atoms in a person's body would not be meaningful, because it is not relevant to that particular person's duration of existence as that person. A meaningful definition for the age of the Earth can thus be formulated as follows: The age of the Earth is the time since its composite materials acquired an organization that could be identified with the present Earth.

Current theories of the formation of the Earth suggest that the atoms of the Earth and all the other members of the solar system formed a cloud of interstellar material that existed in a corner of the Milky Way galaxy several billion years ago. Under the influence of gravity, this cloud of material began to condense in those regions where the concentration of material was sufficiently higher than average. This nebular cloud, as it is called, gave birth to the Earth, the Sun, and the planets. As the material from which the Earth was forming condensed, a number of events occurred: The density increased to the point where the mutual repulsion of the particles balanced the gravity from the newly formed "planet"; the planet became hotter as friction from the now-dense material became a significant source of energy; and energy given off by materials inside the planet was unable to escape into space and was absorbed, further increasing the temperature. The early Earth was therefore very hot and existed in a molten state for many years.

There is thus no unique age for the Earth. Rather, there is a time period that can realistically be described as the "birth" of the Earth. This time period was millions of years long, and any dates given for the age of the Earth must necessarily reflect this ambiguity. Fortunately, the age of the Earth is measured in billions of years, so the uncertainties surrounding the exact time of its birth do not significantly affect measurements of its age.

Since the initial formation of the Earth, many processes have been taking place: Unstable (radioactive) materials have been decaying into other elements; the initial rotation rate has been declining as friction from the tides and the Moon has worked to slow the rotation of the Earth; mountains have been rising under the influence of global tectonics, and rivers have been formed from the ceaseless activities of erosion; and evolution has been transforming the planet, changing sterile compounds into organic, and barren wasteland into ecological congestion as the phenomenon of life has manifested itself over the face of the globe. As these various physical processes traverse the Earth, they leave footprints as evidence of their passing. When these footprints are studied, the history of the Earth can be reconstructed. In some cases, this reconstruction can lead all the way back to the origin of the Earth, thus providing an answer to the question "How old is the Earth?"

Methods of Study

Current estimates put the age of the Earth at about 4.6 billion years. This figure is firmly supported by a number of measurements—some very direct and straightforward and some rather subtle. Life itself can be used as a clock. For example, trees add distinguishable layers of growth at a rate of one a year; these are the familiar "rings" that can be counted on a stump of wood. Counting these rings provides a very accurate clock for determining the age of the tree. Giant sequoias in California are regularly dated at about three thousand years old, and the bristlecone pine has been dated at almost five

Geologic Time Scale
(ages in millions of years)

Eon	Era	Period	Epoch	Age
			Recent	
		Quaternary	Pleistocene	1.6
	Cenozoic		Pliocene	5.3
			Miocene	23.7
		Tertiary	Oligocene	36.6
			Eocene	57.8
			Paleocene	66.4
		Cretaceous		144
Phanerozoic	Mesozoic	Jurassic		208
		Triassic		245
		Permian		286
			Pennsylvanian	320
		Carboniferous		
			Mississippian	360
		Devonian		408
	Paleozoic			
		Silurian		438
		Ordovician		505
		Cambrian		570
	Late			900
Proterozoic	Middle			1,600
	Early			2,500
	Late			3,000
Archean	Middle			3,400
	Early			3,800 ?

thousand years. Samples of sedimentary rock, which form yearly layers called varves, can extend back as far as twenty thousand years. Unfortunately, all these annual processes that provide a direct year-by-year chronicle of Earth history provide no useful data beyond a few tens of thousands of years.

There are other, less direct, uniformitarian processes, however, that perform somewhat better in this regard. Measurements of erosion, the salinity of the ocean, the strength and direction of the Earth's magnetic field, and the internal heat of the Earth can all yield values for the "age" of the Earth, measured in millions rather than thousands of years. The validity of each of these indirect measurements requires a strict uniformitarian character for the nature of the process; this assumption, however, is not legitimate for most of these processes, which explains why the ages determined from their application are so discordant and unreliable.

The most consistent geological chronometer is based on radioactive decay, an atomic/nuclear phenomenon. All atoms consist of a densely packed nucleus housing a number of protons, which have a positive charge, and neutrons, which have no charge. Because the protons are all positively charged, they repel one another; an atomic nucleus would immediately explode if it were not for a different nuclear force, called the strong force, that holds them together. Every nucleus exists in a state of dynamic tension as the electrical force tries to blow it apart and the strong nuclear force tries to hold it together. Certain nuclei are frequently unstable; that is, they have a tendency to disintegrate spontaneously into other, more stable, nuclei. This disintegration is initiated by yet another nuclear force, the weak force.

Usually the protons in the nucleus of an atom are paired with a particular number of neutrons in such a way that the nucleus will be stable. For the first few elements on the periodic table, the neutron/proton ratio is equal to one, but for larger atoms, the ratio increases as the neutrons start to outnumber the protons. For almost all the elements, there are certain nuclear combinations of protons and neutrons that are stable. By definition, members of the same atomic species have the same number of protons in the nucleus and thus the same atomic number. Atoms with differing numbers of neutrons are called isotopes of that element. Carbon, for example, normally has twelve particles in the nucleus—six protons and six neutrons—and is therefore designated carbon 12. A common isotope, however, has two extra neutrons and is designated carbon 14.

The detailed structure of a particular nucleus determines its long-term stability. Most of the nuclear configurations found in nature, such as hydrogen and helium, are stable indefinitely, or at least for a time that is much longer than the age of the universe (about 20 billion years). Unstable nuclei, on the other hand, are stable for only a finite period of time, which can be either very short (a fraction of a second) or very long (billions of years), depending on the composition of the particular nucleus.

The period of stability for an unstable nucleus is known as its half-life. A half-life is defined to be the time period during which one-half of the nuclei of a given sample will spontaneously decay into another nuclear species. The half-life of carbon 14, for example, is about 5,730 years. This means that in 5,730 years, one-half of an original carbon 14 nucleus, called the parent, will spontaneously decay into another element, nitrogen 14, called the "daughter" element. Over time, the parent element will gradually transform into the daughter. The ratio of daughter to parent can be used to determine how long the parent has been decaying and thus how old the material containing the parent is. It is important to note that the assumption of uniformitarianism for radioactive decay rates is considered very reasonable. Unlike the other processes mentioned above, there seems to be very few mechanisms in nature that can disturb the constancy of the radioactive "clock."

A number of radioactive materials are found in nature, all with differing half-lives. Each can be used to find the ages consistent with their half-lives; that is, a material with a long half-life, such as uranium 238 (whose half-life is almost 5 billion years), can be used to date objects that are billions of years old, and carbon 14 can be used to date objects that are thousands of years old.

Radioactive dating has been applied to many rocks found on the Earth. The oldest rocks believed to have formed on the Earth are from a volcano in western Greenland and have been dated at about 3.8 billion years, using uranium 238. It is difficult to find very ancient rocks on the surface of the Earth, because most of the Earth's surface has been rebuilt many times since the Earth was born. There are probably older rocks in the deep interior of the Earth.

The currently accepted age for the Earth, 4.6 billion years, was obtained by dating meteorites that fall to Earth from space. These meteorites are believed to have been formed at the same time as was the Earth and to have existed in the vacuum of space until they were captured by the gravity from the Earth. Similar dates have been obtained from the rocks brought back from the Moon, which is believed to have formed at about the same time as the Earth.

While many questions remain about the details of the formation of the Earth, two facts seem clear: First, the Earth owes its origin to the same processes that brought the solar system into existence; second, those processes can be dated with a high degree of confidence at between 4 and 5 billion years ago.

Context

The problem of the age of the Earth is part of a much larger scientific question, which exists at the interface between the very practical study of the Earth and its various properties and the more esoteric question of the origin and evolution of the universe as a whole. On the practical side, knowledge of the Earth's various and occasionally delicate properties is important for the future of the human race. By knowing how long the Earth has been in existence, scientists are better able to understand the processes that have shaped the surface of the Earth into the form that it has today. Predicting earthquakes, hunting for oil, monitoring the spread of the sea floor—all these practical questions require knowledge of large-scale planetary processes, the same kind of knowledge that illuminates the question of the age of the Earth. Furthermore, knowing that the Earth is billions of years old and can easily survive for billions more should encourage human societies to take better care of the planet.

From a more esoteric or speculative point of view, the age of the Earth is important because it speaks to the most fundamental questions that are asked about the place of human beings in the universe. How old is this planet? How was it formed? In the century or so since geological science overthrew the seventeenth century notion of a much younger Earth, people have struggled with finding a new place in the universe. The argument that began centuries ago is still heard in courtrooms across the United States as "creation science" once again argues that the Earth is thousands, not billions, of years old. Legal battles rage over the issue of whether high schools across the country should teach geochronology that is based on religious dogma rather than on scientific research. Research is still being done on this very important scientific question and no doubt will continue into the foreseeable future as the human mind strives to learn more about the Earth. The growing awareness of how dependent humans are on the continued health of the Earth is a powerful incentive to learn more about their planetary home.

Karl Giberson

Basic Bibliography

Haber, Frances C. *The Age of the World: Moses to Darwin.* Baltimore: Johns Hopkins University Press, 1959. Reprint. Westport, Conn.: Greenwood Press, 1978. This interesting book does not focus on current estimates of the age of the Earth but rather on the historical controversy that emerged when nonbiblical values for the age of the Earth began to be accepted. Provides insight into the conflict between science and dogma.

Hurley, Patrick M. *How Old Is the Earth?* Garden City, N.Y.: Doubleday, 1959. One of the few full-length books on geochronology for the layperson. Even though published thirty years ago, it is still valid, as most of the material relevant to the age of the Earth has not changed appreciably since its publication.

Ozima, Minoru. *The Earth: Its Birth and Growth.* Cambridge, England: Cambridge University Press, 1981. A translation of a Japanese book that was written by a scientist whose specialty is geochronology. Written at an introductory level.

Stearn, Colin W., et al. *Geological Evolution of North America.* New York: John Wiley & Sons, 1979. Several excellent chapters discussing the age of the Earth. Contains an excellent chapter on geological time and the various ways it can be measured.

Stokes, William Lee. *Essentials of Earth History: An Introduction to Historical Geology.* 4th ed. Englewood Cliffs, N.J.: Prentice-Hall, 1982. A standard introductory text on historical geology. All the various methods for determining the age of the Earth are discussed in the first few chapters.

Stokes, William Lee, et al. *Introduction to Geology: Physical and Historical.* Englewood Cliffs, N.J.: Prentice-Hall, 1978. Textbook similar to Stokes's other book in terms of its discussion of geochronology.

Thackray, John. *The Age of the Earth.* New York: Cambridge University Press, 1989. A very short publication, about forty pages long, published by a British geological museum. Contains more pictures than text, but the pictures, most in color, are helpful and make this an interesting source.

Current Bibliography

Brownlow, Arthur H. *Geochemistry.* 2d ed. Upper Saddle River, N.J.: Prentice-Hall, 1996.

Krauskopf, Konrad Bates. *Introduction to Geochemistry.* 3d ed. New York: McGraw-Hill, 1995.

Cross-References

Earth-Sun Relations, 107; Earth System Science, 115; Earth's Atmospheric Evolution, 130; Earth's Composition, 139; Earth's Magnetic Field: Origins, 176; Earth's Magnetic Field: Secular Variation, 184; Earth's Magnetic Field at Present, 192; Earth's Origins, 213; Life's Origins, 440.

Earth's Atmospheric Evolution

The chemical composition of the atmosphere has changed significantly over the 4.6-billion-year history of the Earth. The composition of atmosphere has been controlled by a number of processes, including the "outgassing" of gases or volatiles originally trapped in the Earth's interior during its formation; the geochemical cycling of carbon, nitrogen, hydrogen, and oxygen compounds between the surface, the ocean, and the atmosphere; and the origin and evolution of life.

Overview

Some 4.6 billion years ago, a cloud of interstellar gas and dust, called the primordial solar nebula, began to condense under the influence of gravity. This condensation led to the formation of the Sun, the Moon, Earth, the other planets and their satellites, asteroids, meteors, and comets. The primordial solar nebula was composed almost entirely of hydrogen gas, with a smaller amount of helium, still smaller amounts of carbon, nitrogen, and oxygen, and still smaller amounts of the rest of the elements of the periodic table. About the time that the newly formed Earth reached its approximate present mass, gases that were originally trapped in the Earth's interior were released through the surface, forming a gravitationally bound atmosphere. (It is believed that the atmospheres of the other terrestrial planets, Mars and Venus, also formed in this manner.) The release of these gases is called volatile outgassing. The period of extensive volatile outgassing may have lasted for many tens of millions of years. The outgassed volatiles or gases had roughly the same chemical composition as do present-day volcanic emissions: 80 percent water vapor by volume, 10 percent carbon dioxide by volume, 5 percent sulfur dioxide by volume, 1 percent nitrogen by volume, and smaller amounts of hydrogen, carbon monoxide, sulfur, chlorine, and argon.

The water vapor that outgassed from the interior soon reached its saturation point, which is controlled by the atmospheric temperature and pressure. Once the saturation point was reached, the atmosphere could not hold any additional gaseous water vapor. Any new outgassed water vapor that entered the atmosphere would have precipitated out of the atmosphere in the form of liquid water. The equivalent of several kilometers of liquid water released from the Earth's interior in gaseous form precipitated out of the atmosphere and formed the Earth's vast oceans. Only small amounts of water vapor remained in the atmosphere—ranging from a fraction of a percent to several percent by volume, depending on atmospheric temperature, season, and latitude.

The outgassed atmospheric carbon dioxide, being very water soluble, readily dissolved into the newly formed oceans and formed carbonic acid. In the oceans, carbonic acid formed ions of hydrogen, bicarbonate, and carbonate. The carbonate ions reacted with ions of calcium and magnesium in the ocean water, forming carbonate rocks, which precipitated out of the ocean and accumulated as sea-floor carbonate sediments. Most of the outgassed atmospheric carbon dioxide formed carbonates, leaving only trace amounts of gaseous carbon dioxide in the atmosphere (about 0.035 percent by volume). Sulfur dioxide, the third most abundant component of volatile outgassing, was chemically transformed into other sulfur compounds and sulfates in the atmosphere. Eventually, the sulfates

SEPTEMBER 5, 1974

A view of Earth and its oceans. The oceans influence Earth's atmosphere through the geochemical cycling of carbon, nitrogen, hydrogen, and oxygen compounds. *(National Aeronautics and Space Administration)*

131

formed atmospheric aerosols and diffused out of the atmosphere onto the surface.

The fourth most abundant outgassed compound, nitrogen, is chemically inert in the atmosphere and thus was not chemically transformed, as was sulfur dioxide. Unlike carbon dioxide, nitrogen is relatively insoluble in water and, unlike water vapor, does not condense out of the atmosphere. For these reasons, nitrogen built up in the atmosphere to become its major constituent (78.08 percent by volume). Therefore, outgassed volatiles led to the formation of the Earth's atmosphere, oceans, and carbonate rocks.

The molecules of nitrogen, carbon dioxide, and water vapor in the early atmosphere were acted upon by solar ultraviolet radiation and atmospheric lightning. In the process, molecules of formaldehyde and hydrogen cyanide were chemically synthesized in the early atmosphere. These molecules precipitated and diffused out of the atmosphere into the oceans. In the oceans, the formaldehyde and hydrogen cyanide entered into chemical reactions, called polymerization reactions, which eventually led to the chemical synthesis of amino acids, the building blocks of living systems. The synthesis of amino acids from nitrogen, carbon dioxide, and water vapor in the atmosphere is called chemical evolution. Chemical evolution preceded and provided the material for biological evolution.

For many years, it was thought that the early atmosphere was composed of ammonia, methane, and hydrogen, rather than of carbon dioxide, nitrogen, and water vapor. Experiments show, however, that ammonia and methane are chemically unstable and are readily destroyed by both solar ultraviolet radiation and chemical reaction with the hydroxyl radical, which is formed from water vapor. In addition, ammonia is very water soluble and is readily removed from the atmosphere by precipitation. Hydrogen, the lightest element, is readily lost from a planet by gravitational escape. Thus, an early atmosphere composed of methane, ammonia, and hydrogen would be very short-lived, unless these gases were produced at a rate comparable to their destruction or loss rates. Today, methane and ammonia are very minor components of the atmosphere—methane at a concentration of 1.7 parts per million by volume and ammonia at a concentration of 1 part per billion by volume. Both gases are produced solely by microbial activity at the Earth's surface. Clearly, microbial activity and microbes were nonexistent during the earliest history of the planet. The atmospheres of the outer planets—Jupiter, Saturn, Uranus, and Neptune—all contain appreciable quantities of hydrogen, methane, and ammonia. It is believed that the atmospheres of these planets, unlike the atmospheres of the terrestrial planets—Earth, Venus, and Mars—are captured remnants of the primordial solar nebula. Because of the outer planets' great distance from the Sun and their very low temperatures, hydrogen, methane, and ammonia are stable and long-lived constituents of their atmospheres. This is not true of hydrogen, methane, and ammonia in the Earth's atmosphere.

Layers of the Earth's Atmosphere

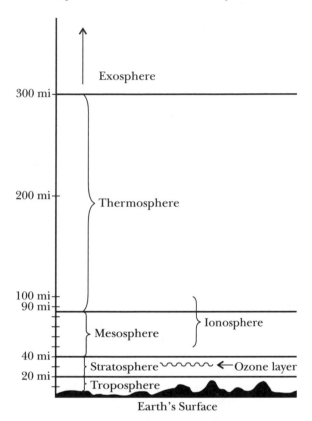

Some have suggested that at the time of its formation, the Earth may have also captured a remnant of the primordial solar nebula as its very first atmosphere. Such a captured primordial solar nebula atmosphere would have been composed of mostly hydrogen (about 90 percent) and helium (about 10 percent), the two major elements of the nebula. Even if such an atmosphere had surrounded the very young Earth, it would have been very short-lived. As the young Sun went through its T Tauri phase of evolution, very strong solar winds (the supersonic flow of protons and electrons from the Sun) would have quickly dissipated this remnant atmosphere. In addition, there is no geochemical evidence to suggest that the early Earth ever possessed a primordial solar nebula remnant atmosphere.

There is microfossil evidence for the existence of fairly advanced microbial living systems on the Earth by about 3.8 billion years ago. Photosynthesis evolved in one or more of these early microbial species. In photosynthesis, the organism utilizes water vapor and carbon dioxide in the presence of sunlight and chlorophyll to form carbohydrates, used by the organism for food. In the process of photosynthesis, oxygen is given off as a metabolic by-product. The production of oxygen by photosynthesis was a major event on the Earth and transformed the composition and chemistry of the early atmosphere. As a result of photosynthetic production, oxygen built up to become the second most abundant constituent of the atmosphere (20.90 percent by volume). It has been estimated that atmospheric oxygen reached only 1 percent of its present atmospheric level 2 billion years ago, 10 percent of its present atmospheric level about 550 million years ago, and its present atmospheric level as early as 400 million years ago.

The evolution of atmospheric oxygen had very important implications for the evolution of life. The presence and buildup of oxygen led to the evolution of respiration, which replaced fermentation as the energy production mechanism in living systems. Accompanying and directly controlled by the buildup of atmospheric oxygen was the origin and evolution of atmospheric ozone, which is chemically formed from oxygen. The evolution of atmospheric ozone resulted in the shielding of the Earth's surface from biologically lethal solar ultraviolet between 0.2 and 0.3 micron. The development of the atmospheric ozone layer and its accompanying shielding of the Earth's surface permitted early life to leave the safety of the oceans and go ashore for the first time in the history of the planet. Prior to the evolution of the atmospheric ozone layer, early life was restricted to a depth of several meters below the ocean surface. At this depth, the ocean water offered shielding from solar ultraviolet radiation. Theoretical computer calculations indicate that atmospheric ozone provided sufficient shielding from biologically lethal ultraviolet radiation for the colonization of the land once oxygen reached about one-tenth of its present atmospheric level.

Calculations indicate that the atmospheres of Venus and Mars also evolved as a consequence of the volatile outgassing of the same gases that led to the formation of Earth's atmosphere—water vapor, carbon dioxide, and nitrogen. In the case of Venus and Mars, however, the outgassed water vapor never existed in the form of liquid water on the surfaces of these planets. Because of Venus' closer distance to the Sun (108 million kilometers versus 150 million kilometers for Earth), its lower atmosphere was too hot to permit the outgassed water vapor to condense out of the atmosphere. Thus, the outgassed water vapor remained in gaseous form in the atmosphere and, over geological time, was broken apart by solar ultraviolet radiation to form hydrogen and oxygen. The very light hydrogen gas quickly escaped from the atmosphere of Venus, and the heavier oxygen combined with surface minerals to form a highly oxidized surface. In the absence of liquid water on the surface of Venus, the outgassed carbon dioxide remained in the atmosphere and built up to become the overwhelming constituent of the atmosphere of Venus (about 96 percent by volume). The outgassed nitrogen accumulated to comprise about 4 percent by volume of the Venus atmosphere. The carbon dioxide and nitrogen atmosphere of Venus is very massive—it produces an atmospheric surface pressure of about 90 atmospheres (the surface pressure of Earth's atmosphere is only one atmosphere). If the outgassed carbon dioxide in the atmosphere of Earth did not leave via dissolution in the oceans and carbonate formation, its surface atmospheric pressure would be about 70 atmospheres, with carbon dioxide comprising about 98-99 percent of the atmosphere and nitrogen about 1-2 percent. Thus, the atmosphere of Earth would closely resemble that of Venus. The carbon dioxide-rich atmosphere of Venus causes a very significant greenhouse temperature enhancement, giving the surface of Venus a temperature of about 750 Kelvins, which is hot enough to melt lead. The surface temperature of Earth is only about 288 Kelvins.

Like Venus, Mars has an atmosphere composed primarily of carbon dioxide (about 95 percent by volume) and nitrogen (about 3 percent by volume). The total atmospheric surface pressure of Mars, however, is only about 7 millibars (one atmosphere is equivalent to 1013 millibars). It is thought that because of Mars' greater distance from the Sun as compared to Earth's (228 million kilometers versus 150 million kilometers), the temperature of the surface of Mars was too low to support the presence of liquid water. There may be very large quantities of outgassed water in the form of ice or frost below the surface of Mars. In the absence of liquid water, the outgassed carbon dioxide remained in the atmosphere. The smaller mass of the atmosphere of Mars compared to the atmosphere of Venus and Earth may be attributable to the smaller mass of Mars and, therefore, the smaller mass available for the trapping of gases in the interior of Mars during its formation. In addition, it appears that the amount of gases trapped in the interiors of Venus, Earth, and Mars during their formation decreased with increasing distance from the Sun. Venus appears to have trapped the greatest amount of gases, and was the most volatile-rich planet, Earth trapped the next greatest amount, and Mars trapped the smallest amount.

Methods of Study

Information about the origin, early history, and evolution of the Earth's atmosphere comes from a variety of sources. Information on the origin of Earth and other planets is based on theoretical computer simulations. These computer models simulate the collapse of the primordial solar nebula and the formation of the planets. Recent astronomical observations of what appears to be the collapse of interstellar gas clouds and the possible formation of planetary systems have provided new insights into the computer modeling of this phenomenon. Information about the origin, early history, and evolution of the atmosphere is based on theoretical computer models of volatile outgassing, the geochemical cycling of the outgassed volatiles, and the photochemistry/chemistry of the outgassed volatiles. The process of chemical evolution, which led to the synthesis of organic molecules of increasing complexity, the precursors of the first living systems on the early

Earth, is studied in laboratory experiments. In laboratory experiments on chemical evolution, mixtures of gases simulating the Earth's early atmosphere are energized by solar ultraviolet radiation and atmospheric lightning. The resulting products are analyzed by chemical techniques. A key parameter affecting atmospheric photochemical reactions, chemical evolution, and the origin of life was the flux of solar ultraviolet radiation incident on the early Earth. Astronomical measurements of the ultraviolet emissions from young sunlike stars have provided important information about ultraviolet emissions from the Sun during the very early history of the atmosphere.

Geological and paleontological studies of the oldest rocks and the earliest fossil records have provided important information on the evolution of the atmosphere and the transition from an oxygen-deficient to an oxygen-sufficient atmosphere. Studies of the biogeochemical cycling of the elements have provided important insights into the later evolution of the atmosphere. Thus, studies of the origin and evolution of the atmosphere are based on a broad cross section of science, involving astronomy, geology, geochemistry, geophysics, and biology as well as atmospheric chemistry.

Context

Studies of the origin and evolution of the atmosphere have provided new insights into the processes and parameters responsible for global change. Understanding the history of the atmosphere provides better understanding of its future. Today, several global environment changes are of national and international concern, including the depletion of ozone in the stratosphere and global warming caused by the buildup of greenhouse gases. The study of the evolution of the atmosphere has provided new insights into the biogeochemical cycling of elements between the atmosphere, biosphere, land, and ocean. Understanding this cycling is a key to understanding environmental problems. Studies of the origin and evolution of the atmosphere have also provided new insights into the origin of life and the possibility of life outside the Earth.

Joel S. Levine

Basic Bibliography

Cloud, Preston. *Cosmos, Earth, and Man: A Short History of the Universe.* New Haven, Conn.: Yale University Press, 1978. A very readable, nontechnical account of cosmic evolution covering the evolution of stars, the Earth, life, and humankind. The volume defines various scientific terms such as elementary particles, chemical bonding, isotopes, periodic table, and mass. The author assumes that the reader does not have a scientific background, only an interest in our cosmic roots.

Henderson-Sellers, A. *The Origin and Evolution of Planetary Atmospheres.* Bristol, England: Adam Hilger, 1983. A technical treatment of the variation of the climate of the Earth over geological time and the processes and parameters that controlled it. The chapters in the book include the mechanisms for long-term climate change, the atmospheres of the other planets, planetary climatology on shorter time scales, and the stability of planetary environments.

Holland, H. D. *The Chemical Evolution of the Atmosphere and Oceans.* Princeton, N.J.: Princeton University Press, 1984. A comprehensive and technical treatment of the geochemical cycling of elements over geological time and the coupling between the atmosphere, ocean, and surface. The book covers the origin of the solar system, the release and recycling of volatiles, the chemistry of the early atmosphere and ocean, the acid-base balance of the atmosphere-ocean-crust system, and carbonates and clays.

Levine, Joel S., ed. *The Photochemistry of Atmospheres: Earth, the Other Planets, and Comets.* Orlando, Fla.: Academic Press, 1985. A series of review papers dealing with the origin and evolution of the atmosphere, the origin of life, the atmospheres of Earth and other planets, and climate. The book contrasts the origin, evolution, composition, and chemistry of Earth's atmosphere with the atmospheres of the other planets. It contains two appendices that summarize all atmospheric photochemical and chemical processes.

Lewis, John S., and Ronald G. Prinn. *Planets and Their Atmospheres: Origin and Evolution.* New York: Academic Press, 1983. A comprehensive, textbook treatment of the formation of the planets and their atmospheres. This monograph begins with a detailed account of the origin and evolution of solid planets via coalescence and accretion in the primordial solar nebula and then discusses the surface geology and atmospheric composition of each planet.

Schopf, J. William, ed. *Earth's Earliest Biosphere: Its Origin and Evolution.* Princeton, N.J.: Princeton University Press, 1983. A comprehensive group of papers on such subjects as the early Earth, the oldest rocks, the origin of life, early life, and microfossils. Chapters include those on the oldest known rock record, prebiotic organic syntheses and the origin of life, Precambrian organic geochemistry, the transition from fermentation to anoxygenic photosynthesis, the development of an aerobic environment, and early microfossils. Very technical.

Current Bibliography

Ahrens, C. Donald. *Essentials of Meteorology: An Invitation to the Atmosphere.* Minneapolis/St. Paul, Minn.: West, 1993.

Anthes, Richard A. *Meteorology.* 6th ed. New York: Macmillan, 1992.

Barry, Roger Graham. *Atmosphere, Weather, and Climate.* 6th ed. New York: Routledge, 1992.

McIlveen, J. F. R. *Fundamentals of Weather and Climate.* 2d ed. London: Chapman and Hall, 1992.

Singh, Hanwant B., ed. *Composition, Chemistry, and Climate of the Atmosphere.* New York: Van Nostrand Reinhold, 1995.

Cross-References

Auroras, 25; Earth-Sun Relations, 107; Earth's Magnetic Field: Origins, 176; Earth's Magnetic Field: Secular Variation, 184; Earth's Magnetic Field at Present, 192; The Greenhouse Effect, 338; The Van Allen Radiation Belts, 1032.

Earth's Composition

Understanding the processes that have evolved the Earth can help to unify various Earth and biological sciences. The theories about Earth's evolution are speculative, and much of the Earth's earliest history is unknown. Using meteorites and some of the oldest-known crustal rocks, geochemists are trying to unravel the mysteries of the early Earth's composition.

Overview

About 4.5 billion years ago, scientists believe, a massive star exploded in a supernova event that shined as brightly as a whole galaxy of stars. Shock waves from the celestial fireworks overtook a cloud of gas and dust a few light-years away and triggered its contraction, simultaneously seeding the nebula with heavy elements (those heavier than iron on the periodic table). The solar nebula's collapse led to the formation of the Sun (which swept up most of the matter), and the planets formed by the accretion of small bodies called planetesimals. As the planetesimals grew into protoplanets, their gravitational fields increased, so they continued to sweep up material not garnered by the protosun. The innermost planets, Mercury, Venus, Earth, and Mars, contained the dense metals and rocks, while the outer planets were mostly made of gases and volatile ices. During the protoearth's initial accretion process, small, cold bodies collided to form a large mass of homogeneously heterogeneous composition. By the process of differentiation, the heavier metallic elements, such as iron and nickel, migrated to the core of the early Earth, while the lighter elements migrated to the outer portions of the contracting planet.

Meteorites offer clues to the composition of the Earth. Extraterrestrial pieces of an asteroid or planetesimal, meteorites are remnants of the earliest period of planetary formation and come in three basic types. Stony meteorites comprise the most abundant group and are composed of silica-associated, or lithophile, elements such as those found in the Earth's crustal materials. Stony-iron meteorites are composed of roughly equal parts of rock (typically olivine) suspended in a matrix of iron. Iron meteorites are composed of siderophile elements, iron being the major constituent, along with (perhaps) 10-20 percent nickel. Iron meteorites are of particular interest to scientists attempting to model the composition of the Earth's core. The mean density of the Earth is about 5.5 grams per cubic centimeter. The mean density of crustal rocks, however, is only about 2.7 grams per cubic centimeter (water is conveniently 1 gram per cubic centimeter), which indicates a core density of ten to twelve times that of water. The only known objects approaching these densities are the iron meteorites.

After the initial accretion of the planetesimal materials and just prior to differentiation of the lithophile and siderophile elements, the Earth's thermal history began through the process of radioactive decay. During this early thermal period, short-lived radioactive nuclides (atoms of a specific isotope, distinguished by their atomic and mass numbers) produced heating seven times greater than that of today's molten core. Most of the heating was attributable to the decay of potassium 40 as well as of the short half-lived elements such as aluminum 26. After about 100,000 years, the planet separated into the iron-nickel core and magnesium-iron-silicate lower mantle. Over a longer time scale (probably more than 10 million years), the high-volatility compounds, such as lead, mercury, thallium, and bismuth, along with the noble gases, water in hydrated silicates, and carbon-based organic compounds, all condensed. This volatile-rich material migrated to the surface, where it was melted into magmas in a continuous period of crustal reprocessing that lasted for about 1 billion years.

The Earth's original inventory of gases appears to have been lost, based on the relative present abundances of the rare gases (helium, neon, argon, krypton, xenon, and radon) compared to the present silicon content of the Earth. Later periods of volcanic outgassing and perhaps impacts with volatile-rich cosmic objects such as carbonaceous chondritic meteorites and comets may also have played a role in the evolution of the atmosphere and oceans. Separated into three main layers—the crust, mantle, and core—the Earth is an active body, its internal heat far from exhausted. The complexity of the chemical composition increases as one examines each successive outward layer. This generalized model gives a starting point with which to examine the complex nature of Earth materials. Earth's wide range of pressure and temperature regimes helps explain why there are more than two thousand distinct minerals and numerous different combinations of minerals in rock types.

The core is actually composed of two basic parts: the solid inner core, with a density equal to twelve times that of water and a radius of 1,300 kilometers, and a molten outer core, 2,200 kilometers thick, with a density of about 10 grams per cubic centimeter. This model consists of an essentially iron-nickel inner core at high pressure and a metallic outer core that also contains iron sulfide and light elements such as silicon, carbon, and oxygen. As a whole, the core unit comprises about 32 percent of the Earth's mass. Comprising the outer 68 percent of the Earth's bulk, the mantle makes the crust, atmosphere, and oceans insignificant by comparison. The mantle is rich in dense, or mafic, rocks such as olivine and pyroxene (which comes in two basic types, calcium-rich or calcium-poor), with olivine the dominant mineral.

Basic Earth materials are derived via reaction series from mafic magmas melting and settling out in the mantle's upper regions. As the temperatures drop in the melt zone, a discontinuous series (a set of discrete reactions) occurs. Magnetite, an oxide of iron and titanium, is the first to settle out, with the highest melting point at about 1,400 degrees Celsius. Olivine, a mineral whose silicate structure is a simple tetrahedron, is the next to solidify out of the melt, with a density of 3.2-4.4, followed by the single chain structure pyroxene, with a density of 3.2-3.6. As temperatures in the magma drop to near 1,000 degrees Celsius, the amphibole group forms with a lesser density, 2.9-3.2. As the cooling progresses, the structures increase in complexity with the micas—biotite and muscovite, which form in planar sheets. Next in the cooling sequence would be orthoclase, or potassium feldspar, and plagioclase, or calcium feldspar, and, finally, quartz, which are all distinguished by their characteristic three-dimensional diamond shapes and varying colors. The calcic through sodic plagioclase to muscovite, biotite, and quartz occurs in a smooth, or continuous, transition rather than the stepwise, or discontinuous, reactions that characterize the formation of olivine through biotite.

An estimate of the crustal elemental composition of the Earth indicates that only a handful of elements (oxygen, silicon, aluminum, iron, magnesium, calcium, sodium, and titanium) make up more than 99 percent of the Earth's crust. The simple oxide quartz is the most common of the silicate minerals, which account for 95 percent of the crust. With these facts in mind, one can start to hypothesize about how the continents evolved. About 700 million years after the initial formation of the Earth through accretion and differentiation, the first rocks of the Archean eon formed. They are composed of olivine, pyroxene, and anorthite (calcium-rich plagioclase feldspar), which settled out of the basaltic magma. The lighter plagioclase would rise to the surface to form a hardened crust of anorthosite, the same material that comprises the Moon's ancient highlands, which are about 3.8 billion years old.

The anorthosite formed a thick sheet that was fractured into pieces and subjected to further heating through radioactive decay, leading to an essentially granitic rock layer 10-15 kilometers thick. Extensive volcanic activity and high surface temperatures gradually diminished until the hydrosphere (water cycle) was established. The Earth's crust is divided into two main types: the dense, or mafic, oceanic crust and the lighter, or sialic (silica-aluminum), continental crust. Archean rocks (up to 3.5 billion years old) found in the stable interiors of the continents contain massive anorthosite inclusions and may be viewed as the nuclei of the continents.

About the time of the formation of the continental nuclei, or cratons (relatively stable portions of crust), the oldest-known sedimentary rocks accumulated as the rock cycle began, eroding the parent igneous rocks into secondary types of rock. This occurrence may coincide with the beginning of plate tectonics, as the lithosphere (rock crust) of the Earth broke into plates and began its hallmark active motion. Life is thought to have arisen at about the same time, with primitive blue-green algae found in strata 2.8

billion years old. With the oceans growing in volume and salinity and the development of oxygen-releasing blue-green algae, Earth's geochemistry became more complex. Chemically precipitated rocks of calcium carbonate, commonly known as limestones, are an example of the evolving rock cycle.

Life-forms shaped the Earth's chemical composition. By the end of Precambrian time, oxygen levels had reached 1 percent of its present value. Multicelled animals in the oceans scrubbed the carbon dioxide from the atmosphere and locked it up in the carbonate rocks, forming biochemically precipitated limestones. By the late Paleozoic era, coal formations grew as a result of the first land forests being periodically inundated by ocean transgressions.

Methods of Study

Perhaps no other Earth science is as speculative as that of early Earth history and the geochemical evolution of the Earth. Varying models for crustal development are advanced and overturned annually. Despite the problems of extrapolating back to a time before there were solid rocks, the established models are based on some solid lines of evidence as well as on conjecture. In 1873, American geologist James D. Dana made one of the initial advances in the study of the Earth's internal chemical composition when he suggested that analogies could be drawn from the study of meteorites. Believed to be pieces of differentiated bodies that were later disintegrated into smaller pieces, meteorites come in differing types that are analogous to the Earth's interior. Because meteorite types approximate elemental distribution in the Earth, they are valuable samples for laboratory examination by scientists. Geochemists studying meteorites have derived radiometric dates of 4.6 billion years—corresponding to the initial time of accretion and differentiation of the planets.

Geophysicists use seismic waves to study the Earth's interior. Changes in velocity and deflections of the waves passing through the Earth have revealed a differentiated Earth with a very dense core, less dense mantle, and a light crust "floating" on top. The well-established theory of plate tectonics has shown that the crust is broken into pieces, or plates, that are moving, driven by convection currents in the upper mantle. Some of the major challenges confronting Earth scientists are the questions about how the Earth's crust formed and about when plate movement began.

During the 1960's, interest in Archean crustal evolution was aroused by the discovery of Archean era magnesium-oxygen-rich lavas similar to those found in the early Precambrian. Called komatiites, these rocks date back to 3.7 billion years ago and represent ultramafic lavas that form at 1,100 degrees Celsius. Komatiites are generally found around greenstone belts, an agglomeration of Archean basaltic, andesitic, and rhyolitic volcanics, along with their weathering and erosion derived sediments. One hundred million years older than any previously known rocks, the finds led to further exploration of Archean formations by field geologists in West Greenland-

Labrador, Zimbabwe, Transvaal-Swaziland, Ontario-Quebec, southern India, Western Australia, and, more recently, China and Brazil.

Important work by field geologists in these regions launched a new era in Precambrian geology. The primary targets for study are the greenstone belts and granitic-gneiss associations. An important twentieth century find included detrital zircon, discovered in Australia. An age of 4.2 billion years for the zircons was determined using precise ion microprobe analysis. The zircon find is significant because it places an approximate birth date for the continental crust, as zircon is a mineral constituent of granite (recall that oceanic crust is composed of mafic and ultramafic rocks while continental crust is granitic).

The drive to study Archean rocks was further fueled by the United States' Apollo missions to the Moon, which returned rocks of slightly older age from the lunar surface. At the same time, geochemists were able to refine their study of these ancient rocks with more sophisticated methods to determine ratios of isotopes in the samples. Instruments common in the geochemical lab today are X-ray diffraction and gamma-ray spectrometers, which probe the nuclei of atoms to determine the spectral fingerprint of elements and their various isotopes. Isotopic ratios in rocks are of particular interest to geochemists because they provide clues as to chemical cycles in nature, such as the sulfur, chemical, nitrogen, and oxygen cycles. The equilibria of these cycles, as indicated by the isotopic ratios, offer insights into volcanic, oceanic, biological, and atmospheric cycles and conditions in the past.

It is generally accepted by most Earth scientists that crustal formation and heat flow were substantially greater in Archean times. The question is whether this crust was broken into moving lithospheric plates as it has been for the past 900 million years. The question of plate motion during this early period has generated debate among scientists and has led to two general theories of early crustal evolution. If plate tectonics was occurring 4 billion years ago, one would expect to find formations of arc deposits and complexes similar to the Franciscan formation in California's coast range. Oölite and arc deposits are terranes that accumulate near zones of subduction, where dense mafic rocks are recycled into the mantle. Such formations have not been found to date—geologic evidence arguing against rapid plate motion.

If crustal rock production was great and yet plate tectonics minimal, what process shaped the early Earth? An answer may have emerged from one of the Earth's sister planets. Shrouded in clouds, Venus did not give up the mysteries of its geology until the radar maps generated by Soviet and American spacecraft. Like Mars, with its giant volcanoes in the Tharsis region, Venus appears to have great shield volcanoes and continentlike regions the size of Africa and Australia. Hot-spot volcanism, in which plumes of magma rising from the planetary interior erupt to form shield volcanoes at the surface, may indeed be the key to understanding incipient plate tectonics on the early Earth. The question of whether hot-spot magmatism and some form of plate movement is occurring on Venus would be answered by the NASA Magellan mission, planned to arrive at the planet in the 1990's.

Context

Perhaps no other area of scientific study is as intriguing and controversial as that of the origin and evolution of the Earth. Geochemists have been at the forefront of the quest for understanding the Earth's present geology in terms of its past. Before the 1960's, little was known of the Earth's history during early Precambrian times. This lack is significant when one realizes that the Precambrian comprises about 87 percent of the geologic time scale.

It is likely that new techniques used to analyze rocks and minerals in the laboratory will lead to a better understanding of the formation of the Earth's crustal materials and the evolution of moving crustal plates. Precise dating of zircons from ancient rocks, isotope analysis, and high-resolution seismic data will help scientists to comprehend the relationships between the granite-greenstones and gneiss terranes (crustal blocks) that typify Archean formations.

Studying materials on other solar system bodies will also lead to a better understanding of the early Earth and its evolution. The U.S. NASA Mars Observer will carry a gamma-ray spectrometer designed to study the surface composition of Mars' crust and its distribution of elements. The question of whether the Earth's early history was dominated by hot-spot volcanism (the case on Mars with its huge volcanoes) will receive valuable evidence from this and future studies of asteroids, meteorites, the Moon, Mars, and Venus.

David M. Schlom

Basic Bibliography

Burchfiel, B. Clark, et al. *Physical Geology.* Westerville, Ohio: Charles E. Merrill, 1982. An excellent and comprehensive textbook covering all aspects of geology suitable for the lay reader or liberal studies college student. Of special interest are chapter 2 on mineralogy, chapter 7 on the Earth's interior, chapter 9 on crustal materials and mountain building, and chapter 10 on the origin and differentiation of the Earth and early geologic time.

Fyfe, W. S. *Geochemistry.* Oxford, England: Clarendon Press, 1974. Part of the Oxford Chemistry series, this work was written for lower-division college chemistry students. Although in some respects dated, it is nevertheless a brief (about one-hundred-page) and excellent introduction to the science of geochemistry. Of special interest is chapter 9, "Evolution of the Earth." The book has a bibliography, glossary, and index.

Gregor, C. Bryan, et al. *Chemical Cycles in the Evolution of the Earth.* New York: John Wiley & Sons, 1988. A systems approach to geochemistry, this book is suitable for the serious college student. Although filled with graphs, tables, and chemical equations, sections are very readable for the layperson. Discussions of mineralogical, oceanic, atmospheric, and other important chemical cycles are extensive and the work is well referenced.

Kroner, A., G. N. Hanson, and A. M. Goodwin, eds. *Archaean Geochemistry: The Origin and Evolution of the Archaean Continental Crust.* Berlin: Springer-Verlag, 1984. A collection of reports by the world's leading geochemists studying the geochemistry of the world's oldest rocks. Although many of the articles are technical in nature, the abstracts, introductions, and summaries are accessible to a college-level reader interested in the work of top international scientists.

Levin, Harold L. *The Earth Through Time.* 3d ed. Philadelphia: Saunders College, 1988. An excellent and very readable text dealing with historical geology. Filled with illustrations, photographs, and figures, this book is suitable for the layperson. Chapters on planetary beginnings, origin and evolution of the early Earth, and plate tectonics are of special interest. Contains an excellent glossary and index.

McCall, Gerald J. H., ed. *The Archean: Search for the Beginning.* Stroudsburg, Pa.: Dowden, Hutchinson and Ross, 1977. A superb collection of thirty-eight papers by outstanding geologists, arranged under topical headings. The papers are at times technical, but the editor provides an introduction and integrating commentary that helps bridge the gap for the nontechnical reader. Contains a subject index.

Ponnamperuma, Cyril, ed. *Chemical Evolution of the Early Precambrian.* New York: Academic Press, 1977. A collection of papers from the second colloquium of the Laboratory of Chemical Evolution of the University of Maryland, held in 1975. Written by experts in the field, the papers are still, for the most part, accessible to the nontechnical reader. The volume contains a subject index.

Salop, Lazarus J. *Geological Evolution of the Earth During the Precambrian.* Berlin: Springer-Verlag, 1983. A top Soviet geologist conducts an exhaustive survey of Precambrian geology. Suitable for a college-level reader with a serious interest in the subject. Contains numerous graphs and tables, with extensive references.

Tarling, D. H. *Evolution of the Earth's Crust.* New York: Academic Press, 1978. Written for the undergraduate-level college reader with some background in geology, this volume is an excellent collection of nontechnical, well-written essays covering the origin and evolution of the Earth's crust and plate tectonics. Contains references and an index.

Wedepohl, Karl H. *Geochemistry.* New York: Holt, Rinehart and Winston, 1971. An accessible and brief introduction to geochemistry fundamentals. Contains an excellent chapter on meteorites and cosmic abundances of the elements. Suitable for the nontechnical reader, with index and references. A good starting point for those unfamiliar with mineral formation.

Wetherill, George W., A. L. Albee, and F. G. Stehli, eds. *Annual Review of Earth and Planetary Sciences.* Vol. 13. Palo Alto, Calif.: Annual Reviews, 1985. Three articles of interest to the Earth history student are "Evolution of the Archean Crust," by Alfred Kroner, and "Oxidation States of the Mantle: Past, Present, and Future" and "The Magma Ocean Concept and Lunar Evolution," by Richard Arculus. Kroner's article is particularly readable for the college-level audience, with an excellent overview of the historical views on Precambrian geology. References at the end of each article.

Current Bibliography

Cloud, Preston. *Oasis in Space: Earth History from the Beginning.* New York: W. W. Norton, 1988.

Navrotsky, Alexandra. *Physics and Chemistry of Earth Materials.* New York: Cambridge University Press, 1994.

Rohr, Anders, ed. *Concise Earth History.* Translated by Jim Manis and Randy Morse. Denver, Colo.: Earthbooks, 1991.

Schindewolf, Otto H. *Basic Questions in Paleontology: Geologic Time, Organic Evolution, and Biological Systematics.* Translated by Judith Schaefer. Chicago: University of Chicago Press, 1993.

Stearn, Colin William. *Paleontology: The Record of Life.* New York: John Wiley, 1989.

Cross-References

Earth's Core, 147; Earth's Core-Mantle Boundary, 154; Earth's Crust, 161; Earth's Differentiation, 169; Earth's Mantle, 207; Earth's Shape, 228; Earth's Structure, 234.

Earth's Core

The core is the Earth's densest, hottest region and its fundamental source of internal heat. The thermal energy released by the core's continuous cooling stirs the overlying mantle into slow, convective motions that eventually reach the surface to move continents, build mountains, and produce earthquakes.

Overview

The Earth's core extends from a depth of 2,900 kilometers to the center of the Earth, 6,371 kilometers below the surface. The core is largely liquid, although toward the center, it becomes solid. The liquid part is known as the outer core; the solid part, the inner core. Ambient pressures inside the core range from 1 million to nearly 4 million atmospheres, and temperatures probably reach more than 5,000 degrees Celsius at the Earth's center.

Being almost twice as dense as the rest of the planet, the core contains one-third of the Earth's mass but occupies a mere one-seventh of its volume. Surrounding the core is the mantle. The boundary between the solid mantle and the underlying liquid core is the core-mantle boundary (CMB), a surface that demarcates the most fundamental compositional discontinuity in the Earth's interior. Below it, the core is mostly made of iron-nickel oxides. Above it, and all the way to the surface, the mantle is made of silicates (rock-forming minerals). The solid inner core contains 1.7 percent of the Earth's mass, and its composition may simply be a frozen version of the liquid core. The boundary between the liquid and the solid cores is known as the inner core boundary (ICB); it appears sharp to seismic waves, which easily reflect off it.

The core has lower wave-transmission velocities and higher densities than the mantle, a consequence of its being of a different chemical composition. The core is probably composed of 80 to 90 percent (by weight) iron or iron-nickel alloy and 20 to 10 percent sulfur, silicon, and oxygen; it therefore must be a good electrical and thermal conductor. The mantle, in contrast, is composed mainly of crystalline silicates of magnesium and iron and is therefore a poor conductor of electricity and a good thermal insulator.

This sharp contrast in physical properties is a major end product of the way in which the Earth evolved thermally, gravitationally, and chemically. It is difficult, however, to tell whether the Earth's core formed first and the Earth was accreted from the infall of meteorites and other gravitationally bound materials or, alternatively, the core differentiated out of an already

formed protoearth, in which silicates and iron were separated after a cataclysmic "iron catastrophe." This event may have occurred when iron, slowly
heated by radioactivity, suddenly melted and sank by gravity toward the
Earth's center, forming the core. Unfortunately, the two scenarios are
equally likely, and both give the same end result; moreover, there probably
are other scenarios. Calculations show, however, that iron sinking to the core
must have released great amounts of energy that would have eventually
heated and melted the entire Earth. Cooling of the outer parts proceeded
rapidly, by convection, but as the silicate mantle solidified, it created a
thermal barrier for the iron-rich core, which, not being able to cool down
as readily, remained molten. The inner core began then to form at the
Earth's center, where the pressure was greatest and solidification was
(barely) possible.

The most tangible consequence of the existence of a fluid, electrically
conducting core is the presence of a magnetic field in the Earth that has
existed for at least 3.5 billion years with a strength not very different from
what it has today. The process that generates and maintains the geomagnetic
field is attributable to a self-exciting dynamo mechanism—that is, an electromagnetic induction process that transforms the motions of the conducting fluid into electric currents, which in turn induce a magnetic field that
strengthens the existing field. (For the system to get started, at least a small
magnetic field must be present to initiate the generation of electric currents.) The increased magnetic field in turn induces stronger currents,
which further strengthen the field, and so on. As the magnetic field increases beyond a certain high value, it begins to affect the fluid flow; there
is a mechanical force, known as the Lorentz force, that is induced in a
conductor as it moves across a magnetic field. The stronger the magnetic
field, the stronger the Lorentz force becomes and the more it will tend to
modify the motion of the fluid so as to oppose the growth of the magnetic
field. The result is a self-regulating mechanism which, over time, will attain
a steady state.

A dynamo mechanism is needed to explain the geomagnetic field, because there can be no permanently magnetized substances inside the Earth.
Magnetic substances lose their magnetism as their temperature increases
above the so-called Curie temperature (around 500 degrees Celsius for most
magnetic substances), and most of the mantle below the depth of 30
kilometers and all the core is at temperatures well above the Curie point.
The basic problem, then, is to find a source of energy that can maintain the
steady regime of flow in the core against decay by somehow maintaining the
fluid currents that induce the field. A favored view is that the necessary
energy to maintain the flow is provided by the growth of the inner core as it
is fed by the liquid core. According to some researchers, this process would
provide enough gravitational energy to stir the core throughout. Thermally
and compositionally driven flows can also be invoked as possible models of
core fluid dynamics, but there is still no evidence that decides the question.

A most extraordinary feature of the core-generated magnetic field is that, at least over the past few hundred million years, it has reversed its polarity with irregular frequency. For example, it is known that at times the field has reversed as frequently as three times every million years, but in other cases, more than 20 million years went by without a noticeable reversal. A reversed geomagnetic field means simply that the magnetic needle of a compass would point in the opposite direction as it does today. (For convenience, the present orientation of the needle is considered normal.) The important point is that the rocks that form (for example, lavas that cool below the Curie point as they become solid rock) during either a reverse or a normal period acquire and preserve that magnetism. Unlike the swinging compass needle, a rock keeps the magnetic field direction that existed at the time of its formation forever frozen in its iron-bearing minerals. Therefore, rocks formed throughout geologic time have recorded the alternating rhythms of normal and reverse Earth magnetism. This sequence of magnetic reversals contains the clue to the core's nature.

Geophysicists are anxious to learn whether the core is vigorously convecting as a consequence of the inner core's growth. If that were the case, the core would be delivering a great amount of heat to the mantle, whose low thermal conductivity would create a barrier to the upcoming heat. As a result, the local temperature gradient at the base of the mantle would probably be very high, so that a layer 100 kilometers thick, say, at the base of the mantle, would be gravitationally unstable. From this layer, thermal inhomogeneities would rise through the mantle in the form of plumes of buoyant, hot, lower-mantle material. Several such plumes might reach the upper mantle or set the entire mantle into convection. These convection currents would be responsible for the motion of the tectonic plates on the Earth's surface and, consequently, for the uplifting of mountain ranges, the formation of oceanic basins, and the occurrence of volcanic eruptions and earthquakes. Continental drift and plate tectonics, the most visible effects of the internal cooling of the Earth, would thus be linked to the growth of the inner core and to Earth's earliest history. This view of the Earth is very speculative, but it is favored by many geoscientists, who recognize its beauty and simplicity.

Methods of Study

Knowledge of the structure, physical properties, and composition of the core is entirely based on indirect evidence gathered mostly from analyses of seismic waves, the study of the Earth's gravitational and magnetic fields, and laboratory experiments on the behavior of rocks and minerals at high pressures and temperatures. The first evidence for the existence of the core was presented in a paper suggestively entitled "The Constitution of the Interior of the Earth, As Revealed by Earthquakes," published in 1906 by Richard D. Oldham, of the geological survey of India. Thirty years later, Inge Lehmann, from the Copenhagen seismological observatory, presented seismic evidence for the existence of the inner core. In the past few decades, with the advent of high-speed computers and technological advances in seismometry, seismologists have developed increasingly sensitive instrumentation to record seismic waves worldwide and sophisticated mathematical theories that allow them to construct models of the core that explain the observed data.

Seismic waves provide the most important data about the core. Earthquakes or large explosions generate elastic waves that propagate throughout the Earth. These seismic waves may penetrate deep in the Earth and, after being reflected or transmitted through major discontinuities such as the CMB and ICB, travel back to the surface to be recorded at the seismic stations of the global network. The most direct information that seismic or elastic waves carry is their travel time. Knowing the time it takes for elastic waves to traverse some region of the Earth's interior allows the calculation of their velocity of propagation in that region. The velocity of seismic waves strongly depends on the density and rigidity, or stiffness, of the material through which they propagate, so estimates of the mechanical properties of the Earth can in principle be derived from seismic travel time analyses. Seismic waves that propagate through the deep interior of the Earth are of two types: compressional waves (also called P waves) and shear waves (also called S waves). Compressional waves produce volume changes in the elastic medium; shear waves produce shape distortion without volume change. If the medium has some rigidity, both P and S waves can be transmitted. If the medium has no rigidity, it offers no resistance to a change in shape; no elastic connection exists that can communicate shearing motions from a point in the medium to its neighbors, so S waves cannot propagate, although P waves can.

After many years of careful observations, it has been determined that S waves are not transmitted through the outer core. Therefore, the outer core material has no rigidity, but behaves as a fluid would. Similar observations suggest that the inner core is solid; the actual rigidity of the inner core is very difficult to estimate, however, since shear waves inside the inner core are isolated from the mantle by the outer core and can only travel through it as P waves converted from S waves at the ICB. Nevertheless, when the whole Earth is set into vibration by a very large earthquake, the average rigidity of the inner core can be estimated by comparing the observed frequencies of oscillation with those theoretically computed for models of the Earth that include a solid inner core. Model studies have indicated that the inner core is indeed solid, because a totally liquid core model does not satisfy the observations.

The average velocity of P waves in the Earth is about 10 kilometers per second, whereas the average P-wave velocity in the rocks accessible to measurement at the Earth's surface is 4 to 5 kilometers per second. The S-wave velocity is nearly half that of P waves in solids and zero in perfect fluids.

The velocity of P waves drops abruptly from 13.7 kilometers per second at the base of the mantle to 8.06 kilometers per second across the CMB, at the top of the core. From this point down, the velocity steadily increases to 10.35 kilometers per second at the ICB, where it jumps discontinuously to 11.03 kilometers per second at the top of the inner core. From there to the center of the Earth, the velocity of P waves increases slowly to reach 11.3 kilometers per second. The S-wave velocity increases from zero at the ICB to around 3.6 kilometers per second at the Earth's center. The core's density abruptly increases from 5,500 kilograms per cubic meter at the base of the mantle to nearly 10,000 kilograms per cubic meter just underneath the CMB. From there, the density increases slowly to nearly 13,100 kilograms per cubic meter at the Earth's center. In comparison, the density of mercury at room temperature and ambient pressure is 13,600 kilograms per cubic meter.

That the core is mostly iron is consistent with iron's being cosmically more abundant than other heavy elements and with the high electrical conductivity the core needs to have in order to generate the Earth's magnetic field. The fluidity of the outer core has been demonstrated by measurements not only of seismic wave transmission but also of the oscillation period of gravitational waves in the core excited by the lunisolar tides. The existence of a sustained, steady magnetic field is also consistent with a fluid outer core.

Seismic data can probe the inner core only partially from the Earth's surface, unless the source of the seismic waves and the receivers are located antipodally to each other. Such an arrangement would allow scientists to measure seismic waves that had penetrated the center of the Earth. It would be possible to construct a global experiment to investigate the inner core by deploying an array of highly sensitive seismic sensors antipodal to either a seismically active region or an underground nuclear explosion testing ground. Despite the wealth of unique data that would be obtained from such an experiment, it would be a very expensive endeavor, and not devoid of risk.

New views of the Earth's interior are produced, sometimes unexpectedly, by the analyses of data collected by satellite missions. Data from orbiting satellites that measure tiny variations of the Earth's gravitational field, combined with computer-aided seismic tomography of the Earth's interior, have revealed large-density anomalies at the base of the mantle and a large relief of more than 2 kilometers on the CMB. Seismic tomography uses earthquake-generated waves that penetrate the mantle in a multitude of directions to map the three-dimensional structure of its deep interior, just as computerized medical tomography uses multiple X-ray images to create a three-dimensional view of internal organs of the body. Essential to the success of these studies, however, is the installation of dense networks of seismic sensors all over the surface of the Earth; this installation, however, is another very expensive procedure.

Context

It is almost certain that whether or not geophysicists discover the actual cause of the geomagnetic field will not affect the everyday life of the people of the world.

Any study of the Earth's physical environment is likely to provide insight into the nature and future of the planet and, consequently, the future of mankind. If geophysicists come to understand how the Earth's core works, they will be able to predict the geomagnetic field's activity for years to come. Thus, they will be able to predict an upcoming reversal. According to the best estimates, a reversal does not occur suddenly but takes about ten thousand years. That means that during a reversal, there is a time of very small or even zero field intensity. Under such conditions, the magnetic shielding that prevents the highly energetic solar wind particles from reaching the Earth's surface will disappear, leaving the Earth directly exposed to lethal radiations.

The inner core has not yet been sufficiently explored with seismic waves. One reason is that it is the remotest region of the Earth and therefore the most difficult to reach; another is that it is hidden beneath the "seismic noise" created by the crust, mantle, and outer core. The inner core, however, holds the key to the understanding of the Earth's early history and its subsequent development as a planet.

J. A. Rial

Basic Bibliography

Bolt, Bruce A. *Inside the Earth: Evidence from Earthquakes.* San Francisco: W. H. Freeman, 1982. An elementary treatment of what is known about the Earth's interior, mostly through the study of seismic waves, the author's major field of research. The book contains abundant diagrams that illustrate accurately important results of the investigation of the core and mantle. For readers with some knowledge of mathematics, the book includes brief derivations of important formulas, separated by "boxes" from the main text. It is well written and includes anecdotal descriptions of great scientific discoveries along with personal views of the history and development of seismology. Illustrated.

Clark, Sydney P. *Structure of the Earth.* Englewood Cliffs, N.J.: Prentice-Hall, 1971. Although slightly out of date, this short review of the Earth's structure and composition is an excellent first reading to gain a global perspective on geology and geophysics. Illustrations are abundant and very clear. The text is simply written, yet the author manages to convey complex concepts about tectonics, wave propagation, and ray theory with ease. The chapter dedicated to seismology is the best and most carefully written section of the book.

Hamblin, W. Kenneth. *The Earth's Dynamic Systems: A Textbook in Physical Geology.* New York: Macmillan, 1989. This geology textbook offers an integrated view of the Earth's interior not common in books of this type. The illustrations, diagrams, and charts are superb. Includes a glossary and laboratory guide. Suitable for high school readers.

Jacobs, J. A. *The Earth's Core.* 2d ed. New York: Academic Press, 1987. This is a highly technical text, but it is perhaps the best reference for a detailed description of the most accepted core models. The tables—which give the numerical values of the density, temperature, rigidity, and wave velocity distributions within the Earth—are of interest to anyone wanting a quantitative description of the core. A long list of research articles is included.

Jeanloz, Raymond. "The Earth's Core." *Scientific American* 249 (September, 1983): 56-65. The best elementary treatment of the structure and composition of the core. Jeanloz is a leading expert in the field. In this article, the origin, evolution, and present state and composition of the core are discussed in detail. The language is precise but not too specialized. The entire issue is dedicated to the Earth and Earth dynamics, so it should be of great interest to some readers.

Press, Frank, and Raymond Siever. *Earth.* 3d ed. San Francisco: W. H. Freeman, 1985. The most geophysical and probably the best written of all elementary geology textbooks. It includes an intriguing description of the evolution of the Earth, the iron catastrophe, and the formation of the atmosphere. Well illustrated. Includes a glossary.

Current Bibliography

Brown, G. C. *The Inaccessible Earth: An Integrated View to Its Structure and Composition.* 2d ed. New York: Chapman and Hall, 1993.

Fowler, C. M. R. *The Solid Earth: An Introduction to Global Geophysics.* New York: Cambridge University Press, 1990.

Jacobs, John Arthur. *The Earth's Core.* 2d ed. Orlando: Academic Press, 1987.

James, David E., ed. *The Encyclopedia of Solid Earth Geophysics.* New York: Van Nostrand Reinhold, 1989.

Cross-References

Earth's Core-mantle Boundary

The core-mantle boundary is a pronounced discontinuity separating the outer core from the mantle of the Earth. It is a chemical and mineralogical as well as a thermal boundary. The topography of the core-mantle boundary is believed to be controlled by the dynamic processes in the mantle and the outer core.

Overview

The core-mantle boundary (CMB) is a prominent discontinuity within the Earth. The mantle above the boundary is largely solid, of relatively low temperature, and primarily composed of magnesium and iron silicates. The outer core below the boundary is liquid, of higher temperature, and composed of dense materials such as iron oxides and iron sulfide alloys. This boundary separates two dynamic systems: one operating in the mantle as hot spots and convection cells, the other—in the outer core—consisting of convection currents and eddies of the core fluid. The motions of the core fluid appear to be responsible for the Earth's magnetic field. The approximate depth of the CMB is 2,885 kilometers.

Detailed studies of the seismic velocities in the Earth led K. E. Bullen to divide the interior of the Earth into seven concentric, spherical zones termed A through G. For an earthquake occurring in the crust or the upper mantle, the downgoing waves pass through the different zones of the Earth before they emerge at the surface. To study the CMB, the effects of these zones on seismic propagation need to be considered. It has been found that the Earth is laterally heterogeneous, particularly the crust (zone A), the low-velocity zone of the upper mantle (B), and the lowermost part of the mantle (D″). The D″ zone, known as the core-mantle transition zone, is approximately 200-300 kilometers thick and is located just above the CMB. A suggestion was made that the D″ zone was thinly layered, which resulted in variations in the reflected amplitude of waves from the CMB. However, accurate analysis of the short-period seismic waves recorded by seismological arrays indicated that such is not the case. Studies utilizing inversions of seismic waveforms and travel times indicate large-scale variations (more than 1,000 kilometers) in the velocities in the D″ zone. The P-wave velocity varies as much as 1.5 percent, which is three to four times more than in the middle part of the mantle. The longitudinal (P) waves appear to travel faster in the portions of this zone that are located below North America, China, the eastern part of the Indian Ocean, and off the Pacific coast of Chile. Lower P-wave velocities are observed below the southern part of Africa, the New Hebrides Islands, the South Pacific Ocean, and the Argentine Basin.

Similar large-scale variations have also been observed for shear (S) waves. The D″ zone under the American continents, Asia, the northern Indian and Pacific oceans, and Antarctica are characterized by higher S-wave velocities. Lower S-wave velocities are observed underneath the Central and South Pacific Ocean, the Atlantic Ocean, the major parts of Africa, and the southern part of the Indian Ocean. These long wavelength velocity variations in the D″ zone appear to continue upward in the mantle. Thus, the thermally induced convection currents and hot spots in the mantle appear to be related to large-scale, lateral velocity variations in the D″ zone. The lateral heterogeneity of the D″ zone is also evident in the short-scale (less than 100-kilometer) and the intermediate-scale (100-1,000-kilometer) lengths, determined primarily through studies of scattered core phases and waveform modeling techniques.

Improvements in instrumentation have enabled scientists to simulate in the laboratory the physical and chemical conditions of the lower mantle and the outermost core. It appears that the lower mantle is primarily composed of magnesium-iron silicates present in the perovskite structure. Although some amount of aluminum-calcium silicates and magnesium-iron oxides may also be present, their relative abundance is not known. Measurement of the melting point of silicate perovskite led scientists to estimate the temperature of the D″ zone in the range of 2,600-3,100 Kelvins. Similar studies of outer core materials, which are primarily iron sulfides and iron oxides, indicate that the temperature of the outermost core is at least 3,800 Kelvins. Thus, the temperature increases by about 700 Kelvins in the D″ zone, resulting in partial melting of some minerals and thereby making the zone soft with anomalous characteristics.

Seismologists studying the core-mantle boundary (CMB) by means of reflected waves from the core have long been frustrated by the strong scatter of the reflected amplitudes. A major part of this scatter is believed to be the result of undulations of the core-mantle boundary. The lateral extent of these undulations is of the order of thousands of kilometers. The elevation of the boundary may change as much as 5-8 kilometers above or below its normal depth. Topographic highs of the CMB have been observed beneath the Indian Ocean, the Pacific Ocean, and the Atlantic Ocean (particularly in the North Atlantic). The CMB is depressed below the Tonga-Karmadec area, the China-Japan region, Central Africa, and off the west coast of South America. Because most of these areas are associated with the subduction of oceanic plates, the CMB structure is believed to be caused by the dynamic processes in the mantle, which may again be related to the convection processes in the outer core. Subduction of a crustal plate is caused by the

Earth's Major Plates and Mid-Ocean Ridges

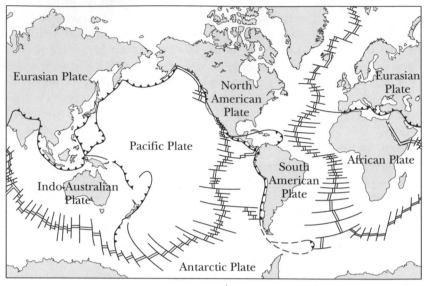

Types of Boundaries: Divergent // Convergent ⤳ Transform /

downwelling convective flow in the mantle. When the convective flow reaches the core boundary, it depresses the CMB into the hot, liquid core. Core fluids may partially invade the "topographic low" of the CMB, altering the chemical composition of the D″ zone. Similarly, beneath an upwelling zone of mantle flow, liquid core material may be "sucked" up into the mantle, creating a topographic high of the CMB. The "lows" of the CMB, being subjected to the higher temperatures of the outer core, may melt and recrystallize at the topographic "highs" of the CMB. Thus, the overall effect is to smooth the CMB, which is continually disturbed by the convective circulations in the mantle. With heat dissipation in the mantle, the outer core slowly cools and the core materials crystallize and underplate the mantle. Thus, the outer core slowly shrinks with time, and the CMB gets deeper.

Although near the Earth's surface the temperature increases quickly with depth, the rate of increase slows below 200 kilometers depth. The core-mantle boundary not only is a compositional boundary but also appears to be a thermal boundary, where the temperature increases by at least 700 Kelvins. Thermal coupling between the mantle and the outer core, however, may change laterally, resulting in a variable heat flow across the boundary. Although no consensus has been reached among scientists, it is possible that the mantle dynamics are at least partially responsible for controlling the heat flow.

The Earth behaves like a large magnet. The magnetic field of the Earth—that is, the geomagnetic field—undergoes a slow change known as the secular variation. The origin of the geomagnetic field appears to be related to motions of the outer core fluid. Studies suggest that the deep mantle and the outer core play a significant role in shaping the secular variations. Upwellings in the outer core material are associated with the hot and seismically slow regions of the D″ zone; downwellings are associated with the cold and higher-velocity portions of D″. Cold regions in the mantle transmit greater amounts of heat from the outer core, thereby setting up mantle circulations. The topography of the CMB is controlled by the circulations in the mantle as well as in the outer core. The topographic relief of the CMB may also set up a lateral temperature gradient which may be responsible for the secular variation of the magnetic field.

Methods of Study

Various subdisciplines of geophysics are being utilized to determine the nature and the structure of the core-mantle boundary (CMB). They include, among others, seismology, geodesy, and geodynamics, high-temperature and high-pressure mineral physics, geothermometry, and geomagnetism. Seismology has been the most important among all these subdisciplines and has contributed most of the information about the Earth's interior.

Seismology deals with earthquakes and the propagation of earthquake waves through the Earth. Whenever an earthquake occurs, different types of waves are generated. Surface waves travel along the Earth's surface, and longitudinal (P) waves and shear (S) waves travel through the interior of the Earth. It is often helpful to visualize P and S waves in the form of rays originating from an earthquake focus, or hypocenter, and radiating in all directions through the Earth. Because of the increased rigidity and incompressibility of rocks downward, the velocities of these waves increase with depth. As a result, the downgoing seismic rays (except for vertical or near-vertical rays) are curved back to the surface. Thus, the seismographic stations that are farther away from the epicenter record direct seismic rays, which penetrate through the deeper layers in the mantle.

The outer core has no rigidity, as it is liquid. Consequently, the velocities of seismic waves decrease abruptly as they cross the CMB. P waves decrease from 13.5 to 8.5 kilometers per second and are steeply refracted in the outer core. S waves do not propagate through the outer core. As a result, shadow zones are produced for both direct P and S waves recorded at the ground surface beyond 12,000 kilometers from the epicenter. The presence of liquid outer core was discovered through the existence of the shadow zones and the absence of core-transmitted shear waves.

Seismic rays emerging at steep angles from the hypocenter encounter the CMB. Part of the incident energy is reflected back from the boundary, and the rest is refracted through the outer core. A P wave can be reflected back as a P and as an S wave, called PcP and PcS waves (or phases) respectively. Similarly, an S wave reflected back from the CMB as a P or an S wave is called ScP or ScS. These core-reflected phases have been important in the study of the nature, shape, and depth of the CMB. Because S waves cannot transmit through liquid, the refracted energy in the outer core propagates in the form of P waves. These waves are designated as a K phase. Thus, PKP is a phase that travels from the hypocenter in the mantle as a P wave, propagates as a P (that is, K) in the outer core, and reemerges in the mantle as a P wave. Similarly, SKS and other combinations, such as PKS and SKP, are often observed in the seismic records. A joint study of the core-reflected phases (for example, PcP) and the core phases (for example, PKP) is often important in resolving the depths and topography of the CMB. Seismic rays incident at a large angle on the CMB are diffracted. Study of these diffracted waves provides important information on the D″ zone above the CMB. Using the waveform modeling techniques, scientists are determining the thickness and fine structures of the D″ zone.

Another important tool is seismic tomography. It utilizes the same principle used in CAT-scan X rays of humans. In a CAT scan, the X-ray source and the camera are rotated around the body and a large number of images are produced. A computer processes these images and forms a three-dimensional image of the internal organs of the subject. The seismological data collected worldwide can similarly be processed to form a three-dimensional image of the Earth's interior. Seismic tomography is providing valuable information on the CMB as well as the Earth's mantle.

A large earthquake sets the Earth vibrating like a bell. If the Earth were perfectly spherical with uniform layering, it would produce a pure tone, vibrating at a preferred frequency. Departures from the spherical shape of the Earth, as well as depth-related discontinuities, produce additional tones involving distortions of the Earth. Thus, recordings of these various modes of the Earth's vibrations, known as free oscillations, can furnish information about the shape of the CMB.

Satellite measurements of the Earth's gravity field and the geodetic observations of the geoid can also provide us with information on the CMB. Theoretical models of the Earth's interior, particularly the mantle, the D″ zone, and the CMB, can be constructed to match observed geoidal undulations and the gravity anomalies. It appears that a 2-3-kilometer change in elevation of the CMB can explain 90 percent of the observed large-scale gravity anomalies. Astronomical observations of the Earth's wobble also furnish additional constraints on the shape of the CMB. The Earth has an equatorial bulge caused by its rotation. The Moon pulls at the bulge and attempts to align it along the orbital plane of the Moon, generating a wobble, or a nutational motion, of the Earth's axis. (This motion is similar to the wobble of a spinning top or a gyroscope.) Deformation of the CMB, which is not formed by rotation, produces certain irregularities in the nutational motion. Studies of these irregularities indicate that the undulations of the CMB are less than 1 kilometer in height.

Major developments in instrumentation have made it possible to simulate in the laboratory the temperature and pressure conditions of the deep mantle. Scientists can now study how the crystal structures of minerals change with increased temperature and pressure. Measurements on the electrical properties of rocks under high pressure, and possible alloying of iron by sulfur and oxygen that may occur in the outer core, are also being studied. These investigations are important for complete understanding of the mineral compositions, structure, temperature, and pressure environment of the Earth's deep interior.

Context

The study of the core-mantle boundary (CMB) is important from several perspectives. The CMB is believed to be associated with deep mantle plumes, the mantle convection currents that drive the lithospheric plates, and may be responsible for secular variations of the geomagnetic field. As the most pronounced discontinuity within the Earth, the undulations at the CMB may also cause regional gravity anomalies and can affect the transmission of seismic waves. The transmission effects of seismic waves crossing the CMB should be determined in order to study the geometry and the physical and chemical parameters of materials at the boundary as well as the outer and inner core of the Earth. Furthermore, because core-reflected phases travel along vertical or near vertical paths in the mantle, they are often utilized to study heterogeneity and the seismic behavior in the mantle. Knowledge of the nature of the CMB is necessary to determine these mantle characteristics.

Scientists from various geophysical subdisciplines have made a concerted effort to investigate the structure and nature of the CMB and the deep interior of the Earth. A committee on Studies of the Earth's Deep Interior (SEDI), under the auspices of the International Union of Geodesy and Geophysics (IUGG) and the American Geophysical Union (AGU), was formed to stimulate exchange of scientific information about the Earth's interior. The first meeting of SEDI was held in Spain in 1988; starting with the fall of 1987, special sessions on the Earth's deep interior have been held at most of the AGU meetings. The Twenty-fifth General Assembly of the International Association of Seismology and Physics of the Earth's Interior (IASPEI) also held a symposium on this subject at its meeting in Istanbul, Turkey, in August, 1989.

D. K. Chowdhury

Basic Bibliography

Bolt, Bruce A. *Earthquakes.* New York: W.H. Freeman, 1988. This volume presents information on the Earth's interior obtained from seismological studies. Suitable for high school and college levels.

_____. *Inside the Earth.* San Francisco: W. H. Freeman, 1982. A good introduction to seismology for the nonscientist, this well-illustrated, concise book summarizes the seismological methods and the results.

Eiby, G. A. *About Earthquakes.* New York: Harper & Row, 1957. Lucidly written, this book provides the historical perspective of seismological discoveries. Suitable for high school and undergraduate students.

Hodgson, J. H. *Earthquakes and Earth Structures.* Englewood Cliffs, N.J.: Prentice-Hall, 1964. This volume summarizes the important seismological observations prior to 1960. Suitable for high school and undergraduate students.

Kerr, Richard A. "Continents of the Core-Mantle Boundary." *Science* 233 (August 1, 1986): 523-524. This short, well-written article provides some of the results of current research about the core-mantle boundary. Appropriate for readers at any level.

Lay, T. "Structure of the Core-Mantle Transition Zone: A Chemical and Thermal Boundary." *EOS: Transactions of the American Geophysical Union* 70, no. 4 (1989): 44-59. This is an important review article on the transition zone at the core-mantle boundary. Suitable for university-level audience with some background in the geosciences.

Lay, T. "Structure of the Earth: Mantle and Core." *Reviews of Geophysics* 25 (June, 1987): 1161-1167. This important review article summarizes major works on the mantle and the core. Appropriate for university-level readers.

Young, C. J., and T. Lay. "The Core-Mantle Boundary." *Annual Review of Earth Planetary Sciences* 15 (1987): 25. A summary of recent research in the core-mantle boundary. The treatment is at a university level.

Current Bibliography

Fowler, C. M. R. *The Solid Earth: An Introduction to Global Geophysics.* New York: Cambridge University Press, 1990.

Knapp, Ralph W., ed. *Geophysics.* Exeter, England: Pergamon, 1995.

Vogel, Shawna. *Naked Earth: The New Geophysics.* New York: Plume, 1996.

Cross-References

Earth's Crust

Humankind's existence and modern society depend upon the crust of the Earth. The dynamic changes involved in the creation and destruction of crustal rock also liberate gases and water that form oceans and the atmosphere, cause earthquakes, and create mineral deposits essential to society.

Overview

The crust of the Earth is the outermost layer of rock material of the Earth. It is distinct from the region of rocks lying beneath it, called the mantle, in that the rock materials that comprise the crust are of a different composition and a lower density. Density may be described as the weight per unit of volume of solid materials. Therefore, if a cubic centimeter of granite, which makes up much of the crust of the Earth of continents such as North America, could be weighed, it would total 2.7 grams. Deeper crustal rocks under continents have higher densities, some approaching the 3.3 grams per cubic centimeter characteristic of upper mantle rocks. A sample of crustal rock underlying the ocean basins would reveal that it is a rock type known as basalt, with a density of about 2.9 grams per cubic centimeter.

Compared with the rocks of the mantle, the rocks of the Earth's crust are quite varied. The rocks of the crust can be classified as belonging to one of three broad groups: igneous, sedimentary, and metamorphic. Both granite and basalt are igneous rocks. Such rocks are formed by cooling and crystallization from a high-temperature state called magma or lava. Other igneous rock types of the Earth's crust that are intermediate in rock composition and density between granite and basalt include andesite and granodiorite. Igneous rocks may form by melting of other igneous and metamorphic rocks in the crust or upper mantle, or by melting of sedimentary rocks.

Metamorphic rocks are formed from other rocks that have been subjected to pressures and temperatures high enough to cause the rock to respond by change in the crystalline structure of the rock materials. These temperatures are not high enough to melt the rock. Such changes often occur in the deep parts of the crust, where heat is trapped and great pressure occurs from the weight of the overlying rock. As a consequence of this high pressure, densities of metamorphic rocks of the lower crust average about 2.9 grams per cubic centimeter.

Sedimentary rocks of the Earth's crust are formed by chemical change and physical breakdown into fragments of other rocks exposed to the

Metamorphic Rock Classification
Based on Texture and Composition

Texture	Nonfoliated			Foliated			
	Nonlayered			Layered	Nonlayered		
	fine to coarse grained	fine to coarse grained	fine grained	coarse grained	coarse grained	fine grained	very fine grained
Composition	calcite					chlorite	
			mica		mica		
		quartz					
		feldspar					
				amphibole			
				pyroxene			
Name	MARBLE	QUARTZITE	HORNFELS	GNEISS	SCHIST	PHYLLITE	SLATE

atmosphere and water of the Earth's surface. The density of sedimentary rocks is generally less than that of igneous rocks, ranging from about 2.2 to as high as 2.7 grams per cubic centimeter.

The boundary between the rocks of the crust and the mantle is known as the Mohorovičić discontinuity, or simply Moho. The nature of this boundary varies from place to place. Under parts of the crust that have recently been stretched or compressed by mountain-building forces, such as under the great desert basins of the western United States, the Moho is a very sharp, distinct boundary. Elsewhere, in the interior of continents that have not been deformed for long time periods, the Moho appears to be an area of gradual density change with increasing depth rather than a distinct boundary. The position of the Moho, and thus the thickness of the crust, varies widely. The crust is thickest under the continents, reaching a maximum of 70 kilometers beneath young mountain chains such as the Himalaya. Under the ocean basins, the crustal thickness varies from 5 to 15 kilometers.

Thickness of the crust is directly related to its formation and evolution through geologic time. Only within the last twenty-five years have geoscientists understood this relationship. The crustal rocks of the Earth are constantly being created, deformed, and destroyed by a process known as plate tectonics. Plate tectonics is a theory that suggests that the crust and upper mantle of the Earth are divided into a number of separate rock layers that resemble giant plates. These plates are in motion, driven by heat from the Earth's interior. Where the heat reaches the surface along boundaries between plates on the ocean floor, new rocks are formed by rising lava, creating new ocean basin crust. Because new crust is being created, crust must be consumed or destroyed elsewhere so that the Earth's volume will remain constant. The sites where crust is consumed also lie on the ocean floor. Topographically, such sites are deep trenches where the crust bends down into the mantle to be heated and remelted. Such a process of recycling ocean-basin crust means, first of all, that ocean-basin crust is never geologically very old. The oldest sea-floor crust in the western Pacific is 175 million years old as compared to about 4.5 billion years for the age of the Earth. Second, it suggests that since ocean-basin crust goes through a geologically short life and uncomplicated history, it has a rather uniform thickness of about 5 to 15 kilometers, unchanged between the time it is born and the time it is destroyed.

Continental crust has a much longer life and a more complicated history, reflected in a highy variable crustal thickness. It is initially created at the sites where oceanic crust is consumed, also known as subduction zones. As the crust and upper mantle, or lithospheric plate, is bent back down into the Earth, it is heated up. Eventually, melting of part of this rock material occurs, creating volcanoes near trench sites. Such volcanoes have lavas rich in elements such as calcium, potassium, and sodium. When these lavas cool to form rock, the rock type that results is an andesite, named for volcanic rocks abundant in the Andes of South America. These continental volcanic rocks are less dense than basalts and, once created, remain on the top of a lithospheric plate, where they are carried along by the motion of the sea floor and underlying lithospheric plate as it moves away from the ocean ridge boundaries. Eventually, the sea-floor motion may cause pieces of this continental crust to collide and weld together, forming larger pieces of continental crust. Thus, continents grow with time by two processes: volcanism above subduction zones and collision. The process of collision causes rocks to pile up like a throw rug pushed against a wall, creating high mountains that also extend downward with roots that increase crustal thickness. Continents thus grow along their edges where young mountain belts, called orogenic belts, are found, such as the Andes and the mountain systems of the western United States. The crust is relatively thick under young mountain belts, piling upward and sinking downward simultaneously to form a thick wedge of rock. In this sense, it is much like a buoyant iceberg, with the majority of its mass below the water or, in this case, below sea level. The buoyancy of the lighter continental rocks above the denser mantle rocks is known as the principle of isostasy, or flotational equilibrium. Just as the iceberg must reach a flotational level by displacing a volume of water equal to its mass, so must the continental crustal rocks displace a volume of denser mantle rocks to reach their buoyancy level. Thus, under higher mountainous terrain thicker crust is found, whereas at lower elevations, such as under the ocean basin, the thinnest crust is found.

Toward the center of continental landmasses are core areas of older rocks known as cratons. The age of rocks found in the cratons range from about 500 million to an extreme of 3.8 billion years. The cratons of the world compose about one-half of the area of the continental crust and have been free of deformation and mountain-building forces for long periods of time. Consequently, their surfaces tend to be relatively flat as a result of surface processes such as weathering and stream-cutting acting on the exposed rocks over a geologically long period of time. The thickness of the continental crust in cratonic areas is variable, which is a reflection of their long and complex histories. These areas were at one time thickened because of mountain-building activity, but long and varying periods of stability have caused them to lose some crustal thickness as well. Figures for central Canada and the United States show a range of from 30 to 50 kilometers for thickness of the craton.

Methods of Study

Elastic waves are created by both earthquakes and artificial sources and may be used to study the crust of the Earth. This branch of Earth science is

Comparison of Zones of Oceanic and Continental Crust

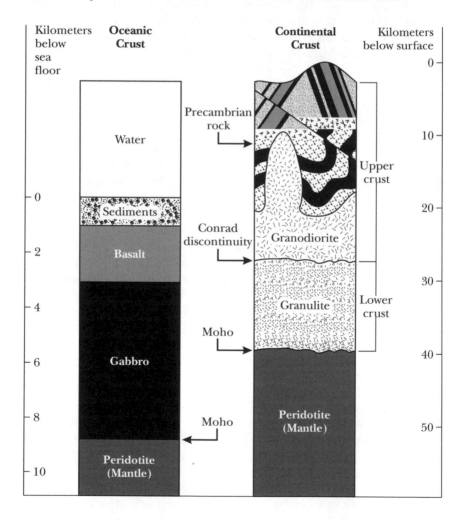

called seismology. When energy is released in rock by a source, the rock is set in motion with an up-and-down or back-and-forth wavelike motion. These waves force the rock to respond like a rubber band, stretching and compressing it without permanently deforming it. Such a response is called elastic. This response can be used as a key to studying the physical properties of the rocks because of a wave generated by a seismic relationship between velocity and rock properties. The fastest elastic wave is the primary, or P, wave. This wave is basically an acoustic wave or sound wave traveling in rock, compressing and stretching rock materials in its path. Therefore, the density, rigidity, and compressibility of a material determine wave velocity. A simple example would be to compare the velocity of an acoustic wave in air, called the speed of sound, to that in rock. The result is that in air near sea level, an acoustic wave travels at about 0.3 kilometer per second, whereas in rocks near the Earth's surface, the same kind of wave travels at about 5 kilometers per second. Air is much less dense than rock and has no rigidity (no permanent shape).

Rocks of the lower crust beneath the continents have P-wave velocities of between 6.8 and 7.0 kilometers per second. It can be shown in the laboratory that metamorphic rocks known as granulites, when placed under the pressures and temperatures of the lower crustal depths, have velocities in this range. Other rocks under the same pressures and temperatures (600 to 900 degrees Celsius, 5,000 to 10,000 atmospheres) may have similar velocities. Samples of lower crustal rocks known as xenoliths, however, exist at the surface, having been brought up by volcanic activity. These samples also suggest that granulite is a good choice.

Rocks of the upper crust in continental areas have P-wave velocities of around 6.2 kilometers per second. Here, rocks at the surface of a granite to granodiorite composition suggest the appropriate choice of rock. When such rocks are velocity-tested in the laboratory under the appropriate range of pressures and temperatures, there is a good match between rock type and velocity.

The composition of the oceanic crust is well known. Here, basalts yield a velocity of around 6.7 kilometers per second, reflecting the rather uniform composition of the geologically simpler oceanic crust. Finally, part of the continental crust is mantled by sedimentary rocks. This material has among the lowest velocities, ranging from less than 2 kilometers per second up to an extreme of about 6 kilometers per second and reflecting a wide range of compositions as well as the presence of open space and fluids contained therein.

The thickness of continental crust has been determined by the study of seismic waves that bounce off (reflect) or bend (refract) when they cross the Moho. The density contrast and resulting change in velocity of seismic waves when they cross the Moho from crust to mantle cause the wave path to change angle or bend. The same phenomenon occurs when light crosses from air to liquid in a glass. This can be shown by placing a straight straw in the liquid and gazing along its length. The straw will appear bent even though it is actually the light wave that has bent.

Waves that leave the source at one critical angle will cross the boundary and travel along beneath it, radiating energy back to the surface at the same angle. This is the critically refracted ray path, and the sine of the critical angle can be predicted from Snell's law of refraction to be the ratio of the crust and mantle velocities. The geometry of this wave path is determined by two factors, the ratio of the crust and mantle velocities, and the thickness of the crust. The thicker the crust, the longer the travel time of the wave for a particular pair of velocities. Using critically refracted P waves, thicknesses have been estimated for much of the crust.

It has been possible in many areas to check the crustal thickness determined by critically refracted waves by using information from reflected waves. This has been applied with particular success to the study of Earth's crust in continental areas. The technique is similar to that of depth sounding in ships, in which an acoustic wave is sent down from a ship, bounces off the bottom, and returns. The depth is proportional to the time of travel of the wave, also called the two-way time. The depth can be found by multiplying water velocity by travel time. The same basic procedure has been used under the continents with artificial acoustic wave sources such as explosives and vibrator trucks.

Context

An understanding of the geometry, evolution, and composition of the Earth's crust increases humankind's knowledge of the nature of the world. It is easy to show that humankind's very existence, as well as the material wealth of modern societies, is totally dependent on the crust of the Earth. The crustal state is one of dynamic evolution, with rock materials being created, deformed, and destroyed at plate tectonic boundaries. The process that makes creation and destruction of rocks possible is that of crystallization and melting of the mineral compounds that compose rock, a process known as volcanism. Volcanic activity over the billions of years of the Earth's existence has, by the expulsion of gases trapped in lavas that reach the surface, provided the water vapor and other gases necessary to form the oceans and atmosphere, which are necessary to support life.

An understanding of volcanoes, of the how, why, and where they occur, requires an understanding of the Earth's crust and of crustal dynamics. Certainly, this can be important as viewed from the perspective of Mount St. Helens and other volcanoes of the northwestern United States. Mount St. Helens is a volcano formed by remelting of part of the oceanic crust that is slowly being taken back into the interior of the Earth. As this process of subduction and remelting of the oceanic crust will continue into the future for millions of years, so will eruptions continue to occur at Mount St. Helens, as well as at other volcanoes of the Cascade Mountains. Thus, an understanding of the crust of the Earth shows that the disastrous May 18, 1980, eruption of Mount St. Helens was not a onetime event.

The dynamic evolution of the Earth's crust is also accompanied by the movement of large plates of the crust and upper mantle, up to 100 kilometers thick, against one another. The San Andreas fault of California is one place where two of these plates of crustal material rub against each other. The forces created by this motion are released as energy in large earthquakes, posing a threat to life and property. Eventually, knowledge of how crustal rocks change and respond to these forces before an impending earthquake may allow their prediction.

Exploration for important economic minerals is guided by knowledge about the evolution and composition of the crust. The creation of valuable metal deposits, such as gold and copper, during volcanic activity at ocean ridge sites where new oceanic crustal rocks are also being created is occurring in the Red Sea between Africa and Asia. Consequently, exploration efforts for such metallic ores can be directed toward identifying ancient ridge site deposits. The formation of continental sedimentary rocks in the Gulf of Mexico is trapping organic materials that will be turned into oil and natural gas. Looking for similar types of sedimentary rocks in the appropriate crustal environment would be worthwhile for explorers in the petroleum and natural gas industries.

David S. Brumbaugh

Basic Bibliography

Bally, A. W. *Seismic Expression of Structural Styles.* Tulsa, Okla.: American Association of Petroleum Geologists, 1983. An excellent visual treatment of the structure and layering of primarily the upper crust throughout the world. Sections into the crust of offshore Scotland and northwest Germany show the Moho. Suitable for a broad audience from general readers to scientific specialists.

Bott, M. H. P. *The Interior of the Earth.* New York: Elsevier, 1982. This book was intended for undergraduate and graduate students of geology and geophysics as well as for other scientists interested in the topic. The plate tectonic framework of the outer part of the Earth is strongly emphasized.

Brown, G. C., and A. E. Mussett. *The Inaccessible Earth.* London: Allen & Unwin, 1981. A good general introduction geared toward the undergraduate college student. The primary topics are the internal state and composition of the Earth. Included is background material on seismology and three chapters discussing the Earth's crust.

Phillips, O. M. *The Heart of the Earth.* San Francisco: Freeman, Copper, 1968. An excellent and well-written book intended for a general college and noncollege audience with no background in geophysics. The book has an excellent chapter on seismology and the way in which earthquake waves are used to determine physical properties from velocity and to infer crustal structure by refracted waves.

Smith, David G., ed. *The Cambridge Encyclopedia of Earth Sciences.* Cambridge, England: Cambridge University Press, 1981. This general reference provides an excellent overview of the Earth sciences. Chapter 10 is an extensive discussion of the Earth's crust, including useful illustrations and diagrams. Contains a glossary, an index, and recommendations for further reading.

Taylor, Stuart R., and Scott M. McLennan. *The Continental Crust: Its Composition and Evolution.* Boston: Blackwell Scientific, 1985. A text aimed at undergraduate and graduate geology and geophysics students as well as general Earth scientists. It is clearly written and up-to-date and has excellent, well-rounded scientific references.

Current Bibliography

Brown, G. C. *The Inaccessible Earth: An Integrated View to Its Structure and Composition.* 2d ed. New York: Chapman and Hall, 1993.

Fowler, C. M. R. *The Solid Earth: An Introduction to Global Geophysics.* New York: Cambridge University Press, 1990.

James, David E., ed. *The Encyclopedia of Solid Earth Geophysics.* New York: Van Nostrand Reinhold, 1989.

Knapp, Ralph E. *Geophysics.* Exeter, England: Pergamon Press, 1995.

Vogel, Shawna. *Naked Earth: The New Geophysics.* New York: Plume, 1996.

Cross-References

Earth's Composition, 139; Earth's Core, 147; Earth's Core-Mantle Boundary, 154; Earth's Differentiation, 169; Earth's Mantle, 207; Earth's Structure, 234.

Earth's Differentiation

Earth's differentiation describes the formation of "layers" within the early Earth when it originated more than 4 billion years ago. A core surrounded by a mantle overlain with a crust, on which humans now live, was created by chemical and physical processes as the Earth cooled from a hot molten sphere.

Overview

The Earth today is a spherelike body composed of layers arranged according to density. The highest-density ("heaviest") material, mainly nickel and iron, is at the core, which is about 3,400 kilometers (2,100 miles) thick with an average density of about 10-13 grams per cubic centimeter. The lightest elements are dominant in the crust, the outermost layer at the surface of the Earth. This layer is very thin—only 5-60 kilometers (3-37 miles) thick. The average density of the crust is about 2.8 grams per cubic centimeter. The common elements of the crust include silicon, aluminum, calcium, potassium, and sodium. They combine to form various silicate minerals, especially the feldspars and quartz. These minerals are major components of granites and other abundant rocks. Between the crust and the core is the mantle, which is intermediate in density (4.5 grams per cubic centimeter). It is very thick, about 2,900 kilometers (1,800 miles).

There are two major theories on how the Earth became differentiated in this way: the homogeneous accretion theory and the inhomogeneous accretion theory. The homogeneous accretion theory states that the Earth formed by randomly sweeping up debris (meteors, dust) in its orbit around the Sun. This process, which occurred about 4.6 billion years ago, caused the debris to be added on (accreted) to the early Earth in a sort of "snowball" effect that made the Earth progressively larger. The bigger it became, the more its gravity increased and the more debris it accumulated. According to this theory, because the debris was accreted at random, the Earth at this time was undifferentiated; that is, it was homogeneous, meaning it was roughly the same throughout. At some time (scientists are uncertain exactly when) during or after the accretion, differentiation occurred when this body became molten. The liquid state allowed heavier (denser) elements to sink to the core so that it became enriched in iron and nickel. The lighter elements rose to the surface to form the crust, while elements of intermediate density stayed below them. This process would also explain why radioactive elements such as uranium and thorium are common in the crust, because they would have tended to combine with the low-density crustal minerals at this time.

For the homogeneous accretion theory to be correct, there must have been some process which heated up the originally solid body, causing it to become molten liquid. Scientists agree that there were probably three processes that could have caused this heating. First, radioactive isotopes were much more common in the early Earth; radioactive decay of these isotopes would have produced much heat. This heat source has greatly decreased through time as the isotopes have decayed to more stable states. Second, during accretion of debris, the energy released as the debris impacted the Earth was converted to heat energy. Third, much heat is created by gravitational compression. As more and more material was added to the Earth, progressively greater temperatures were generated at the core. Some scientists have estimated that the combination of these three processes would have raised the temperature of the Earth by as much as 1,200 degrees Celsius. While this theory has many supporters, it is far from conclusively proven. Current research based on computer models of physical laws indicates that even with all three of these processes operating, there might not have been enough heat generated to warm a cold planetary body to a molten state.

To provide an alternative to the problems of the homogeneous accretion theory, the inhomogeneous accretion theory was proposed. The main difference is that this latter theory states that the differentiation of layers occurred as accretion was occurring. Instead of accreting as an originally homogeneous body, which then became layered through density gradients, the Earth is thought to have accreted the layers in sequence. First, a naked core developed from dense matter in the debris of the orbit. Later, a less dense mantle and an even lighter crust accreted around the core as lighter debris in the orbit was encountered. Yet why should progressively lighter matter be encountered in such a cloud of debris? Calculations show that in a cooling cloud of hot gas and dust, such as that in the early Earth's orbit, iron and nickel would condense first to form the core. As the cloud cooled further, silicates of progressively lighter elements would condense so that they would be accreted in that order.

In spite of their differences, the two theories agree on a number of major points about the Earth's differentiation, the most basic being the assumption that the Earth originated from condensation of a large cloud of dust and debris around the Sun. The theories also agree that the differentiation must have been well under way by 3.8 billion years ago. The oldest rocks on Earth date to this age, and they contain remanent magnetism, which indicates that the Earth had a magnetic field by then; therefore, scientists know that the core had formed. Rotation of the core produces the field. Another major point of agreement is that the different melting points of the various elements played a key role in the origin of layering. In both theories, undifferentiated matter formed separate layers because the denser materials tended to solidify first. Thus, nickel and lead condense early in the homogeneous accretion theory and then sink to the core, or condense early in the dust cloud in the inhomogeneous theory and are accreted first as the core.

Scientists are currently debating the evidence for the two models and, presumably, a consensus will someday be reached. Whichever of the two models is correct, it must be noted that the differentiation of the Earth did not end with the formation of merely these three layers. The early crust almost certainly consisted mainly of ultramafic minerals, which are relatively heavy minerals high in magnesium and iron. Nevertheless, today's crust, composing the continents, contains much lighter sialic minerals, which are high in silicon and aluminum. Experimental evidence shows that in order for this continental crust to differentiate, the ultramafic crust would need to undergo remelting, which would cause the lighter minerals to separate from the heavier ones. There are two theories as to how this remelting came about. One relies on convection currents within the very hot early Earth itself. For millions of years after it formed, the Earth stayed extremely hot compared to today's interior temperatures. Therefore, as the crust began to harden and surface cooling began, there was much volcanism as hot magma from the interior sought release through the crust. Volcanoes created some local density differences in the crust and also led to erosion as some of the higher areas were exposed to weathering. It is thought by many scientists that these density differences together with accumulating sediment along the volcano margins led to remelting as convection in the underlying magma carried up great amounts of heat. In addition, convection currents return to deeper depths when they cool off, so they may have carried ultramafic crust and sediment down with them to be remelted. This recycling of rock by convection cells in hot magma was probably the beginning of plate tectonics. This same recycling process continues, although at a much slower pace because the convection currents are driven by heat and the Earth is much cooler today. The second theory about the differentiation of the crust states that meteorite impacts were involved. Scientists know that the early Earth was (with all the planets) heavily bombarded with debris. This theory says that large meteors penetrated the original ultramafic crust, remelting some of the crust and causing a large rim to form around the crater. The remelting, along with the rim formation, might have led to a continental "nucleus" that formed the center onto which later continental material was accreted. This theory is not exclusive of the first theory because the nuclei created by the impacts would then participate in convection recycling, helping to create still more continental crust. Whether impacts were involved or not, it is clear that the amount of continental crust has continued to increase since the original differentiation to form the land masses as they are known today. At the same time, the amount of ultramafic crust has diminished because it is readily destroyed by the erosion and remelting process. Instead there remains only oceanic crust, underlying the ocean basins. The oceanic crust is more mafic than the continental crust but not as high in magnesium and iron as the original ultramafic crust. It consists of crust that has not been as completely recycled as is continental crust and is therefore somewhat denser. Today, the crust is composed entirely of the lighter continental crust, with a density of about 2.7 grams per cubic centimeter, and the denser oceanic crust, with a density of about 3.0 grams per cubic centimeter.

Methods of Study

It is not possible to study directly the differentiation of the Earth because the process occurred at least 4 billion years ago. If technology ever becomes adequate, it may be possible to study the differentiation of other planets in other solar systems. Astronomers have recently discovered debris around other stars that appears to represent a solar system in the process of formation. Until then, there are two less direct methods of studying Earth's differentiation: observations of the current internal structure of the Earth to see what changes continue to occur and laboratory and field study of the Earth and meteorites to make inferences about those processes involved in differentiation.

The core, mantle, and even the deeper crust are far too deep to be reached by conventional drilling; therefore, no one has ever seen rocks from those parts of the Earth. Instead, all scientists know of them comes from the study of seismic waves produced by earthquakes, which provide a kind of X ray of the interior. For example, if an earthquake occurs on one side of the planet, the seismic vibrations traveling to stations on more distant parts of the planet not only travel rapidly but follow refracted (curved) paths. This high speed indicates that the Earth's interior becomes denser with depth, because vibrations travel faster in denser material—which refraction confirms, because the changing density will cause waves to travel at different speeds depending on where they are. Even more telling is the behavior of different kinds of seismic waves. P (primary) waves move back and forth in the direction of travel and will go through solid or liquid material. S (secondary) waves, which move at right angles to the travel direction, will go through solids but not through liquids. Observations show that S waves are not received at locations directly on the other side of the Earth to an earthquake. This "shadow zone" indicates that the Earth has a core that is composed of liquid. On the other hand, P waves are received on the opposite side of the Earth, but they are refracted in some parts but not in others. Calculations show that this phenomenon occurs because the core is divided into two layers: a solid inner core and a liquid outer core. Similar refractions are used to locate the top of the mantle, where "seismic discontinuities" cause waves to change speed beween the mantle and crust.

Laboratory studies used to model differentiation show that iron and nickel will differentially separate from silicate minerals at an early stage in cooling. This finding is confirmed by the study of metallic meteorites, which are composed mostly of nickel and iron. These meteorites appear to have formed under extremely high temperatures and pressures such as exist in planetary cores. In fact, such meteors are thought to have originated from early planets that were shattered in collisions shortly after the solar system formed. The next major group of minerals to separate are olivine and pyroxene. These are silicates that are high in iron and magnesium and that form the rock called peridotite. This observation, plus density estimates of the mantle itself using seismic velocity data, indicates that the mantle is composed largely of that rock. (The rate of seismic wave travel can be related to what the medium is composed of chemically.) Laboratory studies of peridotite also indicate how oceanic and continental crust would differentiate from it. As peridotite rises up from the mantle at divergent plate boundaries, the pressure and temperature of the magma's environment begin to decrease dramatically. This temperature decrease leads to partial melting of the magma, which produces minerals of basaltic composition. These minerals become accreted onto the oceanic basin floor to become oceanic crust. At convergent plate boundaries where subduction is occurring, the oceanic crust, along with many sediments on it, is being pushed underneath the other plate and is being remelted. Laboratory studies of magmas of this composition show that its partial melting will create a new magma that is rich in silica and other minerals found in granites and in other common rocks making up continental crust.

Context

It is difficult to appreciate the importance of an event that occurred at least 4 billion years ago, but there are two good reasons to do so. On a personal level, each human being needs to have a firm grasp of how he or she and the planet arrived at this moment. Many of the problems facing humankind today arise because decision makers fail to consider long-term consequences.

On a more immediate, practical level, the events involved in Earth's differentiation very much shaped the Earth as humans now live on it; the better those events are understood, the better the planet will be understood and its resources used wisely. For example, humankind lives on only a tiny fraction of the crustal thickness, yet the crust itself is only a small fraction of the total planet. How far down will mineral resources be found? A project that had been planned to drill to the mantle to sample it directly was abandoned because it was too expensive. At present, industrialized society is running low on many materials, such as chromium, which is mined from ores naturally enriched by differentiation. If it were not for such differentiation, there would be no civilization, because it costs too much (uses too much energy) to separate the usable minerals in rocks that have not undergone natural enrichment. For example, any average rock (like a granite) contains many valuable elements, such as gold. They are so dilute, however, that the cost of extracting them is too great to be economical. Is petroleum formed by magmatic processes of differentiation as some (only a few) geologists say? It is not known for certain. Of particular relevance is the origin of earthquakes. The processes that formed the mantle and crust played a major role in establishing the processes of plate tectonics. Scientists now know that most earthquakes are directly associated with plate tectonism. Some earthquakes originate at great depths, while others begin nearer to the surface.

On a longer time frame, our knowledge of Earth's differentiation will make it much easier to understand the formation and to utilize the resources of other planets. The other terrestrial planets—Mercury, Venus, and Mars—also underwent planetary differentiation at about the same time as did the Earth. Mars is the most habitable by humans, but all of them, especially Mercury, are rich in minerals and in other materials that humans can use. Comparative planetology can also tell scientists about the geological future of the Earth. It is important to note that Earth's differentiation is not truly complete; plate tectonism means that the crust continues to evolve. Furthermore, physiochemical changes continue to occur in the core and mantle as the interior slowly cools. By looking at other worlds that have already gone through these changes, scientists can draw conclusions about Earth's fate. Mercury, for example, because of its small size (about that of Earth's moon), lost its internal heat billions of years ago, and any movement of crust or volcanic activity has long since ceased.

Michael L. McKinney

Basic Bibliography

Head, James W., Charles A. Wood, and Thomas A. Mutch. "Geologic Evolution of the Terrestrial Planets." *American Scientist* 65 (January/February, 1977): 21. Comparative evolution of Mars, Venus, Mercury, and Earth in a widely read review article. Technical but very informative to the motivated layperson or student.

Kaufmann, William J., III. *Planets and Moons.* New York: W. H. Freeman, 1979. One of the standard and best-respected texts on comparative planetology, this book includes excellent discussions of planetary origins and differentiation. Some parts of this college text are highly advanced, but much is suitable for the interested layperson and the advanced high school student because chapters begin with the basics.

Levin, H. *The Earth Through Time.* New York: Saunders, 1988. A summary of the Earth's growth and differentiation is found in this highly respected and widely used basic freshman text. Very well illustrated and clearly written; an excellent introduction to the subject. Technical references for further research.

Moorbath, Stephen. "The Oldest Rocks and the Growth of Continents." *Scientific American* 236 (March, 1977): 92. A well-illustrated discussion of differentiation processes of the continental and oceanic crusts, including the role of plate tectonism. Especially interesting discussion of earliest known rocks. Suitable for the interested layperson or the advanced high school student.

Ozima, Minoru. *The Earth: Its Birth and Growth.* Translated by J. F. Wakabayashi. New York: Cambridge University Press, 1981. An excellent overview of Earth's differentiation from the beginning of planetary condensation to the present. Suitable for interested laypersons and advanced high school students. Technical in parts, but many basic concepts, too.

Short, Nicholas M. *Planetary Geology.* Englewood Cliffs, N.J.: Prentice-Hall, 1975. A complete introduction to planetary evolution, with detailed description on an elementary level. Comprehensible to interested laypersons and high school students.

Wetherill, George W. "The Formation of the Earth from Planetesimals." *Scientific American* 244 (June, 1981): 162. A well-illustrated account of Earth's origin and subsequent differentiation. Very readable by the motivated layperson or high school student.

Wicander, R., and J. Monroe. *Historical Geology.* St. Paul, Minn.: West, 1989. An up-to-date survey of Earth history, with a good summary discussion of Earth's differentiation. A basic college-level text, but readable for the layperson and the advanced high school student.

Current Bibliography

Consolmagno, Guy. *Worlds Apart: A Textbook in Planetary Sciences.* Englewood Cliffs, N.J.: Prentice-Hall, 1994.

Elder, John. *The Structure of the Planets.* Orlando: Academic Press, 1987.

Encrenaz, Therese. *The Solar System.* 2d ed. New York: Springer, 1995.

Hartmann, William K. *Moons and Planets.* 3d ed. Belmont, Calif.: Wadsworth, 1993.

Cross-References

Earth's Composition, 139; Earth's Core, 147; Earth's Core-Mantle Boundary, 154; Earth's Crust, 161; Earth's Mantle, 207; Earth's Structure, 234.

Earth's Magnetic Field: Origins

The Earth has a magnetic field that scientists believe did not appear spontaneously. The process of discovery leads into other areas of geophysics and into physics and chemistry. A dynamo effect in the outer core of the Earth is perhaps the most likely source of most of the magnetic field.

Overview

Central to study about the Earth's magnetic field are questions concerning its origin. Is it the result of a great bar magnet similar in concept, if on a larger scale, to an ordinary, store-bought magnet, or is a more complex process involved? The hypothesis that the source of the Earth's field is a bar magnet can be tested by comparing characteristics of the Earth's field with those of a huge bar magnet. Because the Earth is immense, the magnet must be correspondingly large. The Earth has a strong field that a small bar magnet could not account for anyway, as a magnet's field strength decreases with distance from the magnet. A small magnet at the center of the Earth would produce a field with too low a strength at the surface of the Earth, given the distance involved: 6,371 kilometers.

A bar magnet and the Earth both possess north and south magnetic poles that produce a dipole field. The "di" prefix is from a Greek term for "two": A dipole field is a field produced by two poles. If a bar magnet is located somewhere inside the Earth, the magnetic field at the Earth's surface should not shift position. It is difficult to imagine how a structure such as a large bar magnet could physically move in order to account for the movement of the field. Yet the field at the surface does change. Some of the alteration is the result of outside influences, such as magnetic storms caused by energetic particles from the Sun, and some motion is from some changing conditions within the Earth. One change is difficult to explain: the secular variation of the Earth's field. This variation is the slow shift in the magnetic pole position over periods of years because of the changing of some interior condition that alters the field's position. A bar magnet cannot account for the observed secular variation.

Scientists do not accept an explanation based on one line of evidence, and so they search for other ways to support or refute a hypothesis. In this case, the next step is to look at the temperature change in the Earth's interior. Moving below the Earth's surface, depths are rapidly reached where the temperature is so high that rocks melt. The temperature is above the Curie temperature of all known permanently magnetized materials. The Curie temperature (or Curie point) is the temperature above which a material is no longer permanently magnetic. Heating a magnet above its Curie temperature, for example, causes it to lose its ability to attract iron objects such as pins. When the magnet cools, it once again becomes permanently magnetized but not to the same strength as before.

An alternative theory is that the Earth's outer layer of cool material contains enough magnetic material to account for the magnetic field. There are two problems with this idea: It does not explain the movement of the field, and there is not enough permanently magnetized material to account for more than a minimum percentage of the Earth's magnetic field. As the magnetic bar theory cannot be substantiated, perhaps a look at the manner in which magnetic fields are produced will establish another hypothesis.

The ultimate source of any magnetic field is the movement of electric charges, such as electrons, protons, and ionized atoms. Wires, for example, have magnetic fields around them because electric charges (electrons) move through the wires in the form of the electric current. In a magnet, the electrons surrounding the nucleus of an atom are moving, which denotes electrical current, however minute. All these small currents taken together produce the magnetic field of the material. The conclusion is, therefore, that some electric current within the Earth, other than atomic current, is producing the magnetic field of the Earth.

The current cannot be a passive current, one that was started sometime in the past and allowed to flow, generating a passive magnetic field. A process that could have started such a passive current is unknown. An electrical current encounters resistance that causes a passive current to diminish with time. The resistance converts electrical energy into heat. To sustain the current requires a conductor and a source of energy. The layer of the Earth under the thin surface crust, the mantle, is composed of rock that is an insulator, and, thus, very little current can flow. The innermost layer, the core, is roughly 3,500 kilometers in radius and metallic in composition, most probably iron with a small percentage of nickel and an even smaller percentage of other elements. Therefore, the core is a possible conductor through which the charge can flow.

Some process must actively generate the current. The most probable is a dynamo effect, comparable to the method employed to generate electrical energy for home and industrial use. ("Generate" is not a very accurate term—the process is actually one of converting one form of energy, such as the chemical energy in coal, into electrical energy and not creating the electrical energy from nothing, as "generation" implies.) A length of wire moved across a magnetic field will induce a small current in the wire. One end of the wire is now electrically positive, and the other end is negative.

Take a longer length of wire, form it into loops, and turn these loops in a magnetic field, and the result is an electrical generator, or dynamo, with electrical energy available at the ends of the wire. The actual design of a dynamo is not so simple, but the energy conversion process is very straight-forward and well understood.

The requirements for producing the Earth's field include a source of energy that causes a conductor to move through a magnetic field, which causes an electric current that in turn produces a magnetic field that adds to the original field. Movement is also essential; energy and conductors cannot produce even the smallest magnetic field without free, unimpeded movement between the conductor and the initial magnetic field. These necessary conditions are met by resources within the Earth.

The heat energy of the Earth's interior is more than adequate for the generation of the field. The temperature at the Earth's center is between 4,000 and 6,000 degrees Celsius. Some of this heat energy escapes from the interior through the Earth's surface and is detected as heat flow. It is much smaller than the amount of energy that the surface receives from sunlight, but it is enough. The heat energy is transferred from the interior to the surface by conduction and convection and produces such phenomena as earthquakes, volcanoes, and mountain building.

Convection is important where material is fluid. It is seen in a container of boiling water—heated water expands and rises, and cooler water sinks to replace it. This reaction produces a convection cell that transfers heat from a hot area to a cold one. In molten regions of the Earth, convection transfers heat outward from the hot interior to outer, cooler areas. Earthquake studies indicate that the inner core, with a radius of 1,200 kilometers, is solid, but the outer core, with a thickness of 2,300 kilometers, is molten. An earth-quake produces waves known as S waves that cannot travel through liquids, and they do not travel through the outer core of the Earth. This molten material is free to move and transfer heat, or convect.

The Earth has an average density 5.5 times that of water, and it is much denser than rock. The Earth is not entirely rocky material and must have a denser portion to give a high average density. Therefore, the Earth has a mantle of lower-density rock and a core of much higher-density conductive metal that is most probably iron in composition. (The metallic nature of the core can be deduced from the unique high-density composition of metal.)

With a source of energy—heat—that causes molten iron to move in convection cells, all that is needed is a magnetic field to start the process. Magnetic fields, however weak, are always present in the universe. The outer core's liquid iron moves through a weak field and produces a weak electrical current. When electric charge flows, it produces a magnetic field. The weak electric current can produce a magnetic field that reinforces the initial field. Molten iron moves through this stronger field and generates more current, which then yields a stronger magnetic field.

Although it may seem like a perpetual-motion, or closed, system, that is not the case. The energy comes from the Earth's heat supply, which is a finite source of energy. Also, the process does not continue generating an increasingly stronger field. The process reaches a steady-state condition at which the current and field achieve stable levels. It becomes harder to produce more magnetic field because the electric and magnetic fields interact to slow the process to a steady state. A bicycle with an electric light powered by a generator spun by one of the bicycle's wheels demonstrates this principle: It is harder to pedal with the light operating than without. A similar effect is operating in the outer core.

This process can explain features seen in the Earth's field. The shifting of the field's position is caused by alterations in the convection cells within the core. The core is free to move inside the Earth, and changes in the Earth's motion through space can cause the mantle to shift position relative to the core, which will affect the convection currents of the outer core and the generation of the field. Curie temperature does not pertain to electromagnets, and in fact a high temperature in the core is required as an energy source for the convection. Studies indicate that the Earth's magnetic field has reversed polarity many times in the past, the last occurring about 700,000 years ago. The dynamo process is unstable over long periods of time and can change polarity. Models of dynamos can be constructed that are simple versions of the Earth's dynamo, which, when set in operation, reveal changes in the field's intensity and polarity.

This dynamo process can be used to explain the presence or absence of a magnetic field for the planets, their moons, and the Sun. Mercury, Venus, Mars, and the moons do not have substantial magnetic fields; they do not possess a molten conductive core. The Earth, the Sun, and the larger planets have substantial fields. The Earth has a molten iron core; the Sun is a fluid, conductive plasma; and Jupiter and the other outer planets contain thick layers of liquid, metallic hydrogen. The dynamo effect explains the origin of about 95 percent of the Earth's magnetic field; the rest comes from the magnetic fields associated with magnetic minerals in the Earth's crust and from external sources such as electrical charges flowing in the atmosphere. They, however, are minor considerations in comparison to the main field generated by the dynamo in the Earth's outer core.

Methods of Study

The study of the magnetic field's origin involves many areas of science. Earthquakes may be destructive, but their waves act as probes of the Earth's interior. Various types of earthquake waves travel from the starting point of the earthquake, the focus, into the Earth's interior. Their speed and direction of travel are determined by the density and elastic properties of the material through which they are traveling. The waves reflect off the core-mantle boundary and return to seismic stations, where the waves are recorded on a seismograph. Calculations, using data from these seismograms, reveal the thickness of the mantle and the size of the outer core. They also reveal that the seismic wave known as an S wave cannot travel through the outer core of the Earth. S waves cannot travel through a liquid, and, therefore, it can be inferred that the outer core of the Earth is liquid.

In determining the volume of the Earth and its mass, the Earth's density can be ascertained by dividing the mass by its volume; the average density of the Earth is five and a half times that of water. This figure may not seem very significant, but rocks are only three times the density of water. A portion of the Earth's interior must be much denser in order to yield such a high average. Only metals have the required density, but some metals, such as aluminum, are too low in density, and others, such as uranium, are too high. Still others are closer to the required density but are too rare, as is the case with gold or silver. Iron is a good candidate, as it has the right density and is fairly common. Therefore, the core of the Earth is concluded to be mostly iron, with some nickel and other elements: a conclusion reached mainly with simple mathematics and previously established scientific knowledge.

Studies of magnetic characteristics of materials determine the Curie temperatures and types of magnetism the materials possess. Heating a permanently magnetized material in a magnetic field and recording the temperature when the material is no longer strongly pulled by the field establishes the Curie temperature. Other studies investigate the manner in which magnetic fields are generated, such as moving charges producing magnetic fields. These are areas of study for physicists or engineers, whose work can have great implications in a discipline such as geophysics.

Those studying the Earth's heat flow, a subdiscipline of geophysics, also advance study on the connection between heat and magnetism. In the ocean, the heat flow is determined by placing two temperature probes several meters apart on a tube that is lowered into the sediment on the ocean bottom. The system is allowed to come to equilibrium with its surroundings, and the temperature of each probe is read. There is a mathematical formula that is used to ascertain the heat flow from the temperature difference, the distance between the probes, and the heat-conduction characteristics of the surrounding sediment. The calculated heat flow permits the determination of the temperature change with depth for the Earth and the fact that there is enough heat energy to produce the magnetic field.

Magnetometers such as the spinner magnetometer are used to determine the characteristics of the Earth's magnetic field in the past, and this information places constraints on the methods by which the field is produced. Some igneous and sedimentary rocks are good recorders of the field. Igneous rock samples are collected and taken to the laboratory for analysis. Basalt, an igneous rock, has a strong magnetization that is measured using a spinner. The sample is placed in the instrument and spun at a high speed. Surrounding the sample are coils of wire in which an electric current is induced by the spinning magnetic field of the sample. The current is proportional to the magnetic field strength, and the electronics of the magnetometer convert it into a reading of that strength. This work has established that the magnetic field has changed polarity many times in the past.

Context

For civilization in general, the simple knowledge of how to generate electric current from a moving magnetic field or a magnetic field from a moving electrical charge is fundamental. Without the laws governing electric and magnetic fields, most of the world's standard of living would collapse. There would be no electric motors for drills, mixers, fans, and automobile starters. No electric generators would produce electricity, with no electric heaters for water and house, no electric lights, and no television. Moreover, beyond creature comforts, the electromagnetic force is one of the four basic forces in the universe, along with gravity and the two nuclear forces (strong and weak). A universe without magnetic fields is incomprehensible.

The fact that the Earth has a magnetic field indicates that the Earth is a dynamic planet with many geological processes taking place. Without this activity, there would be no earthquakes, no volcanoes, no moving plates, and no mountains. It is doubtful that the varied life-forms that presently exist could survive on such a planet, and they most certainly could not have originated on such an Earth. The active generation of the Earth's magnetic field thus symbolizes the vitality of the Earth.

Stephen J. Shulik

Basic Bibliography

Busse, F. H. "Recent Developments in the Dynamo Theory of Planetary Magnetism." In *Annual Review of Earth and Planetary Sciences*, edited by W. W. Wetherill, vol. 11. Palo Alto, Calif.: Annual Reviews, 1983. This article gives the reader the opportunity to see the advances a particular discipline has made in seven years when compared with the article by Levy, cited below. An outline of the dynamo theory is given, with models of the dynamo for various planets. The observation evidence is discussed, along with the paleomagnetic data, geomagnetic reversals, and secular variation. References are listed, along with a number of figures.

Garland, G. D. *Introduction to Geophysics*. 2d ed. Philadelphia: W. B. Saunders, 1979. Used as a text for introductory geophysics, this book covers, in sections 17.4 and 17.5, the cause of the main field and the dynamo theory. A few equations, but many figures and graphs that are of interest to the less technically informed reader. At the end of the chapter is a listing of thirty-two references.

Gubbins, D., and T. G. Masters. "Driving Mechanisms for the Earth's Dynamo." In *Advances in Geophysics*, edited by B. Saltzman, vol. 21. New York: Academic Press, 1979. This article looks at such topics as the physical and chemical properties of the core and the power sources for the magnetic field. References are located at the end of the article. Mathematics and numerous figures and tables are included.

Kennett, J. P. *Marine Geology*. Englewood Cliffs, N.J.: Prentice-Hall, 1982. Kennet devotes pages 21-23 to a brief discussion of the subdivision of geophysics called paleomagnetism, the study of the Earth's magnetic field, from generation to magnetization methods such as TRM. Not exhaustive but very readable, with no mathematics and some figures. The text is a veritable encyclopedia on marine geology: plate tectonics, oceanic structure, sediments, margins, and history.

Lapedes, D. N., ed. *McGraw-Hill Encyclopedia of Geological Sciences*. New York: McGraw-Hill, 1978. Pages 704-708, under the heading of "Rock Magnetism," provide a concise description of many aspects associated with rock magnetism: how rock magnetization occurs, the present field, magnetic reversals, field generation, secular variation, and apparent polar wandering, among other subjects. Very readable, with no mathematics and a fair number of graphs, tables, and figures.

Levy, E. H. "Generation of the Planetary Magnetic Fields." In *Annual Review of Earth and Planetary Sciences*, edited by F. Donath, vol. 4. Palo Alto, Calif.: Annual Reviews, 1976. This article presents an overview of how the generation of magnetic fields within the various planets affects the dynamo effect. Some mathematical equations and a number of figures, along with many references at the end of the book.

Merrill, R. T., and M. W. McElhinney. *The Earth's Magnetic Field*. New York: Academic Press, 1983. The authors cover much of the material associated with the Earth's field. Chapters 7 and 8 deal with the origin of the field, and chapter 9 covers the origin of secular variation and field reversals. Mathematical equations and thirty-eight pages of references. Numerous tables and figures.

Motz, L., ed. *Rediscovery of the Earth*. New York: Van Nostrand Reinhold, 1979. As a collection of articles for the nonscientist by scientists renowned in their respective fields, the text makes very interesting reading, augmented with many colorful illustrations. The chapter "The Earth's Magnetic Field and Its Variations" is written by Dr. Takesi Nagata, who has authored hundreds of articles on diverse aspects of geophysics besides the Earth's magnetic field, and covers a wide range of magnetic field topics. Two pages are devoted to the origin of the field. A small amount of mathematics; only a few references.

Smith, D. G., ed. *The Cambridge Encyclopedia of Earth Sciences*. New York: Crown Publishers, 1981. Chapter 7, "The Earth as a Magnet," contains a discussion of the field's origin. The term "encyclopedia" is not the best term for this publication because it is broken into chapters that are grouped into six parts pertaining to general categories of the Earth sciences. The text is well written at a nontechnical level, with many colorful diagrams and figures.

Stacey, F. D. *Physics of the Earth.* New York: John Wiley & Sons, 1977. Under section 8.4, "Generation of the Main Field," the author provides a short, technical description of the origin of the field, which will be of interest to the more advanced student. Equations are rather formidable, but several figures illustrating the dynamo effect are included. A large number of references at the end of the text. Many other areas of geophysics are covered at a technical level.

Current Bibliography

Bhattacharya, B. B., ed. *Advances in Geophysics.* New Delhi: Oxford and IBH, 1988.

Brown, G. C. *The Inaccessible Earth: An Integrated View to Its Structure and Composition.* 2d ed. New York: Chapman and Hall, 1993.

Chapel, Paul. *I.E.G. Handbook of Exploration Geophysics.* Rotterdam: A. A. Balkema, 1992.

Fowler, C. M. R. *The Solid Earth: An Introduction to Global Geophysics.* New York: Cambridge University Press, 1990.

James, David E., ed. *The Encyclopedia of Solid Earth Geophysics.* New York: Van Nostrand Reinhold, 1989.

Cross-References

Earth's Magnetic Field: Secular Variation, 184; Earth's Magnetic Field at Present, 192; Earth's Magnetosphere, 199.

Earth's Magnetic Field: Secular Variation

The Earth's magnetism manifests itself at every point on the Earth and above it. It has a direction, as indicated by a freely suspended compass needle, and an intensity. This direction and intensity change slowly over decades and centuries, a process known as secular variation.

Overview

The secular variation of the Earth's magnetic field is a long-term change in the magnetic forces produced in the Earth's core. The phenomenon is observable anywhere on the Earth's surface. Its most familiar example is a gradual alteration of the direction in which an ordinary compass needle points. It also is seen in the change of the inclination; that is, the angle at which a magnetic needle suspended by its center of gravity dips below the horizon. Finally, the intensity of the force which returns a magnetized needle to its rest position is changing. Secular variation differs from other variations in the Earth's magnetism. For example, the diurnal (or daily) variation repeats cyclically. The secular variation, on the other hand, is a constant drift of direction and intensity which never repeats. These slow changes are termed "secular" changes, in analogy with similarly named gradual drifts in astronomical variables. Although its effects are seen best over periods of decades or even centuries, with modern methods secular variation can be detected across a much shorter interval.

The needle of a magnetic compass points generally north and south, but it does not point exactly so. The angle between geographic and magnetic north was originally called magnetic variation, meaning the variation from true north. Declination, as it is now called, was discovered around the twelfth century, although it was originally believed to be caused by abnormalities in the needle's magnetization or in its suspension. By the sixteenth century, Europeans had accepted declination as a phenomenon of the Earth's magnetism. Inclination was also discovered during that century. Hence William Gilbert could write in 1600 of both declination and inclination as natural phenomena. The needle indicated the direction of the Earth's magnetic field. By the early sixteenth century, Europeans had noticed that the declination varies from place to place, though this discovery can be attributed to no single observer. The discovery arose in the practices of navigation, chart making, and "dialing," or the crafting of sundials and magnetic compasses—all activities connected with exploration. Perhaps Christopher Columbus, and certainly Sebastian Cabot, noted that while the compass pointed east of north near Europe, it pointed west of north in the New World.

Indeed, all three magnetic elements—declination, inclination, and intensity—vary over the planet. If places with the same declination are connected by curved lines, maps of equal declination, called isogonic maps, can be produced. The first such printed map was produced by Edmond Halley in about 1701. Similar maps displaying equal inclination or equal intensity are also drawn. One line which early attracted much attention was the agonic line, or "line of no variation"; that is, a line along which the compass pointed to geographic north. It engendered hope for determining longitude by compass. Meanwhile, Henry Gellibrand announced in 1635 that declination changed over time as well as space. In his case, the declination had shifted from longitude 11.3 degrees east for London in 1580 to longitude 4.1 degrees east in 1634. Later investigators discovered that the inclination and the intensity of the magnetic field also gradually change. Between 1700 and 1900, the inclination at London decreased from almost 75 to 67 degrees. The intensity of the dipole field is decreasing at the rate of 8 percent per century.

Secular variation has been characterized by the westward drift of the agonic line. This drift can be visualized another way. As one can map the magnetic elements, one can map how these elements change. Curved lines connect points that are changing at a certain rate. For example, all points where the declination is shifting, say, eastward at 1 degree per century, might be connected together. These charts, known as isoporic charts, came into wide use in the mid-twentieth century. Areas of most rapid change are called isoporic foci. These isoporic foci are drifting westward, just as the agonic line is. While this drift has been a prominent feature of secular variation since Gellibrand, some evidence exists for eastward drifts during prehistoric times.

Secular variation is distant from direct experience. First, its very description presumes a system of mathematical analysis. The geomagnetic field and its secular change are often described in terms of dipoles, that is, idealized bar magnets superimposed on each other, or one dipolar field superimposed on a nondipolar field. Second, the effects produced by causes inside the Earth are always discussed in isolation from those caused by external processes, even though measurements cannot separate the two types of effects. Last, any discussion of the cause of secular variation is necessarily indirect, as is any discussion of the cause of the main field. Ultimately, separation of the description of geomagnetic secular variation from its mathematical analysis and theory is difficult.

Theories of geomagnetic secular variation have been extremely diverse. That is predictable, given the inaccessibility of the cause of the Earth's magnetism. Gilbert had suggested that the Earth behaves as if it had an ordinary bar magnet of extraordinary intensity at its center. From worldwide declination data, Halley discerned in 1683 a pattern dependent on four magnetic poles, not merely two. Robert Hooke proposed in 1674 that the magnetic axis of the Earth is tilted about 10 degrees from the axis of rotation and that this axis revolves around the rotational axis every 370 years. In 1692, Halley suggested that his four poles could explain secular variation. Two of these poles he assigned to the Earth's outer crust and the other two to a nucleus, which rotated slightly more slowly than the crust, on the same axis. The crustal magnetic poles were, he said, fixed in place, though as the nucleus drifted slowly westward under the crust, so did its magnetic poles. This motion explained, he thought, drift of the agonic line. The idea that the core is permanently magnetized was later ruled out by its temperature; it is too hot to be magnetic. Current discussion of dipoles in the core do not assume permanent magnets.

Two theories that have attracted attention in the twentieth century are that the Earth's very rotation causes its magnetism and that the Earth acts as an electromagnet. The former hypothesis reached its highest state of development around 1950 in work by Patrick M. S. Blackett, but the latter approach has proven more fruitful. In its rudimentary early nineteenth century form, this model assumed that the Earth's magnetism was produced by electrical currents flowing inside the Earth, from east to west, as in an electromagnet made up of a coil of wire. The model of electric currents flowing inside the core became adequately sophisticated to address the data only with the theoretical investigations of Walter Elsasser, from 1939 on, and of Sir Edward Crisp Bullard, starting in 1948. Elsasser proposed that the combination of the movement of molten materials and the simultaneous flow of electricity in these materials produced both the Earth's main magnetic field and the secular variations in it. This dynamo was driven, he suggested, by the heat generated by radioactive materials. Convection of hotter materials upward and of colder materials downward, he said, produced the dynamo. Various models have been advanced to show that such convection cells can produce the observed effects, and many debates are still waged over the character and cause of the dynamo.

There is significant agreement that the Earth's field and its secular variation are the result of motions in the core. It is also agreed that, for the most part, the magnetic field lines (or lines of force) travel with the moving fluid; that is, the lines are frozen. Similarly, the dynamo is a self-exciting (or better, self-sustaining) dynamo. Most scientists accept the two most probable energy sources for the dynamo to be heat from radioactive materials and convection caused by the settling of denser materials to the inner core. As any other dynamo must be driven—perhaps by a waterfall or by steam from coal or by a nuclear reactor—so, too, the geodynamo requires a source for its power. The Earth does not create its magnetic field; rather, it converts some other form of energy into it. The Earth's magnetic field is not a perpetual motion machine.

In the end, one must emphasize that theories of the geomagnetic dynamo and of its power sources are tentative. Their connection to secular variation is also exploratory. This area of geophysical theory is a most active and challenging one, and it is in rapid flux.

Methods of Study

Because detection of geomagnetic secular variation requires measurement of an invisible force, special apparatus is required. The simplest way to detect this slow change is to observe the declination of a magnetic compass over some decades; until the twentieth century, that was the only way. All the instruments employed by famous students of geomagnetism, from Gilbert in 1600 to C. F. Gauss in the 1830's, used adaptations of the compass to measure the magnetic elements. Among other goals, these scientists aimed to measure these elements more accurately, so as to reveal secular change in a shorter interval. During the twentieth century, however, there has been a sustained trend to replace magnetic needle instruments with ones based on new principles. Around 1900, research-quality Earth inductors were developed to replace the dip circle in measuring inclination. The idea behind this first electrically based geomagnetic instrument is simple: If a coil of wire is rotated in a magnetic field, and if its axis differs from the direction of that field, an electric current circles through the coil. Let the axis coincide with the field, however, and the current will cease. Magnetic scientists used this "null" method to determine inclination more accurately and more conveniently. The Earth inductor was followed in the 1930's by the flux-gate magnetometer. This instrument is based on a high-permeability alloy, that is, one that magnetizes readily. Around two cores of such material are wound two coils of wire, in opposite directions, that carry the same alternating current. When placed in the Earth's field, the changes in the magnetic fields of these two cores do not cancel each other. The net effect indicates the Earth's magnetic element in one direction. When, however, this magnetometer is oriented parallel to the Earth's field, no current is produced. The flux-gate magnetometer has seen wide use in aerial geomagnetic surveys.

Other generations of magnetic instruments have appeared since the flux-gate. Some of the most useful are the proton precession, the Rubidium vapor, and the superconducting magnetometers. These devices take advantage of principles of quantum physics. Some of them, like the proton precession instrument, measure only the total intensity of the Earth's field. Others, like the superconducting magnetometer, are directional. Both types are many times more sensitive than older instruments and also perform much faster.

Magnetic surveys have been an essential part of the method of studying

Earth's Magnetic Field Has Reversed During Its History

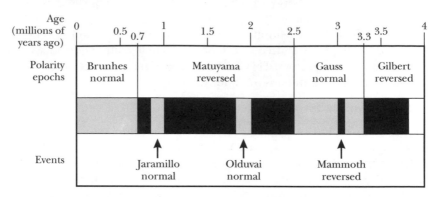

secular variation. All over the world, teams of observers have established "repeat stations," or places for careful observation of the magnetic elements at times separated by, say, several decades. These global data have then been analyzed according to one of several mathematical approaches. Magnetic surveys have been greatly facilitated not only by the new instruments mentioned above but also by the way those instruments are used. Surveys are now often conducted very quickly with instruments carried by airplanes and satellites (such as MAGSAT). Data that once took decades to gather are now collected in months. Moreover, calculations have been accelerated unimaginably by computers. That is critical, as the utility of the data depends on extensive calculations. Worldwide magnetic charts are produced much more frequently now than in 1900, and the study of secular variation is thus much more fine-grained.

Equally impressive changes have been wrought by the use of geomagnetic methods to study the magnetic properties of rocks. Many rocks provide a record of the Earth's magnetic field at the time they were deposited. The phenomenon is called remanent (or fossil) magnetism, and the science is called paleomagnetism. Until this development, mostly since 1950, secular variation studies were limited to data obtained by direct measurement of the Earth's field. Little was known of the magnetic field before 1600. New phenomena that have been revealed by these methods include reversals of the magnetic field and geomagnetic excursions. These findings are, however, mainly an extension of scientists' understanding of secular variation.

The study of geomagnetism has come a long way with the rapid development of new instruments and methods. No longer is the purpose restricted to a description of the main field and its variations. With the new sensitivity and portability made possible by electronics, geomagnetic secular variation has become a tool for understanding many other phenomena: archaeological dating, sea-floor spreading, continental drift, and magnetostratigraphic dating in sedimentation, in addition to the traditional effort to understand events in the Earth's core. New methods yet to appear will certainly expand our knowledge of the Earth.

Context

One cannot sense the magnetic field of the Earth directly, unaided by scientific instruments. Even so, most people are familiar with the magnetic compass, and many know roughly how to use it. Two areas which require greater familiarity with geomagnetic phenomena are the reading of topographic maps and navigating at sea. These activities demand close attention to declination and its secular variation.

In the lower left-hand corner of topographic maps produced by the U.S. Geological Survey there are three arrows, which point to true north, to magnetic north, and to "grid" north, respectively. With this declination information, one can adjust field readings to correspond to the map. In areas where secular variation of geomagnetism proceeds at a high rate, it may also be necessary to know when declination readings were last taken and the rate of their change. For example, near Tay River in the Canadian Yukon Territory, the declination was listed as longitude 33 degrees 25 feet east in 1979 and decreasing at 3.3 feet per year. Thus, if secular variation continued at its current rate, in eighteen years the declination would decrease to longitude 32 degrees 25 feet east. In a century this could mean a change of more than 5 degrees. Secular variation cannot be predicted reliably over so long a period, however, and maps are therefore updated regularly in magnetic surveys.

Information regarding declination at sea and especially near the coast is of even greater importance. Every vessel is sometimes beset by fog, and thus an essential bit of navigational data is the declination. With it and a known starting point, one can at least know the direction toward which the ship is pointing. Up-to-date charts are, again, the best means to circumvent secular variation. As the date of the magnetic declination data recedes into the past, however, reliable information concerning its secular change becomes more important.

The deep interior of the Earth is more inaccessible than the surfaces of Mars and Venus. Man can fly to these planets, but he can only scratch at the Earth's surface. Thus, scientists must watch closely the faint but distinct signals received at the Earth's surface for clues to the processes that drive this planet. Magnetic secular variation provides one of the few methods by which such information can be obtained. Perhaps the most exciting implications of secular variation are related to reversals of the Earth's main magnetic field. Reversals have happened scores of times over geological history. They tie geomagnetic secular variation in with the chronology of the planet and with sea-floor spreading and plate tectonics. The magnetism impressed upon minerals as they formed and on sedimentary beds as they settled has been preserved over hundreds of millions of years. When these records are gathered from around the world, they provide a unique look at the past state of the Earth's magnetic field. As scientists expand this record, it becomes a key to solving more geochronology problems and may even aid in archaeological investigations.

Gregory A. Good

Basic Bibliography

Carnegie Institution. *The Earth's Core: How Does It Work?* Washington, D.C.: Author, 1984. This 32-page pamphlet, available from the Carnegie Institution of Washington (1530 P Street NW, Washington, D.C. 20005), discusses active research undertaken by the institution's scientists in the study of the Earth's core. A nontechnical account of the core in many perspectives: seismological, geochemical, and geomagnetic. Suitable for high-school-level readers.

De Bremaecker, Jean-Claude. *Geophysics: The Earth's Interior.* New York: John Wiley & Sons, 1985. This well-written text is intended for college-level students with some calculus and some physics background. Nevertheless, the author is careful to explain difficult concepts or mathematical statements. Chapter 10, "Magnetostatics," and chapter 11, "The Earth's Magnetic Field," can be read separately from the rest of the book to provide an in-depth survey of geomagnetism, its measurement, and its secular variation. Especially useful are the technical appendices on mechanical quantities, magnetic quantities, data about the Earth, notation, and some relevant mathematics. One of the best treatments available.

Hoffman, Kenneth A. "Ancient Magnetic Reversals: Clues to the Geodynamo." *Scientific American* 258 (May, 1988): 76-83. This article provides a fine update on how paleomagnetic data are providing a new understanding of the geodynamo. A nonmathematical account, with clear graphical representations of the main field, the timetable of magnetic reversals, and the wandering of the virtual (apparent) geomagnetic poles during several important reversals of the Earth's magnetic field. The discussion of how the geodynamo can or could reverse the field it produces is an especially useful summary of ideas of the 1980's.

McConnell, Anita. *Geomagnetic Instruments Before 1900.* London: Harriet Wynter, 1980. This short book provides one of the clearest expositions of the basics of geomagnetism for the lay reader. Includes illustrations of many of the basic early forms of instrumentation, especially European.

Multhauf, Robert P., and Gregory Good. "A Brief History of Geomagnetism and a Catalog of the Collections of the National Museum of American History." *Smithsonian Studies in History and Technology* 48. Washington, D.C.: Smithsonian Institution Press, 1987. This monograph, available in many libraries, has two parts. The first section sketches discoveries in geomagnetism from about 1600 to World

War II, with an emphasis on work done in America. The second section illustrates and discusses more than fifty magnetometers, dip circles, Earth inductors, and other magnetic instruments in the collection of the Smithsonian Institution.

Thompson, Roy, and Frank Oldfield. *Environmental Magnetism.* London: Allen & Unwin, 1986. This book captures the broad range of possible applications of knowledge of magnetism in the study of the Earth that have appeared since the 1950's, from the study of magnetic minerals to biomagnetism. This is an introductory, nonmathematical, college-level text. Although its chapters on basic magnetic principles are valuable, the most unusual feature of the book is the many application chapters. Especially relevant to secular variation are chapter 5, "The Earth's Magnetic Field"; chapter 6, "Techniques of Magnetic Measurements"; chapter 13, "Reversal Magnetostratigraphy"; and chapter 14, "Secular Variation Magnetostratigraphy." The schematic illustrations of apparatus and experiments are another useful feature of this book.

Current Bibliography

Backus, George. *Foundations of Geomagnetism.* New York: Cambridge University Press, 1996.

Jacobs, J. A., ed. *Geomagnetism.* Orlando: Academic Press, 1987.

Subbarao, K. V., ed. *Magnetism: Rocks to Superconductors.* Bangalore: Geological Society of India, 1994.

Cross-References

Earth's Magnetic Field: Origins, 176; Earth's Magnetic Field at Present, 192; Earth's Magnetosphere, 199.

Earth's Magnetic Field at Present

The study of the Earth's magnetic field—its origin, its history, and other characteristics—has vast implications for humanity, ranging from the location of ore deposits to the disruption of communication systems. The Earth is the only planet of the inner solar system with a strong magnetic field, which has implications for the formation of the Earth and the solar system as well as for the existence of life.

Overview

The study of the Earth's magnetic field is a subdiscipline of geophysics, which is the study of various physical characteristics of the Earth. Geomagnetism is the study of the field as viewed over the past several centuries, when measurements were taken of the field. Prior to that time, the study known as paleomagnetism examines various rock layers to determine the field's history. Subdivisions of geomagnetism include rock magnetism, magnetic reversals, and magnetic stratigraphy.

The ultimate source of a magnetic field is a moving electrical charge, which is an electrical current as in the electron flow in home wiring. Approximately 90 percent of the Earth's magnetic field found at any location is produced by electrical currents in the Earth's outer core. A dynamo effect is thought to be the origin of this main field.

The main field is predominantly a dipole field, or a field resulting from two charges (the prefix "di" is derived from the Greek word meaning "two")—in this case, two magnetic charges. A bar magnet has a dipole field because it has a north end, representing one charge, and a south end, representing the other charge. A magnetic field line leaves the Earth's surface in the Southern Hemisphere, arcs over the Earth, and enters the Earth in the Northern Hemisphere. On the Earth's surface, many of these lines, emerging and penetrating at angles from 0 to 90 degrees to the horizontal, make up the dipole field of the Earth. The magnetic south pole of the Earth, which lies in the Northern Hemisphere, is located where the lines penetrate the Earth at 90 degrees, and the magnetic north pole (in the Southern Hemisphere) is where they leave at 90 degrees. The field's strength is 0.6 gauss (the unit of magnetic induction) at the poles and 0.3 gauss at the magnetic equator. (A small magnet has about a 1-gauss field strength.) The difference results from the field lines bunching together at the poles and spreading apart around the magnetic equator. The number of field lines present in a particular area determines the magnetic field strength.

The magnetic poles are not located at the geographical poles of the Earth, which are the points where the imaginary spin axis of the Earth penetrates the surface. They are not stationary; rather, they apparently wander around the polar regions. The south magnetic pole is located approximately 11 degrees from the geographic pole in the islands north of Canada.

Magnetic anomalies contribute another portion of the interior field. They distort the dipole shape of the main field. Some of these anomalies are associated with the outer core. Other anomalies result from rock bodies, with the strongest known located at Kursk in Russia, 400 kilometers south of Moscow. An anomaly can arise from an igneous rock body such as basalt, which has a large amount of the magnetic iron oxide, magnetite, or, for smaller anomalies, from man-made objects such as a plowshare. An important set of anomalies associated with the oceanic ridges are known as the magnetic sea-floor stripes. They support the concept that the Earth's magnetic field has reversed polarity many times in the past and also the concept that plates, or segments of the Earth's outer rock layer, the lithosphere, have moved.

Other portions of the field are external to the Earth and tend to vary rapidly in direction and magnitude with a time period of hours to days. The gravitational fields of the Sun and the Moon cause shifts in the atmosphere of the Earth, which move charged particles within the atmosphere, thus producing a magnetic field that changes with the motion of the Sun and Moon.

The Sun pushes electrons, protons, and, to a lesser extent, other particles, outward from its surface. These particles are collectively known as the solar wind, and they hit the Earth's magnetic field at speeds of hundreds of kilometers per second. Because they are charged as well as in motion, they have their own magnetic fields that interact with the Earth's magnetic field and contribute to it. Normally, a magnetic field extends to infinity, but because of these interactions, the Earth's field has a boundary known as the magnetopause that surrounds the magnetosphere, or the magnetic field of the Earth. The solar wind also changes the shape of the field: The area pointing toward the Sun is pushed in toward the Earth so that the magnetopause is ten Earth radii from the Earth, and the field pointing away from the Sun is elongated into a teardrop shape that is more than one thousand Earth radii long.

Some of the solar wind particles, particularly electrons and protons, are trapped in the Earth's magnetic field. These form the Van Allen belts, which were discovered in the late 1950's by Dr. James Van Allen while he was analyzing magnetic data from satellites. The inner belt is a broad ring, about 3,000 kilometers above the magnetic equator; the outer ring is about 14,000 kilometers above the equator and is much larger in volume. The belt's particles are traveling at high speeds, and if they hit an object, they disturb its atomic structure.

The Sun follows a sunspot cycle, in which the number of sunspots increases and decreases over a period of eleven years. The sunspots are associated with the magnetic field of the Sun. During times of maximum sunspot activity, the Sun is very active, and solar flares erupt from its surface. These flares are large plumes of hot gases traveling along the magnetic field lines of the Sun. Some of these particles travel out from the Sun and hit the Earth's magnetic field, producing magnetic storms that cause wild variations in the Earth's field. They also cause disruptions in various communication networks on Earth as a result of the changes in the Earth's upper atmosphere.

In the late winter and early spring of 1988-1989, many solar flares were produced, and they were so violent that they were off the scale used to rank solar flare intensity. It is at these times that auroras are common, as charged particles from the Sun enter the Earth's atmosphere near the magnetic poles and hit air molecules, causing them to glow. The particles enter near the poles because they are moving parallel to the field and it does not affect them. If they enter farther away from the magnetic poles, they are moving across the field lines, and therefore the field changes their direction of travel so that they are scattered. Auroras were observed in the northern sky as far south as Florida in solar flare events in the late 1980's.

Another external field is a very rapidly changing one: the magnetic field associated with a lightning strike. Lightning is caused by the flow of electrical charges from the ground to clouds or vice versa. Locally, this current produces a very large increase and then decrease to normal field strength. The field can induce electrical currents in metal objects and can cause their destruction as a result of the heating produced by the current. After a strike, wire segments a foot long may be found lying on the ground; the heat caused changes in their structure that caused them to become very brittle so that they easily broke.

These variations are of an external nature, but the internal field also varies, though over a period of tens or hundreds of years. This phenomenon is referred to as secular variation and is caused by changes in the outer core of the Earth, where the Earth's main field is produced. The variation is also linked to the shifting of the magnetic pole position around the geographic pole position. The magnetic pole wanders around the geographic pole along a looping and twisting path, but, recorded over a long period of time, the pole's position averages out to be the location of the geographic pole.

An interesting change in the magnetic field occurred in 1969: a rapid, worldwide change in the field known as a jerk. Geomagnetists still do not understand its cause, and some believe that, rather than a "real" change, it is a glitch in the processing of the data. A small error in a computer program or a malfunctioning component of an instrument can generate faulty data. Scientists repeat experiments and process data by different methods in order to eliminate these difficulties.

In addition to these various field changes measurements of the field's strength since the mid-nineteenth century indicate that it is decreasing at a rate of 5 percent per century. Intensity readings obtained from rock samples reveal that the field peaked at an intensity of one and a half times the present value around eleven hundred years ago, and before that it was one-half the present strength at 3500 B.C. With these changes in mind, scientists cannot predict what the field will do in the future. It may continue to decrease for a few years or hundreds of years and thereafter increase. It may change polarity, as it has been known to have done many times in the past.

Methods of Study

In order to study the Earth's magnetic field scientifically, measurements must be made, as they enable scientists to observe changes in a phenomenon and, therefore, to develop theories about it. In order to determine the field's orientation, scientists obtain two angles and a magnitude. A compass gives one angle, as it measures the horizontal angle between geographic north, once true north is determined for a location, and the needle direction. This angle is called declination. The vertical angle between the horizontal plane and the field line is the inclination. For example, at longitude 80 degrees west and 40 degrees north latitude (the location of Pittsburgh, Pennsylvania), the declination is 9 degrees west of geographic north, and the inclination is approximately 70 degrees from the horizontal into the Earth. In the Southern Hemisphere the inclination is upward. The magnetic equator is located where the inclination is 0 degrees. At the magnetic poles, the inclination is 90 degrees up for the pole in the Southern Hemisphere and 90 degrees down for that in the Northern Hemisphere.

There are two categories for studying the Earth's magnetic field: either on a permanent or on a temporary basis. Around the world, 130 permanent magnetic observatories were established to observe the everyday changes in the magnetic field and to report any significant changes, such as the apparent jerk of 1969, in the scientific literature. Per area, Europe has the most observatories and Asia the fewest. Japan has nine, and Antarctica has twenty-four. A number of others are scattered around the globe on islands. It was at observatories in London and Paris, established centuries ago, that the secular variation of the field was first observed. These early observatories could measure only the vertical and horizontal directions of the field. The horizontal was determined by a compasslike device and the vertical by a small, magnetized rod placed so that it could pivot in the vertical direction.

Starting in the mid-nineteenth century, magnetometers were developed for the measurement of the field's intensity. There are a number of different magnetometers used to measure the field. One is the rubidium magnetometer, which applies the fact that a magnetic field affects the frequency of light given off by an electron moving from a higher to lower energy level around the nucleus of the rubidium atom. The change in the light is proportional to the strength of the magnetic field. The change is measured by the electronics of the magnetometer, and the strength of the field is displayed. In conjunction with the stationary posts, satellites carry magnetometers for the measurement of the field at various heights above the surface, and they provide readings for virtually the entire globe.

The study of the field on a temporary basis is performed on a small area of Earth's surface. In this context, scientists are interested in what the field has to reveal about objects under the surface. A magnetic iron ore deposit affects the magnetic field near it, and thus scientists can discover the deposit's location. In historic archaeology, researchers are interested in determining where to dig for artifacts. A magnetic survey of the area may provide interesting magnetic anomalies worthy of further investigation.

A common magnetometer used in survey work is a proton precession magnetometer. This formidable name belies a rather simple procedure for measuring a magnetic field. A closed cylinder, filled with water and surrounded with coils of wire, is attached by wires to a box containing the electronics and the power supply of the magnetometer. A current is passed through the coil, and this produces a very strong magnetic field in the water-filled cylinder. The magnetic field forces the protons in the hydrogen atoms to align with the field. The field is then removed, but the Earth's weaker field is still present to affect the protons. The protons naturally spin so that it is difficult to change their orientation with a weaker magnetic field; thus, they start to precess around the Earth's magnetic field. (The wobble seen in a spinning top is precession that is caused by the pull of the Earth's gravity on the top.) The proton precesses at a frequency that depends on the strength of the magnetic field. This frequency is measured by the magnetometer electronics, and the strength of the field is displayed. This value is recorded along with the position of the magnetometer on the grid laid out in the survey area. The data are plotted on a piece of paper and patterns of high- and low-intensity field strength are noted. High-intensity areas indicate a buried magnetic object such as iron shot for a cannon. Using this method, the archaeologist can concentrate on areas that have a higher potential for containing artifacts, instead of digging by trial and error, with subsequent savings in time and funds.

Context

When magnetic storms strike the Earth, communication networks, such as radio, are disrupted. When these storms occur, auroras are very prominent in the polar regions, and nature's version of painting with light can be observed. When lightning strikes, radio waves are produced that spiral along the magnetic field lines and bounce into the Southern Hemisphere, where they can be heard on a radio receiver as a "whistler."

The magnetic field also affects cosmic rays, or charged particles moving through space that enter the Earth's atmosphere and even the solid Earth. Some of the particles are prevented from entering the atmosphere because of their interaction with the magnetic field. Scientists are not sure if a decrease in the field would lead to more cosmic rays reaching the surface and possibly producing greater numbers of genetic mutations or even death. Changes in the field strength have been posited as the cause of the mass extinctions that have occurred in the distant past.

Perhaps most important to Earth scientists is the role the Earth's magnetic field has played in lending support for the theory of plate tectonics, which describes the lithosphere as composed of shifting, or moving plates; thus, the continents have shifted position on the globe. Geophysicists have determined that rocks record the position of the Earth's magnetic field for various periods of the Earth's history. The results of their studies provided direct evidence, previously lacking, that the continents have shifted position over hundreds of millions of years and are continuing to do so. The theory of plate tectonics has led to a better understanding of how the Earth operates, how various ores are produced, how mountains originate, why certain areas are good oil producers and others are not, and why earthquakes occur in patterns.

Stephen J. Shulik

Basic Bibliography

Chapman, Sydney, and Julius Bartels. *Geomagnetism.* 2 vols. Oxford, England: Clarendon Press, 1940. Although outdated, this book contains virtually all there was to know about the Earth's magnetic field at the time it was published. It is of value to browse through to gain historic perspective on the discipline of geomagnetism.

Courtillot, V., and J. L. Le Mouel. "Time Variations of the Earth's Magnetic Field: From Daily to Secular." In *Annual Review of Earth and Planetary Science*, vol. 16, edited by G.G. Wetherill. Palo Alto, Calif.: Annual Reviews, 1988. This source covers the geomagnetic field in general and then launches into an in-depth study of its variations, from short-term to very long-term. Very little mathematics, and many figures. At the end of the chapter is a listing of over a hundred references.

Garland, G. D. *Introduction to Geophysics.* 2d ed. London: W.B. Saunders, 1979. Used as a text for introductory geophysics, this book contains in chapter 17, "The Main Field," very readable material on the main field and its generation. Time variations are discussed in chapter 18; chapter 19 covers the external field; chapter 16, methods of measurement. Some equations. Many figures and graphs of interest to the less well informed reader. References are placed at the end of each chapter.

Jacobs, J. A., R. D. Russell, and J. T. Wilson. *Physics and Geology.* 2d ed. New York: McGraw-Hill, 1974. This introductory geophysics textbook is formidable for the average student because there is considerable mathematics in some chapters, but chapter 8, "Geomagnetism," has sections on the present field and contains a minimum of equations but many figures and graphs. Auroras and the magnetosphere are discussed in chapter 9. One problem is the method of reference citation: The author's name and the reference date are placed within the text, which makes for tiresome reading, as there are many citations.

Knecht, D. J., and B. M. Shuman. "The Geomagnetic Field." In *Handbook of Geophysics and Space Environment*, edited by A.S. Jursa. Springfield, Va.: National Technical Information Service, 1985. This source covers the geomagnetic field and its various aspects: terminology, coordinate systems, sources of the field, measurements, the main field, and sources of geomagnetic data. Some sections have no mathematics, but others have a small amount. Many figures help the reader to understand the authors' narratives. A number of references are listed at the end of the chapter. Excellent.

Motz, Lloyd, ed. *Rediscovery of the Earth*. New York: Van Nostrand Reinhold, 1979. As a collection of articles for the nonscientist by scientists renowned in their respective fields, the text makes very interesting reading, augmented with many colorful illustrations. The chapter "The Earth's Magnetic Field and Its Variations" is written by Dr. Takesi Nagata, who has authored hundreds of articles on diverse aspects of geophysics besides the Earth's magnetic field.

Smith, David G., ed. *The Cambridge Encyclopedia of Earth Sciences*. New York: Cambridge University Press, 1982. Chapter 7, "The Earth as a Magnet," contains information about the Earth's present-day magnetic field, geomagnetic field changes, and magnetic anomalies. The term "encyclopedia" does not characterize this publication well, as the book is organized by chapters that are grouped into six parts pertaining to general categories of the Earth sciences. The text is well written at a nontechnical level, with many colorful diagrams and figures. Excellent.

Stacey, F. D. *Physics of the Earth*. New York: John Wiley & Sons, 1977. In section 8.1, "The Main Field," the author provides a short, technical description of the main field that is of interest to the more advanced student. As a textbook for geophysics, it covers many other areas on a technical level.

Current Bibliography

Brown, G. C. *The Inaccessible Earth: An Integrated View to Its Structure and Composition*. 2d ed. New York: Chapman and Hall, 1993.

Fowler, C. M. R. *The Solid Earth: An Introduction to Global Geophysics*. New York: Cambridge University Press, 1990.

James, David E., ed. *The Encyclopedia of Solid Earth Geophysics*. New York: Van Nostrand Reinhold, 1989.

Knapp, Ralph W., ed. *Geophysics*. Exeter, England: Pergamon Press, 1995.

Vogel, Shawna. *Naked Earth: The New Geophysics*. New York: Plume, 1996.

Cross-References

Earth's Magnetic Field: Origins, 176; Earth's Magnetic Field: Secular Variation, 184; Earth's Magnetosphere, 199.

Earth's Magnetosphere

Earth's magnetic field controls the motions of cosmic rays and of charged particles emanating from the Sun, protecting life from their harmful effects. The magnetosphere, the region where Earth's magnetic field is dominant, extends toward the Sun for a distance of about ten times Earth's radius and away from the Sun for millions of kilometers.

Overview

Earth's magnetic field has been used in navigation for centuries. William Gilbert, in the seventeenth century, turned the study of magnetism into an experimental science. Carl Friedrich Gauss, in the mid-nineteenth century, invented improved ways of measuring and describing Earth's magnetic field. In the twentieth century, Sydney Chapman compiled records of measurements of Earth's magnetic field. A true understanding of the magnetosphere's importance and structure, however, first became possible with the United States' launch of Explorer 1 on January 31, 1958. A completely unexpected belt of charged particles, girdling Earth and trapped by Earth's magnetic field, was discovered by James Van Allen, who analyzed the signals sent back from a Geiger counter on board the satellite. These belts were named "the Van Allen radiation belts" in his honor.

Since Explorer 1, myriad spacecraft have explored Earth's magnetosphere, measuring the field's strength and direction and the numbers and energies of the charged particles in it. The Explorer satellites and the Pioneer space probes supplied much of the information scientists now have about the magnetosphere and the interplanetary magnetic field. Practically every scientific space probe or satellite has discovered something new or added to the knowledge gained from previous flights.

The source of the magnetosphere is believed to be electric currents in Earth's molten core, which produce a magnetic field in the same way that a current passing through a loop of wire produces an electromagnet. The strength of Earth's magnetic field changes with time, and measurements of the magnetic fields that became trapped in rocks as they formed have shown that it disappears and then reverses direction over periods of hundreds of thousands of years. Above Earth's surface, the magnetic field may also change over hours, days, or years in response to currents of charged particles.

When charged particles such as electrons or ions (atoms which have lost one or more electrons) move in a magnetic field, they follow corkscrew paths. The center of the corkscrew is the "guiding center," and for a uniform magnetic field, the guiding center moves in the field's local direction, along a magnetic "field line." The field lines of a simple bar magnet may be visualized by placing iron filings near the magnet on a sheet of paper. The field lines converge on the magnet's north and south poles and spread out in between, making a flattened, doughnut-shaped, "dipole" pattern.

The magnetic field near Earth is similar to a dipole field, as if a bar magnet inside Earth were tilted with respect to the axis of rotation and displaced from Earth's center a few hundred kilometers toward the Pacific Ocean. The "north" pole of this magnet is really nearer Earth's south pole, and vice versa, because a magnet's "north" and "south" poles are the north-seeking and south-seeking poles of a magnet used as a compass. Such a compass points to the north and south magnetic poles of Earth, located about 11 degrees in latitude away from the true north and south poles. If a compass needle is suspended so that it may tilt, the "dip angle" of the local magnetic field toward Earth's surface may also be seen.

When a charged particle corkscrews around a magnetic field line, the angle its path makes with the field line (its "pitch angle") increases as it moves into regions of greater magnetic field strengths, until it is moving in a circle perpendicular to the field line and can go no farther in the direction of the field. It has reached its "mirror point" and must now return in the direction from which it came.

The field lines of a magnetic dipole reach out from regions of high field strength near one pole to weaker regions, and then return to strong field regions near the opposite pole. Thus, a particle finding itself corkscrewing around one of these field lines will be mirrored near one magnetic pole, travel back to the vicinity of the other pole and be mirrored again, and so on. High-energy particles can reach farther in toward the pole than low-energy particles, and they may even enter the atmosphere, producing the beautiful auroras, or northern and southern lights. Less energetic particles are trapped on the magnetic field lines outside the atmosphere, and they can only escape by colliding with other particles or by slowly moving across field lines in response to electric fields or changing magnetic fields. As Earth rotates, these trapped particles swing around with the rotating magnetic field.

Earth has two invisible belts of trapped energetic particles, the Van Allen belts. The inner belt, which extends from 1,000 to 5,000 kilometers above the equator, is kidney-shaped in cross section and contains mainly high-energy protons. The outer belt, 15,000 to 25,000 kilometers from Earth, is crescent-shaped in cross section and contains mainly high-energy electrons. Because the particles are trapped in the magnetic field, they cannot easily leave the belts. They pose a danger to astronauts or sensitive electronic equipment orbiting for long periods within the Van Allen belts.

Earth's sun-side magnetic field lines are distorted by the flow of the charged particles in the solar wind, which streams out from the Sun carrying the bent-back spirals of the solar magnetic field (also called the interplanetary magnetic field). Earth's closed magnetic field lines—that is, those which start at Earth and return to Earth—usually extend about 65,000 kilometers toward the Sun. This boundary, the magnetopause, limits the extent of the charged particles trapped in Earth's magnetic field.

Outside the magnetopause is a shock wave, a region where the density and velocity of particles changes drastically over a short distance because of the interaction of the rapidly moving solar wind particles and the interplanetary magnetic field with Earth's trapped particles and magnetic field. Most of the particles in the solar wind flow past Earth around this "bow shock." The magnetopause and its accompanying shock wave fit around Earth like a sock with a golf ball in its toe. Some of Earth's field lines originating near a magnetic pole extend through the magnetopause into the magnetosheath, the region between the magnetopause and the bow shock. It is along these field lines, called the polar cusps or clefts, that some of the charged particles in the solar wind may enter Earth's magnetosphere.

Away from the Sun, the magnetosphere stretches out into a "magnetotail" of nearly parallel field lines extending for millions of kilometers. The magnetic field lines that do not bend around and return to Earth but continue out into the magnetotail, or that extend through a polar cusp into the magnetosheath, are called open field lines. At the magnetic poles, the boundary between the open field lines and the closed field lines is the

Earth's Magnetosphere

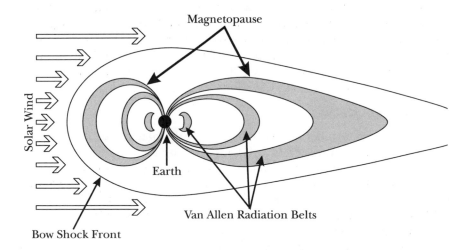

Solar Wind

Magnetopause

Earth

Van Allen Radiation Belts

Bow Shock Front

auroral oval. Within this oval, a current consisting mainly of helium ions—the polar wind—flows out to distant regions of the magnetosphere. Because the auroral oval is the dividing line between field lines where particles may be trapped and those where trapping is impossible, it is where the energetic particles of the solar wind and outer magnetosphere may reach into Earth's atmosphere during auroras. Spacecraft have shown that the auroras are fairly continuous phenomena around the auroral ovals.

In the center of the magnetotail runs a flattened "plasma sheet" of ions and electrons, separating the regions of magnetic field lines originating from Earth's north and south magnetic poles. Currents flow crosswise in the plasma sheet and maintain the magnetic field configuration. At a great distance from Earth, the magnetotail may sometimes undergo a magnetic field line reconnection—or a collapse—whereby it releases a large amount of stored magnetic field energy, which in turn accelerates the charged particles in the magnetosphere. Such an event is called a geomagnetic substorm.

During a substorm, high-energy electrons enter the atmosphere near the auroral oval, producing particularly strong auroras and disrupting the ionosphere and long-range radio communications, which depend on reflection in the ionosphere. At these times, "ring currents" flow around the equator at a distance from Earth of about 12,500 kilometers. Magnetometers on the ground can measure changes in the magnetosphere produced by these currents.

At times of increased solar activity, near the maximum of the solar sunspot cycle, solar flares or other disturbances may send out strong bursts of charged particles in the solar wind which strongly compress the magnetosphere on the Sun side, and the magnetopause may come as close to Earth as 12,000 kilometers. At these times, geosynchronous satellites orbiting at an altitude of about 15,000 kilometers (where the satellite revolution period equals Earth's rotation period) may sometimes enter the magnetosheath and become subject to interactions with solar wind particles. Geomagnetic substorms, most likely when the magnetosphere is compressed by solar activity, may cause geosynchronous satellites to charge suddenly to high voltages. Some communications satellites have been disabled or have had their signals disrupted by internal sparks at these times.

Knowledge Gained

Earth's magnetosphere is made up of Earth's magnetic field and the charged particles controlled by it. The magnetic field is a result of electric currents flowing within Earth's molten core. The field loses some strength and reverses direction every few hundred thousand years, as revealed by magnetization in volcanic rocks; near Earth it is approximately a dipole field, but its structure is modified by electric currents within it.

Charged particles in a magnetic field must follow corkscrew paths around magnetic field lines. These paths are mirrored in regions of high magnetic field strength, turning back particles in the direction from which they came. Charged particles which enter Earth's magnetic field from the solar wind or distant space are prevented by mirroring from reaching Earth's surface, except near the magnetic polar regions, where small amounts of very high-energy particles may reach into the atmosphere. Earth's magnetic poles are displaced from the rotational poles by about 11 degrees in latitude.

Earth's magnetic field has trapped two radiation belts of charged particles, the Van Allen belts. Although these belts would be dangerous to astronauts or electronic instruments orbiting for long periods within them, they pose no threat to life on Earth, because the charged particles are effectively trapped within them by the magnetic field. Charged particles may only be trapped in the magnetosphere on closed field lines, which intersect Earth at both poles. Along open field lines, which originate in the auroral ovals around Earth's magnetic poles and which stretch far into space, never to return, electric currents may flow out of the polar caps and energetic particles from the solar wind and space may enter the ionosphere.

The limit to the closed field lines that extend toward the Sun is the magnetopause, usually about 25,000 kilometers from Earth, where the Sun's spiral magnetic field and the solar wind interact with Earth's magnetic field. Outside the magnetopause is the bow shock, a shock wave where the solar wind is turned aside to flow around Earth's magnetosphere. Between the bow shock and the magnetopause is the magnetosheath, where high-energy particles from the solar wind may enter the magnetosphere.

Away from the Sun, the magnetosphere is elongated into a magnetotail, millions of kilometers long. Open field lines from the magnetotail and from the Sun-side magnetopause carry charged particles down to Earth's auroral ovals. When the magnetosphere is compressed by bursts of charged particles from solar flares or other solar activity, the magnetopause may be pushed to within 12,000 kilometers of Earth, and the magnetotail may "collapse." Geomagnetic substorms, associated with the collapse of the magnetotail, accelerate charged particles in the magnetosphere, producing strong auroras and disrupting long-range radio communications on Earth.

Context

Earth's magnetosphere performs the vital function of protecting living things from the possibly harmful effects of the high-energy charged particles that come from the Sun and from outer space. The Van Allen belts, however, pose dangers for spacefarers, and events on the Sun may disrupt the magnetosphere and damage or disable geosynchronous satellites in orbit around Earth. Furthermore, when space travelers leave the protective field lines of the magnetosphere, they must be shielded against the full intensity of the charged particles found in solar flares.

At times in Earth's history when its magnetic field became very weak and reversed direction, living things may have been subjected to intense cosmic rays emanating from solar flares, which could have led to increased rates of cancer and genetic mutation. Periods of rapid evolution, including some since human beings appeared, may have occurred during those times.

Despite these fluctuations, the magnetosphere acts as a buffer for changes in the solar output of charged particles that can influence Earth. Some theorists believe that changes in the amount of solar particles entering Earth's atmosphere, or changes in the direction of the solar magnetic field as it interacts with Earth's magnetic field, may influence the weather on Earth. Perhaps, they suggest, auroral currents modify polar air currents, leading to periods of drought or the flooding of different regions on Earth's surface. Discovery of a "hole" in the ozone layer over Antarctica has led to renewed interest in the dynamics and chemistry of the polar atmosphere.

It is important to understand the processes that occur in Earth's magnetosphere, because conditions on Earth are strongly affected by those processes. Scientists are gaining an understanding of how the magnetosphere responds to human activities even as those activities are becoming energetic and pervasive enough to have negative effects on it. For example, scientists have studied the possible effects a nuclear war—with its immense outpouring of charged and radioactive particles—would have on the magnetosphere by working with the same technology that would be involved in waging such a war. If enough evidence of the impossibility of winning a nuclear war is discovered, nations may be less likely to begin one. Humans may even be able to prevent or survive natural disasters because of an increased understanding of the environment. Perhaps by changing the composition of the atmosphere and magnetosphere, scientists may someday be able to prevent another ice age or help mankind survive the impact of a giant comet or the explosion of a nearby supernova. It is only since the space age began that the structure of Earth's magnetosphere has been revealed.

Dale C. Ferguson

Basic Bibliography

Akasofu, S. I., ed. *Dynamics of the Magnetosphere.* Dordrecht, Netherlands: D. Reidel, 1980. A collection of contributions to a 1979 meeting of magnetospheric scientists in Los Alamos, New Mexico. Includes up-to-date results of experiments and readable, condensed, technical summaries. This volume is mostly concerned with the disturbed magnetosphere, as during geomagnetic substorms. Well illustrated. Bibliographies and references are included. Indexed.

Akasofu, S. I., and Y. Kamide, eds. *The Solar Wind and the Earth.* Dordrecht, Netherlands: D. Reidel, 1987. Written by experts, this is a collection of chapters about the Sun and Earth and their interactions. Includes sections on Earth's ionosphere and thermosphere. The book is somewhat technical, but nevertheless clear; the history of each subtopic is well treated. Contains lists for further reading.

Allen, Oliver E. *Atmosphere*. Alexandria, Va.: Time-Life Books, 1983. A popular book that covers all aspects of the atmosphere. A good treatment of the history of atmospheric studies. The interested layperson will find the relationship of the magnetosphere to Earth's atmosphere well explained. Contains photographs, illustrations, a bibliography, and an index.

Friedman, Herbert. *Sun and Earth*. San Francisco: W. H. Freeman, 1986. A volume that lucidly describes the Sun's effects on Earth's magnetosphere and ionosphere. Written for the layperson by a pioneer in spacecraft exploration. Of moderate length, the book contains photographs, drawings, and an appendix of references to specific topics.

Hargreaves, John K. *The Upper Atmosphere and Solar-Terrestrial Relations*. New York: Van Nostrand Reinhold, 1979. This textbook delves into the physics of the magnetosphere. It may profitably be read by specialists in the field, other physical scientists, or mathematically inclined students. Includes useful line drawings, numerous equations and references, and questions for study.

Johnson, Francis S., ed. *Satellite Environment Handbook*. 2d ed. Stanford, Calif.: Stanford University Press, 1965. An excellent technical reference that has lost little value with age. It covers the near-Earth environment, from the magnetic field to micrometeoroids, and has a good section on the magnetosphere. Includes graphs, tables, line drawings, and references. Written by many knowledgeable contributors.

McCormac, Billy M., ed. *Earth's Magnetospheric Processes*. Dordrecht, Netherlands: D. Reidel, 1972. A collection of contributions to the 1971 Summer Advanced Study Institute in Cortina, Italy, this work features readable, condensed, technical summaries and details the results of experiments carried on spacecraft. Contains graphs, line drawings, bibliographies, references, and a glossary.

Smith, Robert E., and George S. West, comps. *Space and Planetary Environment Criteria Guidelines for Use in Space Vehicle Development*. Vol. 1. NASA TM-82478. Springfield, Va.: National Technical Information Service, 1983. This authoritative source provides information about the environments of Earth, the Moon, the inner planets, and interplanetary space. Although highly technical, it condenses information relevant to spaceflight near the terrestrial planets into a readable volume of moderate length. Contains tables and graphs, line illustrations, and many references.

Current Bibliography

Brown, G. C. *The Inaccessible Earth: An Integrated View to Its Structure and Composition*. 2d ed. New York: Chapman and Hall, 1993.

Fowler, C. M. R. *The Solid Earth: An Introduction to Global Geophysics.* New York: Cambridge University Press, 1990.

James, David E., ed. *The Encyclopedia of Solid Earth Geophysics.* New York: Van Nostrand Reinhold, 1989.

Knapp, Ralph W., ed. *Geophysics.* Exeter, England: Pergamon 1995.

Vogel, Shawna. *Naked Earth: The New Geophysics.* New York, N.Y.: Plume, 1996.

Cross-References

Earth's Magnetic Field: Origins, 176; Earth's Magnetic Field: Secular Variation, 184; Earth's Magnetic Field at Present, 192.

Earth's Mantle

The mantle is that portion of the inner Earth that lies between the crust and the outer core. It is composed of rocks that are of greater density than those of the crust. The mantle contains a zone in which the rock is under such great temperature and pressure that it exists in a plastic state. It is upon this zone that the major plates of the Earth's crust slide.

Overview

The mantle is that portion of the interior of the Earth that extends from the base of the crust to the boundary of the outer core. This distance is approximately 2,900 kilometers, roughly 45 percent of the radius of the Earth. Since the thickness of the Earth's crust is not uniform, the distance from the ground surface to the upper boundary of the mantle varies significantly. It has been determined that the thickness of the crust in continental areas is approximately 40 kilometers, while in the ocean basins the thickness is only some 5 kilometers.

Evidence for the existence of differentiation, layering within the Earth caused by density differences, was first observed from the study of earthquake waves. In 1906 a seismologist, Andrija Mohorovičić, studied the records of an earthquake that had taken place in Yugoslavia. At a certain distance from the actual focus of the earthquake, two types of earthquake waves were received. Those types were the primary waves, P waves, and the secondary waves, S waves. Although there was only a single shock, a short time later another set of P and S waves were received by the same seismograph. Mohorovičić concluded that the second set of waves were actually reflections of the original waves. When the rock was stressed and broken at the focus, P and S waves were sent out in all directions. The P and S waves initially received by the seismograph traveled by the most direct route. Waves directed downward into the Earth were reflected back from a surface and were recorded. This reflecting surface is called a discontinuity. A discontinuity is a rapid change in the properties of rock with increased depth. Knowing the velocities of seismic waves in the rocks nearer to the surface, Mohorovičić calculated the distance from the surface to the discontinuity. This boundary between the crust and the mantle is known as the Mohorovičić discontinuity, or Moho, named in his honor.

Unlike rocks of the crust, rocks of the mantle have never been directly observed, and therefore only indirect evidence of their nature or composi-

207

tion exists. At one time in the mid-1960's, a project to drill down through the Earth's crust to the mantle was begun. The undertaking was appropriately named Project Mohole. Unfortunately, because of lack of funding, the idea was abandoned.

The greatest source of information on the nature of mantle materials comes from the study of earthquake waves. Since the velocity of seismic waves through the mantle is known, the types of rock that conduct waves at this known velocity are primary candidates for being mantle materials. These rocks are peridotite and eclogite, which both occur to some extent in the crust. Peridotite is a heavy, dark-green rock from the igneous rock family. Igneous rocks are those that have cooled and solidified from a molten state. Peridotite consists of the elements magnesium, oxygen, and silicon. The second possibility, eclogite, is composed of the minerals garnet and jadeite. Eclogite is very similar chemically to basalt, which is a lava commonly associated with worldwide volcanic activity. Since the source of volcanic activity is believed to be in the mantle, eclogite might well be the material that is transformed into basalt as pressures are reduced. Since the crust is far less dense than the mantle, as the molten material moves upward toward the surface, the lithostatic pressure exerted by overlying rock layers would be significantly less.

There is a third type of material that is believed to originate in the mantle. This is the rare substance known as kimberlite. Kimberlite occurs in pipe-shaped deposits and is mined extensively for diamonds. Diamonds are a form of carbon that has been placed under great pressure. These pressures have been calculated, and it has been concluded that pressures of this magnitude could occur only 100 kilometers or more within the Earth. The diamond pipes must have originated within the mantle.

By the use of seismic wave information, it has been shown that the mantle is not uniform throughout. It is assumed that greater depths in mantle rock would produce greater pressures and, therefore, greater rock density. If this is true, seismic wave velocity would also increase. Primary wave velocities in the upper mantle are approximately 8 kilometers per second and gradually increase with depth to a velocity of roughly 8.3 kilometers per second. At this depth, the velocity of the waves begins to drop to a value of somewhat less than 8 kilometers per second. It has been concluded that the rock composition at that depth does not change but that its physical state does. Because of the geothermal gradient, temperatures at this depth and pressure have risen to near the partial melting point of the rock. The material then assumes plastic or flow properties. This low-velocity layer was first identified by Beno Gutenberg in 1926.

According to the theory of continental drift, the Earth's surface consists of pieces called tectonic plates. These eighteen or so lithospheric plates slide over a plastic zone in the mantle. Apparently the low-velocity layer of the mantle is the asthenosphere, the plastic zone upon which the plates move. The asthenosphere has been found to vary significantly in depth from the surface of the Earth. It has been found to be as close as 20 kilometers in depth near an ocean ridge; the asthenosphere averages some 100 kilometers in depth under continents.

Beneath the asthenosphere the wave velocity begins to increase again. Sharp increases at depths of 400 kilometers and 650 kilometers have been noted. Scientists believe that these increased velocities are caused by polymorphism. Polymorphism is a term that means "many different forms." When a rock or a mineral is subjected to increasing temperature and pressure, it may rearrange its internal structure to compensate for this added stress. As a result, the density of the substance is increased, and therefore the velocity of the seismic waves passing through it is also increased. From the 650-kilometer anomaly, the wave velocities gradually increase until reaching the boundary of the outer core, where the S wave is no longer conducted.

Critical to the modern explanation of how the continents move is the topic of heat flow in the mantle. Although the mechanism of heat flow in the mantle is not completely understood, it is known that the Earth's interior heat was left over both from its original formation and from the decay of radioactive elements. It is believed that this heat causes rock to rise in the form of a current from the depths. It cools nearer to the surface and then plunges back deep within the mantle. This process is known as convection and is easily explained with the heating of a beaker of water or a container of a gas. A convection current is the density flow of a liquid or a gas. The hot material is less dense and rises, cooler material moves in to replace the rising material. As surface material cools, it plunges below to be replaced by more rising material. This concept of a convection current is the modern explanation of heat flow in the mantle and of the mechanism that drives continental movements.

It has been known since the nineteenth century that the age of the Hawaiian islands increases from southeast to northwest. In the early 1960's, when the theory of continental drift was becoming more acceptable to Earth scientists, it was suggested that these volcanic islands recorded the movement of the sea floor. It was postulated that there existed a magma, molten rock, source deep within the mantle. This hot spot, or plume, was a long-lived source of magma. During an eruption of the hot spot, volcanic material would be extruded out onto the sea floor. Eventually the material would break the surface of the ocean and an island would be formed. Since the Earth plates were in constant motion, the newly created island would then move away from the hot spot. Further eruption would create new islands and therefore a chain of islands like Hawaii. More than one hundred hot spots have been found worldwide.

Methods of Study

Although the Earth's mantle cannot be directly observed, it can be studied indirectly by various techniques. The primary method of study is by use of seismic waves. These waves may be generated by an earthquake or a large explosion such as that produced by a nuclear test. At the point of rock fracture, energy is released in the form of several types of waves traveling outward in all directions and at velocities that depend upon the density of the conducting medium. The waves that travel deep into the Earth increase in velocity as they encounter denser material. Since the mantle is much denser than the crust, wave velocities in the mantle are higher than those velocities in the crust. The study of velocities of seismic waves helps scientists determine the type of rock through which the waves are traveling. When calculated velocities of waves are compared with known velocities in various types of rock, the subsurface material can be identified. The study of wave velocities can also be used to identify discontinuities in the subsurface.

When an earthquake or a large explosion occurs, energy waves travel outward from the point of energy release in all directions. These energy waves are of three main types: P waves, S waves, and L waves (surface waves). The P waves are similar to sound waves in that they are compressional in nature. The particles in a compressional wave vibrate back and forth parallel to the direction in which the wave is traveling. Primary waves will pass through any type of material. The secondary waves are transverse types of waves similar to the wave form of electromagnetic radiation. The particles of matter that make up an S wave travel perpendicular to the direction of wave propagation. The S waves are considerably slower than P waves, so at a recording station the P waves always arrive first. The L waves are also transverse waves that travel along the surface; these types are the slowest of the three waves.

As these waves travel through rock, their velocity depends on the density of the material. Since pressure increases with depth, and increased pressure results in rocks of greater density, the velocity of seismic waves is in general greater with depth. As waves encounter boundaries between rock layers of different density or composition, some of the waves are reflected back toward the surface. It is this reflection of waves that allows scientists to determine the depth of various parts of the Earth's interior, including the mantle.

Not all waves are reflected at a discontinuity. Some waves are refracted into the newly encountered material. If the material is denser, the velocities are higher. Waves reaching the surface after being refracted through an area of greater density may arrive in a shorter time interval than those that traveled a shorter distance but through a less dense medium.

Another modern method of studying the subsurface was first used in the field of medicine. The CAT (computerized axial tomography) scan is a composite image of X rays taken from a number of different angles. The computer assembles these images into a three-dimensional representation of the particular organ under study. The Earth science equivalent of the CAT scan is known as seismic tomography. Seismic data from all over the world are analyzed. These data provide pictures of the Earth from many different angles. The goal of seismic tomography is to assemble these pictures into a three-dimensional image of the interior of the Earth. Although this technology is in its infancy, it holds promise for future studies.

Context

By studying the change in velocities of waves, scientists are able to determine the nature and the composition of the Earth's mantle. The behavior of the material of the mantle has a direct bearing on much of the activity of the Earth's surface; consideration of the role of the mantle is essential in studying such concerns as earthquakes, volcanism, movement of the continents, and even diamond mining.

A low velocity zone in the mantle is referred to as the asthenosphere. It is upon the plastic rock of this zone that the tectonic plates of the Earth's crust move. It is these moving plates that make the active fault zones and areas of extensive volcanism that exist on the Earth's surface. For example, Southern California is prone to earthquakes because it lies upon two different plates. The city of Los Angeles lies on the Pacific plate while the city of San Francisco lies upon the North American continental plate. As the Pacific plate moves to the north, it rubs against the boundary of the continental plate. The result is an earthquake.

In areas where one plate is moving below another plate, volcanism is common. The plate that is being subducted into the mantle undergoes remelting. This molten material then finds its way up to the surface through cracks and fissures. The result is a volcano. The eruption of Mount St. Helens is an example of this type of action.

The mechanism that causes the movement of the continents upon the asthenosphere is heat. Scientists believe that a convection current operates within the mantle. Hot rock rises into zones of less temperature and pressure, gives off heat, and then plunges below to be re-heated again. This endless motion of rock is a "conveyor belt"-like action and causes the movement of the continents.

Of economic importance is the mining of diamonds. Diamonds are a polymorphic form of carbon and are found in deposits of kimberlite, an igneous rock that originates deep within the mantle. As molten material it works its way to the surface through cracks and fissures, thus, knowledge of the activity of the mantle and its action on the crust aids in finding likely areas for diamond mining.

David W. Maguire

Basic Bibliography

Cailleux, André. *Anatomy of the Earth.* Translated by J. Moody Stuart. New York: McGraw-Hill, 1968. A complete, well-illustrated volume describing the Earth's interior and how it is studied. The book also treats such topics as the origin of the Earth and continental drift. The book is for general readers.

Compton, R. R. *Interpreting the Earth.* New York: Harcourt Brace Jovanovich, 1977. This well-illustrated volume discusses the geology of the Earth's surface. It also offers chapters on tectonics and continental drift. The book is suitable for general readers.

Jacobs, John A., Richard D. Russell, and J.T. Wilson. *Physics and Geology.* 2d ed. New York: McGraw-Hill, 1974. A technical volume covering such topics as composition of the Earth, geochronology, isotope geology, thermal history of the Earth, magnetism, and seismic studies. The text is intended for college-level students of geology or physics. Some differential equations are used in the book.

Phillips, Owen M. *The Heart of the Earth.* San Francisco: Freeman Cooper, 1968. A technical volume covering various topics in geophysics, such as gravitation, mass, earthquakes and seismic waves, volcanism, continental drift, and Earth magnetism. The volume is well illustrated with drawings and numerical tables. The reader should have a working knowledge of college algebra.

Skinner, B. J., and S. C. Porter. *The Dynamic Earth.* New York: John Wiley & Sons, 1989. A well-written, well-illustrated, and very colorful volume on the geology of the Earth. It would be suitable for the college student beginning geology.

Tennissen, A. C. *The Nature of Earth Materials.* 2d ed. Englewood Cliffs, N.J.: Prentice-Hall, 1983. A complete, well-illustrated volume covering the nature and structure of rocks and minerals. The volume would be suitable for the college student of geology, mineralogy, or petrology.

Weiner, Jonathan. *Planet Earth.* New York: Bantam Books, 1986. A colorful, well-illustrated, well-written book describing the Earth and how it is studied. This volume is the companion to the PBS television series of the same name. It is suitable for general readers.

Current Bibliography

Fowler, C. M. R. *The Solid Earth: An Introduction to Global Geophysics.* New York: Cambridge University Press, 1990.

Knapp, Ralph W., ed. *Geophysics.* Exeter, England: Pergamon Press, 1995.

Vogel, Shawna. *Naked Earth: The New Geophysics.* New York: Plume, 1996.

Cross-References

Earth's Composition, 139; Earth's Core, 147; Earth's Core-Mantle Boundary, 154; Earth's Crust, 161; Earth's Differentiation, 169; Earth's Structure, 234.

Earth's Origins

The Earth's early evolution, its subsequent internal differentiation, and its external weathering have left little substantive evidence intact for direct study. Much about the formative processes involved in the planet's origin can be learned, however, from the study of seismology, space exploration, meteoritics, and geomagnetics.

Overview

In order to understand the origins of the Earth, it is necessary to be aware of the sources of the materials from which it is made. It must also be kept in mind that the Earth is a geologically active body and, as such, is still evolving; the final product of the origin processes has yet to be reached. In the cores of stars, hydrogen nuclei are fused together to form the heavier elements. The first product of this fusion, in addition to energy release, is helium. As the amount of helium increases in the star's core, opportunities to form the heavier elements, such as lithium, beryllium, and carbon, arise. For average, sunlike stars, carbon is usually the last major element to be formed before the star flickers out to end its life as a white dwarf and ultimately as a black cinder body. For the more massive stars, the demise is more spectacular. As the carbon state is reached, the core collapses with such force that the star explodes in what is known as a supernova. It is during this time that the heavier elements are produced and thrown out into interstellar space. The expanding shell of gas and other debris from the supernova forms a planetary nebula. This material continues to expand and mix with interstellar hydrogen, eventually forming a large, irregular nebula many light-years across.

According to the nebular hypothesis, the Sun, planets, and other bodies of the solar system formed as the result of the contracting and cooling of such a nebula. The hypothesis suggests that this cloud was composed primarily of hydrogen and helium along with a small percentage of the other naturally occurring, heavier elements. The forces responsible for the initiation of the nebula's contraction, some 5 billion years ago, are not well understood. It is generally agreed that the gravitational effects within the nebula or that of nearby stars must have been instrumental in the process. A rotational component was established that increased its speed with the compaction of the nebula as a result of the conservation of angular momentum. (The same effect is seen on spinning figure skaters. As their arms are drawn in, their speed of rotation increases.) The rotation caused the nebula first to become oblate and eventually to form a flattened disk known as the solar nebula. Most of the solar nebula's mass concentrated at the center of the disk, which, when heated by gravitational pressure, formed the protosun. It has been shown by some studies that perhaps there was a compositional gradient across the nebula that may have given rise to the different planet types.

Not very long after the protosun's formation, temperatures within the remaining disk were significantly decreased. With a decrease in temperature, fractional condensation began—a process in which substances with the highest melting points solidify first into small sand-sized particles. Iron and nickel were the initial elements to solidify, followed by substances, such as the silicates, that form rocky materials. These solidified particles collided with one another and accreted in the small eddylike concentrations of the disk. As the accretion process continued, the resulting masses increased in size so that, within the span of a few tens of millions of years, the protoplanets, their satellites, and other smaller bodies of the solar system were formed.

As the protoplanets and other large mass objects in the accretion disk continued to grow, their gravitational influence grew as well. They could attract greater amounts of disk materials, thus accelerating their expansion while at the same time sweeping the surrounding interplanetary space clean. Solar radiation could then penetrate the distances between the Sun and the planets, bringing light and heat to their still-evolving surfaces. It was during this time that the planets started to evolve in different ways. The Earth, like its inner solar system neighbors, had a relatively weak gravitational field, which, coupled with its now high surface temperature and exposure to the solar wind, caused it to lose significant amounts of the lighter gaseous elements. These gases, such as hydrogen and helium, were vaporized from the planet's surface and blown away from the inner parts of the solar system by the Sun's emanations. The outer planets, beyond Mars, were not so affected because of their cold temperatures, greater masses, and the lessened influence of the solar wind. As a result, they are now recognized as the low-density, giant, gaseous planets with small, rocky cores.

As the Earth continued to grow by accretion, certain processes were under way that would lead to the melting of its interior. Radioactivity levels were much higher in the formative periods of the Earth's history as a result of the fact that many of the radioactive elements with the shorter half-lives had not yet decayed. When the protoplanet Earth was smaller and not as consolidated, the energy released during the spontaneous breakdown of the radioactive elements could escape into outer space. A larger Earth would tend to insulate itself, making it more difficult for the energy released deep within it to reach its surface and to escape. Thus, the insulation effect helped in increasing the growing planet's internal temperature. Another source of heat energy for the forming planet Earth was meteoritic impact. As the Earth attracted more and more material, the influx rate increased tremendously.

As each colliding body struck the Earth's surface, its energy of motion was converted into heat energy. The impact pressures of the larger masses were also transmitted into the Earth, generating heat not only at the surface but also in its depths. There was yet another major source of heat for the Earth's interior: pressure. As the accretion continued, the crushing weight of the overburden on the inner materials caused molecular friction and heat. The combined effect of all these thermal sources was the melting of the Earth's interior. Once the materials of the Earth were in a liquid form, they became mobile, and the process of differentiation could proceed.

The heavier elements, particularly iron and nickel, sank to form the core, while the lighter rock-forming components floated up toward the planet's surface. Also occurring at this time was the release of vapors either trapped in the solid materials or held under pressure in the molten phases or through simple sublimation or vaporization of the frozen and liquid gases. These processes were thus responsible for the generation of the Earth's first atmosphere, which was primarily composed of hydrogen, helium, methane, and ammonia. The fate of this first atmosphere was quickly evident. The hydrogen and helium were swiftly lost to outer space because of insufficient gravity, while the other gases were chemically altered in the harsh environment of the rapidly evolving planet's surface. The segregation process is an ongoing one for the Earth, but on a greatly reduced scale. As a result of differentiation, the interior structure of the Earth consists of concentric spheres, or shells, made of materials possessing different physical and chemical properties. It has also been proposed that the Earth went through a two-stage accretion process in which first 80 percent of the planet accumulated and the metallic core differentiated. During the second stage, the remaining nebular material cooled further, and the outer 20 percent of the Earth accreted to form the lighter element-enriched mantle.

As time went on, the gases that were released rose to the planet's surface in a process known as outgassing. They were expelled at the surface through volcanoes, fissures (large cracks in the crust), and fumaroles (vents expelling gases of steam and sulfurous vapors). Ninety-five percent of the released gas was composed of steam and carbon dioxide and a small percentage of nitrogen. These emissions supplanted the original atmospheric gases already on the Earth's surface, giving the Earth its second-generation atmosphere. As several hundreds of millions of years passed, the atmosphere gradually cooled. The outpouring of gas from the Earth's interior continued, however, and provided an abundant supply of water vapor that would eventually condense to form rain clouds. As the rains fell, the rivers, lakes, and seas were formed. All this water caused large amounts of carbon dioxide to be absorbed from the atmosphere by dissolving. As more gaseous material was taken up by the water, nitrogen remained, eventually becoming the major atmospheric constituent.

Thus all the criteria had been established to bring the Earth through its formative stage to maturity. A phase in its existence is now in place where life as it is now known thrives, where rocks are formed and weathered, and where an evolving sea and atmosphere are present to keep the planet dynamically alive on its surface as well as in its depths.

Methods of Study

Much of what is known about the origins of the Earth is derived from studies of meteorites and comets, space exploration programs, seismology, and geomagnetics. In meteorites and space exploration, scientists have two pristine, unadulterated data sources—early solar system materials to observe and study. Meteorites, Moon rocks, photographs, and other remote-sensing data are being derived from sources that have not been exposed to the destructive forces of chemical and physical weathering that are at work on the Earth's surface. These materials give investigators a glimpse of the composition and element distribution of the ancient solar nebula and of the various types of bodies that were formed from it. Seismology and geomagnetics give researchers clues about the internal structure of the planet. Thus, between the heavenly sources and the plutonic sources, scientists have been able to piece together an acceptable hypothesis of the Earth's origin.

Meteorites have been described as miniature asteroids that have survived the rigors of an encounter with the Earth. Not all meteorites fit into this description; some have been recovered that suggest lunar and Martian origins. All meteorites, however, can be classified into two major categories based on composition: The iron-nickel types have a density of about 7.5 and comprise 25 percent of all the falls; the stony types have a density average of 3.5 and comprise 75 percent of all the falls. When the combined total composition of all meteorites is calculated, the resulting values compare quite favorably with those for the terrestrial planets. The difference in composition lends support to one interpretation of the nebular hypothesis: that all protoplanets differentiated approximately at the same time. It is believed that the nickel-iron meteorites are representatives of a metallic core, while the stony types were derived from the rocky mantle of some embryonic planet that was torn apart early in its formative period.

Comets provide evidence of the more volatile components of the early solar system. They are composed of ice and gravel, remnants of materials blown out from the inner solar system some 4-5 billion years ago by the solar wind but not before a portion was incorporated into the accreting protoplanets.

Data obtained from seismological studies led to the discovery that the Earth's interior is divided into several distinct zones. Observations of the discontinuous transmission of earthquake shock waves near the Earth's surface led to the discovery of the Mohorovičić (Moho) discontinuity zone. Below this zone, wave propagation accelerates. A more fundamental low seismic velocity zone is now recognized below the Moho and is used to define the lower boundary of the Earth's lithosphere. Another seismic discontinuity 2,900 kilometers below the surface delineates where the solid mantle is separated from the fluid outer core. Later work revealed the existence of a solid inner core.

Studies of the magnetic nature of the Earth have also given support to the zonal nature of the planet's interior. Hypotheses concerning the generation of the magnetic field within the Earth take into account an iron-nickel-rich core (not unlike the iron-nickel meteorites) with a solid interior surrounded by a mobile liquid outer part. This combination of phenomena would provide for an electric dynamo that could sustain a magnetic field.

All these disciplines support the nebular hypothesis in its modified state. As more data are obtained, the picture of the Earth's origin becomes clearer and more refined. The story of the planet's birth is not linked to one or two sources, but encompasses all the major scientific disciplines.

Context

An understanding of the genesis of ore bodies and the processes that produce them can be of invaluable use to prospecting and mining technology, perhaps even leading to the synthesis or recycling of important minerals or elements. Planetary engineering would also benefit from such information for the modification or preservation not only of planet Earth but also of the other planets. By knowing the products of various processes in the past, one is better able to predict technological impact on the present Earth. Astronomers are now prepared to look for similar processes elsewhere in the galaxy, not only to find proof of the hypothesis but also to discover and refine existing ideas about the Earth's origins.

Technological spinoffs from the investment in research projects relative to learning about the origins of the Earth also play an important role in the daily routine of life. Instrumentation developed to analyze the various objects involved in solving this mystery has been applied to medical, forensic, and other disciplines requiring sensitive and accurate analyses. Meteorite size and shape studies, made long before the space age, were employed by space engineers in designing reentry vehicles and in studying their aerodynamic properties. Theories about material behavior in zero-gravity conditions similar to those in the solar nebula have led technologists to experiment in outer space in preparing perfect ball bearings and other substances impossible to produce on Earth.

Bruce D. Dod

Basic Bibliography

Beatty, J. Kelly, and Brian O'Leary. *The New Solar System.* 2d ed. New York: Cambridge University Press, 1981. A general overview of the solar system and its components, this book has been organized around comparative planetology. A discussion of the various aspects of the genesis of the planets is scattered throughout. Draws heavily on the results of space exploration and on the interdisciplinary use of science to illustrate many concepts. Contains abundant illustrations, such as full-color photographs, artwork, graphs, and charts. An excellent source of material for the general reader.

Hutchison, Robert. *The Search for Our Beginning*. London: Oxford University Press, 1983. The author addresses the problem of determining the processes involved in the formation of the Earth and other solar system bodies through the analyses of meteorites. Links astrophysics, geology, cosmochemistry, organic chemistry, and astronomy to one another using meteoritics as the common ground. Also, fact is resolved from theory using historical perspectives and recent space exploration results. Contains some fine illustrations, both in color and in black and white. Suggested for college-level readers.

McCall, G. J. *Meteorites and Their Origins*. New York: John Wiley & Sons, 1973. This book serves as a general text for college students as well as for amateur scientists. In addition to discussions on meteorite fall phenomena, petrology, mineralogy, and astronomical phenomena, special sections are included concerning their origins and planetological considerations. Also of interest are discussions of the possibility of life in meteorites and age-dating results. Contains many fine illustrations in the form of graphs, charts, and photographs.

Morrison, David, and Tobias Owen. *The Planetary System*. Reading, Mass.: Addison-Wesley, 1988. Designed as a text for a college course in planetology, this book contains many references to the origins of the solar system and its individual components. Comparative planetology based on space exploration results, meteoritics, and other sources are utilized throughout the text to illustrate some of the evolutionary phases in the development of the planets and other solar system objects. Extensively illustrated.

Ozima, Minoru. *The Earth: Its Birth and Growth*. Translated by J. F. Wakabayashi. New York: Cambridge University Press, 1981. This book traces the genesis of the Earth and its growth while highlighting problems that are rapidly being solved through isotope geochemistry. The past 4.5 billion years are sketched out for the reader in terms that are easy to comprehend. Other hypotheses are introduced and are compared to, or used to amend, the general hypothesis. Suitable for advanced high school or college students.

Smart, William M. *The Origin of the Earth*. 2d ed. New York: Cambridge University Press, 1953. This older reference is included for those interested in the earlier forms of the nebular hypothesis. Quite inclusive of the major concepts while omitting many of the details that would be of interest only to scientists. Divided into three major topics: a general description of the solar system's components, chronology and how it is derived, and a synopsis of other theories. Easily understood by high school and lower-division college students.

Wasson, John T. *Meteorites: Their Record of Early Solar-System History.* New York: W. H. Freeman, 1985. Written as a text for a course on solar-system genesis, this book includes topics on meteorite classification, properties, formation, and compositional evidence linking meteorite groups with individual planets. Several techniques are revealed that describe how researchers use meteorites to determine conditions in the formative periods of the Earth and other planets. Includes many graphs, charts, and illustrations that are closely tied to the subject at hand. Suggested for upper-division college students.

Current Bibliography

Brush, Stephen G. *Nebulous Earth: The Origin of the Solar System and the Core of the Earth from Laplace to Jeffreys.* New York: Cambridge University Press, 1996.

Horton, E., and John H. Jones, eds. *Origin of the Earth.* New York: Oxford University Press, 1990.

Cross-References

Earth System Science, 115; Earth's Age, 123; Earth's Atmospheric Evolution, 130; Earth's Composition, 139; Earth's Magnetic Field: Origins, 176; Life's Origins, 440.

Earth's Rotation

The rotation of the Earth produces the days and nights that provide the daily rhythm of life. Rotation causes the Earth to be flattened at the poles and to bulge at the equator. The Coriolis force, which influences the circulation of the atmosphere and oceans, is a result of this motion.

Overview

The spinning of the Earth on its polar axis is called rotation. The ancient Greeks who studied the motions of the universe considered the Earth to be a motionless body in the center of a geocentric (Earth-centered) universe. An exception was Heracleides (fourth century B.C.) who thought that the Earth did rotate. In general, the Greeks reasoned that a stationary object (in their experience, the Earth) tends to remain at rest, and they had no physical theory of gravitation to account for planetary motions. Later, the work of Nicolaus Copernicus, Galileo, Johannes Kepler, and culminating with Sir Isaac Newton's law of universal gravitation, explained how moving bodies tend to remain in motion. In other words, the Earth's rotational motion is imparted to the objects that move along with the Earth as it rotates and revolves around the Sun. Today, it is commonly accepted that the Earth rotates around a heliocentric (Sun-centered) system.

The polar axis of rotation, which is inclined 23½ degrees from the perpendicular (90 degrees) to the plane of the orbit of the Earth, passes through the center of the Sun and the Earth. The axis of the Earth, therefore, makes an angle of 66½ degrees with the plane of the ecliptic, or path of the Earth. The inclination has an effect on the length of days and nights as the Earth orbits the Sun. The Earth rotates from west to east, or in a counterclockwise direction, thus making the Sun, Moon, planets, and stars appear to move from east to west across the sky. Rotation produces the nights and days of the year and the sunrises and sunsets of each day. People refer to the Sun as rising and setting because it appears that the Sun is moving around the Earth, when in fact, the Earth is moving around the Sun.

The velocity of rotation is 1,038 miles per hour (mph) at the equator; it decreases to 899 mph at 30 degrees latitude, to 519 mph at 60 degrees latitude, and to 0 mph at 90 degrees latitude (the polar axis of rotation). Because the Earth's velocity is 1,038 mph at the equator and because 1 degree of longitude at this latitude equals approximately 69 miles, division of 1,038 mph by 69 miles gives 15 degrees. The Earth then rotates through

15 degrees of longitude every hour; consequently, the Earth's rotation is also important from the standpoint of time.

The Earth is not a good timepiece. Its rate of rotation varies through the course of the year. A day may be defined as the interval of time between successive passages of a meridian, or line of longitude from the North to South Pole, under a body of reference (the Sun or a star). A day with reference to the Sun is called a solar day, and a day with reference to a star is called a sidereal day. (The solar day is approximately four minutes longer than the sidereal day.) Therefore, we have solar and sidereal time. The difference between the two is a result of the Earth's revolution around the Sun in a counterclockwise manner. This motion makes the Sun appear to shift eastward about 1 degree per day. The Earth in fact makes one complete revolution (360 degrees) once every 365¼ days; the rotation velocity varies because of the elliptical orbit of the Earth, which brings it closer to the Sun (perihelion) around January 3 and takes it farthest from the Sun (aphelion) on July 4. The apparent solar day, which is not constant, measures the time interval between successive passages of the Sun over the same meridian. This is the time indicated by a sundial. Mean solar time is the average solar day, or the twenty-four-hour clock day that consists of 86,400 seconds. The solar day would coincide with the Earth's if the Earth were not inclined and moved at a constant velocity as it revolved.

If the Earth were a true sphere, it would have a constant diameter of 7,927 miles and a circumference of 24,901 miles. Because of rotation, however, the Earth is flattened in the polar regions and it bulges at the equator, thus making it slightly elliptical. This form is known as the ellipsoid of rotation, or the oblate spheroid (flattened sphere), and results in objects located at the equator being at a greater distance from the center of the Earth than those at the poles. The centrifugal force developed as a result of rotation is consequently greater at the equator than at the poles. The gravitational pull is 289 times greater than the centrifugal force and is increased slightly at the polar axis due to rotation. Because the Earth is slightly flattened, the length of a degree of latitude changes from 68.70 miles at the equator to 69.40 miles at the poles. The Coriolis force or effect, named after a nineteenth century French mathematician who studied this phenomenon, is caused by the Earth's rotation. It is an apparent force that affects free-moving bodies (wind, water, missiles). For example, if a missile were fired in a northerly direction, it would be seen veering to the right in the Northern Hemisphere because the observer, along a certain meridian, has rotated westward with reference to the missile's path. In the Southern Hemisphere, objects would veer to the left. At the equator, where an object would be farthest from the axis of rotation, the Coriolis deflective force is zero, and therefore free-moving bodies would not be deflected. At 30 degrees latitude, the deflective force is 50 percent greater, and at 90 degrees, at the axis of rotation, the deflective force is 100 percent.

Overall, the rotation velocity of the Earth is decreasing. Astronomers agree that the length of the day is increasing by milliseconds per century, as the rotational velocity is decreasing by that amount. Thus the amount of days in a year has decreased through geologic time. The decrease in velocity is a result primarily of the tidal friction caused by the gravitational pull of the Moon. Evidence for a slowing rotational velocity comes from the study of fossils. Paleontologists have found that living corals produce approximately 365 growth lines on their shells versus about 400 growth lines for Devonian fossil corals about 370 million years old. There are numerous detailed studies that show that the Earth's rotation varies constantly in minute proportions for various reasons. The reasons for these variations include the speeding up of the rotation of the mantle (this is more likely in reference to the asthenosphere, which is part of the mantle that behaves in a plastic manner), the transfer of momentum (motion) between the mantle and outer core, movements of air masses, changes in wind patterns, periodic exchange of angular momentum between the atmosphere and the Earth's mantle, transfer of angular momentum between the atmosphere and the oceans, monsoons, earthquakes, volcanoes, and the plate tectonics (crustal plate movements). The periods of variation on the Earth's rotation vary. There are short-term and seasonal variations attributed to wind velocities. Length of day variations are mainly attributed to atmospheric changes. Decade variations may be attributed to climatic variations, which may be related to volcanism. Length of day changes caused by earthquakes amount to only 1 percent of the total causes of variation. Monthly changes in the length of day result from changes in the distance of the Moon with reference to the Earth because of changes in the Earth's tidal bulge. It is evident from many studies that the Earth's rotational velocity has varied throughout geologic time and continues to change on a daily, weekly, monthly, seasonal, yearly, or even longer-term basis.

It may be assumed that the Earth's axis of rotation points towards Polaris—our present North Star; however, because of the slowing of the Earth's rotational speed, the Earth's axis is becoming more and more inclined from the perpendicular to the plane of the ecliptic. Like a spinning top, as it begins to slow down, its axis begins to tilt and wobble. Because the axis of the Earth's equinoxes precess (shift) by 50 seconds of arc a year along the ecliptic, it takes the axis of the Earth 25,800 years to complete one precession, or wobble. In other words, the rotation axis of the Earth will again point to the same position in the sky in 25,800 years. Changes in the orientation of the Earth's axis as a result of precession cause the polar axis to inscribe a large imaginary upside-down cone in the sky. As the axis points to different parts of the sky, other stars serve as north stars. Because of precession, star charts have to be changed every 50 years. The seasons of the year will be reversed, because as the Earth revolves, the polar axis of rotation will be pointing to a different position in the sky. Superimposed upon the precessional motion are two other motions. One of these small oscillating motions is called nutation, which has a semiamplitude of 9.2 seconds of arc and a period of 18.6 years. This motion is associated with the periodic variation in the angle that the Moon's motion makes with the Earth's equator. The other motion, called Chandler's wobble, has two oscillations. One of the oscillations, the Chandler component, has a period of twelve months. The twelve-month component is a result of meteorological effects associated with seasonal changes in air masses. The second oscillation of the Chandler wobble, the 14.2-month component, is caused by shifts in the Earth's interior mass. Thus, the precession circle is not a smooth, round circle but a squiggly one. These two motions and others caused by various forces affect the Earth's polar motion.

Methods of Study

Scientists have used methods ranging from visual observation to satellites and lasers to fossils to learn about the rotation of the Earth. Visual observations by the early Greeks led them to conclude that the Earth did not rotate. Through the much later contributions of Copernicus, Galileo, Kepler, and Newton, a new physics evolved that explained the planetary motions of the universe. Kepler derived three basic laws of planetary motion. The first two are important with reference to the Earth's rotation. The first law states that the planets move around the Sun in elliptical orbits, with the Sun located at one focus. The second law states that as a planet revolves, a line connecting it to the Sun sweeps over equal areas in equals period of time. The telescope first used by Galileo in astronomical observations allowed scientists to see that heavenly bodies rotate. Telescopic observations showed that other planets were slightly flattened. This led observers to question whether the Earth were similarly shaped. Evidence indicated that the Earth's gravity varied with latitude; when the physical laws of gravity were considered, it became evident that the Earth was oblate in form.

In 1671, Jean Richer, a French astronomer, made time measurements with a pendulum clock both in Paris (49 degrees north) and in Cayenne, French Guiana (5 degrees north) and compared the two. In French Guiana, the clock "lost" two and one-half minutes per day. He attributed this loss to a decrease in gravitational pull toward the equator. It was later determined that, as a result of the Earth's rotation, the polar area of the Earth was flattened and that it bulged at the equator because of centrifugal force. Measurements to confirm the Earth's oblateness were made in the eighteenth century in Lapland (67 degrees north) and near Quito, Ecuador (4 degrees north); it was found that the length of a degree of arc near the equator was less than that in France and even less than that in Lapland. In 1851, the French physicist Jean-Bernard-Léon Foucault hung an iron ball with a 200-foot-long wire—adding a pin at the bottom to make marks in the sand underneath—from the dome of the Panthéon, in Paris. It was observed that the path of the ball moved toward the right. Since the pendulum kept swinging in the same direction, this meant the building underneath the pendulum was rotating. The apparent movement to the right of the pendu-

7:30 A.M.   10:30 A.M.   NOON

3:30 P.M.   7:30 P.M.

Views of South America showing the transition from morning to evening, the result of Earth's rotation on its axis. *(National Aeronautics and Space Administration)*

lum also demonstrated the apparent force called the Coriolis effect. Sundials also help to demonstrate that the Earth rotates as the shadow of the gnomon (stick) moves across the face of the dial. In the 1950's, atomic clocks began to be used to measure time accurately over long periods. When time kept by the clocks was compared to time determined by the rotation of the Earth, new variations in the Earth's rotation were found. An interesting technique used to determine the changing rotational velocity of the Earth through time has been the study of growth lines located between coarse (presumably annual) bands in fossil and modern-day corals.

Until the 1970's, telescopes were used to observe stars to determine length of day and polar motion. This technique was limited by bending of starlight by the atmosphere. New techniques used to determine length of day and polar motion involve the use of satellites and lasers. One method called Lunar Laser Ranging (LLR) involves the emission of light pulses from a laser on Earth to reflectors left on the Moon by Apollo and Soviet spacecraft. The returning pulses of light are received by a telescope. The total travel time is calculated to determine the Earth-to-Moon distance. By observing the time the Moon takes to cross a meridian during successive passages, this method has provided very good length-of-day measurements. Another technique involves the use of the Laser Geodynamics Satellite

(Lageos). This satellite is covered by prisms that reflect light from pulsed lasers on Earth. Again, the returned beam is received by a telescope and the round-trip travel time is used to infer the one-way distance from the Earth to the satellite. Scientists hope that this method, which includes a network of stations on Earth, will be able to tell something about the yearly movement of crustal plates, which is believed to cause variations in the Earth's rotation. A very accurate technique known as Very-Long Baseline Interferometry (VLBI) is also being used to plot continental drifts as well as variations in Earth's rotation and the position of the poles. In this method, radio signals (typically quasars) from space are received by two radio antennas and are tape-recorded. The tapes are compared, and the difference in arrival times of the signals at the two radio antennas is used to calculate the distance between the two. If the distance between the two antennas has changed, the crustal plates have moved. All of these techniques are important to scientists who need accurate data about the Earth's rotation. The layperson, however, needs only to observe the daily east-west motion of the Sun, Moon, planets, and stars as the world turns from west to east on its polar axis of rotation.

Context

The spinning of the Earth on its polar axis once every twenty-four hours is very much a part of the daily rhythm of life. It gives to human reckoning days and nights and daily time references; because there are 360 degrees in a circle and the Earth rotates through 15 degrees of longitude every hour, there are 24 time zones in the world. The rotational velocity of the Earth varies from day to day because of the elliptical orbit of the Earth around the Sun. For day-to-day time-keeping purposes, however, the mean solar day of twenty-four clock hours is used. In addition, the shape of the Earth is affected by the Earth's rotation. The spinning of the Earth on its polar axis sets up a centrifugal force that causes the Earth to bulge at the equator and the polar area to be flattened. Because of this phenomenon, the distance to the center of gravity in the Earth varies, and the gravitational pull on objects on the Earth also varies: Objects weigh slightly less in the equatorial area than in the polar regions of the world. The Coriolis force, an apparent force caused by the rotation of the Earth, causes free-moving bodies to be deflected to the right in the Northern Hemisphere and to the left in the Southern Hemisphere. This force controls the circulation patterns of the atmosphere and the oceans. It governs the direction of winds as they flow in or out of pressure systems. It has set up the wind belts of the world. The force also influences the flow of water, as evidenced by the ocean currents of the world. Consequently, these patterns help to produce certain climatic regions along the borders of continents. Because the Earth's crust is broken into several moving crustal plates, it has been suggested that the shape and location of the continents have been influenced by the Coriolis force. The Coriolis force is believed to be important in producing the convection currents in the liquid outer core, which in turn give rise to the internal magnetic field of the Earth.

Roberto Garza

Basic Bibliography

Gould, S. G. "Time's Vastness." *Natural History* 88 (April, 1979): 18. This article summarizes the reasons for the slowing down of the Earth's rotation. It discusses the use of corals as a proof that the length of the day is increasing and that the number of days in a year are decreasing. Suitable for high-school-level readers.

Hoyle, Fred. *Astronomy*. Garden City, N.Y.: Doubleday, 1962. This book traces astronomical discoveries through time. Of particular value to the study of rotation are the chapters on planetary motion and ancient astronomy, Copernicus and Kepler, and the theory of gravitation. An excellent book for anyone interested in astronomy. It includes an index and numerous illustrations.

King-Hele, D. "The Shape of the Earth." *Scientific American* 217 (October, 1967): 17. This article begins with the historical views of the shape of the Earth. It then discusses, with a good set of illustrations, how satellites have helped scientists to learn more about the shape of the Earth. Suitable for high school and other readers interested in a nontechnical approach.

McDonald, G. E. "The Coriolis Effect." *Scientific American* 186 (1952): 72. The article takes a nontechnical approach to the study of how objects move on the Earth as a result of the Coriolis effect. Suitable for high school readers.

Markowitz, W. "Polar Motion: History and Recent Results." *Sky and Telescope* 52 (August, 1976): 99. This article reviews studies of polar motion. It takes an in-depth look at how the Earth's rotation and precession motions are affected by various forces.

Mulholland, J. D. "The Chandler Wobble." *Natural History* 89 (April, 1980): 134. The article discusses how small movements affecting the Earth's axis may be associated with other terrestrial phenomena. Suitable for high school readers.

Rosenburg, G. D., and S. K. Runcorn, eds. *Growth Rhythms and the History of the Earth's Rotation*. New York: John Wiley & Sons, 1975. This book is a good compilation of studies that can serve as an introduction to the methods of determining the history of the Earth's rotation. The text is suitable for college-level readers not intimidated by technical language. Each study includes a bibliography, and the book is carefully indexed by author, taxonomy, and subject.

Rothwell, Stuart C. *A Geography of Earth Form*. 2d ed. Dubuque, Iowa: Wm. C. Brown, 1973. This book is an introduction to the basic topics of the Earth's shape, map projections, planetary motions, and time and its measurements. It is suitable as a supplement to a college-level physical geography course.

Smylie, D. E., and L. Mansinha. "The Rotation of the Earth." *Scientific American* 225 (December, 1971): 80. This article analyzes measurements indicating that the Earth's wobble may be due to earthquakes. It is a well-illustrated article that can be read by high school readers.

Strahler, A. N. *Physical Geography.* 2d ed. New York: John Wiley & Sons, 1960. This book is written for a freshman college-level course in physical geography. It is an excellent textbook as well as a reference book. Each chapter provides a bibliography. The book has an index and excellent illustrations.

Current Bibliography

McCarthy, Dennis D., and William E. Carter, eds. *Variations in Earth Rotation.* Washington, D.C.: International Union of Geodesy and Geophysics: American Geophysical Union, 1990.

Moritz, Helmut. *Earth Rotation: Theory and Observation.* New York: Ungar, 1987.

Cross-References

Earth-Sun Relations, 107; Earth's Shape, 228; Eclipses, 241; Gravity Measurement, 330; Planetary Orbits, 711; Planetary Orbits: Couplings and Resonances, 718; Planetary Rotation, 725.

Earth's Shape

It has been known for centuries that Earth is not a perfect spheroid. The circumference of the planet is significantly greater at the equator than in the dimension of the meridians, the so-called polar circumference. This oblateness is the result of the substantial centrifugal force generated by Earth's daily rotation around its axis.

Overview

A view of Earth from satellite distance in space would, to the naked eye, suggest that the planet is a perfect spheroid. Yet, finer measurements from space and on Earth itself reveal that the planet is an oblate spheroid, meaning that it is deformed. In other words, Earth is distended at its "waistline," the equator. Earth's flattening at the poles, or its oblateness, is about three one-thousandths in terms of its diameter, which, as measured at the equator, is 12,756 kilometers and, pole to pole, is 12,714 kilometers.

The discovery that Earth is not a perfect spheroid dates to the seventeenth century, when measurements of the distance of 1 degree of latitude (one-ninetieth of the distance from the equator to a pole) demonstrated inconsistencies from one place to another. It eventually became evident that the distance from one latitude to another becomes less the farther from the equator the measurements were taken. Extreme precision in the measurements of Earth's oblateness was not possible until the advent of twentieth century instrumentation.

Earth turns on its axis, making one complete rotation every twenty-three hours, fifty-six minutes, and four seconds, which means that on the equator at sea level, there is rotational velocity of about 1,670 kilometers per hour. At 45 degrees latitude (north or south), however, the surface velocity is approximately one-half that speed, and at the poles there is no rotational velocity. This differential in rotational velocities means that the centrifugal force at work in the low latitudes is great, while in the polar regions the centrifugal force is small or nonexistent. From this differential derives the equatorial deformation and thus Earth's oblate spheroidal shape.

It is necessary at this point to consider why all planets are essentially spheroidal while the hundreds of objects that comprise the asteroid belt lying between Mars and Jupiter are not, which is known as the principle of gravitational equilibrium. Any object that has density also develops its own gravitational force. When the mass of an object is sufficiently large, it cannot sustain any shape other than spheroidal; the fragments of the asteroid belt are not sufficiently large to have met that requirement. On the other hand, Earth, all the other planets of the solar system, and most of the satellites of planets (the Moon, for example) are indeed spheroids. An object with large mass (density times volume) develops its own gravitational force in a direction downward from the surface of the object. This force results in unit weight or specific gravity; the greater the force of gravity, the greater an object's weight. Only a spheroidal shape will permit physical equilibrium in a large mass in which the forces of gravity exceed the strength of the material that makes up the mass.

One is easily misled as to the rigidity of planet Earth. Its solid lithospheric crust has a thickness that approximates an eggshell in relative dimensions. Therefore, it is understandable that the Earth's "shell" has been broken, warped, and distorted through geologic time and into the present. It also becomes comprehensible that Earth is extremely sensitive to distortion and deformation from forces imposed upon it, upsetting gravitational equilibrium, as in the case of centrifugal force created by rotational velocity, especially in the equatorial latitudes where the velocities are highest.

A comparison of the oblateness of Earth with that of other planets in the solar system demonstrates that centrifugal force from rotational velocity is the principal cause of the Earth's equatorial "bulge" (see table). Oblateness is not directly proportional to the surface velocity of rotation at the planet's equator; the strength or rigidity of a planet's material composition affects the degree of warping. Planets Mercury and Mars, however, each with very slow rotational velocities, have no discernible oblateness and are nearly perfect spheroids. Mars has three times more oblateness than Earth, yet with only about one-half of the rotational velocity. The average density of Mars is about 30 percent less than that of Earth, which suggests that its materials have less rigidity, perhaps accounting for Mars' excessive equatorial bulge.

Planet Shapes and Rotational Periods and Velocities

Planet	Oblateness	Rotational Period	Surface Velocity of Rotation
Mercury	0.0	59 days	10.8
Venus	0.0	243 days	6.5
Earth	0.003	23 hours 56' 4"	1,670.0
Mars	0.009	24 hours 37' 23"	866.0
Jupiter	0.06	9 hours 50' 30"	45,087.0
Saturn	0.1	10 hours 14' 0"	36,887.0
Uranus	0.06	11 hours 00'	14,794.0
Neptune	0.02	16 hours 00'	9,794.0
Pluto	?	6 days 9 hours	128.0

Note: Surface velocity of rotation is expressed in kilometers per hour.

Lesser forces imposed upon Earth also affect the shape of the planet, a prime example being Earth tides. The oceans of the world have two huge bulges, or regions where the ocean surface is relatively high. Sea level rises as the bulge is approached and falls as it is passed. Therefore, two high tides and two low tides are recorded each day. The ocean bulges are caused primarily by the gravitational attraction of the Moon, which slightly counters Earth's controlling force, its own gravitational attraction. The Sun also imposes an attraction, although less than that of the Moon. When both the Sun and the Moon are positioned in line with the Earth, the oceans display the highest tides, as the negative attractions of both bodies are imposed collectively. The solid Earth distorts very slightly from the same external force imposed by the Moon and the Sun, but the distortion is so slight as to render great difficulties in actual measurement. The cycle of these Earth tides is much longer than that of ocean tides; they are sufficiently long to be called static tides.

Methods of Study

The passing of geologic time has brought startling changes in the phenomena which control Earth's shape. The distance from Earth's surface to the Moon was far shorter than at present, and Earth's rotational velocity was much faster back in geologic time. Therefore, Earth's shape does not remain constant. About 350 million years ago, Earth appears to have had about 405 days in the year. Fossil coral of that age shows microscopic diurnal growth lines, and the year is measured by seasonal changes in patterns. On the basis of 405 days per year, the planet's rotational velocity must have been at least 10 percent faster. Such a rotational velocity would have generated significantly greater centrifugal force, and Earth's oblateness would have been more severe than at present. One can speculate as to what effect that condition might have had on ancient dynamic processes; couple that thought with the Moon's nearer proximity to Earth, which would have resulted in far more severe ocean tides in the Paleozoic era (about 250-575 million years ago). The two phenomena are scientifically linked. It is the Moon's relatively strong negative gravitational attraction on Earth that is believed to be the principal force causing the slowing of Earth's rate of rotation.

Until recently, it was generally assumed that, other than the two tidal bulges, the surface of the oceans represents the smooth curvature of the planet. Geodesists, however, have hypothesized for decades that the ocean surface should theoretically have highs and lows conforming to the peaks and deeps of the ocean floor. Actual measurements in the early 1980's proved those theories to be correct.

It has become possible to map the topography of an ocean surface to a precision of a few centimeters. The instrument used is the satellite-mounted radar altimeter, which makes continuous measurements of the distance from the satellite to the water surface. Assuming the satellite itself maintains

A full view of Earth showing its shape. *(National Aeronautics and Space Administration)*

a consistent orbital path, a perfectly curved ocean surface should reflect an equally consistent distance. The fact is, with wave crests and troughs averaged out, ocean surfaces show substantial deviations from a smooth curve. Major seamounts and suboceanic ridges are clearly represented by corresponding high places of ocean surface. Likewise, the major deep-sea troughs, as are common in the western Pacific, the Indian Ocean, and the Caribbean, reveal themselves with troughs in the ocean surface above. This phenomenon derives from geographic variations in the acceleration of gravity. In the case of a deep-sea trough, for example, the space within the trough is filled with seawater instead of with rock. The density or specific gravity of seawater is slightly greater than 1.0, whereas the density of suboceanic rock is typically about 2.85—which means that the acceleration of gravity at sea level directly over a deep-sea trough is less than normal. A compensating rise in the ocean surface maintains nature's equilibrium.

Context

Earth's inhabitants suffer little or no effect from the planet's distortion. It cannot be observed with the naked eye, and it does not appear to play a role in weather patterns and climate. The principal cause of deformation, however, affects the entire habitability of the planet. The daily rotation of Earth around its polar axis and its 23.5-degree tilt, with respect to the plane of orbit around the Sun, results in the seasons of the year. If the Earth rotated today at the rate it rotated 350 million years ago, days and nights would be 10 percent shorter. An interesting meteorological challenge is to calculate exactly how shorter days and concurrently shorter nights would affect weather, climates, agriculture, and human health. Conversely, were rotation to slow appreciably, as surely it must in geologic time, the effect would be disastrous. The daytimes would be far hotter, and the nighttimes would be far colder because of longer exposure to solar radiation in daylight and longer nocturnal radiation at night. It is doubtful that the agricultural systems of today's society could be sustained.

Earth's daily turn on its axis results in other familiar phenomena. The ocean currents of the Northern Hemisphere always flow clockwise, while those of the Southern Hemisphere flow counterclockwise. Witness the Gulf Stream of the north Atlantic and the Japanese (Alaskan) current of the north Pacific, always turning to the right, while the south Atlantic flow is to the left in rotation. This phenomenon is caused by Earth's west-to-east rotation. If Earth rotated in the opposite direction, the Sun would rise in the west and set in the east, and the phenomenon would also be reversed. The planet's oblateness, however, would be unchanged, as the equatorial bulge results from centrifugal force. That force has no regard to compass direction, deriving as it does solely from the difference in surface velocity of the land surface: very high speed in the equatorial belt, diminishing to zero speed at the poles.

John W. Foster

Basic Bibliography

Dott, R. H., and R. L. Batten. *Evolution of Earth.* 3d ed. New York: McGraw-Hill, 1981. Describes the physical and paleontological evolution of Earth from pre-Paleozoic to the present. Designed as an introduction to the natural history of the planet and to the fossil evidence of the past.

Heacock, John G., ed. *The Structure and Physical Properties of the Earth's Crust.* Geophysical Monograph 14. Washington, D.C.: American Geophysical Union, 1971. Contributors were drawn from pertinent disciplines of geophysics, physics, geochemistry, and geology. Serves primarily as a reference for advanced students of Earth science.

Melchior, Paul. *The Earth Tides.* Oxford, England: Pergamon Press, 1966. A sophisticated treatment of the physical phenomenon of small distortions of Earth resulting from gravitational forces imposed by the Moon and the Sun.

Munk, W. H., and G. J. F. MacDonald. *The Rotation of Earth: A Geophysical Discussion.* New York: Cambridge University Press, 1960. A detailed analytical treatment of the physics of Earth's rotation. Designed for professional geophysicists. Includes discussion of the small fluctuations in rotation as a result of redistribution of angular momentum, thought to be caused by dynamics in the fluid outer core.

Plummer, Charles C., and David McGeary. *Physical Geology.* 4th ed. Dubuque, Iowa: Wm. C. Brown, 1988. An introductory textbook designed for the college student and the general reader. Contains excellent overviews of planet Earth and its interior.

Siever, Raymond. *The Solar System.* San Francisco: W. H. Freeman, 1975. A comprehensive and readable compendium of twelve parts by twelve authors, including part 6, "The Earth." This work is unique in that it could serve as a reference, as a textbook, or simply as reading for the inquiring mind.

Stacey, Frank D. *Physics of Earth.* 2d ed. New York: John Wiley & Sons, 1977. A reference volume on solid-earth geophysics, including radioactivity, rotation, gravity, seismicity, geothermics, magnetics, and tectonics. Carries detailed numerical tabulations on dimensions, properties, and unit conversions.

Current Bibliography

Brown, G. C. *The Inaccessible Earth: An Integrated View to Its Structure and Composition.* 2d ed. New York: Chapman and Hall, 1993.

James, David E., ed. *The Encyclopedia of Solid Earth Geophysics.* New York: Van Nostrand Reinhold, 1989.

Cross-References

Earth-Sun Relations, 107; Earth's Composition, 139; Earth's Rotation, 220; Earth's Structure, 234; Gravity Measurement, 330.

Earth's Structure

Processes that are occurring in the interior of the Earth have profound effects upon the surface of the Earth and its human population. The results of processes operating in the interior include earthquakes, volcanic activity, and the shielding of life-forms from solar radiation.

Overview

Evidence that comes primarily from the study of earthquake waves reveals that the interior of the Earth is not homogeneous. It is instead divided into a number of layers of varying thickness, some of which show a change in composition. The thinnest layer is the outermost one known as the crust. The crust of the Earth varies in thickness from about 5 kilometers under parts of the ocean basins up to about 70 kilometers under the highest mountain ranges of the continents. The rock materials of the crust are composed of a number of different rock types, but if an average continental rock could be chosen, it would probably be best represented by a granite. Granite is an igneous rock, formed by crystallization from a hot liquid known as a magma. It characteristically is rich in the element silicon, which comprises about 68 percent of its composition. The ocean basin areas of the crust, on the other hand, are characterized by an igneous rock type known as basalt. Basalt is not as rich in silicon (48 percent of its composition) but does have a greater abundance of the elements magnesium and iron.

The base of the crust is marked by a boundary known as the Mohorovičić discontinuity, or Moho. In places, the Moho is quite sharp, such as under the Basin and Range province of the western United States. It is marked by a change in density of rock types on either side of the boundary. Density is the weight per unit of volume of materials. Thus, if a cubic centimeter of rock of a granitic composition under the continents and just above the Moho could be sampled, it would weigh 2.9 grams. Rocks below the Moho, however, would weigh 3.3 grams per cubic centimeter. This suggests a change in composition to a denser type of material. It is believed this material below the Moho is probably a rock type known as peridotite. Peridotite is similar to basalt in composition, but the former is richer in magnesium while having slightly less silicon than basalt.

Peridotite is believed to represent the basic composition of the layer of the Earth underlying the crust known as the mantle. The mantle comprises the bulk of the Earth, representing about 80 percent by volume. The mantle is also heterogeneous. In the upper mantle at depths beneath the surface ranging from 100 to 350 kilometers is a zone of less rigid and more plastic, perhaps even partially melted material. This zone has been termed the asthenosphere. The mantle and crust above it, acting as a more rigid unit or plate, are known collectively as the lithosphere. The change in physical properties in the asthenosphere occurs because at about 100 kilometers, temperatures in the upper mantle are close to the melting point of peridotite. Although temperature continues to increase below 350 kilometers, the tremendous pressures at those depths are high enough to keep melting of peridotite from occurring.

The asthenosphere has been suggested to play an important role in changes taking place in the lithosphere above. The theory of plate tectonics suggests that the lithosphere is divided into a number of plates about 100 kilometers thick that are in constant motion, driven by hot, convective currents of material moving slowly in the plastic asthenosphere. The heat rises along plate boundaries marked at the surface by volcanic mountain ranges in the ocean basins known as mid-ocean ridges. The slowly moving currents in the asthenosphere then move laterally away from the ocean ridges beneath the lithospheric plates, perhaps helping to carry the plates above away from the ridges. As they move laterally, these asthenospheric convection currents cool, eventually becoming denser and sinking back downward. The sites where the convection currents sink are also sites where lithospheric plates dive into the mantle, perhaps pulled by the sinking currents. At these sites, marked at the surface by gashes or trenches in the ocean-basin floor, crustal rocks may be carried into the upper mantle as deep as 670 kilometers.

Two other changes in properties occur within the mantle. At 400 and 670 kilometers below the surface, increases in density occur. Although one might suspect a change in composition to account for the jump in density, laboratory studies of rocks under pressure suggest a simpler explanation. The primary constituent of peridotite is olivine. At pressures that exist at 400 kilometers and again at 670 kilometers, there is a change that occurs that causes collapse of the crystalline structure and, as a result, produces a denser mineral compound with the same composition of iron and magnesium silicate. At pressures existing at 400 kilometers olivine converts to the denser mineral compound spinel. At the even higher pressures at 670 kilometers, spinel will convert to yet a denser mineral compound with the same composition, known as perovskite.

Thus, the changes occurring in the mantle to produce the asthenosphere and the 400-and 670-kilometer boundaries or discontinuities are not related to changes in composition but to changes related to temperature and pressure. Recall that crustal materials may be carried downward into the mantle no deeper than 670 kilometers. Although some difference of opinion exists on this point, if it is true, as most believe, it may suggest that the rock below this level is simply too dense for the lithospheric plates to penetrate.

The next layer beneath the mantle is called the outer core. This layer begins at a depth of about 2,900 kilometers beneath the surface and continues to a depth of 5,100 kilometers. There is a large density increase across the core-mantle boundary. At the base of the mantle, density has increased to a value of 5.5 grams per cubic centimeter, compared to about 3.3 grams per cubic centimeter at the Moho. At the top of the outer core, the density is estimated to be 10 grams per cubic centimeter. Iron is the only abundant element that would have the required density at the tremendous pressure of millions of atmospheres at these depths. Thus, the core-mantle boundary represents a composition change from the silicate perovskites of the lower mantle. Pure iron would give too high a density, so an iron alloy has been suggested with silicon or possibly sulfur.

At the pressures and temperatures that must exist at the depths in the outer core, iron compounds would be in a liquid state. Complex currents of metallic iron alloy, generated in the fluid outer core by the Earth's rotation, give rise in some complex and, as yet, poorly understood way to the Earth's main magnetic field. Some of the changes in the Earth's magnetic field, such as a slow westward drift, are a direct consequence of this rotation-generated magnetic field.

The outer core-mantle boundary is a sharp one, but whether it is a smooth, spherical shape or irregular with hills or peaks on its surface is not well known. There is also some evidence from seismology that the lower mantle within 100 kilometers of the core boundary represents a transition zone with a change of properties. It is not known whether this represents a mix of mantle and core material or some other composition that is less rigid than the mantle rocks above it.

The innermost layer of the Earth's interior is the inner core. This region has a radius of about 1,200 kilometers and has a sharp boundary with the outer core. Increasing pressures at these depths within the Earth require that the iron and perhaps nickel of the inner core exist in the solid state. There is some controversy as to whether the inner core has remained relatively constant in size throughout much of Earth's history or has grown at the expense of the outer core.

Methods of Study

Much of what is known about the structure of the interior of the Earth comes from the study of earthquake waves that pass through the body of the Earth. These waves are of two varieties, the primary, or P wave, and the secondary, or S wave. The P wave is the same as an acoustic or sound wave. As the P wave travels through rock material, it causes the material to move back and forth in the line of wave travel, stretching and compressing it. Since the rock is not fractured by this response, or permanently deformed, this is called an elastic response, as with the stretch and release of a rubber band. It can be shown in the laboratory that there is a relationship between the amount of elastic response, or the specific physical property, and the velocity of the P wave. The ability to maintain a fixed shape, or the rigidity of the material, is one of these physical properties, while the resistance to squeezing or a change in volume is another. The S wave, however, which moves material in the path from side to side, is sensitive only to rigidity. Therefore, an S wave cannot travel across a substance that is not rigid, such as a gas or liquid, while a P wave can, but with reduced velocity. It has been found for the interior of the Earth that both P waves and S waves cross the asthenosphere of the upper mantle, but with reduced velocity, suggesting lower rigidity but not a liquid state, since the S wave is propagated through the zone. Therefore, it seems that the asthenosphere may represent a plastic but still solid region.

Elsewhere in the Earth's interior, only the Earth's outer core shows a sharp drop in velocity of the P wave as it crosses the mantle outer core boundary. At this point, the S wave disappears, suggesting no rigidity of the material of the outer core. Since it is known that gases cannot exist at pressures at the depth of the outer core, the material of this region must consist of a liquid.

Still in other locations, the interior of the Earth is marked by increases in velocity for both the P wave and S wave. There is a sharp increase in velocity at the base of the crust. Above the Moho, the P-wave velocities are around 7 kilometers per second, while below it they jump to 8 kilometers per second or more. Below the asthenosphere, the P-wave velocity increases gradually to a depth of about 400 kilometers. At this depth, there is a rather sharp increase in P-wave and S-wave velocities. Studies of wave velocities in rocks under pressure in the laboratory indicate that peridotite is an appropriate choice for upper-mantle rocks. At 400 kilometers, pressures are such that peridotite collapses to form spinel. This change in mineral compounds could account for the increased velocity in 400 kilometers.

At 670 kilometers depth in the mantle, a second discontinuity or increase in wave velocities occurs. Here, pressures may cause a second collapse to produce the yet denser mineral compound, perovskite. Once again, P and S waves passing through a mantle composed of perovskite would show an increase in velocity. Moreover, the velocities for this part of the mantle match those obtained in the laboratories from waves passing through perovskite samples placed under the kinds of pressures found at 670 kilometers. A final increase in velocity may be observed at the outer to inner core boundary. This could be explained by a phase transition from liquid to solid iron. Such a proposal is supported by the reappearance of the S wave in the inner core.

Another way in which the existence of structural boundaries within the Earth can be shown from a study of seismic waves is to examine the behavior of the waves when they encounter the boundaries. Depending on the angle at which the waves approach the boundary, as well as on the properties of materials on both sides of the boundary, a seismic wave may bounce off or reflect from such a boundary, or refract or bend as it crosses the boundary. The same bending occurs when light crosses from air to liquid in a glass.

This can be shown by placing a straight straw in the liquid and looking down along it. The straw will appear bent when it is actually the light wave that has bent. P waves are reflected off the Moho, mantle-core, and outer-inner core boundaries, providing clear evidence that there are sharp boundaries between these layers. Waves have also been detected bouncing off of the 670-kilometer discontinuity.

The bending or refraction of waves yields further evidence. As P waves cross the mantle-core boundary, they are refracted away from the center of the Earth because of the change in density. This lenslike focusing action for waves passing through the outer core leaves a gap on the other side of the Earth where the earthquake waves emerge. This gap is known as the P-wave shadow zone because no P waves will reach the surface in this area. This shadow zone is also evidence of the existence of a liquid outer core.

Advances in computer science have allowed the identification of even subtler details about the Earth's interior. Computerized tomography is a technique used in medicine, in which X rays from all directions are analyzed in a computer to give a three-dimensional picture of the human body. Seismic tomography is an analogous approach that uses seismic waves that travel from earthquakes to seismographs around the world to map the Earth's interior. This includes both P and S waves in the interior as well as the results of the study of surface waves, which can also move rock material at great depths. By looking at the time of travel between two points, scientists are able to compare velocities along different paths. Such an approach has already resulted in maps of slow and fast regions of the mantle that probably represent warmer (less rigid) and colder (more rigid) regions.

Context

The interior of the Earth has profound effects on humans and their environment. The interior acts as a complex great engine. The heat energy released affects the crust of the Earth. This release of energy is the driving force behind plate tectonics that results in the formation and evolution of oceanic and continental crustal rocks. In the process, earthquakes and volcanic activity occur that create hazards for the human population on the Earth's surface. Complete acceptance of the plate tectonic theory could not occur without the discovery of the asthenosphere, which makes the movement of the lithospheric plates more plausible.

The Earth is fortunate to have a magnetic field. Without it, the age of discovery and exploration would not have been possible, for navigation by magnetic compasses allowed voyages across uncharted oceans. Modern-day navigation is equally dependent on the magnetic field. It is now known that the Earth's magnetic field is generated from deep inside in the region of the outer core. Another important implication of the core-generated magnetic field is the changes it undergoes through time. In particular, at rather irregular intervals the magnetic poles switch places between north and south. The details of such a switch are uncertain; however, it is known that the magnetic field decreases in strength. Since the magnetic field shields life-forms on the Earth's surface from extremes of solar radiation, there is some concern for the effect on the human population. Some scientists suspect that genetic changes occur during polar reversal periods that aid the process of biologic evolution. Thus, the surface of the Earth as well as the life-forms on it depend upon and are strongly affected by changes occurring within the Earth, in its mantle and core.

David S. Brumbaugh

Basic Bibliography

Bolt, Bruce A. "Fine Structure of the Earth's Interior." In *Planet Earth*. San Francisco: W. H. Freeman, 1974. An extremely well-illustrated review of how seismic waves have been used to discover and define the various layers of the Earth's interior. This collection of articles from *Scientific American* is written at a general-interest college level. Little background or expertise in mathematics is required.

Bolt, Bruce A. *Inside the Earth: Evidence from Earthquakes*. San Francisco: W. H. Freeman, 1982. This book is written for undergraduate college students in physics and the Earth sciences and for nonspecialists interested in a more detailed summary of knowledge of the Earth's interior. The text is relatively free of mathematics and is clearly and well illustrated. It is a rather concise, up-to-date, and readable treatment of the use of seismic waves to discover and interpret the Earth's interior. A large list of useful references is included.

Cromie, W. J. "Windows to the Earth." *Mosaic* 15, no. 6 (1984): 28-37. The articles in this journal are written for the nonspecialist, providing a very readable review of the latest developments in research of the interior of the Earth. A good summary of seismic tomography.

Heppenheimer, T. A. "Journey to the Center of the Earth." *Discover* 8 (November, 1987): 86-92. A very well-illustrated treatment of planet Earth with color illustrations and clear diagrams. Includes a short treatment of the latest advances in understanding of the Earth's interior, as well as an excellent explanation of seismic tomography. This article describes the development of the relationships between the Earth's interior and its processes and the dynamic changes occurring on the surface of the Earth.

Jeanloz, Raymond. "The Earth's Core." *Scientific American* 249 (September, 1983): 46. This article is geared toward general science and undergraduate college audiences. It is well illustrated with excellent color photographs and diagrams. The references are restricted to a few key ones. Emphasis is on the Earth's magnetic field and on the physical state and chemical composition of the inner and outer core.

McKenzie, D. P. "The Earth's Mantle." *Scientific American* 249 (September, 1983): 67. An excellent companion article to "The Earth's Core."

Again, the color illustrations are excellent and helpful. There is an emphasis on the physical state and composition of the mantle and a strong development of the relationship between processes in the mantle and the dynamics of the crust.

Current Bibliography

Brown, G. C. *The Inaccessible Earth: An Integrated View to Its Structure and Composition.* 2d ed. New York: Chapman and Hall, 1993.
Fowler, C. M. R. *The Solid Earth: An Introduction to Global Geophysics.* New York: Cambridge University Press, 1990.
Knapp, Ralph W., ed. *Geophysics.* Exeter, England: Pergamon Press, 1995.
Vogel, Shawna. *Naked Earth: The New Geophysics.* New York: Plume, 1996.

Cross-References

Earth's Composition, 139; Earth's Core, 147; Earth's Core-Mantle Boundary, 154; Earth's Crust, 161; Earth's Differentiation, 169; Earth's Mantle, 207; Earth's Shape, 228.

Eclipses

Eclipses, occultations, and transits occur when three celestial bodies line up, causing the middle body to block the path of light between those on the ends. Solar and lunar eclipses visible from Earth are spectacular phenomena that have been objects of awe, study, and speculation since ancient times. Once they were understood, they became powerful tools of science which have been and continue to be used to investigate topics as diverse as geodesy and general relativity.

Overview

Eclipses of the Sun and Moon are impressive events. They have captivated people since before recorded history and continue to excite us today. Once considered great omens or portents, they have become among the most powerful means with which science tests theories in a remarkable variety of areas.

A lunar eclipse occurs when the Moon passes into the shadow of the Earth. For this to happen, the Moon must be on the side of the Earth opposite the Sun, so that as the eclipse begins the face of the Moon is almost entirely illuminated by the Sun. Thus, lunar eclipses can only occur when there is a full Moon. Figure 1 shows the geometry of this situation.

Not every full Moon results in an eclipse, since the orbit of the Moon lies in a plane angled about five degrees to the ecliptic plane, which contains Earth's orbit around the Sun and in which the Earth and the Sun always lie. Unless the full Moon occurs just as the Moon is crossing the ecliptic plane, Earth's shadow will miss it entirely and no eclipse will be observed. This fact has been known and used to predict eclipses since ancient times and is the source of the name of the ecliptic plane.

A lunar eclipse is visible from all points on Earth where the Moon is above the horizon and may be either total or partial. During a total lunar eclipse, the entire Moon passes through the Earth's umbra, the total shadow in which Earth blocks light coming from all parts of the Sun. At such times, the previously bright full Moon darkens to a dull reddish glow, illuminated only by indirect light that has been scattered by Earth's upper atmosphere. The amount and quality of this illumination can vary markedly from one eclipse to another, depending on exact atmospheric conditions on Earth. Occasionally, some areas of the Moon can seem less illuminated than others.

Not all lunar eclipses are total. Sometimes only part of the Moon enters the umbra, or the Moon may miss the umbra and pass only through the penumbra. This is a region of partial shadow surrounding the umbra in which Earth cuts off light from some but not all parts of the Sun. An observer on the Moon during this condition would see part of the Sun extending beyond the edge of the Earth. The Moon is slightly dimmed while in the penumbra, but it does not become really dark unless it enters the umbra.

A total lunar eclipse can last several hours. From the time the Moon begins to enter the umbra it takes about an hour for the eclipse to become total. Totality can last up to about 1¾ hours, with another hour required for the Moon to entirely leave the umbra. Earth's shadow is seen to fall first on the edge of the Moon closest to the eastern horizon, and at the end of the eclipse it is this eastern edge that brightens first.

Solar eclipses are somewhat more complex. By coincidence, the Sun and the Moon both have nearly the same apparent size—about one-half degree in diameter—when viewed from Earth. Sometimes the Moon, although actually a much smaller body than the Sun, appears slightly larger, so that when the Moon lines up between Earth and the Sun it entirely (but barely) covers the Sun. This condition is called a total solar eclipse. Figure 2 illustrates the geometry of a total solar eclipse. During solar eclipses the side of the Moon that always faces Earth must be turned directly away from the Sun; thus, solar eclipses can occur only when there is a full Moon. As with lunar eclipses, the Moon must cross the ecliptic plane at the same time as the Earth, or the shadow of the Moon will miss the Earth entirely.

The umbra of the Moon is conical in shape, narrowing to its apex as it nears Earth. Consequently, only a small part of Earth experiences a total solar eclipse at any one time. Because of the orbital motion of the Moon, its umbra sweeps a path across the Earth from west to east at speeds always exceeding 1,700 kilometers per hour. The region within the umbra may be quite small and is never more than a few hundred kilometers across. The maximum duration possible for totality is about 7½ minutes, although the complete eclipse, including partial phases, may take over 4 hours. Because any given solar eclipse is total only for a narrow strip, a given point on Earth will experience a total eclipse only once in three or four centuries.

Slightly more common than total eclipses are annular eclipses. Because both the Earth's orbit around the Sun and the Moon's orbit around Earth are elliptical, the distances from Earth to both bodies vary. Consequently, their apparent diameters change. Most of the time the Moon appears slightly smaller than the Sun. If this is the case at the time of an eclipse, the Moon cannot completely cover the Sun. When the Moon is centered on the Sun, a ring or annulus of the Sun is still visible around it. Thus the name "annular eclipse."

Beyond the region in which a total or annular eclipse is seen, there is an area thousands of kilometers wide in which a partial eclipse, with the disk of the Moon covering part of the disk of the Sun, can be seen.

Never look directly at the Sun or at any solar eclipse without using eye protection manufactured for this purpose. Common sunglasses are insuffi-

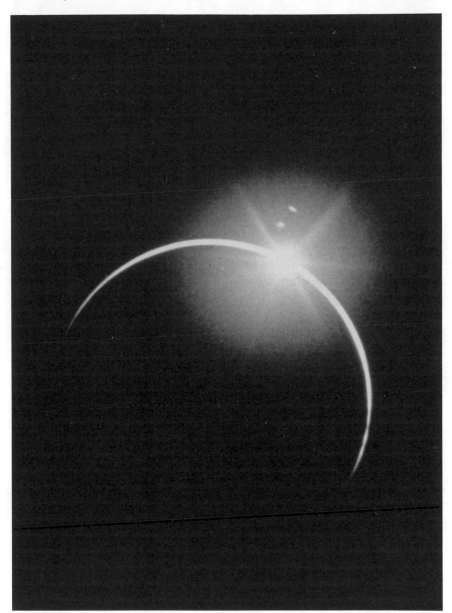

A view of a solar eclipse. *(National Aeronautics and Space Administration)*

cient to prevent injury. Never look at the Sun or any solar eclipse through optical instruments such as telescopes, binoculars, or camera viewfinders unless they are equipped with a filter expressly manufactured for this purpose. Permanent, severe, and painful eye injuries can be instantaneous.

During a total solar eclipse the Moon appears as a dark disk that slowly moves across and obscures the bright, similarly-sized disk of the Sun. Just before the Sun is completely covered, the remaining crescent narrows until it becomes a chain of bright spots along the edge of the Moon. These spots, called Baily's beads, represent a last glimpse of the Sun between mountains on the Moon. At about this time, rapidly moving shadow bands, striations of light and dark a few centimeters across, can be seen on surfaces such as walls. These are believed to be due to atmospheric refraction. The shadow bands and Baily's beads also occur at the end of totality.

The sudden darkness at totality produces uneasiness among some animals, and birds are sometimes seen to go to roost, as at sunset. While the sky overhead turns dark during totality, it remains bright around the horizon as light is scattered in from outside the region of total darkness. The solar corona, a white region of glowing ionized gases, can be seen extending out to about one solar radius around the Sun. Smaller, fiery red prominences can often be seen around the disk of the Moon.

Methods of Study

Ancient peoples, who used astronomical observations to keep track of planting seasons and the like, usually imputed magical or spiritual significance to eclipses and consequently tried to predict them. They did this by watching the position of the Moon against the background of the stars and by recording patterns in the recurrence of eclipses.

A lunar or synodic month is the period from one new Moon to the next, about 29.53 days. Eclipses depend on this cycle and also on the draconic month of about 27.21 days, the time required for the Moon to complete one cycle of crossing and recrossing the ecliptic plane (from south to north and from north to south). Since it is the coincidence of these cycles that produces eclipses, the pattern of eclipses starts again when they return to the same relative phase.

As it turns out, this happens every 223 lunar months, the very simple pattern called the saros cycle, which is almost an integral number of draconic months (241.9986). The cycle lasts 18 years, $11^1/_3$ days (or $10^1/_3$ days if five leap years occur during the interval). The extra $1/_3$ day means that eclipses 223 lunar months apart, although similar, are seen about eight hours later at any given place. In the case of a solar eclipse this means that the path of totality will be about 120 degrees farther west. After three such cycles, somewhat over fifty-six years, eclipses are seen to repeat at almost the same time of day.

These cycles were known to Babylonian astronomers by around the eighth century B.C. and may have been known to some peoples long before that (based on disputed interpretations of a circle of fifty-six pits around the neolithic monument at Stonehenge in England). Knowledge of this cycle enabled the Babylonians to work out in some detail the relative motions of the Sun, Moon, and Earth. The round shadow of the Earth on the Moon during a lunar eclipse was cited by several ancient authors as evidence of Earth's sphericity.

The saros cycle was of limited use in prediction of solar eclipses, because the path of totality is so narrow. Very precise knowledge of the relative motions of the bodies involved was required. This was not possible before Sir Isaac Newton discovered the law of gravity, the laws of motion, and the calculus in the seventeenth century. One of the first tests he applied to his new methods was the calculation of the orbit of the Moon.

Centuries of refinement, both of mathematical methods and of measurements of the position of the Moon, were necessary to achieve modern accuracy of eclipse prediction. Astronomers can now calculate eclipses, including exact times and paths of totality, several years into the future with almost total precision.

Even these calculations are limited by residual uncertainties in the motions of the bodies involved when predictions hundreds of years in the past or future are attempted. With three bodies gravitationally interacting, no exact solution for the orbits is possible, although modern approximation methods are very good. More significantly, the mass within the Earth and the Moon is not uniformly distributed, complicating the calculation. The rate of rotation of the Earth also varies over time. Consequently, comparison of astronomical calculations with historical records is necessary when extrapolating eclipses back into ancient times.

Context

Eclipses of other planetary satellites are observable from Earth. With good binoculars, eclipses of the four largest satellites of Jupiter can be seen as they disappear from view in the huge planet's shadow and reappear as they emerge again. The timing of these eclipses, which seem to occur later than expected when Jupiter is farthest from Earth and earlier when it is nearest, enabled the Danish astronomer Ole Rømer to determine the speed of light in 1675.

On rare occasions it is possible to witness from Earth the transit of Venus or Mercury across the face of the Sun. When this happens, the planets appear like small, black dots moving across the Sun. Like all eclipse observations, the timing and measurement of such transits are very helpful in refining the calculated orbits of the bodies involved.

The term "occultation" is used to describe an apparently large body moving in front of an apparently smaller one. The Moon frequently occults bright stars, which are seen to wink out instantly when touched by the limb of the Moon. The Moon also occasionally occults planets, and on rarer occasions planets are seen to occult bright stars. Astronomers observing the occultation of a bright star by Uranus in 1977, hoping to determine the planet's diameter more precisely, were surprised when the star faded and brightened several times before being occulted. The astronomers had discovered the ring system of Uranus.

Another, related phenomenon is that of eclipsing binary stars. Some of the stars seen in the sky are in fact groups of two or more stars orbiting about

A full solar eclipse. *(National Aeronautics and Space Administration)*

one another. If the Earth lies near the plane of their orbit, the system is seen to vary in brightness as the stars alternately block each other from Earth's view. By observing these variations in brightness and spectrum, astronomers can determine the separate characteristics of the stars and study their interactions.

Eclipses, especially lunar eclipses and those of the satellites of Jupiter, enabled explorers to map the Earth. Although latitudes can be determined easily by astronomical measurements, even with a sextant from the deck of a ship, longitudes cannot be determined astronomically without a time reference. Since eclipses can be observed simultaneously at points far apart, they provide such a time reference and permit the construction of accurate maps.

Solar eclipses have helped resolve some of the most important questions in science. They provide a unique opportunity for observing the Sun and its environment such as its corona and prominences, which, before the development of modern instruments, were otherwise hidden by the brightness of the Sun. Just before totality, only the atmosphere of the Sun is visible, and a flash spectrogram can be made to study this atmosphere's composition. The element helium was first discovered in this way during an eclipse in 1868.

One of the most important eclipse experiments was carried out in 1918. In 1915, Albert Einstein had published his then-controversial general theory of relativity. One of its predictions was that light passing by a massive object, such as the Sun, would be deflected by gravity. By photographing stars close to the Sun during a total eclipse, astronomers verified the theory, which has since stood up to all other observational tests.

Modern instruments, including spacecraft and coronagraphs, can perform many of the observations of the Sun and Moon which at one time could only be performed during some eclipses. Thus, during every eclipse instruments of all types and sizes, professional and amateur, are pointed upward to observe and learn from the most awesome events in the sky.

Firman D. King

Basic Bibliography

Baker, Robert H. *Astronomy*. 7th ed. Princeton, N.J.: Van Nostrand, 1959. Baker's classic astronomy text provides a complete and lucid description of eclipse phenomena, along with related issues in spherical astronomy.

Stevenson, F. Richard. "Historical Eclipses." *Scientific American* 247 (October, 1982): 170-183. This article discusses how historical records and astronomical calculations are compared to resolve questions in both history and astronomy.

Taff, Laurence G. *Celestial Mechanics*. New York: Wiley-Interscience, 1985. Taff describes how orbits are calculated and makes it clear why the process becomes so complicated when long time intervals are involved.

Current Bibliography

Brewer, Bryan. *Eclipse*. 2d ed. Seattle: Earth View, 1991. This book is a good introduction for the general reader to eclipse phenomena and their history.

Zirker, Jack B. *Total Eclipses of the Sun*. Expanded ed. Princeton, N.J.: Princeton University Press, 1995. This book describes how solar eclipses are observed and some of the scientific results that have been obtained from them.

Cross-References

Earth-Sun Relations, 107; Earth's Rotation, 220; Planetary Orbits, 711; Planetary Orbits: Couplings and Resonances, 718; Planetary Rotation, 725.

Europa

Europa is one of the four "Galilean satellites" that orbit the giant planet Jupiter. Only slightly smaller than the Earth's moon, Europa is covered by a relatively smooth layer of highly reflective fractured ice. Tidal forces exerted by Jupiter cause internal heating on Europa that apparently results in the periodic resurfacing of watery "lava" flows, which have over time obliterated most impact craters and other blemishes. Heat flow may be sufficient to maintain a liquid water subsurface layer that could potentially harbor simple life-forms.

Overview

Europa is one of the four large satellites of the planet Jupiter known as the "Galilean satellites" after their discoverer, Galileo Galilei. Jupiter has at least sixteen satellites, but only the Galilean satellites (according to their distance from Jupiter: Io, Europa, Ganymede, Callisto) are large enough to be observed from Earth by small telescopes. With a diameter of 3,138 kilometers, Europa, the smallest Galilean satellite, is slightly smaller than Earth's Moon (3,476 kilometers). By contrast the largest Galilean satellite, Ganymede, measures 5,260 kilometers in diameter, larger than the planet Mercury (4,878 kilometers). Thus, if the Galilean satellites orbited the Sun instead of Jupiter, they would be considered full-fledged planets. Despite its relatively small size compared to its Galilean companions, Europa is nevertheless the sixth largest planetary satellite in the solar system. It is located about 780 million kilometers from the Sun, about 5.2 times the Earth-Sun distance.

Europa orbits Jupiter at an average distance of 670,900 kilometers; its orbital period (time to complete one orbit) is 3.55 Earth days. Its rotational period around its axis is also 3.55 days, which means that Europa always shows the same face toward Jupiter. The other Galilean satellites and our own Moon follow this 1:1 ratio of orbital to rotational period, termed a "synchronous" relationship.

Galileo discovered Europa and two of the other four large Jovian satellites (Io and Callisto) on January 7, 1610, using a crude home-made telescope. At first he believed the tiny points of light in line with Jupiter were small stars, but later he realized that they in fact orbited Jupiter as a miniature solar system. Galileo originally called the moons the "Medicean planets" (after the powerful Italian Medici family) and numbered each satellite with a Roman numeral beginning with the one closest to Jupiter. Europa in this scheme was designated "II." Another observer, Simon Marius (Simon Mayr), who claimed to have discovered the Jovian satellites prior to Galileo (in November, 1609) but was tardy in publishing his results, later named the bodies as we know them today.

The name Europa comes from a Phoenician princess, one of many mortal consorts of the supreme Greek god Zeus, whose Roman name graces the planet Jupiter. The other Galilean satellites are similarly named for mythological characters associated in some manner with Zeus.

The most intriguing aspect of Europa is its unusual and unique surface. Images beamed to Earth in 1979 by Voyagers 1 and 2 space probes showed a relatively smooth ice ball that some scientists compared in appearance to a fractured, antique ivory billiard ball. The planet is covered by a globally encompassing shell of water ice (frozen at −145 degrees Celsius) that gives it an extremely high albedo (light reflectivity). While 64 percent of the light striking its surface (an albedo of 0.64) is reflected back in all directions, rocky surfaces like that of the Moon or Mercury reflect only about 10 percent. Europa's density (3.04 grams per cubic centimeter) suggests that most of the planet is composed of rocky silicate material like the Earth; the icy surface layer, therefore, must be relatively thin. Most estimates lie in the range of 75 to 100 kilometers thick. The surface shows very little topographic relief (nothing higher than 1 kilometer) and displays only a few small scattered impact craters, in dramatic contrast to its highly cratered neighbors, the two outer satellites Ganymede and Callisto. Large craters on the order of 50 to 100 kilometers in diameter are virtually absent on Europa but plentiful on Ganymede and Callisto. Most craters on Europa do not exceed about 20 kilometers in diameter. This suggests that Europa's icy surface is relatively young, indicating that resurfacing by liquid ice floes or other processes have covered over any large craters formed during early, heavy meteoroid impacting in the Jovian system. Estimates of the surface age of Europa range from a high of 3.0 to 3.5 billion years old to more recent estimates of only one hundred million years. The younger age, if true, suggests significant resurfacing of the planet in the later stages of its history.

In 1997 the Galileo orbiter produced images of a large, multiringed impact crater probably buried beneath the ice crust. Evidence for the crater consists of diffuse, dark, concentric, arclike bands and associated fractures that define a structure over 5,000 kilometers in diameter. The presence of this buried crater shows that the rocky surface below the ice layer was subjected to significant impacting early in Europa's history. It further suggests that the ice crust formed at some later time, probably after heavy meteoroid bombardment had greatly diminished.

The most striking aspects of Europa's surface are the mottled, colored terrains and linear fractures that crisscross most of its globe. The mottled terrains, based on color and subtle topographic expressions, are of two varieties: brown and gray. Brown terrains contain numerous pits and depressions from 1 to 10 kilometers in diameter. Several large "plateaus" occur that range from a few kilometers up to a few tens of kilometers wide and up to nearly 100 kilometers long. Some circular depressions, missing raised crater rims, may represent degraded impact craters. Gray terrains are similar to the brown but are generally smoother and less hummocky. The relationship between the two terrains is unknown, but their differences may result from contrasting ages, degree of surface development, or both. The ultimate origin of these mottled terrains is also unknown, but a reasonable hypothesis is that they represent the effects of hydrothermal (hot-water) upwelling, causing heating and expansion of affected crustal areas. The "non-mottled" areas on Europa are very light in color and very smooth in topography. These icy plains contain most of the observed linear surface fractures.

Linear features on Europa's surface may extend for thousands of kilometers. They are classified into three categories: (1) dark triple bands, some containing dark outer bands with a white strip down the center, thought to represent icy geyser deposits erupted along the axis of the fractures; (2)

An image of Jupiter's moon Europa, taken from 1.2 million kilometers (.75 million miles) away. *(National Aeronautics and Space Administration)*

older and brighter lineaments that are crosscut by the triple bands and resemble them in some cases; and (3) very young cracks that crosscut the other two fracture types. Detailed analysis of the orientation of these three fracture types indicates that each type shows a distinct orientation that can be correlated with the relative age of the fractures. The data show that the direction of tidal stresses in Europa's crust has rotated in a clockwise direction over time. This observation has been used to suggest that Europa's rotation is not perfectly synchronous. Over time Europa may rotate faster than the synchronous rate, causing the surface to be progressively reoriented relative to tidal forces.

High-resolution images from the Galileo orbiter show places on Europa resembling ice floes in the Earth's polar regions. Large, angular pieces of ice have shifted away from one another, some rotating in the process, but reconstructions show that they fit together like puzzle pieces. This evidence for motion involving fluid flow, along with the possibility of geyser eruptions, shows that the ice crust has been, or is still, lubricated from below by warm ice, or even liquid water. The source of heating to produce this watery fluid is tidal forces by gravitational interaction with massive Jupiter, along with some escaping heat produced by radioactive minerals in the underlying silicate crust.

Methods of Study

Jupiter and its four largest satellites have been studied using telescopes since Galileo first trained his on the system in 1610. Prior to the advent of interplanetary space probes, telescopic observations resulted in a remarkable trove of data on the Galilean satellites.

For example, in the 1920's the astronomers Willem de Sitter and R. A. Sampson succeeded in obtaining reasonably accurate data on their masses. Their calculations involved observing how each moon disturbed the orbits of the others and by noting the nature of the resonant orbits of the inner three (first described by Pierre-Simon Laplace in the late eighteenth century). These resonant orbits dictate that for every one orbit of Io around Jupiter, Europa revolves two times and Ganymede four. This orbital resonance scheme implies a specific ratio for the masses of the bodies, which assisted de Sitter and Sampson in their calculations.

The diameters of the satellites were not accurately known until star occultation studies in the 1970's (noting how starlight is affected by a passing object) and later spacecraft imaging produced precise values. Prior to that Europa was described by a popular 1950's-era science text as having a diameter of 1,800 miles (2,880 kilometers), only a bit less than the currently accepted value of 1,950 miles (3,138 kilometers).

Although the first Earth-launched space probes were sent to the Jovian system in 1973 (Pioneer 10) and 1974 (Pioneer 11), these spacecraft paid scant attention to the Galilean moons. In 1979, however, our knowledge of these bodies dramatically expanded as images of all four satellites were beamed back to Earth by Voyagers 1 and 2. The first pictures of Europa showed a previously unknown world. They showed a highly reflective, smooth surface mottled by brown and tan patches and crisscrossed by a complicated network of curved and straight lines. Four months later higher-resolution images from Voyager 2 confirmed the presence of even more linear structures, which were interpreted as fractures but having virtually no relief associated with them. In addition to its imaging work, the Voyager probes also made precise measurements of the mass of the Galilean satellites (by analyzing the gravitational affects of the planets on spacecraft trajectories), which, combined with improved size determinations, allowed for more accurate calculations of density. Density, in turn, is used to assess planetary composition.

In 1995 the Earth-orbiting Hubble Space Telescope discovered a thin oxygen atmosphere on Europa. Hubble used its highly sensitive spectrometers to analyze the energy spectrum of light reflected from the planet's surface. Europa's atmosphere is so tenuous that its surface pressure is only one-hundred-billionth that of Earth. It is estimated that if all the oxygen on Europa were to be compressed to the surface pressure of the Earth's atmosphere, it would fill about a dozen Houston Astrodomes.

In late 1996 and again in 1997, another spacecraft, Galileo, visited Jupiter. After launching an atmospheric probe into Jupiter itself, the Galileo orbiter assumed an elliptical orbit that allowed it to make several close passes to all four Galilean satellites. The resolution of the Voyager images, although very good for its day, made it possible to view only those objects no smaller than about 4 kilometers across. In contrast, Galileo swooped down closer than either Voyager craft, and with its more sophisticated cameras it achieved resolutions of around 10 meters per pixel, allowing objects the size of buildings on Earth to be discerned. From these high-resolution images scientists have observed evidence of both tensional (pull-apart) and compression ridges and have documented features like water-ice geysers, possible ice volcanoes, and jumbled, puzzle-like ice flocs. These observations paint a picture of a dynamic planet in which tectonic faulting and flooding by liquid water occur periodically. The dark color of many surface fractures may result from the injection of water or warm ice mixed with darker silicates that well up into the fractures and freeze. Galileo images have generated renewed interest in the idea that a layer of liquid water exists below the ice or existed some time in the recent past.

Galileo also carried a magnetometer to detect the existence of a planet's magnetic field and to measure its strength. During a December, 1996, pass of Europa this magnetometer detected the first evidence of a magnetic field. Ganymede, the next moon out from Europa, also has a magnetic field. Although it is about four times stronger than that of Europa, Europa's field is of substantial magnitude. Combined with gravity data suggesting a dense core, the Europa magnetic measurements indicate the probable existence of a sizable metallic core and a layered internal structure similar to Earth.

Context

The Jovian system has long been of interest to scientists as a possible model analog to the larger solar system of the Sun and planets. In this model Jupiter substitutes for the Sun and the Galilean satellites represent the planets, particularly the rocky planets from Mercury to Mars. The considerable masses and stable orbits of the Galilean satellites suggest that they probably originated along with Jupiter during its formation from the gaseous solar nebula. If so, do these little planets show evidence for having evolved in a parallel manner to the inner planets of the solar system (including Earth)?

In the early 1970's the theoretical planetary scientist John Lewis pointed out that the densities of the two outer satellites, Ganymede (1.93 grams per cubic centimeter) and Callisto (1.83 grams per cubic centimeter), were consistent with condensation of solar-composition gas (the solar nebula), where water ice is a stable compound. He predicted that these two bodies should be composed of about equal parts of water ice and silicate rock, a view generally accepted today. The two inner bodies, Io and Europa, however, have higher densities (3.55 and 3.04 grams per cubic centimeters, respectively) and thus would be expected to contain less in the way of low-density materials like ice (ice density is 1.0 gram per cubic centimeter). In fact, these bodies show evidence of being largely composed of rocky material, with no ice on Io and only a thin crust of ice on Europa. What processes could have produced such a density distribution?

In the early 1950's the astronomer Gerard P. Kuiper suggested that Jupiter had been very hot during its early history. Building on Kuiper's early work, current hypotheses confirm that Jupiter was probably hot enough in its infancy to have forced low-mass, volatile gaseous materials to the outer fringes of the Jovian region, leaving heavier compounds to accrete as planetoids closer to Jupiter. The lighter volatile gas would contain a high proportion of elements that would eventually freeze as ice, compared to denser silicate minerals. These materials would eventually accrete to produce Ganymede and Callisto, while the volatile-poor inner gas would eventually accrete as Io and Europa. Europa, being farther from Jupiter than Io, has more volatiles as ice than Io, which has no ice on its surface. Io probably also lost much of its volatile component as a result of long-term volcanic activity, the result of tidal heating produced by Jupiter's gravitational field.

In a similar fashion the solar system as a whole shows a composition distribution with high-density "rocky" planets near the Sun and more volatile-rich bodies in the outer regions (Jupiter and other "gas giants"). The inner planets (Mercury to Mars) show a similar density distribution. Thus, the Jovian satellite system shows that any evolving planetary system on a scale large enough to have a hot central "star" predictably develops a density distribution where low-density, high-volatile planets dominate the outer regions and high-density "rocky" bodies dominate the inner regions.

The study of Europa is important in terms of its possible role as a site of extraterrestrial life-forms. Images from the Galileo space probe have renewed ideas spawned after the Voyager flybys that Europa may have a globally encircling layer of liquid water beneath its surface ice layer. Where water exists in liquid form on a planet, life as we know it can theoretically evolve. Europa has now joined the ranks of Mars and Saturn's moon Titan as possible sites where primitive life could exist.

John L. Berkley

Basic Bibliography

Beatty, J. K., and Andrew Chaikin, eds. *The New Solar System.* 3d ed. New York: Cambridge University Press, 1990. Chapter 13, "The Galilean Satellites" (by Terrence Johnson), gives a comprehensive overview of these moons based on Voyager data. It is amply illustrated with color images, diagrams, and informative tables. This book is aimed at a popular audience, but it could also be useful to specialists. Contains an appendix with planetary data tables, a bibliography for each chapter, planetary maps (including Europa), and an index.

Greely, R. *Planetary Landscapes.* Boston: Allen and Unwin, 1987. This book concentrates on the nature and origin of planetary surface features. It is packed with excellent monochrome images of planets taken by space probes (mostly Voyagers 1 and 2), diagrams, tables, and maps. Chapter 8 ("The Jupiter System") has a very detailed section on Europa (pages 197-202). Contains an extensive reference section and index.

Morrison, D., ed. *Satellites of Jupiter.* Tucson: University of Arizona Press, 1982. This volume was written for planetary science specialists and is one of the most comprehensive compendiums of Voyager data on the Jovian satellites. It should be a useful reference for any advanced high-school or college student seeking in-depth research material. Contains numerous photographs, diagrams, and tables. Well indexed.

Current Bibliography

Anderson, C. M. "Weird and Wonderful Europa Keeps Her Secrets." *The Planetary Report* 17 (March/April, 1997): 10-14. This article shows very high resolution monochrome images of critical areas on Europa photographed by the Galileo orbiter. These include possible ice volcanoes, areas of recent smoothing, the ringed impact basin, and pressure ridges. Includes discussion of how each feature may have developed.

Beatty, J. K. "Galileo: An Image Gallery II." *Sky and Telescope* 93 (March, 1997): 32-33. This article shows spectacular images from the Galileo spacecraft's encounters with Europa and her fellow moons. Text discusses the nature of features and possible origins.

Cross-References

Extrasolar Planets

Indirect methods of observation have revealed the existence of more than a dozen planets orbiting other stars. These extrasolar planets have surprised astronomers and led to new theories about planet formation, because they differ from the planets in our solar system. This new evidence suggests the uniqueness of our own solar system.

Overview

The discovery of extrasolar planets orbiting sunlike stars has excited the imagination of astronomers and laypersons alike. If it can be demonstrated that planetary systems are a common occurrence among the billions of stars in our galaxy, the possibility of extraterrestrial life in the universe takes on greater credibility. Indeed, the idea that intelligent civilizations may exist on other planets could become more compelling.

Early in the twentieth century spectroscopic evidence from Barnard's star, a nearby red dwarf one-seventh the mass of the Sun, indicated a slight wobble that seemed to imply gravitational interaction by one or two Jupiter-mass planets with decade-long orbits. However, by 1980 further work showed that the wobble of Barnard's star was more likely the result of a companion star too small to observe. The mass of an unseen companion can be estimated from the amount of wobble detected from a visible star.

Double-star systems like Barnard's tend to rotate around their common center of mass in larger orbits than the tiny wobble of a star with a planetary system. Masses between about ten and eighty Jupiter masses usually qualify as brown dwarfs, defined as objects that formed like other stars by gravitational collapse of a dust cloud rather than by accretion from a stellar disk. But they are too small to sustain the nuclear fusion processes that energize the core of most stars.

The first confirmed extrasolar planetary system was discovered in 1991, but it was a far cry from a Sun-like solar system that could support life as we know it. Radio astronomer Alex Wolszczan was observing a millisecond pulsar (PSR 1257+12) that he and Dale Frail had just discovered with the 305-meter Arecibo radio telescope in Puerto Rico. This pulsar, resulting from the collapse of a massive star about a billion years ago, is now a neutron star that spins 161 times each second, generating a radio pulse about every 6.2 milliseconds. However, Wolszczan found that the pulses varied periodically from the usual high degree of regularity of other pulsars.

Analysis revealed two periods in the pulse variations from PSR 1257+12: one lasting sixty-six days and the other ninety-five. Wolszczan and Dale Frail proposed that two Earth-size planets orbit the pulsar, giving it gravitational tugs that move it slightly to-and-fro and causing its radio pulses to arrive slightly earlier and then later than expected. Calculations showed that one planet had at least 3.4 Earth masses at an orbit of 0.36 AU (AU = Earth-Sun distance) and the other at least 2.8 Earth masses at 0.47 AU. By 1994 additional observations revealed a third planet with a period of twenty-three days that had about 0.015 Earth masses at 0.19 AU.

Planet discoveries about sunlike stars began in 1995, revealing two new and unexpected types of planetary objects: small-orbit, hot-Jupiter-type planets and eccentric-orbit, Jupiter-like planets. In October, 1995, Swiss astronomers Michel Mayor and Didier Queloz of the Geneva Observatory announced evidence of a companion object orbiting a star about 40 light years away (51 Pegasi in the constellation Pegasus). A new generation of optical instruments and computers revealed a periodic Doppler shifting of the light from the star, suggesting a tiny wobble caused by a planet of at least 0.46 of Jupiter's mass and a period of only 4.2 days in a circular orbit of just 0.05 AU radius. At this small distance from the Sun the planet orbiting 51 Pegasi has a surface temperature of about a thousand degrees Celsius.

In a 1996 survey of 120 nearby sunlike stars, Geoffrey Marcy of San Francisco State University and Paul Butler of the University of California, Berkeley, used a refined form of Mayor and Queloz's method to discover six new Jupiter-size planets. The existence of the first two planets, announced in January of that year, were discovered from the tiny wobbles of stars in Virgo and Ursa Major, located 46 and 80 light years away, respectively. The planet around the star 47 Ursae Majoris has a minimum mass of 2.3 Jupiter masses with an orbital period of 3.0 years and a radius of 2.1 AU, less than half of Jupiter's distance of 5.2 AU. The planet orbiting 70 Virginis has a minimum mass of 6.6 Jupiter masses and a highly eccentric orbit (0.40 eccentricity) of 117 days at an average radius of 0.43 AU.

The four other planets included three hot-Jupiter planets similar to 51 Pegasi with nearly circular orbits. At 46 light years, 55 Cancri has a planet with mass at least 0.8 that of Jupiter and an orbital period of about 15 days and radius of 0.11 AU. At sixty light years, Tau Bootis has a planet with a minimum mass of 3.87 Jupiter masses, a period of 3.3 days, and a radius of only 0.046 AU. At 55 light years, Upsilon Andromedae has a planet with mass at least 0.68 that of Jupiter, an orbital period of 4.61 days, and a radius of 0.06 AU. Marcy and Butler also announced a possible second planet orbiting 55 Cancri with a minimum mass of about five Jupiters, an orbital period of about twenty years, and a radius of 5 to 10 AU. They have also found some unconfirmed evidence for a second Upsilon Andromedae planet with a period of about 2 years.

Evidence for the nearest planetary system was also announced in 1996 by George Gatewood of the University of Pittsburgh. He has collected

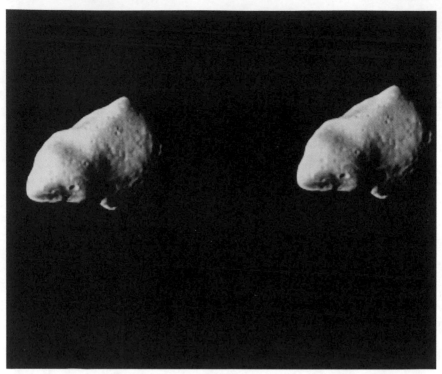

Two views of the asteroid Gaspra. Scientists theorize that life in other solar systems might be dependent on planets as large as Jupiter, which in its present orbit around the Sun sweeps up killer asteroids that would otherwise strike Earth too frequently to permit the development of higher forms of life. *(National Aeronautics and Space Administration)*

photometric data on many of the nearest stars with the 30-inch refractor telescope at Allegheny Observatory. The dim red dwarf star Lalande 21185, the sixth nearest star to the Sun at 8.2 light-years away, appears to have two Jupiter-size planets in orbits similar to those of the gas planets in our solar system. Gatewood analyzed data from fifty years of photographic observations and eight years of photoelectric measurements, revealing tiny accelerations of the star that suggest one planet of about 0.9 Jupiter mass with a period of about 5.8 years in a circular orbit with a radius of about 2.2 AU (similar to the asteroid belt) and a second planet of about 1.1 Jupiter mass with a period of about thirty years in a circular orbit with a radius about eleven AU (similar to Saturn). A third unconfirmed planet may orbit beyond these two Jupiter-like planets. The proximity of Lalande 21185 suggests the possibility of eventually capturing an image of its planets with the Hubble Space Telescope.

Two more eccentric planets were announced in 1997. A group of Harvard astronomers led by David Latham discovered an object in 1988 with a mass of at least nine Jupiters orbiting the star HD 114762 in an 84-day eccentric orbit that varies from 0.22 AU to 0.46 AU (0.35 eccentricity). For eight years this object was classified as the smallest known brown dwarf; but after Marcy and Butler announced the 70 Virginis planet with a very similar eccentric orbit varying from 0.27 to 0.59 AU and a minimum of 6.5 Jupiter masses, the companion of HD 114762 appeared to qualify as a possible planet.

A third eccentric planet has by far the greatest eccentricity of any known planet (0.67). Discovered by Marcy and Butler, it was also independently discovered by William Cochran and Artie Hartzes of the University of Texas at Austin. The planet orbits the star 16 Cygni B, a near solar twin that belongs to a triple star system 100 light-years away. It has a mass of at least 1.5 Jupiters and has a 2.2 year orbit that varies between 0.6 and 2.8 AU, giving it a wild seasonal variation.

Another hot-Jupiter planet orbiting the star Rho Coronae Borealis appears to fill a gap between the very close 51 Pegasi-like planets (less than 0.11 AU) and the 47 Ursae Majoris planet (2.2 AU). It was discovered in 1997 by a Harvard University team of astronomers led by Robert Noyes and has a near circular orbit of radius 0.23 AU, a period of 39.6 days, and a minimum mass of 1.1 Jupiter masses. Given the existence of giant planets with orbits from 0.046 AU (Tau Bootis) to 2.2 AU in a relatively continuous distribution, planet formation theories face dramatic challenges, especially since existing theories predict that Jupiter-size planets cannot form within five AU of their host stars.

Methods of Study

Detecting extrasolar planets from Earth is extremely difficult, requiring a new generation of computers and optical instruments. Planets are about a billion times fainter than their host star, making them virtually undetectable by direct methods. An indirect method involves searching for a tiny wobble in the motion of a star as it and any companions orbit about their common center of mass. Although the gravitational interaction between a star and a planet-size object is too small to observe directly, the radial velocity (back and forth along the line of sight) alternately increases and decreases the wavelength of light from the star, causing an alternating Doppler shift toward the red and then blue end of its spectrum.

The velocity of a star can be determined from the amount of its Doppler shift. The shift in wavelength due to a Jupiter-size planet is only one part in ten million. An absorption cell (consisting of a bottle of iodine vapor placed near the focus of the telescope) absorbs certain known wavelengths of light, producing dark lines in the spectrum that act as a reference for measuring the Doppler shift accurate to within one part in a hundred million. These shifts are recorded by sending light from a star into complex spectrometers consisting of prisms, mirrors, and gratings costing several million dollars.

The periodic variation in the Doppler shift reveals the period of a planet's orbital motion. The velocity of the star and the period of its motion can be analyzed to determine the radius of the orbit (from Kepler's law) and the minimum mass of the planet (from Newton's laws). But the unknown inclination of its orbit allows for a larger wobble than its apparent radial motion and thus a larger possible mass by a factor of about two. The periodic variation in Doppler shift also reveals the shape of the orbit, since a circular orbit produces a perfect sine wave, while an eccentric orbit produces an irregular variation that can be analyzed by computer to determine the orbital shape.

Using these methods, Marcy and Butler have detected radial motions accurate to within plus or minus 3 meters per second, compared to at least the 10 meters per second required to detect a planet. Since Jupiter, which contains most of the mass of the solar system at 318 times the mass of the Earth, causes the Sun to move at a speed of up to 12.5 meters per second, Jupiter-size planets can be readily detected. Most of the new planet discoveries have been based on stars wobbling at speeds between about 10 and 300 meters per second. Planets much smaller than Jupiter cannot be detected with this accuracy, and those with periods of several years require that data be collected over a long enough time span to determine their periodic variations.

Marcy and Butler began collecting Doppler-shift data in 1987 for their survey of 120 Sun-like stars, using Lick Observatory's three-meter telescope; but it was the computer methods used by the Swiss in their discovery of the 51 Pegasus planet that finally yielded results. Their first discoveries resulted from running six computers day and night at the University of California, Berkeley, to analyze data from sixty stars. These methods revealed a variety of planets that shocked astronomers because their orbits were so unexpected. Hot Jupiters and eccentric orbits have initiated a new generation of theories about planetary formation and the uniqueness of our solar system.

Context

The discovery of extrasolar planets may seem at first to offer new hope for the existence of planetary systems like ours that would support extraterrestrial life. But the unexpected nature of these planets has raised new challenges for planet formation theories and new doubts about the possibility that any of them might harbor life. The pulsar planets were probably formed from the remnants of a companion star during a supernova explosion that produced a spinning neutron star, and they are bathed with high-energy radiation that would make life impossible. The other new planets orbit more Sun-like stars but have either extremely small or highly eccentric orbits that make them unlikely candidates for life. Evidence so far seems to indicate that our solar system is highly unusual, if not completely unique.

The strangest of the new planets are the four small-orbit hot-Jupiter planets, including 51 Pegasi, Tau Bootis, 55 Cancri, and Upsilon Andromedae, with short orbital periods (from 3.3 to 14.7 days). These are all massive planets ranging from 0.45 to 3.7 Jupiter masses, all with orbital radii less than 0.11 AU and surface temperatures well above the boiling point of water. Revised theories suggest that they might have formed beyond five AU from their host stars in a dense protoplanetary disk, which then slowed them down and caused them to spiral inward. Such a process would have obliterated any small inner planets congenial to life such as our Earth.

The three eccentric planets, 70 Virginis, HD114762, and 16 Cygni B, have longer periods (84 days to 2.2 years) and larger orbits, but they have huge eccentricities (0.35 to 0.67). New theories suggest that super-Jupiters forming from a dense protoplanetary disk might then interact with each other gravitationally, causing some to be thrown into eccentric orbits or even tossed free of the star. Such eccentric giants would gravitationally disturb and eventually collide with smaller inner planets, again precluding life-supporting planets like Earth.

A few Jupiter-like planets such as those of 47 Ursae Majoris, Rho Corona Borealis, and Lalande 21185 are somewhat more similar to those in our solar system, but they still do not offer the ideal conditions to sustain life. Even though they are in nearly circular orbits and further from their host stars than the hot-Jupiters (ranging from 0.23 AU to 2.2 AU), their huge mass (0.9 to 2.3 Jupiter masses) suggests that they are lifeless gas planets like Jupiter with stormy violent winds and intense surface gravity. They also lie close to the habitable zone of Earth-like planets and would probably disturb the stability of such small planets.

Although current methods can only detect Jupiter-size planets, the orbits so far detected appear to reduce the possibility of smaller life-supporting planets. The majority of the 120 stars surveyed by Marcy and Butler do not appear to have Jupiter-size planets, but they may have smaller undetected planets. However, Jupiter-like planets may be necessary for the development of complex life-forms on smaller planets. About every hundred million years the Earth is struck by asteroids large enough to cause mass-extinctions of species such as the dinosaurs. Without Jupiter in its present stable orbit beyond the Earth to sweep up most of these killer asteroids, this rate would be about every hundred thousand years, too often to permit the development of higher forms of life. Perhaps the most important lesson from extrasolar planet discoveries is the uniqueness of our solar system with its life-sustaining planetary arrangement.

Joseph L. Spradley

Basic Bibliography

Black, David C. "Other Suns, Other Planets." *Sky and Telescope* 92 (August, 1996): 20-26. This is a readable and well-illustrated article with good historical background on the search for extrasolar planets and description of the Doppler method.

Dick, Steven J. *The Biological Universe: The Twentieth-Century Extraterrestrial Life Debate and the Limits of Science.* Cambridge: Cambridge University Press, 1996. Chapter 4 of this book on "Planetary Systems: The Limits of Theory" is a good history of the search for extrasolar planets before 1995, with several illustrations.

Mammana, Dennis, and Donald McCarthy. *Other Suns. Other Worlds? The Search for Extrasolar Planetary Systems.* New York: St. Martin's Press, 1995. This book is a comprehensive history of the search for extrasolar planets through 1995 with several plates, including one describing the January, 1996, discoveries of Marcy and Butler.

Stephens, Sally. "Second Chance Planets." *Astronomy* 24 (January, 1996): 50-55. A good discussion of pulsars and of the discovery of pulsar planets.

Current Bibliography

Goldsmith, Donald. *Worlds Unnumbered: The Search for Extrasolar Planets.* Mill Valley, California: University Science Books, 1997. This is the first book to discuss the new extrasolar planet discoveries in detail, including theories of formation, methods of observation, and possibilities of life. It includes several color plates and an index.

Naeye, Robert. "The Strange New Planetary Zoo." *Astronomy* 25 (April, 1997): 42-49. This article is a comprehensive summary and classification of extrasolar planet discoveries.

Cross-References

Cosmology, 97; Planet Formation, 675; Planetology, 743; The Solar System: Elemental Distribution, 887; The Solar System: Origins, 896.

Extraterrestrial Intelligence

Rapid progress in science and technology justified the initiation, in 1960, of searches for advanced civilizations in the Milky Way. Ten countries have been involved in the Search for Extraterrestrial Intelligence (SETI), a program which uses large radio telescopes to detect signals indicative of intelligent life.

Summary of the Programs

In the spring of 1960, the astronomer Frank Drake used the new 26-meter radio telescope of the National Radio Astronomy Observatory (NRAO) in Green Bank, West Virginia, to conduct the first search for radio signals indicative of life. He looked for signals at the hydrogen emission line from two nearby sunlike stars, Epsilon Eridani and Tau Ceti. Drake made observations for two hundred hours and called the project Ozma (the name of the princess from *The Wizard of Oz* series). His pioneering work marked the beginning of the program known as the Search for Extraterrestrial Intelligence (SETI).

Progress in SETI was slow during the 1960's and the 1970's because the program was viewed with considerable skepticism by the scientific community. As a result, only a few scientists, mostly in the United States and the Soviet Union, continued this important research. Some astronomers conducted radio searches, some wrote books about SETI, and some organized international meetings on the subject.

In 1975, Michael Hart published a paper in which he argued that advanced civilizations are likely to engage in interstellar travel. Thus, according to Hart, space colonies could have become established in all the solar systems of the Galaxy in a time interval of only about 10 million years, a very short period compared to the 10-billion-year history of the Galaxy. Scientists believed that either these space colonies do not exist, or they must be everywhere—including Earth's own solar system. It seems that Enrico Fermi, in the early 1940's, was the first person to make such speculations; for this reason, the apparent absence of extraterrestrials has been called the Fermi Paradox. Although several scholars did offer explanations for the apparent absence of extraterrestrials, these heated debates slowed SETI's progress considerably in the late 1970's and early 1980's.

In 1982, however, there were several important developments. The International Astronomical Union (IAU), which is the world body for astronomical study, established a commission on bioastronomy. Michael Papagiannis was named its first president and Frank Drake and Nikolai Kardashev became the vice presidents. This new IAU commission has grown to include more than three hundred professional members.

Since its origin, the entire SETI program has made tremendous progress. More than fifty SETI projects have been conducted. Most of these projects were radio searches at one or more specific radio lines, such as those of hydrogen (at 21 centimeters), hydroxyl (18 centimeters), and carbon monoxide (2.6 millimeters). The hydrogen line is by far the one most commonly used. Most of the larger radio telescopes of the world and ten of the world's most advanced countries have been involved in these efforts.

SETI radio searches can be divided into three general categories: directed, shared (also known as parasitic), and dedicated. The directed searches are of relatively short duration and are typically conducted at a major university. A characteristic search in this category was Project Ozma. In the Soviet Union, another directed search, one which involved the observation of ten of the nearest stars, was conducted by V. S. Troitskii in 1968. A much larger search program was undertaken in the 1970's involving the simultaneous use of several radio stations around the Soviet Union and occasionally even a Soviet ship equipped with radio telescopes. Researchers sought sporadic radio signals from outer space within the range of 3 to 60 centimeters, their directions being determined from their respective time delays at these widely separated locations.

In the 1980's, the Soviets were planning to embark on Project Obzor, which would have consisted of one hundred or more 1-meter antennae for a wide-angle search of the sky at 21 centimeters. Troitskii, however, became ill, and the project was abandoned. Thus, in the 1980's the Soviets only contributed theoretical work and analysis of data. Nevertheless, there were other directed searches during this period, most of them conducted by Americans. Woody Sullivan of the University of Washington had the idea to "eavesdrop" on nearby stars for radio signals leaking unintentionally into space from advanced civilizations. As a test, Sullivan used the 300-meter Arecibo antenna in Puerto Rico to study the radio leakage from Earth within the range of 150 to 300 megahertz from its reflections from the Moon. Sullivan also eavesdropped on a few nearby stars without any positive results.

Jill Tarter of the Ames Research Center used the Arecibo radio telescope to observe some two hundred solar-type stars at the hydrogen and hydroxyl lines. The Nançay radio telescope in France was used to observe three hundred solar-type stars at the hydroxyl frequencies, extending the previous search to lower declinations that were not accessible from Arecibo. In another project, the radio telescope of the University of Massachusetts was used to search at the carbon monoxide line for powerful beacons along the north rotational axis of the Galaxy, potentially a good location for beacons operated by other civilizations.

Other researchers used the Hat Creek radio telescope in California to search for tritium at its emission line. Tritium is a heavy isotope of hydrogen with a half-life of only 12.5 years. Hence, if tritium is found in the vicinity of normal stars, researchers can be sure it is of artificial origin, probably the by-product of massive nuclear fusion plants. Scientists have also used the 60-centimeter telescope at Kitt Peak in Arizona to look for artifacts and probes at the Lagrangian points of the Earth-Moon-Sun system, the most stable regions in space from which extraterrestrial probes could be observing Earth.

One Soviet astronomer attached a device to a 6-meter optical telescope in Crimea to study twenty-one stellar objects with unusual spectra for very short pulses from optical lasers. In a similar project, a researcher from the University of California, Berkeley, built an infrared laser receiver with one thousand channels to search for interstellar communications with infrared lasers.

The shared, or parasitic, searches either reanalyze data obtained for other purposes or they share, in a parasitic mode, data being obtained by a radio telescope for another purpose. Thus, a group in the Netherlands reanalyzed for SETI maps of the sky that had been obtained by Dutch astronomers. Others have reanalyzed their own radio surveys of globular clusters and data from a pulsar search. During a pulsar search with the 100-meter Bonn antenna, two astronomers also searched for pulsed signals at the hydrogen line.

In a different approach, two Soviet astronomers used Infrared Astronomical Satellite (IRAS) data to search for stellar sources with unusual infrared signatures that could indicate the presence of stellar supercivilizations. Michael Papagiannis of Boston University used the IRAS data on asteroids to look for artificial objects in the solar system.

In a major parasitic project, two researchers from Berkeley built an automated spectrum analyzer to analyze data for narrow-band extraterrestrial intelligence (ETI) signals, data obtained by radio telescopes for other purposes. They call their project Serendip and have attached their equipment on a continuous basis to the 91.5-meter NRAO radio telescope, analyzing for ETI signals all the data it obtains—without using the valuable time of the telescope.

The dedicated searches are conducted by radio observatories that have become SETI-dedicated facilities; through automated processes, these facilities conduct SETI projects on a continuous basis. The oldest dedicated search is the Ohio SETI Program, under the direction of John Kraus and Richard Dixon; it has been in operation since 1973. This project uses the radio telescope at Ohio State University, a telescope which has a collecting area of 2,200 square meters. Slowly, researchers have been examining all the accessible space at wavelengths around the hydrogen line.

Another directed search is the Megachannel Extraterrestrial Assay (META) project at Harvard University, under the direction of Paul Horowitz. This project uses the 26-meter Harvard radio telescope, located near Boston. Started in March, 1983, as Project Sentinel, with a 65,536-channel spectrum analyzer, META acquired an 8.4 million-channel spectrum analyzer in 1985. For the Sentinel project, researchers swept the accessible sky first at the hydrogen line and then at the hydroxyl lines. For META, they swept the sky twice at the hydrogen line and will search again at twice the hydrogen frequency.

The Horowitz SETI search has been supported by the Planetary Society, a public organization chaired by Carl Sagan that will also be supporting two new SETI-dedicated facilities, one in Canada and one in Argentina. With four dedicated facilities and the Serendip parasitic search, SETI will be logging close to forty-five thousand search hours per year.

The SETI program as organized by the National Aeronautics and Space Administration (NASA) under the directorship of Bernard Oliver consists of two parts: the Targeted Search, which will scan with very high sensitivity about one thousand discrete sources (primarily sunlike stars, but also some other interesting objects), and the Sky Survey, which will scan the entire sky, but with a lower sensitivity. The key innovation of the NASA program is that it will search over a wide range of frequencies rather than simply at the spectral lines of certain chemicals. The instrument that will make possible this broad coverage of frequencies is a multichannel spectrum analyzer (MCSA), with 8.25 million channels.

The Targeted Search will cover the so-called water hole, the frequency range between the hydrogen and the hydroxyl lines, with a resolution of about 1 hertz. The Sky Survey, on the other hand, will cover the entire "microwave window" of Earth's atmosphere, the frequency range from 1 to 10 gigahertz with a resolution of 32 hertz. In both cases, the large number of channels required will be provided by batteries of MCSAs.

Knowledge Gained

Advances in astrophysics made possible by modern instruments have revealed that the visible universe contains at least 10 billion galaxies and that the Milky Way contains close to 400 billion stars, several billion of which are very similar to the Sun. Scientists also know that the four most common, most chemically active elements in the universe (hydrogen, oxygen, carbon, and nitrogen) are also the four most common elements in all living organisms and account for more than 98 percent of Earth's biomass. It is difficult, therefore, to accept the idea that in this huge universe, whose members obey the same laws and have the same chemical composition, life managed to start and evolve to an advanced civilization only on the tiny cosmic speck called Earth. Modern discoveries have justified what some ancient people had already guessed only on philosophical grounds.

With the rapid advancement of technology, the data from Frank Drake's first search could be gathered by modern instruments in a mere millisecond. The NASA SETI Program will provide a comprehensive picture of interstellar radio communications in the Galaxy. A confirmed contact would certainly be the most important discovery ever made. Would continuous negative results, though, mean that the civilization on Earth represents the only intelligent life in the universe? Not necessarily, because it may be very difficult to intercept direct communications between other advanced civilizations. Perhaps, too, the closest alien civilization may still have reasons to delay contact.

The advent of the space age has expanded scientists' territory to include the whole solar system. Researchers have already looked for life on the surface of Mars (Vikings 1 and 2 in 1976) and plan to do more in the coming decades. They have also developed new techniques to look for other solar systems, a task that is still very difficult but which will become considerably easier when the necessary measurements can be made from observatories in space. The development of SETI has expanded the domain of communications over the entire Milky Way; with the NASA SETI Program, communications will continue to expand over the celestial sphere.

Context

Even in the days of ancient Greece and Rome, philosophers speculated about the Plurality of Worlds, the existence of many other civilizations in the cosmos, but they could not substantiate their statements with scientific data. (Nor did they have any equipment to conduct actual searches.) Still, some early philosophers showed an amazing level of scientific intuition. Around 400 B.C., the ancient Greek philosopher Metrodorus of Chios wrote, "It seems unnatural in a large field to have only one shaft of wheat and in the infinite universe only one living world." Also, around 50 B.C., the Roman philosopher Lucretius wrote, "Nothing in the universe is unique and alone, and therefore in other regions there must be other earths inhabited by different tribes of men and breeds of beasts."

Contacts with extraterrestrials were contemplated in ancient times too. In the second century B.C., Lucian of Samosata wrote about a voyage to the Moon, which he believed to be inhabited, using a ship with very large sails that was blown away from Earth by cosmic winds.

As science and technology started their rapid advancements in the nineteenth century, people began to formulate more serious ideas about how to communicate with extraterrestrial civilizations. The first one was made around 1830 by the famous German astronomer and mathematician Carl Friedrich Gauss, who suggested that people plant a huge pine forest in the form of an orthogonal triangle in order to show extraterrestrials that Earth is inhabited by intelligent beings who are familar with the Pythagorean theorem.

Following the discovery of radio waves by Heinrich Hertz in 1887, the new field of radio communications grew. The first extraterrestrial radio radiation (radio noise from the center of the Galaxy) was detected by Karl Jansky in 1932 while studying radio interference from terrestrial sources at the Bell Telephone Laboratories in New Jersey. In 1938, Grote Reber built, in the backyard of his home outside Chicago, the first radio telescope. It had a 9.4-meter dish and produced the first radio map of the sky. During World War II, there was great progress in radio equipment which Edward Purcell of Harvard University used in 1951 to discover the first radio line, the line of atomic hydrogen at a wavelength of 21 centimeters. In 1959, Giuseppe

German astronomer Carl Friedrich Gauss, who proposed that people plant a huge pine forest in the form of an orthogonal triangle in order to show extraterrestrials that Earth is inhabited by intelligent beings familar with the Pythagorean theorem. *(Library of Congress)*

Cocconi and Philip Morrison urged scientists to start searching for radio signals from other stellar civilizations at the hydrogen line, which at the time was the only emission line known. Finally, in 1960, Frank Drake conducted the first radio search, thus opening the gates for SETI. Technology, however, continued to advance rapidly, and the equipment used for today's radio searches is to Drake's equipment as the space shuttle is to the Wright brothers' first airplane.

Michael D. Papagiannis

Basic Bibliography

McDonough, Thomas R. *The Search for Extraterrestrial Intelligence: Listening for Life in the Cosmos.* New York: John Wiley and Sons, 1986. An informative but accessible text about the search for intelligent life beyond Earth.

Marx, George. *Bioastronomy: The Next Steps.* Boston: D. Reidel Publishing Co., 1988. The proceedings of IAU Colloquium 99, held in Hungary in 1987. This meeting was the second international convention of the IAU Commission on Bioastronomy.

Papagiannis, Michael D. "Recent Progress and Future Plans on the Search for Extraterrestrial Intelligence." *Nature* 318 (November 14, 1985): 135-140. A comprehensive review article on all aspects of SETI, including descriptions of past projects and plans for the future.

_____, ed. *The Search for Extraterrestrial Life: Recent Developments.* Norwell, Mass.: Kluwer Academic Publishers, 1985. Proceedings of the IAU Symposium held in Boston in 1984. A six-hundred-page volume dealing with all aspects of SETI, with extensive introductions by the editor to each one of its eight sections.

_____. *Strategies for the Search for Life in the Universe.* Norwell, Mass.: Kluwer Academic Publishers, 1979. Proceedings of an international meeting held in Montreal during the 1979 IAU General Assembly. Contains interesting alternative points of view about the number of advanced civilizations in the Galaxy.

Sagan, Carl, ed. *Communications with Extraterrestrial Intelligence.* Cambridge, Mass.: MIT Press, 1973. The proceedings of the first major SETI conference, held in 1971 in the Soviet Union.

Current Bibliography

Goldsmith, Donald. *The Hunt for Life on Mars.* New York: Penguin Books, 1997. An in-depth account of the preliminary results from the study of the meteorite from Mars, which NASA scientists suggest contains indications of possible ancient microbial life.

Hansson, Anders. *Mars and the Development of Life.* New York: Ellis Horwood, 1991. A comprehensive, well-illustrated discussion of the conditions for the development of life and the search for life on Mars.

Milstein, Michael C. "Diving into Europa's Ocean," *Astronomy* 25 (October, 1997): 38-43. An account of the evidence that a water ocean may be hidden beneath Europa's icy surface and that conditions in that ocean might be appropriate for the development of life.

Orgel, Leslie. "The Origin of Life on Earth." *Scientific American* 271 (October, 1994): 76-83. A comprehensive description of how the emergence of RNA is believed to have been critical to the development of life on Earth. Includes a good account of the Miller-Urey synthesis experiment.

Sagan, Carl. "The Search for Extraterrestrial Life." *Scientific American* 271 (October, 1994): 92-99. A clearly written, well-illustrated account focusing on the scientific results of the Viking spacecraft and plans to investigate the atmosphere of Titan using the Cassini/Huygens spacecraft.

Cross-Reference

Extraterrestrial Life in the Solar System, 271.

Extraterrestrial Life in the Solar System

Exobiology is the search for and study of life on solar system bodies other than Earth. The planet Mars, the Jovian moon Europa, and Saturn's moon Titan are all considered possible sites where life might have developed.

Overview

Understanding where life might have developed in the solar system requires comprehending how life developed on the Earth. The earliest evidence of life on Earth is the presence of organic matter derived from biological processes in rocks that are about 3.2 billion years old, indicating that life developed very early in Earth's history. However, much of the fossil record of early life on the Earth has been erased by subsequent geological activity. Biologists have pieced together some of that early history by examining the remaining fossil record and by performing a series of laboratory experiments.

Life on Earth is based on complicated "organic molecules," consisting of chains of carbon, hydrogen, and oxygen. However, organic molecules can be produced by simple chemical reactions as well as by biological activity. Thus, to determine if a process is truly biological, rather than simply a chemical reaction, it is necessary to define the criteria for life. The ability of an organism to reproduce itself is considered to be an essential feature of life. Deoxyribonucleic acid, called DNA, and ribonucleic acid, called RNA, are the organic molecules that control heredity in terrestrial life-forms. Thus, DNA and RNA are considered essential for the reproduction of life on Earth. These two nucleic acids are produced only with the help of proteins. A major focus of exobiology is to understand how DNA, RNA, and the proteins essential in their production were first formed.

A major breakthrough occurred in 1953, when Stanley Miller, a graduate student at the University of Chicago, and his research supervisor, Professor Harold Urey, produced amino acids, the basic building blocks of proteins, in an environment simulating that of the early Earth. Miller and Urey passed electrical sparks through a chamber filled with a gaseous mixture of methane, ammonia, and hydrogen—a composition believed to be similar to that of the early atmosphere of the Earth—and water vapor—representing the

Miller-Urey Experiment

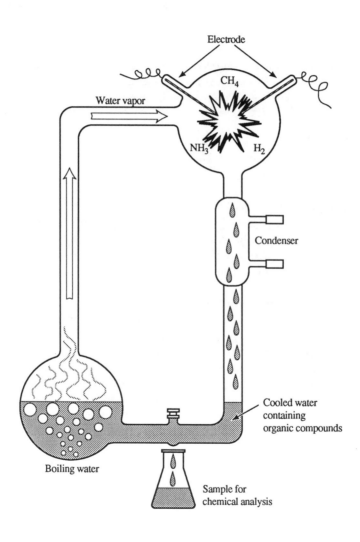

water contributed by the Earth's oceans. After several days they extracted a mixture of organic molecules, including amino acids, from the bottom of the chamber. The Miller-Urey experiment suggested that lightning discharges throughout the Earth's early atmosphere could have deposited amino acids onto the surface of the Earth. Other experiments demonstrated that bombardment of the gas mixture by high-energy particles, simulating cosmic rays, produced similar results. These experiments suggest that three conditions must be met to produce amino acids: A supply of carbon-rich material must be present, liquid water must be available, and some energy source (electrical discharge, high-energy particles, or possibly heat and sunlight) must be present.

Scientists have examined the planets and moons of the solar system, searching for locations where all three conditions are met. Water may be the most critical restriction, since it remains a liquid only over a very narrow range of temperatures. The surfaces of Venus and Mercury are too hot for liquid water to be present, while Jupiter, Saturn, Uranus, Neptune, and Pluto are so far from the Sun that they are too cold to support liquid water. Thus, of the nine planets only the Earth and Mars seem to be suitable candidates for life, because they are in the range of distances from the Sun so that they could support liquid water.

If life is abundant, it can produce changes in the atmosphere of a planet, allowing astronomers to search for unusual signatures of biological activity. The present composition of the Earth's atmosphere, dominated by nitrogen and oxygen, is regulated by the life-cycle processes of respiration and photosynthesis by Earth's living organisms. The atmosphere of Mars, on the other hand, is dominated by carbon dioxide, and it contains only a trace amount of oxygen. Thus, by the 1960's astronomers had observed that at least in the present era living organisms were not present in sufficient abundance to perturb the atmospheric chemistry of Mars.

The beginning of the space age made it possible to employ spacecraft to perform direct measurements on the surface of the planets in the search for evidence of life. The first search was performed by two Viking spacecraft, developed by the National Aeronautics and Space Administration (NASA), which landed on Mars in 1976. Each Viking spacecraft was equipped with instruments designed to examine the soils of Mars for evidence of Earth-like life.

During the 1980's and 1990's developments in terrestrial biology changed how exobiologists looked at the essential conditions for the development of life. Single-celled organisms called archaebacteria, which may have developed very early in Earth's history, were discovered. These archaebacteria live in airless places, such as the hot springs at Yellowstone National Park. Archaebacteria take in carbon dioxide and give off methane, and they cannot live in the presence of oxygen. They have genetic material different from that of other terrestrial life-forms, suggesting that they possibly developed independently from the more common life-forms very early in Earth's history, before the current oxygen-rich atmosphere evolved. Other terrestrial microorganisms were discovered that live on sulfur from geothermal sources rather than by relying on the Sun to supply energy. The discovery of these unusual terrestrial life-forms suggests that the conditions required for development of the common forms of life on Earth may not be required for the development of all life. Thus, some planets or moons previously believed to be unsuitable for the development of life may be habitable by organisms rather different from the common life-forms on Earth. This complicates the search for extraterrestrial life, because many experiments, such as those conducted by the Viking spacecraft on Mars in 1976, look for signatures specific to common terrestrial life.

Methods of Study

One focus of the search for life is to identify the carbon-rich compounds available for life's development. Impacts of meteorites, asteroids, and comets are believed to have contributed a carbon-rich layer to the early surface of the Earth and other planets and moons. One particularly carbon-rich meteorite, called Murchison, fell in Australia in 1969. Detailed studies of Murchison established that it contains numerous organic compounds, including amino acids.

In 1986 three spacecraft, two launched by the Soviet Union and one by the European Space Agency, flew past Halley's comet. Dust analyzers on these spacecraft determined the chemical composition of individual dust particles emitted by the comet. These instruments detected a large number of carbon-rich particles, many of which also contained hydrogen, suggesting the presence of organic molecules in the dust. However, the detailed analysis of organic molecules requires sophisticated scientific instruments too large and complicated to be flown on those spacecraft. NASA plans to launch a spacecraft called Stardust, which will fly to Comet Wild-2, collect dust emitted by the comet, and return samples to the Earth in 2006. Laboratory study of the dust is expected to establish the abundances and types of organic compounds present in Wild-2.

The second focus of the search for life is to perform direct tests for the presence of biological activity on other planets or moons. The Apollo astronauts collected the first samples from the Moon in 1969. When they returned to Earth, the astronauts, their spacecraft, and the lunar rocks were subjected to a twenty-one-day quarantine, during which scientists searched for living microorganisms that might be hazardous to life on Earth. Fragments from the Moon rocks were crushed and placed in a "culture medium," a nutrient-rich soup which promotes the growth of microorganisms. Microscopic examination of these samples showed no evidence of living microorganisms. More detailed studies of the lunar rocks have shown no evidence of fossils of life-forms that might once have developed on the Moon but are now extinct. Examination of the samples returned from the Moon showed them to be exceptionally dry, with none showing any evidence of the presence of liquid water. The absence of liquid water was taken to indicate that the Moon was a lifeless body.

The first experiments in the search for life on another planet were conducted in 1976 by the two Viking spacecraft that landed on Mars. Each Viking carried four instruments to examine the soils for evidence of such life-cycle processes as respiration or photosynthesis. The Gas Exchange Experiment deposited samples of Martian soil in a chamber containing a culture medium and monitored the composition of the gas in the chamber, looking for changes in the abundance of carbon dioxide, oxygen, or hydrogen which would signal metabolic activity by microorganisms in the soil.

In the second experiment, called the Labeled Release Experiment, radioactive carbon atoms were present in the culture medium, and a detector looked for the appearance of radioactive carbon in the gas, signaling that the addition of Martian soil to the nutrient had resulted in a reaction. Both experiments produced positive results, but the effects were much more dramatic than the scientists had expected. These positive results were eventually explained as chemical reactions initiated because of the highly reactive nature of the surface materials on Mars resulting from their exposure to ultraviolet light from the Sun.

The Pyrolitic Release Experiment provided an opportunity to test this explanation. It was also a labeled release experiment, but the apparatus had the additional capability of heating the soil between experiments. Using this apparatus, scientists heated the soil to 175 degrees Celsius, well above the temperature expected to kill any microorganisms present in the soil. Even then the Pyrolitic Release Experiment yielded positive results, suggesting that the release was produced by a chemical rather than a biological process.

The fourth experiment, the Gas Chromatograph Mass Spectrometry Experiment, produced the most convincing evidence that the soils at the Viking landing sites contained no microorganisms. This instrument found no organic molecules in the soil down to a limit of a few organic molecules per million other molecules. Even the organic molecules that would be expected in the soils from the accumulation of meteorites like Murchison were not found. Subsequent studies indicated that the high chemical reactivity of the soils as well as the intense ultraviolet radiation striking the surface would rapidly destroy most organic molecules. Thus, if there is life on Mars, the Viking spacecraft, which were able only to sample the near-surface soils, were probably looking in the wrong place.

Although the instruments on the Viking landers found no evidence of biological activity in the soils, two Viking orbiters that circled the planet, obtaining high-resolution photographs of its surface, produced results that excited exobiologists. Several regions on Mars showed features similar to water flow channels on Earth, leading many geologists to conclude that water had flowed freely on the surface of Mars at some earlier period in its history. Because of the assumed importance of liquid water in the development of life, some exobiologists suggested that life might have developed on

Mars in that earlier era. That life might now be underground, protected from ultraviolet radiation, or it might be extinct, leaving only fossil evidence of its existence.

In 1996 scientists from NASA's Johnson Space Center reported that a meteorite called ALH84001, which is believed to have been ejected from the surface of Mars and deposited in the Antarctic about thirteen thousand years ago, contained microscopic features that might indicate ancient biological activity on Mars. This resulted in a renewed interest in the search for life there.

After the 1997 Mars Pathfinder exploration of the Red Planet returned amazing images of rocks and terrain, NASA has plans for a series of robotic spacecraft to explore Mars. Two of these spacecraft, to be launched in 2001 and 2003, would include small robotic rovers to analyze rocks on the surface and bring them back to the lander. In 2005 a spacecraft would then fly to the landing site of either the 2001 or 2003 lander and return the accumulated cache of rocks to Earth, where they would be examined for evidence of living microorganisms or fossils of extinct microorganisms.

The same techniques used to search for current or fossil life on Mars can be applied to other planets or moons that are identified as suitable candidates for the development of life. Titan, the largest moon of Saturn, has a methane-rich atmosphere believed to be similar in composition to that of the early Earth. High-energy electrons and protons, trapped in the magnetic field of Saturn, continually bombard the upper region of Titan's atmosphere. This bombardment is believed to produce complex organic molecules that rain down onto the Titan's surface. Titan is too cold to have liquid water. However, its surface may be covered with oceans of methane or ethane, which some scientists have speculated might be sufficient to allow primitive life to develop. Titan will be the target of the Cassini spacecraft, which was launched in October, 1997. Cassini was slated to drop its Huygens probe, loaded with instruments to measure the types and abundances of the organic molecules in Titan's atmosphere, in 2004.

The Galileo spacecraft, placed in orbit around Jupiter in late 1995, obtained close-up photographs of Jupiter's four largest moons. One of these moons, Europa, has emerged as another potential site for the development of life. One of Galileo's orbits of Jupiter took it within 363 miles of the surface of Europa, allowing its cameras to photograph objects as small as 75 feet. These images showed evidence of icebergs that had broken from a solid sheet of ice and been displaced, suggesting that they had floated or slipped across a liquid ocean or a layer of slush below. Calculations indicated that the extreme gravitational pull of Jupiter could introduce tidal distortions that produce sufficient heat to allow liquid water to exist beneath Europa's icy surface. Other photographs showed dark deposits, possibly carbon-rich material contributed by meteorites.

Exobiologists were excited to see the possible existence of the three conditions believed necessary for the development of life: carbon-rich material, water, and energy from the Jovian tides. Several follow-on missions have been suggested. A spacecraft placed into orbit around Europa could use radar to see through several miles of ice, detecting any water below and providing a clear test of the ocean model. More ambitious proposals include a spacecraft which would fling a 20-pound projectile into the surface of Europa, catch some of the debris lofted by the collision, and return it to terrestrial laboratories for examination.

Context

The possibility that life might have developed elsewhere in the solar system has been the subject of speculation for hundreds of years. In 1820, Carl Gauss, a German mathematician, suggested cutting geometrical patterns into the Siberian forest large enough to be seen by an observer using a telescope from the Moon or Mars. The idea was to motivate any inhabitants of the Moon or Mars to produce similar geometrical patterns, initiating communication with the Earth. Other suggestions for communication with intelligent life included setting huge fires in the Sahara desert and constructing large mirrors to reflect sunlight back into space. These early ideas of how to communicate with intelligent life elsewhere in the solar system did not focus on particular sites where the conditions were expected to be appropriate for the development of life.

Only in the second half of the twentieth century did biologists begin to develop an understanding of how life originated on Earth. This knowledge provided clues as to the conditions needed for similar forms of life to develop elsewhere in the solar system. The study of terrestrial life indicates that it originated as simple, single-celled microorganisms and that these simple microorganisms might develop quickly and easily on other planets and moons as well. Thus, the focus of solar system exobiology shifted from the search for intelligent life, which has not been seen on any planet other than Earth, to the search for simple microorganisms.

The dawn of the space age inaugurated an era when spacecraft could be used to search for environments favorable to the development of life, perform experiments designed to detect living organisms on the surface of the planets and moons, and return samples so that scientists could examine them for evidence of biological activity or fossil evidence of past life.

Although scientific interest in life elsewhere in the solar system reached a low point after the negative results of the Viking landers in 1976, there was a resurgence of interest by the end of the twentieth century. The discovery of river channels on Mars, possible fossil evidence for ancient microorganisms in a meteorite from Mars, and hints of water ice on the Moon and oceans of Europa suggest that the solar system might not be as inhospitable to the development of life as was believed immediately following the results of the Viking landers.

George J. Flynn

Basic Bibliography

Hansson, Anders. *Mars and the Development of Life.* New York: Ellis Horwood, 1991. A comprehensive, well-illustrated discussion of the conditions for the development of life and the search for life on Mars.

Orgel, Leslie. "The Origin of Life on Earth." *Scientific American* 271 (October, 1994): 76-83. A comprehensive description of how the emergence of RNA is believed to have been critical to the development of life on Earth. Includes a good account of the Miller-Urey synthesis experiment.

Sagan, Carl. "The Search for Extraterrestrial Life." *Scientific American* 271 (October, 1994): 92-99. A clearly written, well-illustrated account focusing on the scientific results of the Viking spacecraft and upcoming plans to investigate the atmosphere of Titan using the Cassini/Huygens spacecraft.

Current Bibliography

Goldsmith, Donald. *The Hunt for Life on Mars.* New York: Penguin Books, 1997. An in-depth account of the preliminary results from the study of the meteorite from Mars, which NASA scientists suggest contains indications of possible ancient microbial life.

Milstein, Michael C. "Diving into Europa's Ocean." *Astronomy* 25 (October, 1997): 38-43. An account of the evidence that a water ocean may be hidden beneath Europa's icy surface and that conditions in that ocean might be appropriate for the development of life.

Cross-Reference

Extraterrestrial Intelligence, 263.

Galactic Structures

The study of the structure of galaxies helps astronomers understand the processes of galaxy formation, which, in turn, gives insights into star formation and the structure of the universe as well as its origin and future.

Overview

Nothing represents the essence of deep space astronomy as much as the majestic form of a spiral galaxy. Like a celestial pinwheel, star-studded arms dusted with interstellar material sweep out from a central core. The form belies its stately motion, which occurs on so vast a scale as to be humanly imperceptible. Although the spiral galaxy is the archetype, there are other types of galaxies with differing structures. To understand the dynamics that form the galaxies is to understand the very basic processes of the universe. This understanding develops a picture of how the universe began, how it evolved, and where these same processes will lead it in the distant future.

Galaxies are the largest individual objects in the universe, vast groupings of stars, gas, and dust, held together by gravitational attraction and their rotation around the nucleus. There are hundreds of billions of galaxies in the universe, each containing from hundreds of thousands to billions of stars. In their groupings, as well as in their structure, they are diverse. They are found in enormous clusters of tens of thousands of galaxies, held together by mutual gravitation, in groupings of only a few, or single galaxies that float solitarily in space. In turn, the clusters of galaxies form larger structures called superclusters. In their activity, galaxies are equally disparate. While some are quiet, others are engaged in inconceivably energetic activity.

The most familiar type of galaxy is the spiral galaxy. Earth's galaxy—the Milky Way—is a spiral galaxy. Other galaxies appear more spherical in shape and are termed ellipticals. Irregular galaxies have no particular symmetrical structure. For these galaxies, it appears that their structure is determined by wrenching gravitational and energetic forces. It was once thought that three-quarters of all galaxies were spirals, including barred spirals, with their arms originating from straight barlike structures running through the central core. In fact, if only the brightest galaxies are studied, this view appears to be true. Considering the number of small elliptical galaxies, however, the percentages are more likely to be 20 percent spirals, 10 percent barred spirals, 60 percent ellipticals, and 10 percent irregulars.

The Great Galaxy in Andromeda, Earth's nearest galactic neighbor. The two smaller Magellanic Clouds are actually satellites of Earth's own galaxy. *(California Institute of Technology and Carnegie Institution of Washington)*

Spiral galaxies vary greatly in size, ranging from giant galaxies such as the Andromeda galaxy, containing at least 2 billion stars, to spirals only a tenth as large. While the details of the spiral structure can vary, the basic design of a spiral galaxy remains consistent. A spiral galaxy has a central core of stars called the bulge, which is spherical or slightly elliptical in shape. Spreading outward from the core and revolving around the bulge is a pancake-shaped disk of material consisting of stars, gas, and dust. The disk of a spiral galaxy is marked by alternating lanes of bright and dark material that form the distinctive spiral arms. Here, new stars are continually being formed from gas and dust. The bright arms of the galaxy indicate the areas of stellar birth. The arms are often fragmented and indistinct, with smaller spurs projecting from the various arms.

A broader structure called the halo is defined by the orbits of both individual stars and spherical clusters of stars called globular clusters. The halo is centered on the central bulge and encompasses the entire disk of the galaxy. It can be as large as 400,000 light-years in diameter. The globular clusters within the halo range in size from 15 to 300 light-years in diameter and contain from tens of thousands to a few million stars.

The motion of spiral galaxies indicates that beyond the visible portion of the galaxy lies a region of dark matter, referred to as the dark halo, which is undetectable by astronomical instruments. Apparently featureless, the dark halo extends another 100,000 light-years beyond the visible halo marked by the orbits of the globular clusters. Although it has never been observed directly, its gravitational effects are manifested in the orbits of stars within spiral galaxies. These effects can be measured, but the actual nature of the dark material remains a mystery.

The proportionate sizes of the galactic disk and the central bulge vary greatly between spiral galaxies. The bulge of some galaxies encompasses a major portion of the disk, extending 100,000 light-years in diameter. Other galaxies are dominated by the disk with its structure of spiral arms, while the central bulge appears a minor protuberance at the center. In a typical spiral galaxy, the disk is only one one-hundredth as thick as it is wide. The bulge of an average spiral galaxy contains about a billion stars. Here, the dust and gas found in the disk are virtually absent, and no new stars are formed. As opposed to the stars in the disk that revolve around the core in nearly circular orbits, the stars in the bulge revolve around the center of the nucleus in highly elliptical orbits. The orbits do not lie parallel to the disk of the galaxy, but are highly inclined. The oldest stars in the galaxy are located in the bulge, at an age of perhaps 10 billion years. These stars are formed in the very early stages of the formation of the galaxy.

While spiral galaxies are common in the universe, their spiral structure is not understood completely. According to the theories of motion, the spiral structure should not exist in galaxies in the numbers it does. While the rotation of a galaxy would be expected to create a spiral structure, it would also be expected to disappear within only a few rotations. A galactic "density wave" has been theorized as a mechanism to explain the enduring shape of spiral galaxies. According to the hypothesis, the density wave is a disturbance that moves through the material in the disk of a galaxy. Spiral in structure, the wave moves through the galaxy at a lower rate than the stars, gas, and dust. Periodically, material in the galaxy catches up with and falls into the density wave, where it slows down and bunches up. The gas that is slowed by the wave compresses, which triggers a burst of star formation. The young, bright stars formed at the boundaries of the density wave define the spiral structure of the galaxy.

Elliptical galaxies have no spiral structure at all. Their three-dimensional shape would appear as a flattened sphere. As opposed to spiral galaxies, they contain little or no interstellar dust and gas. The density of stars in elliptical galaxies increases toward their centers, with a corresponding increase in brightness. The stars in elliptical galaxies are older stars, similar to the stars found in the central bulges of spiral galaxies and globular clusters. Although they have relatively little structure, the largest and most massive galaxies in the universe tend to be elliptical. Ranging to the other extreme as well, some dwarf ellipticals contain fewer than a million stars.

Often, the structure of a galaxy is not symmetrical. These irregular galaxies have undergone some violent process that has wrenched the galaxy out of a symmetrical structure. Many times, the irregularities are caused by interaction with other galaxies, either by the gravitational effects of passing closely by another galaxy or by colliding with one. The likelihood that a galaxy will suffer a collision with another galaxy sometime in its lifetime is relatively high. When galaxies are in a cluster, they generally are grouped many times closer relative to their sizes than are the stars within the galaxies. Therefore, as they orbit around a shared center of gravity, the chances of collision or near-collision are high.

Since the relative distance between stars is great, individual stars are not likely to collide, even though one entire galaxy passes through another. Though individual stars do not interact, nebulas within the galaxies are likely to collide, producing clouds of dense, unstable gas and shock waves. Inside the galaxies, the orbits of stars would be warped and any planetary systems that existed would disintegrate. The primary force between galaxies, however, would be gravitational. The mutual attraction disturbs the arrangement of stars and gas in each galaxy, deforming their structure. The closer the galaxies approach, the greater the gravitational force and resulting deformation. Sometimes galaxies will merge together, or, in other cases, a smaller galaxy will punch a hole through a larger galaxy, carrying away material along with it.

Among the most intriguing objects in the universe are the active galaxies. In a normal galaxy, everything seems to be stable and in equilibrium. In active galaxies, there are strong emissions of energy, or the emissions vary rapidly. There are many types of active galaxies, but they represent different stages in the evolution of a single type of galaxy, which has a black hole at its center. They may indicate galaxies at the early stages of formation. Quasars are the smallest, brightest, and most distant active galaxies. They radiate extremely high levels of energy in the form of visible light, infrared radiation, and X rays. N galaxies are elliptical in shape and have very bright, small nuclei. BL Lacertae objects are a certain type of N galaxy that varies in luminosity. Radio galaxies are distinguished by two enormous regions that emit jets of radio waves from a very compact central source. The likeliest explanation for the source of the radiation is a rotating supermassive black hole at the core of the galaxy. Seyfert galaxies are disk-shaped and are similar to other active galaxies in that they have an extremely bright core. Analysis of the spectra of these galaxies indicates that they are undergoing violent activity in their centers.

Galaxies are fascinating objects to study, mainly because their appearances are deceiving. Analyzing the galaxies at wavelengths ranging from radio through infrared, visible light, ultraviolet, X rays, and gamma rays reveals that even some of the most ordinary of galaxies have extraordinary features.

Applications

The study of the galaxies is the key to the study of the universe. By studying galaxies and clusters of galaxies, deeper insights can be gained into the dynamics and structure of the universe. As the structure of galaxies is studied, astronomers can look at the processes that created these structures.

Once it was understood that the galaxies were moving away from one another, it was natural to look backward in time, when they must have been closer together. Taking this view to its obvious conclusion, it is assumed that at one time the galaxies were merged at some beginning point in time. It was this speculation on the origin of the galaxies that prompted the first serious study of the origin of the first moments of the universe. The most widely accepted theory is that everything that exists began with a colossal explosion some 20 billion years ago. Matter was thrown out in all directions, creating a universe of incredibly hot subatomic particles. As the matter expanded and cooled, it began to clump together into clouds of condensed gas that would eventually become galaxies. Stars began as small turbulences in these clouds, contracting until their mass and density allowed nuclear reactions to begin in their cores. The most massive stars gravitated toward the center to form a galactic nucleus. Gravitational interaction with other forming galaxies causes the galaxy to spin, and as it continues to contract on itself, the rate of its rotation increases. If star formation in the galaxy is very rapid, the gas and dust that make up the stars will be consumed almost completely, and an elliptical galaxy will result. In spiral galaxies, star formation slows once the core of the galaxy has formed. Unused material swirls in random motion around the nucleus, colliding and merging, with the end result as a central disk of the spiral galaxy. The disk represents the most stable condition resulting from the pull of gravity and the centifugal force of the galaxy's motion around the core. The origin of the spiral pattern that forms in the disk is as yet unknown. From the force of the original explosion, or the big bang, the galaxies and the universe continue to expand in the present day. This expansion of galaxies was discovered by Edwin Powell Hubble in the early 1920's.

Most of what is known about the structure of the Milky Way has come from observations at nonoptical wavelengths. Because of the dust and gas that is prevalent in spiral galaxies, much information is hidden from view. Nevertheless, other types of radiation, such as radio waves, infrared radiation, X rays, and gamma rays, do penetrate the clouds of dust and gas and help to reveal the nature of the galaxy. The Milky Way measures 100,000 light-years in diameter and contains at least 100 billion stars. The Sun is located between two major spiral arms about 30,000 light-years from the nucleus of the galaxy. As seen from Earth, the center of the galaxy lies in the direction of the constellation Sagittarius.

Radio studies of the Milky Way have revealed surprising structures in the core of the galaxy. Aside from the disk of the galaxy in which the spiral arms lie, astronomers have found a second disk in the nucleus of the galaxy, which is tilted 20 degrees with respect to the main disk. It is about 8,000 light-years across and rests completely within the central bulge of the galaxy. It seems to be rotating much faster than the material in the spiral arms and is expanding outward. Five powerful radio sources have been discovered in this inner disk and have been named Sagittarius A through E, in order of their discovery.

Within this inner disk lies yet another disk, which is tilted with respect to both the inner and main disks. Inside this disk, at the very core of the galaxy, a supermassive black hole is suspected to reside. It encompasses an area about the size of a large star, yet it contains the mass of at least 4 million suns. The gravity of the black hole pulls in surrounding matter. As the material accelerates into the black hole, its temperature soars, causing it to emit radiation from all ranges of the electromagnetic spectrum. Evidence for black holes has been found in other galaxies. Although they cannot be observed directly and their existence remains theoretical, black holes are thought to be a major mechanism behind the tremendous energy radiated by some galaxies.

Context

Although the galaxies have been observed since the time of Galileo in the 1600's, their nature and the distance of the galaxies was not known until after the first quarter of the twentieth century. Early observers knew them as spiral "nebulas," for the Latin word meaning cloud. Nebulas were believed to be part of the Milky Way. Until astronomers had the tools to measure the distances of these objects they could only guess at their nature.

Galaxies were first cataloged by comet hunters, who would catalog their positions in the sky so that they would not be mistaken for comets, which also appeared as dim, fuzzy patches of light. In 1784, Charles Messier made a list of one hundred of these objects that were not to be confused with comets. Some of the objects in the list were star clusters or glowing clouds of interstellar dust and gas. About a third of the list included galaxies. Sir William Herschel and his son, Sir John Frederick Herschel, continued Messier's work. By 1864, *The General Catalogue of Nebulae* was published with 5,079 objects listed. By 1888, Johan Ludwig Emil Dreyer updated the list to include 7,840 objects and published *The New General Catalogue of Nebulae and Clusters of Stars*. In 1895, two volumes of the *Index Catalogue* were published, listing a total of fifteen thousand objects. These listings are still in use today. Galaxies, clusters, and nebulas are listed by their "M," "NGC," or "IC" numbers, relating back to these important catalogs.

In the 1700's, Sir William Herschel first proposed that instead of the Sun being only one of a random scattering of stars in space, it was part of a disk-shaped system of stars. He drew the first maps of what this system of stars might resemble, and it became known as the galaxy, or the island universe.

Until the 1920's, the accepted cosmology of the universe was that the Milky Way galaxy was the only sizable object that existed. In 1923, Hubble discovered a method of measuring the distances to the galaxies, proving they were much farther away than anyone had seriously imagined before. He discovered that the Andromeda galaxy was a full-fledged star system similar to the Milky Way. By 1930, Hubble's work had changed the perceived face of the universe. In addition to determining the nature of the spiral nebulas, Hubble discovered that rather than being unchanging (as was the theory for

Hubble's Morphological Classification of Galaxies

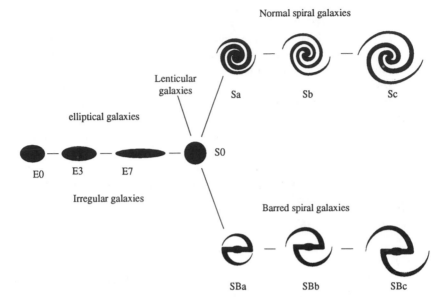

Note: E refers to elliptical galaxies; S to spiral

hundreds of years), the galaxies were rushing apart from one another, and the universe was expanding. With this concept, the modern theories of cosmology were born. Modern astronomers believe that the universe is infinite and that there is nothing unique about Earth's position in space and time. The universe is basically the same everywhere when viewed on the largest scale. The Milky Way is merely one of billions of galaxies scattered across the cosmos.

Divonna Ogier

Basic Bibliography

Editors of Time-Life Books. *Galaxies.* Alexandria, Va.: Time-Life Books, 1989. One volume of a series examining different aspects of the universe. Comprehensively covers theories about galactic structure and formation, active galaxies, the Milky Way, and cosmological theories. Highly illustrated and suitable for the general reader with an interest in astronomy.

Henbest, Nigel. *Mysteries of the Universe.* New York: Van Nostrand Reinhold, 1981. Explores the limits of what is known about the universe. Ranges from theories about the origin of the solar system, galaxies, and the universe; exotic astronomy; and astronomy at invisible wavelengths.

Henbest, Nigel, and Michael Marten. *The New Astronomy.* New York: Cambridge University Press, 1983. Compares optical, infrared, ultraviolet, radio, and X-ray observations of well-known astronomical objects. Highly visual, and written specifically for general readers.

Kaufmann, William J. *Galaxies and Quasars.* San Francisco: W. H. Freeman, 1979. A comprehensive and easy-to-read book that explores the subject of normal and active galaxies. Discusses the history of the discovery of galaxies, the structure of various galaxies including the Milky Way, galactic classification, and cosmological theories. Nontechnical language is geared toward the general reader.

Marten, Michael, and John Chesterman. *The Radiant Universe.* New York: Macmillan, 1980. An overview of imaging that is not accessible in visible wavelengths. Includes electronic processing, as well as infrared and ultraviolet wavelength imaging. Beautiful pictures along with easy-to-read and informative text.

Current Bibliography

Bartusiak, Marcia. "Giving Birth to Galaxies." *Discover* 18, no. 2 (February, 1997): 58-66.

Bertin, G., and C. C. Lin. *Spiral Structure in Galaxies: A Density Wave Theory.* Cambridge, Mass.: MIT Press, 1996.

Tayler, Roger J. *Galaxies, Structure and Evolution.* Rev. ed. New York: Cambridge University Press, 1993.

Visser, Matt. "Energy Conditions in the Epoch of Galaxy Formation." *Science* 276, no. 5309 (April, 1997): 88-91.

Cross-References

Cosmology, 97; Galaxies and Galactic Clusters, 287; Gamma-ray Bursts, 296; Globular Clusters, 310; Interstellar Clouds and the Interstellar Medium, 385; The Milky Way, 584; Quantum Cosmology, 767.

Galaxies and Galactic Clusters

Bound together by gravity, stars compose galaxies, of which there are several distinct types, and their mutual gravitational attraction draws galaxies into clusters. Explaining these formations is one goal of cosmology.

Overview

The study of galaxy and cluster types seeks to explain shared structures and characteristics among the arrangements of luminous matter outside Earth's Milky Way galaxy. The search, astrophysicists believe, will provide essential clues to the origin and development of the universe. This search is almost entirely a twentieth century endeavor. Although some philosophers and scientists had proposed earlier that certain "spiral nebulas" might lie outside the Milky Way, it was not until the 1920's that astronomers accepted the fact that Earth's galaxy is only one of countless "island universes" in the vastness of outer space, each of which comprises billions of stars like the Sun that are bound together by gravity. In 1925, Edwin Powell Hubble announced that he had located Cepheid variable stars in the Andromeda galaxy. The intrinsic brightness of these stars was known, so he was able to compare their apparent brightness with their intrinsic brightness, calculate the distance to Andromeda, and prove it was a discrete system lying far outside the Milky Way. Other astronomers soon made similar discoveries about other galaxies.

Hubble also proposed the first morphological classification system for galaxies. He discerned three basic types: elliptical, spiral, and irregular. Elliptical galaxies are spheroid in structure—almost none appears to be a perfect sphere—and are classified by the difference between their length and width in relation to their axis of rotation on a scale of E0 to E7 (E stands for elliptical). E0 galaxies show a nearly circular outline, while the flattened E7 galaxies resemble fat, stubby cigars in profile. Elliptical galaxies largely lack gas or dust clouds or hot bright stars. The only visible internal structures are globular star clusters, which usually proliferate, and the stars of an elliptical circle its galactic center in complex patterns. Furthermore, analysis of an elliptical's spectrum will suggest that its stars are all old and of moderate size. The largest ellipticals are about five times larger in diameter and fifty times more massive than the Milky Way, which is between 70,000 and 100,000 light-years in diameter; the smallest, called dwarf ellipticals, are about one hundred times smaller and a million times less massive. Astronomers believe that ellipticals account for about 70 percent of all galaxies in the universe, most of which, being dim dwarfs, are difficult to observe.

Spiral galaxies have the basic shape of a discus, as their stars orbit a central

Spiral galaxy NGC 6946. *(National Aeronautics and Space Administration)*

bulge, or nucleus, and are classified in three distinct types: S0 galaxies, normal spirals, and barred spirals. S0 galaxies have little obvious internal structure, showing a uniform disk with a large nucleus, and like ellipticals contain little gas and dust and few hot bright stars. Accordingly, they are considered to be intermediate between spirals and ellipticals. Normal spirals are further classified a to c depending upon how tightly their spiral arms are wound about the nucleus. Sa galaxies have closely wound arms and relatively little dust and gas; Sb galaxies show a definite whirlpool structure, with the ends of the arms loose in intergalactic space, and contain more dust and gas; and Sc galaxies look like pinwheels, and large gas and dust clouds are evident. The Milky Way and the closest spiral to it, Andromeda, are Sb galaxies. Barred spirals are similarly classified as SBa, SBb, and SBc depending on how tightly wound their arms are. They differ from normal spirals in that their nucleus is elongated, so that their arms look like streamers being spun from the ends of a thick central rod. In composition, they otherwise resemble normal spirals. The largest spirals are about one and a half times larger and slightly more massive than the Milky Way; the smallest are about five times smaller and have about 1 percent of its mass. Spiral galaxies are thought to include about 15 percent of all galaxies.

Irregular galaxies have little or no evidence of spiral arms, nuclei, or overall symmetrical shape; instead, they look like dense, chaotic patches of stars. Their most prominent feature is the presence of large clouds of gas and dust, in which are embedded both young and old stars. Irregulars are small—between 5 and 25 percent of the Milky Way's diameter—and account for about 15 percent of all galaxies. The Milky Way's closest neighbors, the Magellanic Clouds, are irregulars and are visible to the naked eye in the Southern Hemisphere.

Hubble's system has been the basic morphological schema since he introduced it, but since World War II, astronomers have observed an increasing array of bizarre galactic phenomena that suggest classifying by appearance alone is insufficient. Consequently, they also distinguish "normal" galaxies, classified by the Hubble system, from "peculiar" or Arp galaxies (if they are contained in Halton C. Arp's *Atlas of Peculiar Galaxies*, 1966), which either emit intense energy or have novel structures. Energy emitters are also known as "active" galaxies.

Those with strange structures are relatively rare and may be the result of interactions between galaxies. For example, some extremely large, apparently elliptical galaxies are now designated "cD." The D indicates in astronomical notation that the central sphere is surrounded by an envelope of stars, and the c denotes unusual size. Some contain multiple nuclei, so that cD's are suspected to be mergers of two or more galaxies, as if an elliptical has swallowed but not completely digested smaller neighbors, a process called galactic cannibalism. Other structural peculiarities include ring galaxies, which either show no nucleus or have an off-center nucleus; polar-ring galaxies; and galactic arcs. These may result from a close encounter with another galaxy or be the product of a rare phenomenon called a gravitation lens, in which a distant galaxy's image is distorted when a nearer galaxy's gravitational field bends the former's light.

When astronomers began using radio telescopes in the 1950's, they found that some galaxies broadcast very high levels of energy. These were dubbed "radio galaxies," and subsequent observations found galaxies that similarly emit intense amounts of ultraviolet, X ray, and infrared radiation. The discoveries prompted a host of new, sometimes overlapping designations. Radio galaxies include those that emit tens of thousands of times more radio radiation than normal galaxies. Most are giant ellipticals, in which a central object shoots out beams of high-energy particles hundreds of thousands of light-years beyond the border of their visible stars. These beams often terminate in pear-shaped lobes that contain regions of intense radio emissions.

Megamaser galaxies produce strong emissions because their interstellar gases amplify the radiation from their stars in the same way a maser does (maser, a predecessor of the laser, stands for *m*icrowave *a*mplification by the *s*timulated *e*mission of *r*adiation). Seyfert galaxies are spirals with very small cores that fluctuate in brightness and can be radio or X-ray sources; many show disturbances in the spiral structure, perhaps caused by the gravity of a nearby galaxy. Markarian galaxies have abnormal amounts of blue light and strong continuous ultraviolet radiation. By 1986, astronomers had cataloged about fifteen hundred of these galaxies. Others with unusual visible light characteristics, suggesting intense activity in the nucleus, include liner galaxies (an acronym for *l*ow-*i*onization *n*arrow *e*mission-line *r*egion) and starburst galaxies.

Finally, astronomers identify two galaxy-like phenomena that may represent early stages in galactic evolution. The first is the protogalaxy—that is, a galaxy in the process of forming. They are believed to have been common in the distant past, but it is disputed whether any exist now. The second is the quasar, a blend of "quasi-stellar object," so called because the first were mistakenly thought to be starlike objects inside the Milky Way. Although a controversial subject, most astronomers accept them as the most distant visible objects in the universe; the farthest are as much as 15.5 billion light-years away and, judging from the redshifts in their spectra, speeding away from Earth at more than half the speed of light.

Not only does gravity gather stars into galaxies but also it gathers galaxies into clusters. Those containing fewer than a thousand galaxies are called poor clusters or groups. Their resident galaxies are loosely associated, there is little intergalactic gas, and they have a large proportion of spirals. The Milky Way, Andromeda, and twenty-seven other galaxies belong to a poor cluster called the Local Group, which is about 1 megaparsec in diameter and is probably only a suburb of the much larger Vega cluster. Clusters that contain more than a thousand galaxies are called rich clusters. Their galaxies tend to condense toward a central point, often occupied by a cD galaxy; regions of hot, sometimes X-ray-emitting gases lie between galaxies; and ellipticals predominate. Rich clusters range up to 10 megaparsecs in diameter.

Applications

The investigation into galaxy and cluster types has helped scientists to understand their evolution and mass. Although fundamental questions remain unanswered about these matters, the latter half of the twentieth century has seen startling developments because of computer simulations and new types of ground-based and space-borne telescopes that greatly increase the range and accuracy of extragalactic observations.

Hubble proposed that galaxies have evolved in a uniform pattern during the history of the universe: He theorized that spheroid ellipticals flatten until they become tight spirals, which gradually unwind until they become irregular galaxies. While the evidence has proved this schema to be incorrect, Hubble did stimulate astronomers to explain the relation between the various types. They have approached the problem by first observing the properties of structure and composition in galaxies and then preparing mathematical models and computer programs based on the information to test various theories of evolution. Furthermore, computer graphic displays have helped astronomers visualize evolutionary processes in minutes that require millions of years in actuality.

From these techniques, two basic theories have emerged. The first assumes that galaxies originally formed when clouds of gas collapsed as a result of gravity; however, astronomers now believe that this theory alone cannot account for the variety of galaxy types. The second theory proposed that collisions, mergers, and gravitational interactions among galaxies have determined their structures. It may seem unlikely that galaxies ever come close enough to affect one another, much less collide, but actually collisions and mergers are relatively common. The average distance between any two galaxies is only twenty times their diameter, not very much more than the average distance between cars on an interstate highway, and observations, in fact, have detected galaxies that have already collided and others that appear destined to collide. Computer simulations suggest that a head-on, high-speed collision should produce a ring galaxy, and a near miss or glancing collision can start spiral structures in elliptical galaxies. When a small galaxy passes through a larger one, the complex gravitational forces derange the former's structure, sending its stars into random motions; the result is an irregular galaxy.

Computer simulations also suggest that often galaxies never entirely escape each other's gravitational field after they collide, especially when they approach at low velocities; instead, they slow, fall back, and pass through each other again and again until they finally merge into a single large galaxy. This is the case especially if one galaxy is much larger than the other. Mergers are particularly common in rich, dense clusters, which often have giant ellipticals at their center, but even though the Milky Way is in a poor

An image of hot blue stars at the core of the star cluster M 15. The blue stars are believed to be evidence that the core of the star cluster has contracted to an extremely dense condition, or "gravitational collapse." *(National Aeronautics and Space Administration)*

cluster, astronomers believe it, too, has benefited from this galactic canni-balism, having partially digested the Magellanic Clouds as they passed through millions of years ago.

Clusters are believed to evolve—as poor clusters converge into rich clusters because of mutual gravitational attraction—and gravitationally re-lated structures larger than clusters have been identified: superclusters, or clusters of clusters. Computer simulations and large-scale surveys indicate that superclusters, in turn, may outline bubbles connected by long, narrow filaments of galaxies, between which are immense voids, as if the universe were structured like a sponge.

Because their redshifted spectra indicate that galaxies are speeding away from one another, astronomers have theorized that there is a relation between a galaxy's distance from Earth and its evolutionary stage. Since light travels at a constant value, once a galaxy's distance is estimated, its age relative to Earth is apparent. For example, when a galaxy is observed a million light-years away, one is actually seeing light that was produced a million years ago. So, galaxies at the limit of observation may represent the structures assumed shortly after the origin of the universe. The most distant known objects are quasars; they may therefore be either intensely active galactic nuclei, suggesting that such activity is normal in young galaxies, or interacting galaxies, similarly suggesting that galactic interaction has been a feature of the universe from early epochs.

Attempts to calculate the masses of galaxies have raised unexpectedly daunting problems since the 1970's. The most astonishing is that visible matter accounts for only about 10 percent of the mass needed to make galaxies and clusters gravitationally stable. The rest of the mass, astrophysicists have hypothesized, is invisible to current telescopes. This phenomenon is called the dark matter, or missing mass, problem.

Context

The primary goals of cosmology are to explain the origin, evolution, and structure of space-time, and for this reason the structures and composition of galaxies and clusters have been studied intensively to yield data upon which to base a unified theory. A fundamental assumption behind this effort is the cosmological principle. It postulates that the universe should look the same in all directions from any vantage point (or isotropy) and that matter should be evenly distributed (or homogeneity). The fact that galaxies have been detected in every direction and as far as instruments can detect supports isotropy, but homogeneity has been more difficult to reconcile with observation.

Most cosmologists subscribe to variations of the big bang theory, first proposed by Georges Lemaître in 1927 to explain why galaxies are hurtling away from one another at high velocities. The theory states that the universe began with the explosion of a "primal atom," and about 1 million years later, its radiation began cooling enough to congeal into the present galaxies. After radical revisions, the big bang theory has succeeded in accounting for structures the size of clusters, but complexes of superclusters and voids makes it appear that matter is not evenly distributed throughout the universe, despite what the theory predicts. Accordingly, cosmologists have supposed that as yet undetected phenomena exist whose forces lie behind large-scale structure. For example, some have suggested that one-dimensional faults exist in space-time, remnants of the big bang. These "cosmic strings" are thought to be either infinitely long or looped and to have gravitational fields strong enough to draw matter into galaxies and clusters.

Another unresolved question is whether—given the assumptions about the big bang—the universe will continue to expand forever or gradually slow to a stop and then reverse direction until it squeezes back into a single object. To answer the question, cosmologists need to know the amount of matter in the universe; the studies of galaxies that have indicated that only about 10 percent of the matter is visible greatly complicate the problem. Combining subatomic particle theories with cosmological theories in grand unified theories (GUTs), cosmologists have predicted many exotic particles within and between galaxies that could constitute the missing mass, but experiments designed to detect them have proved ambiguous or negative.

Galaxies and clusters are likely to remain a focus of investigations into the nature of the universe for some time. In the meantime, their magnificent forms testify to the rich diversity of space and the great depth of time.

Roger Smith

Basic Bibliography

Bartusiak, Marcia. *Thursday's Universe.* New York: Times Books, 1986. This highly readable overview of modern astronomical discoveries relates the general classifications of galaxies and clusters to theories of the large-scale structure and origin of the universe. Nevertheless, the details of galaxy and cluster variation are superficially described.

Ferris, Timothy. *Coming of Age in the Milky Way.* New York: William Morrow, 1988. Ferris presents a history of the ideas and observations that led to modern cosmological theories, including both astronomical and sub-atomic phenomena. Although only two of the twenty chapters pertain directly to galaxies, the book is particularly valuable and entertaining for anecdotal information about the controversies that shaped modern knowledge.

Hodge, Paul W. *Galaxies.* Cambridge, Mass.: Harvard University Press, 1986. The single best book for general readers coming to the subject for the first time. Through orderly, lucid explanations and a delightful style, Hodge discusses the composition, structures, and formation of galaxies and clusters. Photographs and diagrams are well placed to help the reader visualize the information in the text.

Hubble, Edwin. *The Realm of the Nebulae.* New Haven, Conn.: Yale University Press, 1936. Now largely of historical interest, the book—collecting a series of lectures delivered at Yale University in 1935—is Hubble's first thorough presentation to a general audience of his foundation-laying observations and theories. Many of Hubble's ideas still under-lie astronomical measurement and morphology, although in revised form.

Schorn, Ronald A. "The Extragalactic Zoo." 4 parts. *Sky and Telescope* 75 (January, 1988): 23-27; 75 (April, 1988): 376-388; 76 (July, 1988): 36-37; 76 (October, 1988): 344-345. This well-titled article attempts to sort out the often duplicative terminology relating to phenomena that astronomers are trying to explain, such as radio galaxies and quasars. Well illustrated with photographs and diagrams.

Seeds, Michael A. *Foundations of Astronomy.* 2d ed. Belmont, Calif.: Wadsworth, 1990. This large introductory-level college textbook devotes three chapters to galaxies and their modern astronomical theory: "Galaxies," "Peculiar Galaxies," and "Cosmology." Contains clear, simple explanations of complicated phenomena, and includes a wealth of photographs, diagrams, graphs, and drawings.

Current Bibliography

Combes, F., et al. *Galaxies and Cosmology.* Translated by M. Seymour. New York: Springer, 1995.

Smail, Ian, Alan Dressler, and Ray M. Sharples. "A Catalog of Morphological Types in Ten Distant Rich Clusters of Galaxies." *The Astrophysical Journal* 110, no. 2 (June, 1997): 213.

Tayler, Roger J. *Galaxies, Structure and Evolution.* Rev. ed. New York: Cambridge University Press, 1993.

Yungelson, L., M. Livio, and A. Tutukov. "On the Rate of Novae in Galaxies of Different Types." *The Astrophysical Journal* 481, no. 1 (May, 1997): 127.

Cross-References

Cosmology, 97; Galactic Structures, 279; Gamma-ray Bursts, 296; Globular Clusters, 310; Interstellar Clouds and the Interstellar Medium, 385; The Milky Way, 584; Quantum Cosmology, 767.

Gamma-ray Bursts

Gamma-ray bursts are a still-unexplained phenomenon in high-energy astrophysics. A variety of spacecraft have detected and studied these random, brief, and intense bursts of gamma rays which come from all parts of the sky. Most current theories associate them with neutron stars in the Galaxy, but an extragalactic source cannot be excluded.

Overview

Gamma-ray bursts are a unique phenomenon in astronomy. During their brief appearance, they are brighter than all other objects in the sky, including the Sun. About a hundred strong gamma-ray bursts occur every year. It is not known how many weaker bursts occur. Years after their discovery, their source is still one of the greatest mysteries in astrophysics. They occur at random times and appear to be randomly distributed over the sky. There is no particular clustering of gamma-ray bursts in any region, nor have they been associated with any known objects. As a result, they are extremely difficult to study, since it is never known when or where a gamma-ray burst will occur.

In recent years it has become recognized that there are distinct classes of gamma-ray bursts, with different properties, that may be caused by entirely different objects or emission mechanisms. The situation is analogous to the recognition, long after the first telescopes came into use, that not all nonstellar objects should be classified simply as "nebulas," since they include objects as diverse as supernova remnants, galaxies, star clusters, and planetary nebulas. It is believed that, similarly, the phenomena that scientists call "gamma-ray bursts" will be found to be caused by more than one process or object.

The discovery of gamma-ray bursts in 1972 by the Vela spacecraft was a classic case of a serendipitous discovery, a discovery made while looking for something else. The Vela spacecraft were designed and operated to detect nuclear explosions from space. This series of small spacecraft, built by TRW and launched in the mid-1960's, contained a wide variety of sensors which "looked" in all directions. The spacecraft were launched into high, eccentric orbits so that they could even scan the area behind the Moon for clandestine nuclear explosions.

The gamma-ray detectors aboard the Vela spacecraft were designed and built at the Los Alamos National Laboratory. They consisted of small scintillation detectors, the output of which was continuously monitored for an increased rate above background. After several years of operation, occasional triggers were detected, but they were dismissed since no other sensors on board the spacecraft recorded the events and because such "glitches" were common to detectors on other spacecraft. It was not until the Los Alamos scientists began studying these triggers in greater detail that their nature became known. In many cases, two or more spacecraft would record a trigger at nearly the same time. It was first suspected that a source of gamma rays from Earth, the Sun, or another object or region within the solar system was causing the gamma-ray bursts. When precise gamma-ray-burst timing analysis was performed, it became evident that the triggers were caused by a plane wave of gamma rays striking the array of widely separated spacecraft. This type of wave could be caused only by a powerful point source of gamma rays far beyond the solar system.

The Los Alamos scientists announced their discovery at a meeting of the American Astronomical Society in Columbus, Ohio, in 1973 and published their findings in an astrophysical journal. Almost immediately, there was a flurry of activity to try to explain the gamma-ray bursts and to obtain more experimental data. As experimenters began to look through old data and data from still-operating spacecraft, many confirmed gamma-ray bursts were detected in addition to those detected by the Vela spacecraft. Among the earlier spacecraft that confirmed the existence of gamma-ray bursts were the Orbiting Solar Observatories, the Orbiting Geophysical Observatories, the Small Astronomy Satellites, the Interplanetary Monitoring Platform, Kosmos 461, Apollo 16, and TD 1, a German spacecraft. It should be noted that none of these spacecraft had detectors that were designed to detect gamma-ray bursts; it was only because of the intensity of the bursts and their coincidence with other observations that they were detectable by instruments designed for other purposes.

By the late 1970's, a network of small detectors on Interplanetary spacecraft was established in an attempt to locate the source of the gamma-ray bursts more precisely. Included in this network were instruments aboard the Pioneer Venus Orbiter; International Sun-Earth Explorer 3 (ISEE 3); Veneras 11, 12, 13, and 14; Prognoz 7; and Helios 2. For the first time, these spacecraft provided the long interplanetary baseline distances required to locate the gamma-ray bursts within one arc minute. Unfortunately, with one important exception, no unusual objects were detected near the burst sources. The exception was the gamma-ray burst of March 5, 1979. It occurred in or near a supernova remnant in the Large Magellanic Cloud. This burst was unusual in other respects, however, so it may have been part of a separate class of gamma-ray bursts, as mentioned previously.

A number of experiments have been designed expressly for the study of gamma-ray bursts. The more important of these have been experiments aboard the following spacecraft: Veneras 11, 12, 13 and 14, the Pioneer Venus Orbiter, Ginga, ISEE 3, the Solar Maximum Mission, Prognoz, and the Italian-Dutch Beppo-SAX satellite. In the late 1980's, scientists were planning to operate some very large, sensitive gamma-ray burst experiments on the Granat and Gamma Ray Observatory spacecraft in Earth orbit. Experiments on several interplanetary spacecraft, including Phobos, Ulysses, Mars Observer, and Wind, were also planned.

Knowledge Gained

Since gamma-ray bursts have not been identified with known objects, their distance is highly uncertain. This, in turn, makes it difficult to speculate on their origin. Since the distance to the burst sources is not known, the intrinsic luminosity of the source is even more uncertain. Many of the early theories of gamma-ray bursts posited exotic phenomena or objects to explain them. In later years, most models have associated gamma-ray bursts with explosive events near, or at the surface of, neutron stars within the Galaxy. These explosions could be caused by thermonuclear reactions resulting from the collision of interstellar material, comets, or asteroids with neutron stars or from the annihilation of strong magnetic fields near such stars. Another theory attributes gamma-ray bursts to a sudden shift of the solid crust that is thought to be present in neutron stars. There are also models of gamma-ray bursts which attribute them to enormous explosions occurring at cosmological distances, or distances near the edge of the observable universe. At these distances, the luminosity of a gamma-ray burst would be equivalent to that of a supernova, although all of its energy would be emitted at gamma-ray wavelengths and within the duration of a gamma-ray burst.

The Gamma-Ray Observatory. *(National Aeronautics and Space Administration)*

The three observable properties of gamma-ray bursts that are most often studied are their time histories, their energy spectra, and the statistical properties of their intensity and distribution over the sky. Attempts to locate a gamma-ray burst and identify it with a known object have thus far been unsuccessful. Very sensitive optical, radio, and X-ray searches have been made of precisely located gamma-ray-burst "error boxes" (the region of uncertainty in the position of a celestial source). These searches have been either inconclusive or controversial. A search of old photographic plates from telescopes in the Southern Hemisphere, however, has shown two or three transient starlike optical images at the location of gamma-ray bursts. The authenticity and the significance of these observations are still being debated.

The time history of a gamma-ray burst refers to the intensity variations of the burst as a function of time. Some gamma-ray bursts show extremely rapid fluctuations over their entire duration, which may encompass a minute or two. Other bursts last a few seconds, during which time only smooth variations are seen. Still others exhibit a single spike lasting only a fraction of a second. The rapid variations indicate that the source of a gamma-ray burst is a very small region or compact object, such as a neutron star or a black hole. The gamma-ray burst of March 5, 1979, was unique in that it had a single, intense spike that was followed by a lower-level emission with an eight-second period that lasted for more than two hundred seconds.

The spectra of gamma-ray bursts indicate that the sources contain regions of extremely high temperatures—perhaps the highest in the universe. In many cases, the gamma-ray energies extend up to 100 megaelectron volts. Extremely rapid variations are observed in the spectra of most gamma-ray bursts. In addition, gamma-ray line features are observed which may be explained by the gamma rays coming from regions with extremely high magnetic fields, such as those expected near neutron stars. There is also a class of gamma-ray bursts that have softer spectra, or lower temperatures, and are observed to be repetitive. Soviet researchers also reported gamma-ray line features near 400 kiloelectronvolts, which some interpreted as being caused by the annihilation and redshift of electron-positron plasma near the surface of a neutron star.

Update

In February, 1997, telescopes sighted the source of a burst, a diffuse, elongated object with a bright core. Astronomers thought the object might be a very distant galaxy, but they could not be certain without more data.

Context

The field of high-energy astrophysics is a product of the space age. It is necessary to carry instruments and telescopes above Earth's atmosphere in order to observe the universe at X-ray and gamma-ray wavelengths. This relatively new branch of astronomy not only has taught scientists more about objects that they already knew to exist but also has revealed new types of objects and phenomena, including X-ray stars, black holes, and gamma-ray bursts. These objects are among the most energetic and violent in the universe. Most of them are associated with the final stages in the life cycles of massive stars.

Gamma-ray bursts represent one of the greatest unsolved problems in high-energy astrophysics today. Their distance and luminosity are unknown. They are difficult to study because of their random and transient nature. Although the initial discovery and studies of gamma-ray bursts were made by groups in the United States, the Soviets, often with French collaborators, also obtained many of the gamma-ray-burst data. The establishment of an international gamma-ray-burst observation network, combining data from as many as nine spacecraft, has become a model for international collaboration in space exploration. It is expected that the continued study of gamma-ray bursts not only will help astrophysicists in their understanding of these objects but also will enable scientists to study conditions of extreme temperature, pressure, and density that are unavailable anywhere else.

Gerald J. Fishman

Basic Bibliography

Fichtel, Carl E., and Jacob I. Trombka. *Gamma-Ray Astrophysics: New Insight into the Universe.* NASA SP-453. Washington, D.C.: Government Printing Office, 1981. A comprehensive survey of the methods and objectives of gamma-ray astronomy, this book describes how gamma rays are formed in the solar system and the Galaxy and the various methods used to detect them. Suitable for general audiences.

Hillier, Rodney. *Gamma-Ray Astronomy.* Oxford: Clarendon Press, 1984. This well-illustrated and well-referenced book provides a comprehensive, college-level overview of the objects and methods of gamma-ray astronomy.

Katz, Johnathan I. *High Energy Astrophysics.* Reading, Mass.: Addison-Wesley Publishing Co., 1987. A well-organized book covering all aspects of high-energy astrophysics but concentrating on emission mechanisms. For advanced readers.

Liang, Eddison P., and Vahe Petrosian, eds. *Gamma-Ray Bursts.* New York: American Institute of Physics, 1986. This book summarizes the observational and theoretical status of gamma-ray bursts as of 1985. The authors of the various chapters have distilled the contents of more than thirty papers that were presented at a workshop on gamma-ray bursts at Stanford University in 1985. Written at an advanced level but comprehensible to the educated reader.

Lingenfelder, Richard E., H. S. Hudson, and D. M. Worrall, eds. *Gamma-Ray Transients and Related Astrophysical Phenomena.* New York: American Institute of Physics, 1982. This book contains forty-four papers on gamma-ray bursts, X-ray bursts, solar transients, and instrumental concepts. Many of the papers are quite detailed and technical, but there arc a few papers of a summary nature.

Schaefer, Bradley E. "Gamma-Ray Bursters." *Scientific American* 252 (February, 1985): 52-58. A broad summary of the observed properties of gamma-ray bursts and their possible origins, this article has well-produced illustrations of models of gamma-ray bursts and describes how they may be formed near neutron stars. Aimed at the educated general reader.

Woosley, Stanford E., ed. *High Energy Transients in Astrophysics.* New York: American Institute of Physics, 1984. This book contains seventy-four papers that were given at a special two-week meeting at the University of California at Santa Cruz in July, 1983. The primary topics were X-ray bursts and gamma-ray bursts, from both an observational and a theoretical viewpoint. The topics are covered by overviews and by detailed technical papers.

Current Bibliography

Charles, Philip A., and Frederick D. Seward. *Exploring the X-Ray Universe.* New York: Cambridge University Press, 1995.

Jelley, John V., and Trevor C. Weekes. "Ground-Based Gamma-Ray Astronomy." *Sky and Telescope* 90, no. 3 (September, 1995): 20-25.

Parker, Barry. "Where Have All the Black Holes Gone?" *Astronomy* 22, no. 10 (October, 1994): 36-40.

Ramana Murthy, Poolla V., and Arnold W. Wolfendale. *Gamma-Ray Astronomy.* 2d ed. New York: Cambridge University Press, 1993.

Tanaka, Yasuo. "Recent Advances of X-Ray Astronomy." *Science* 263, no. 5143 (January, 1994): 42-45.

Cross-References

Cosmic Microwave Background Radiation, 84; Cosmic Rays, 91; Cosmology, 97; Galactic Structures, 279; Galaxies and Galactic Clusters, 287; Neutron Stars, 614; Novas, Bursters, and X-ray Sources, 628; Quantum Cosmology, 767; Thermonuclear Reactions in Stars, 983; X-ray and Gamma-ray Astronomy, 1068.

General Relativity

The general theory of relativity is a theory describing the effects of acceleration and gravity on bodies, as well as the structure of space and time. Developed by Albert Einstein in 1915, it is the basic theory of gravity on which astronomers, cosmologists, and theoretical physicists base their study of the universe.

Overview

The general theory of relativity is a model of how gravity works. Considering the large-scale structure of the universe, gravity is the governing force. Gravity is what holds the solar system together and what dominates the interactions between stars and galaxies. It also dictates theories of the past and future of the universe as a whole. Any model of the universe, then, must have its basis in a theory of gravity. The general theory of relativity has stood the test of time and experimentation to become the basis of modern cosmological theory.

The motivation of Albert Einstein (1879-1955) in working out the principles of relativity was the belief that it is impossible to detect motion relative to any fixed point in space and that, therefore, there is no absolute motion. The general theory is the second of two stages of a larger picture of relativity theory. The first stage is special relativity, which deals with the laws of physics as seen by observers in uniform, or unaccelerated, motion. The general theory goes beyond the special theory to deal with accelerated motion and gravity.

General relativity describes the universe in the terms of four dimensions: three dimensions in space and the fourth in time. This concept becomes clear when one thinks about the relationship between time and space. Since light travels at a finite pace, the objects that humans can see in the night sky are not seen as they are now, but as they were when their light originally left them. Light from the closest star to Earth has taken about four years to reach this planet, while the light from the nearest galaxy has taken more than 2 million years. From frames of reference located elsewhere in the universe, the relative positions of the stars and galaxies change, as does their relative distance in time. Therefore, space cannot be referred to without reference to time. In general relativity, the fabric of the universe is referred to as space-time.

A fundamental concept in the general theory of relativity is the principle of equivalence. Einstein showed that the effects of acceleration and the

Albert Einstein, father of the general theory of relativity. *(Library of Congress)*

effects of gravity are indistinguishable. This principle is often demonstrated with the use of a "thought experiment." Imagine that a man is in an elevator which has no windows. Now imagine that the elevator is in deep space where there is no gravitational effect. As long as the elevator is in constant motion, he floats around freely inside, experiencing weightlessness. If a constant force is applied to the bottom of the elevator, then it accelerates at a uniform pace and the contents of the elevator (the man) are pushed against the floor. This accelerating force can be adjusted to exactly match the downward pull that he would experience if the elevator were on the surface of the Earth. Without a window to determine the motion relative to the outside world, it would be impossible to tell if the force that he felt was attributable to gravity or to the acceleration of the elevator. From this type of thought experiment, Einstein concluded that gravity and accelera-tion were equivalent.

Following from the principle of equivalence, Einstein proposed that the idea of gravity as the force that attracts separate masses is entirely unneces-sary. Instead, he described a more accurate way of looking at gravity by showing that the presence of mass changes the nature of space-time. Gravity changes the very geometry of space by curving, or warping, it. In the absence of matter, then, the shape or curvature of space-time is flat. Near massive objects, however, space-time is strongly warped. The larger is the amount of matter at any location, the greater is the curvature of space-time at that location. The extent of the curvature is greatest near the massive object, and the curvature becomes progressively less with increasing distance.

Effectively, then, the curvature of space-time around massive objects determines the path of bodies traveling through space. In other words, the curvature of space causes objects to follow curved paths. The Earth, therefore, orbits the Sun not because of the gravitational force of the Sun, but because the mass of the Sun curves the space immediately around it.

Another thought experiment is useful to picture the curvature of space. Imagine a pool table whose surface is not rigid but is made of a thin rubber sheet. When a large weight is placed on such a pool table, the normally flat sheet would stretch, curving around the weight. The heavier is the weight, the more curved is the surface of the pool table. Attempting to play pool with this weight distorting the surface of the table, one finds that balls passing near the weight are deflected from their straight paths. This is a two-dimensional analogy describing how radiation, light, and material objects are deflected by the curvature of space-time around massive objects. When the universe is taken as a whole, the size, shape, structure, and dynamics of the whole is determined by the net effect of curvature caused by every massive object it contains.

While the basic principles of general relativity are straightforward, some of the implications of the theory defy common sense and ordinary experience. Einstein found that the laws that are used to describe the behavior of objects in most circumstances do not hold when very strong gravitational fields are involved or when velocities approach the speed of light. In special relativity, one finds that uniform motion at speeds approaching that of light affects the measurements of the length of objects or the time that it takes for events to occur. In an accelerated frame of reference, or a gravitational field, similar effects take place. Time actually slows as a result of acceleration, and experiments have repeatedly shown this effect to be true. An atomic clock positioned near a massive object will run slower than a clock farther away. Researchers also have found, for example, that clocks in Boulder, Colorado, a mile above sea level, gained about fifteen-billionths of a second per day as compared with clocks near sea level. The difference is attributed to Boulder's greater distance from the Earth's center of gravity.

There is another unusual prediction arising from the general theory of relativity which surprised and disturbed even Einstein. One of the early solutions of the complex sets of equations Einstein created indicated that, if an object were sufficiently compressed, then its gravitational field would be so strong that not even light could escape it. The equations of the theory of general relativity also allowed for mass to be squeezed into an infinitely small space. The implications of this curiosity would wait almost fifty years to be realized. It then became the basis for the fascinating theory of black holes.

Another result predicted by general relativity is that the wavelength or color of a light will be affected by gravity. For example, if blue light is emitted from the surface of a very massive star, then the theory predicts that its wavelength will be lengthened and the color of the light will move toward the red end of the visual spectrum. Experiments using light emitted by the Sun, light emitted by white dwarf stars, and measured gamma rays have succeeded in confirming that this shift actually does take place.

There have been many experimental tests of the validity of the general theory of relativity. In one experiment, the curved path of light near the edge of the Sun was measured during a solar eclipse. The stars near the edge of the Sun were photographed near the edge of the darkened Sun during the eclipse, and their positions were compared with their positions under normal conditions away from the Sun. It has been found that the apparent positions of the stars are shifted by an amount which is consistent with the predictions of general relativity. During the eclipse, the stars appear to shift because the path of their light is warped as it passes the massive body of the Sun. Other variations of this test have been performed and also have confirmed the predictions of general relativity.

Another test is related to the motion of the planet Mercury. Based on the traditional theory of gravity, when all gravitational influences on the planet are taken into account, the observed path of Mercury still fails to correspond to the predicted path. According to general relativity, however, another factor is brought into the equation: Because of the distortion of space around the Sun, Mercury's orbit will not always be the same, but the whole orbit will slowly revolve around the Sun. A comparison of the predicted amount of this added motion with observations of the actual motion of Mercury agree nearly precisely.

While it may be impossible to prove that the general theory of relativity is correct, the experiments that have been used to test it so far have failed to disprove it. It remains the most accurate theory by which to measure and predict the effects of gravity.

Applications

The importance of the general theory of relativity lies not so much in the ability to measure and predict with accuracy, but in the way in which humans think about the universe. The theory is of fundamental importance to astronomy because it alters views about space, time, and matter. In particular, the theory has surprising and profound implications when applied to very massive compact stars and when used to understand the large-scale structure of the universe.

Massive compact stars are objects like neutron stars and white dwarf stars. A neutron star is a very dense body composed of tightly packed neutrons. It is thought to be one possible end result of a supernova. A neutron star represents a mass greater than that of the Sun compressed into a sphere only 16 kilometers wide. A white dwarf star is an old, extremely dense star about as large as the Earth but with a mass as great as the Sun. It is the final result of a star that has used all its fuel. At the extreme end of density lies a black hole, whose intense gravity has compressed it into a singularity (a mass that has been compressed into an infinitely small point). A singularity was one of the early solutions of the general relativity equations. Because the results defied common sense, the idea that objects such as these might actually exist was rejected by Einstein himself and by most scientists as aberrations of the theory. With new techniques in astronomy, however, amazing new observations began to be made which required explanations using these aspects of relativity theory. Extremely dense objects powered by gravitational fields are universally accepted. Although they have not yet been observed directly, even black holes are commonly considered to be bonafide members of the cosmic family—bizarre objects that even Einstein himself could not imagine but that were predicted by his theory of general relativity.

Einstein believed that the universe was static. Although the equations that he worked with did not indicate a static universe, his belief caused him to introduce changes in his equations which would keep it as a steady state model. It is now known that the universe is not static, that the galaxies and all the matter in the universe are rushing outward as part of the expansion of the universe. Armed with this knowledge and a working theory of gravity—the general theory of relativity—a new cosmology was created.

Since gravity is the force that governs the large-scale dynamics of the universe, general relativity has been used to create models of the universe that roughly fit observations. It helps to describe how the universe might have expanded from a singularity (in which all the matter in the universe was compressed into a single, infinitely small point) to form galaxies, stars, and planets. It allows scientists to formulate answers to the biggest questions of all: How did the universe begin? Will it end, and if so, how?

All models begin with the assumption that the universe is expanding, having its origin in the cosmic explosion known as the big bang. Although this theory has been contested, no other theory has yet become as widely accepted. According to modern models of the universe, its fate ultimately depends on the average density of matter in the universe. This density determines whether gravity will act to stop the expansion of the universe.

If the average density of the universe is below a critical value, then the universe is considered to be "open." In this case, gravitation cannot act to stop expansion and the universe will continue to expand forever, its atoms spreading farther and farther apart until it is nearly energyless. If the average density is above the critical value, then gravity will eventually cause the universe to halt its expansion and to begin contracting until it eventually is returned to the state of a singularity. If the average density of the universe is equal to the critical value, then gravity will slow the expansion of the universe but will never quite be able to stop it. For all these models, quite different geometries prevail. Ultimately, it is mass which determines the shape and therefore the geometry of the universe, as explained by Einstein's theories. Direct observation reveals about ten times less than the critical density value of matter to close the universe, but scientists suspect that the reason humans do not see more matter in the universe is that it radiates in a form which cannot yet be detected. These questions lie on the frontiers of modern astronomy.

Context

The theory of relativity emerged as a logical step forward in the understanding of space and time and the relationship of the Earth to the rest of the universe. It arose out of the inability of Newton's laws of gravity and motion to describe the observed universe in certain circumstances. At very high velocities or in the presence of very strong magnetic fields, Newton's laws of gravity break down.

The general theory of relativity arose out of Einstein's earlier special theory of relativity. The concept of relativity was extremely important for the development of theories about the universe because it described two fundamental truths: All motion is relative, and there is no preferred frame of reference in which space and time are defined absolutely. Einstein wrote his first paper on relativity in 1905. He was motivated by the conviction that it is fundamentally impossible to detect motion relative to absolute space. Relativity also abolishes the commonsense notion of a basic universal time.

Although the importance of relativity theory was recognized from the start, it lay mostly dormant for nearly forty years. Theoretical work was being done, but little experimental work. In the early 1960's, when increased technology allowed for the discovery of unexpected types of astronomical objects, relativity theory went through a renaissance. Explanations of the behavior of distant objects could only be explained on the basis of Einstein's theories.

Einstein's goal was to develop a unified theory of the universe. He spent the last years of his life searching for the universal force that would link gravitation to electromagnetic and subatomic forces. This remains a major goal of physics, although it has become even more complex since Einstein's day. At the end of the twentieth century, the attempt was to merge the general theory of relativity with quantum mechanics, the theory that describes how subatomic particles interact. The goal was also to develop a theory which encompasses the forces and all the elementary particles of nature (the fundamental, irreducible components that make up all the matter in the universe).

Relativity has stood the test of time and experimentation to become the foundation of modern cosmology and physics. It is a cornerstone of the attempts to create a unified theory of the universe. Much of the focus of future study centers on the predictions and consequences of general relativity. It is one more tool in the continuing efforts to describe and predict events in the world and, if possible, to understand the nature of the universe.

Divonna Ogier

Basic Bibliography

Calder, Nigel. *Einstein's Universe.* New York: Viking Press, 1979. A well-written book directed toward a general audience. Details the principles of special and general relativity in reference to Einstein's life and a general philosophy of the universe. Useful analogies and popular language make a difficult subject more easily understandable.

Chaisson, Eric. *Relatively Speaking.* New York: W. W. Norton, 1988. A highly readable book giving an overview of Einstein's work on special and general relativity and how it relates to modern astronomical and cosmological questions. Gives a nonmathematical analysis of cosmology and singularity theory.

Hawking, Stephen. *A Brief History of Time.* New York: Bantam Books, 1988. An excellent overview of relativity theory as it applies to modern cosmological inquiry. An excellent resource for the reader who has an interest in the theories but does not have a strong background in science. Written by one of the foremost researchers of cosmological theory of the twentieth century.

Parker, Barry. *Einstein's Dream.* New York: Plenum Press, 1986. A perspective of relativity theory related to Einstein's ultimate goal of a unified theory of the universe. Gives a good historical analysis of relativity and unification theory. Devotes chapters to the origin of the universe, the ultimate fate of the universe, black holes, and quantum theory. Nonmathematical, but recommended for the reader with a background in physics.

Schwartz, Joseph, and Michael McGuinness. *Einstein for Beginners.* New York: Pantheon Books, 1979. A delightful introductory book for those intimidated by the usual presentations of scientific theory. Written in simple language with comic book style drawings, it gives a basic overview of Einstein's life, the political and social environment from which he emerged, and the basic principles of his work.

Time-Life Books editors. *The Cosmos.* Alexandria, Va.: Time-Life Books, 1988. Part of the Voyage Through the Universe series, which examines the universe from the big bang theory to space exploration. A richly illustrated volume that explores the study of the large-scale structure of the universe from a historical perspective. Does a very good job of presenting a complete picture of the subject, although the language and concepts are advanced for the general reader.

Current Bibliography

Barbour, Julian B., and Herbert Pfister, eds. *Mach's Principle: From Newton's Bucket to Quantum Gravity.* Einstein Studies 6. Boston: Birkhauser, 1995.

Foster, J., and J. D. Nightingale. *A Short Course in General Relativity.* 2d ed. New York: Springer-Verlag, 1995.

Glendenning, Norman K. *Compact Stars: Nuclear Physics, Particle Physics, and General Relativity.* New York: Springer, 1997.

Martin, J. L. *General Relativity: A First Course for Physicists.* Rev. ed. New York: Prentice-Hall, 1996.

Sartori, Leo. *Understanding Relativity: A Simplified Approach to Einstein's Theories.* Berkeley: University of California Press, 1996.

Cross-References

Globular Clusters

Globular clusters are spherically symmetrical compact systems containing several tens of thousands of stars that share a common origin; thus, globular clusters are important because they contain a mix of variously sized stars that all lie at the same distance from Earth and all evolved from the same cloud of gas at the same time.

Overview

Globular clusters are spherically symmetrical compact stars located in the halo of the galaxy, are some of the oldest stars in the galaxy, have low metal content, and contain more than a million stars with typical radii of 1 to 10 parsecs. An example of a globular cluster is the Great Cluster in Hercules.

When the Milky Way galaxy was first condensed from a huge cloud of gas, it was roughly spherical. As the collapse proceeded, the rotation of the cloud began to take effect, eventually causing it to become a flattened disk rather than a ball. In the earliest stages of the collapse, however, stars formed in some locally denser sections. These stars—the oldest in the galaxy—occupy a more nearly spherical distribution known as the galactic spheroid or halo. These globular clusters are usually red giants; they typically have diameters of 40 to 50 light-years. A light-year is the distance that light travels in a year: 10 trillion kilometers or 102,000 astronomical kilometers. A globular cluster is an impressive sight. Looking through a large telescope, astronomers have discovered that globular clusters consist of many thousands of stars and are concentrated so tightly that they cannot be fully separated by any ground-based telescope. Globular clusters are better studied from the Southern Hemisphere, except for M13 in Hercules.

Globular clusters have an enormous range in chemical composition. Few are close enough for analysis of their individual stars. The brightest and nearest stars are only of the tenth magnitude. Globular clusters are so populous and their total magnitude is so bright that collective spectra have been recorded for most of them. The interpretation of such spectra presents special problems because they are made of contributions of many stars that differ in luminosity and temperature. These stars have a very large range in metal content, far larger than anything that has been found among open clusters. Globular clusters are rich sources of variable stars whose periods range from about an hour and a half to little more than a day. The period of a variable star is the interval in light variations from maximum-to-minimum-to-maximum amount of light received from the star. Variable stars were first detected in 1895 by Solon Irving Bailey on photographs of certain globular clusters. The brightest of the globular clusters—Omega Centauri (NGC 5139)—lies in the Southern Hemisphere and resembles a hazy star of about fourth magnitude. In reality, it is an immense ball-shaped swarm of at least several hundred thousand stars. Sir John Frederick Herschel (1792-1871), an English astronomer, described it as a "noble globular cluster, beyond all comparison the richest and largest object of the kind in the heavens."

Globular clusters are stellar population II systems, in that all the stars within them are relatively old, actually older than Earth's sun, and have a very low metal content. The distribution and other characteristics of globular clusters indicate that they were formed early in the life of the galaxy, probably around 12 billion years ago, before the main body of the galactic disk had evolved. Globular clusters can be seen around other galaxies; however, they are extremely faint spots of light and can be separated from foreground stars only by extremely close observations. There are always more globular clusters around elliptical galaxies than spiral galaxies. The Milky Way is typical of spirals having fewer than 150 globular clusters. Some globular clusters occupy the flattened disk of the Milky Way. A problem with globular clusters lying near the plane is that they are difficult to detect and, as a consequence, a few remain to be discovered. Globular clusters move in orbits around the galactic center under the gravitational control of the whole system. They have highly inclined eccentric orbits, and many have large velocities. Globular clusters pass in and out of the plane of the Milky Way, suffering total disturbance as they pass through the most massive regions of the system.

Since most of the members in a globular cluster will have evolved away from the main sequence, the Hertzsprung-Russell (H-R) diagram for stars of a globular cluster will differ greatly from the conventional H-R diagram. The turnoff point, or the point on the main sequence where the giant branch originates in the H-R diagram, gives a measure of the age of a cluster. Distances to globular clusters are usually calculated from the apparent magnitudes of the variable RR Lyrae stars in the globular cluster. RR Lyrae stars appear as a nearly horizontal grouping in the H-R diagram, known as a horizontal branch. The intrinsic brightness of the RR Lyrae stars in globular clusters can be determined and can be recognized in other locations. Because the stars of a globular cluster lie at the same distance from Earth, H-R diagrams can be plotted for them simply by measuring their color and their apparent magnitude; however, it is very important to consider that there is a constant difference between the apparent and absolute magnitude according to the cluster's distance. Apparent magnitude represents the relative brightness of a star or starlike object. A star of the first magnitude is said to be one hundred times brighter than one of the sixth magnitude. A difference of 1 in magnitude corresponds to a ratio in brightness of 2.512. On the other hand, absolute magnitude is the magnitude that a star would have if it were at a distance of 10 parsecs from Earth; it corresponds to a parallax of 0.1 second of arc. The H-R diagram clearly shows which stars have begun their transformation into red giants, which leads to a determination of the age of the cluster.

Applications

The most important feature of globular clusters is their value as a means of estimating distances. The presence of globular clusters in the halo of other galaxies presents one of the better ways to measure distances between galaxies. Globular clusters contain a particular type of variable—the RR Lyrae stars—that have brightnesses that can be determined and recognized in other galaxies; astronomers use this variable to measure intergalactic distances.

Globular clusters are important because they contain a mixture of stars of various sizes that all lie at the same distance from Earth and all evolved from the same cloud of gas at the same time. Therefore, they play a vital role in understanding the life history of stars. They have facilitated the develop-

Globular cluster G1 in Galaxy M31. *(National Aeronautics and Space Administration)*

ment of the H-R diagram, particularly the red giant and main sequence. For example, since the stars of a globular cluster lie at the same distance from Earth, an H-R diagram can be plotted for them by measuring their color and their apparent magnitude. It is important to know that there is a constant difference between the apparent and the absolute magnitude according to the cluster's distance. That distance can be determined by comparison with a standard H-R diagram because the main sequence will appear in the correct place only if the distance is right.

There are virtually no main sequence stars in globular clusters that are brighter by about one magnitude than the Sun. Main sequence theory premises that if stars near the Sun are arranged in order of increasing luminosity, most of them form a sequence of increasing mass, surface temperature, and size. These stars are also referred to as dwarf stars. The giant sequence, when stars are more luminous and, therefore, larger than the dwarf stars of the same spectral type, is joined to the main sequence by an almost vertical bridge. There is sometimes a narrow branch of white and blue stars of about absolute magnitude zero. When color-magnitude arrays of globular clusters are compared, significant differences are noted: Spectra of the brightest stars in a globular cluster often show extremely weak lines of heavy elements, ranking from 0.1 to 0.01 percent; however, in open clusters, the strength of the lines of heavy elements is between 1 and 4 percent.

The spectra of the individual stars in globular clusters can be studied only with a powerful 508-centimeter telescope, for example. A careful study of the spectra of stars of a given intrinsic brightness in different globular clusters differs not only from those stars near the Sun but also from one cluster to another. The differences occur in the sense that the metal-to-hydrogen ratio often was smaller in globular clusters than in the Sun.

Stellar evolution can be explained from cluster color-magnitude diagrams, which are a plot of the magnitudes (apparent and absolute) of the stars in a cluster against their color indices. For example, if one assumes that star clusters composed of differing masses were formed at about the same time, that their masses ranged from 10 solar masses to 0.1 solar mass (solar mass is 1.989×10^{30}), and that they were shining on the main sequence, then their luminosities would be correlated with their masses; however, the more massive the star, the more rapidly it would liberate energy.

Each gram of the most massive stars would liberate energy about a hundred times as fast as a gram of the Sun. Taking this a step further and assuming that the total amount of energy that can be squeezed out of each gram is the same for all matter everywhere, then the more massive stars will exhaust their fuel more quickly, leave the main sequence, and eventually disappear. Older clusters show this sequence: The brightest, most profligate stars have used up their energy resources and have disappeared, at least from the main sequence. Further, giants and supergiants represent stars that have evolved from the main sequence, and white dwarfs represent the final stage of evolution.

The Great Cluster M 13 in Hercules, an example of a globular cluster. *(National Aeronautics and Space Administration)*

Another important role of globular clusters is that they are found in all parts of the sky, not merely within the disk of the Milky Way. The distribution as seen from Earth is not uniform, since there appears to be more in the region of the constellation Sagittarius than in the diametrically opposite direction.

Context

The ancient Greeks first noted the existence of clusters of any type when they described the Hyades, Pleiades, and Praesepe. These clusters are the most visible northern open clusters; however, it was not until the first telescopic surveys by Edmond Halley (1656-1742), a seventeenth century English astronomer, and Charles Messier (1730-1817), an eighteenth century French astronomer, that the existence of globular clusters was made known. It was believed initially that these objects were nebulous; however, the spectroscopic observations of Sir William Huggins (1824-1910), an English astronomer, and Pietro Angelo Secchi (1818-1878), an Italian astronomer, in the late nineteenth century showed how to distinguish nebulas from clusters. Bailey and later Harlow Shapley (1885-1972), an American astronomer with Harvard University, noted that there is a distinct class of variable stars associated with the clusters. These RR Lyrae stars are a group of horizontal branch stars with periods of about one-half day that display a distinctive period-luminosity relation.

Globular clusters are found in all parts of the sky, are useful in estimating distances, and have value in determining the age of galaxies. They have played a role in the history of astronomy as a result of the fact that early attempts to determine the location of the Sun within the galaxy were based on observation of the distributions in space of stars of similar brightness; however, the conclusions drawn were invalid because the absorption of light by interstellar dust had been overlooked. The first reliable results were obtained in 1917 from Shapley's studies of the globular clusters.

Globular clusters will continue to function in the future as they have in the past; as more powerful space-based telescopes are perfected and placed in orbit, new globular clusters will most certainly be identified. They will be measured, and the history of the galaxy in which they are found will be revealed.

Earl G. Hoover

Basic Bibliography

Allei, Lawrence H. *Atoms, Stars, and Nebulae.* Rev. ed. Cambridge, Mass.: Harvard University Press, 1971. The book explains in nontechnical language the physical processes at work in the interiors and exteriors of stars, touching on the evolution of stars, production of novas and supernovas, the interstellar medium, quasars, and pulsars. Geared for the beginning student of astrophysics. Numerous illustrations help clarify the text.

Gaposchkin, Cecilia H. Payne. *Stars and Clusters.* Cambridge, Mass.: Harvard University Press, 1979. Copiously illustrated with diagrams, drawings, and photographs, this book contains a complete atlas of stars, nebulas, and clusters to a minimum magnitude of 6.05. Good reference for the high school and college student. The chapter on globular clusters is recommended.

Glasstone, Samuel. *Sourcebook on the Space Sciences.* Princeton, N.J.: D. Van Nostrand, 1965. Represents a comprehensive account of the principles and applications of space science. Intended for the reader with an

elementary knowledge of physics and chemistry. Mathematics is kept
to a minimum. There are more than three hundred illustrations to
facilitate understanding. Each paragraph is individually numbered for
quick reference.

Kaufmann, William J., III. *Stars and Nebulas.* San Francisco: W. H. Freeman, 1978. The first of a trilogy on astronomy written for a general
audience. Brings the fascination of modern astronomy to light. Although there is minimal reference to globular clusters, this book is
recommended for its clear and interesting writing style. Contains a
brief reading list at the end of the book and an appendix of monthly
star charts.

King, Henry C. *Pictorial Guide to the Stars.* New York: Thomas Y. Crowell,
1967. Gives a reasonably clear and well-balanced account about the
stars. Most of the text is concerned with astrophysics. King writes in a
descriptive manner and has held technicalities to a minimum. A very
good glossary at the end of the book complements the numerous
photographs, drawings, and diagrams. A good reference for the advanced high school and lower-level college student.

Current Bibliography

Burgella, Denis. "Globular Clusters at Low and High Redshift." *Science*
276, no. 5317 (May, 1997): 1370-1375.

Djorgovski, S. G., and G. Meylan, eds. *Structure and Dynamics of Globular
Clusters.* San Francisco, Calif.: Astronomical Society of the Pacific, 1993.

Jakiel, Richard. "Southern Skies Hoard the Giants: A Treasury of Giant
Globulars Lies Buried in the South." *Astronomy* 25, no. 5 (May, 1997):
78-82.

Santa Cruz Summer Workshop in Astronomy and Astrophysics. *The Globu-
lar Cluster-Galaxy Connection: Globular Clusters Within the Context of Their
Parent Galaxies.* Edited by Graeme H. Smith and Jean P. Brodie. San
Francisco: Astronomical Society of the Pacific, 1993.

Verschuur, Gerrit L. "In the Beginning." *Astronomy* 21, no. 10 (October,
1993): 40-46.

Cross-References

Cosmology, 97; Galactic Structures, 279; Galaxies and Galactic Clusters, 287;
The Milky Way, 584; Quantum Cosmology, 767.

Gravitational Lensing and Einstein Rings

A gravitational lens is a very massive object which, because of its strong gravitational field, warps the fabric of space and time. This curvature of space around a massive object, such as a black hole, results in a distortion of background images. The light from a single star will produce two or more separate images. If the background light source, the observer, and the massive object are perfectly aligned, the gravitational lensing will result in a ringlike image of the distant object. This image is called an Einstein ring.

Overview

Gravitational lensing is an effect observed near very massive objects such as black holes and clusters of galaxies which is caused by the general relativistic curvature of space produced by these massive objects. Such compact, massive objects deflect light rays passing through them much as an optical lens bends light to form an image. Multiple images will be formed of the distant object. These images formed by the lens will be magnified, brightened, and distorted. The magnification and brightening of the images provide a powerful "zoom lens" for viewing galaxies that are so far away that they could not normally be observed with the largest available telescopes.

Einstein showed that it was not necessary to think of gravity as a force. The principle of equivalence of general relativity states that in a small volume of space the downward pull of gravity can be accurately and completely duplicated by an upward acceleration of the observer. Gravity can be described entirely by its effect on space and time. Near a strong source of gravity clocks slow down and space is curved. One way of understanding the curvature of space around a strong gravitational source is to consider an observer in an accelerating spacecraft who will not be able distinguish between his spacecraft's acceleration and its condition of rest near a source of gravity (a planet, for instance). Consider the path of a light beam that is shot across the spaceship perpendicular to its direction of travel. As the spaceship accelerates past the beam of light, it will appear to the observer that the beam is following a curved path. Since the light beam is composed of photons, which have no mass or charge, it will curve only if space itself is curved. Since this effect is observed in an accelerating system, it must also hold in a gravitational system because of the principle of equivalence. Thus, one effect of a large gravitational source is the curvature of space around the source.

Imagine holding a sheet at each corner so that it is stretched tightly, forming a flat surface. Now drop a baseball on this surface. The weight of the ball will make an indentation in the sheet, curving the "space" to form a depression. If a bowling ball is now dropped on the sheet, the depression, or gravitational well, will be deeper and more difficult to flatten out. If one drops an object the size of a BB with the mass of several thousand bowling balls, it will make a hole in the sheet. Anything entering this well will be unable to escape. For a very massive star, the fabric of space becomes so severely curved that a hole is essentially punched through it. The dying star disappears into this hole along with anything else entering it, including light. It will thus appear black. The point of no return, at which nothing, including light, can leave the black hole, is called the event horizon.

If an object is rolling along the flat surface of space between gravitational wells (dents in our sheet), it will travel in a straight line. As the object just skims the horizon of a well it will be deflected around the curvature of the top of the well. It will curve around the well and then continue in a straight line. Gravitational lenses have much the same effect on light. As the light approaches a region of space where a very massive object is located, it gets bent around the curve or the edge of the gravitational well. However, when we view the light that has been deflected around the sides of a gravitational well, our perceptions are deceived. We know that light can travel only in a straight line under normal circumstances, and we trace it back to where it would have originated had it traveled in a straight line. Thus, several images of the same object may be formed as the light follows different paths around the well.

In addition to distorting space, a strong gravitational source will also slow down time. As seen from a distant observer, time will seem to stop entirely within a black hole. As an object accelerates toward the black hole, its velocity will approach the speed of light. However, no object can travel faster than the speed of light. Thus, in order to keep the velocity of the object from exceeding the speed of light, time must become dilated until it essentially seems to stand still.

If the massive object creating the gravitational lens is a galaxy in which the mass is spread out over some volume of space, multiple images of a distant object, such as a quasar, will form. An Einstein cross is such an image, whereby the gravitational lens formed by a galaxy creates four images of a distant quasar. If the distant object emitting the light is an extended object such as a galaxy viewed past a black hole, then the images of the object will become elongated into arcs that will encircle the location of the lensing black hole. Einstein was the first to suggest that the image of a remote source of light would be formed into a ring of some sort. Thus, these images are known as Einstein rings.

Methods of Study

In 1979 Dennis Walsh, Robert Carswell, and Ray Weymann observed a very surprising phenomenon. They found what they thought were two very faint quasars separated by only six seconds of arc. Observing the spectra of the two quasars, they found that their composition was identical. They concluded that they had not observed two separate quasars after all, but two images of the same quasar. Later observations revealed a galaxy between the quasar and Earth. The gravitational distortion of space due to the massive galaxy was bending the light from the distant quasar, thus acting like a lens.

Since 1979 many more observations are believed to be examples of gravitational lensing. In all of the cases that have been confirmed as gravitational lenses, light from a remote quasar is split by a galaxy located between Earth and the quasar. In some of these observations three or four images of the quasar are produced because the mass of the galaxy is spread out over a large volume of space. These images, known as an Einstein cross, produce four images of the quasar distributed in a cross around a faint image of the intervening galaxy.

In 1987, Roger Lynds at Kitt Peak National Observatory and Vahe Petrosian of Stanford University observed a large luminous arc over three hundred thousand light-years long in a remote cluster of galaxies. This arc is the image of a distant quasar or galaxy that has been stretched out by the gravitational lensing of a galaxy closer to Earth. Anthony Tyson at Bell Labs/Lucent Technologies has shown that detailed observations of such arc-shaped images can be used to map the mass of galaxy clusters that created the gravitational lens. This work is very important in the current search for dark matter in the universe.

In 1988 Jacqueline Hewitt of the Massachusetts Institute of Technology (MIT) discovered a ringlike image of a remote radio galaxy. Such images, known as Einstein rings, are very difficult to detect, because the distant quasar or galaxy, the galaxy forming the gravitational lens, and the Earth must be almost perfectly aligned. Any slight deviation from perfect alignment will decrease the intensity of the rings, often rendering them undetectable through the atmosphere. Since the launch of the Hubble Space Telescope in 1990 many more gravitational lenses have been observed. Hubble's high resolution allows astronomers to extend the search to include images much fainter than those observable through ground-based telescopes. These fainter images originate from much more distant objects, thus expanding our range of knowledge about the universe. Hubble can also explore a larger volume of space than Earth-bound telescopes, providing enough examples of all types of gravitational lensing so that astronomers can address such fundamental cosmological questions as the amount and composition of dark matter and achieve a more accurate determination of the Hubble constant.

A view of a gravitational lens in galaxy cluster 0024+ 1654. *(National Aeronautics and Space Administration)*

Context

As a star approaches the end of its life span, its core begins to cool and die out. As it cools, its gases no longer try to rise from the core. Without this outward pressure of rising hot gases, the gravitational pull of the mass of the star makes it begin to collapse. At this point, a star the size of our Sun will collapse into a neutron star or a white dwarf. However, if the mass of the star's burned-out core is greater than three solar masses, the overpowering weight of its matter will force it to collapse under its own gravity to a sphere roughly 18 kilometers in diameter. The star virtually disappears, collapsing to a single point of infinite density called a singularity. When the star has become this small, the escape speed will exceed the speed of light; nothing, not even light, can escape from it. The star has become a black hole.

Observations of gravitational lensing effects are the only means available to detect such objects. Since nothing can escape from a black hole, it is essentially an "information sink." It is impossible for information about the interior of a black hole to be transmitted outside the event horizon. Once matter falls into a black hole, its physical properties are no longer accessible to observers. These properties cannot affect the black hole, because it is essentially of infinite depth. This presents a difficult problem. Because it is impossible to detect any of the physical properties of a black hole, its only measurable characteristics are its mass, its electrical charge, and its angular momentum— effects these properties have on nearby objects. The extent to which the light from a distant object is separated into multiple images yields information about the size of the massive object which created the gravitational lens.

Clusters of galaxies also exhibit a gravitational lensing effect on distant objects. Using the separation of the images of distant quasars it is possible to reconstruct the projection of clusters' mass density on the sky. Such observations have led to a discrepancy in the data. The total mass of the galaxy clusters as observed through gravitational lensing is a factor five to ten times greater than the total mass of all of the stars and gas in the individual galaxies. The gas and stars we see in galaxies throughout the universe seem to be only a fraction of the mass actually present. The remaining unobservable mass is referred to as "dark matter." Determining the amount of dark matter in the universe is important to cosmologists, for if there is enough matter in the universe its gravitational pull will eventually stop its expansion.

Dark matter in the universe may take the form of stars whose mass is too low to cause fusion in their cores. Such nonshining stars are called brown dwarfs or "Jupiters" and must have a mass less than 7 percent of the mass of the Sun. Even though they do not emit radiation of their own, they can be detected by magnifying the light from a background star—another effect of gravitational lensing. By observing such magnification caused by gravitational lenses, cosmologists have determined that brown dwarfs cannot account for all of the dark matter in the universe.

Study of Einstein crosses can yield important information about the Hubble constant, a fundamental and still not well-determined standard for the measurement of the distance scale of the universe. Each of the four images of an Einstein cross is formed by light that has traveled a slightly different path from the quasar to Earth. This distance may be as great as eight billion light-years, so that even a "slightly" different path length between images can be as large as a light-year. Thus, when the light from the quasar undergoes a sudden change in intensity, the brightness of the four images will also exhibit the same magnitude of change. However, since the light that forms each image has traveled a different distance to Earth, the changes in brightness of the images will occur at different times. Precise measurements of these changes and the time lags between them will determine the distance scale of the gravitational lens system of the galaxy and the quasar being imaged. This information can be used to obtain a value for the Hubble constant.

Linda McDonald

Basic Bibliography

Chaffee, Frederick H., Jr. "The Discovery of a Gravitational Lens." *Scientific American* 243 (November, 1980): 70-78. This article was written soon after the observation of the first gravitational lens. It describes the lens phenomenon and includes some excellent diagrams.

Chaisson, Eric, and Steve McMillan. *Astronomy Today.* Englewood Cliffs, N.J.: Prentice-Hall, 1993. This is a basic introductory text in astronomy. It is written with very little mathematics and covers the basic methods of astronomy, the solar system, stars and stellar evolution, galaxies, and beyond.

Thorne, Kip S. *Black Holes and Time Warps: Einstein's Outrageous Legacy.* New York: W. W. Norton, 1994. A recipient of the American Institute of Physics Science Writing Award, this book is a very readable, thorough treatment of the subject of black holes and their resultant curvature of space.

Turner, Edwin. "Gravitational Lenses." *Scientific American* 259 (July, 1988): 54-60. This article is an excellent description of gravitational lensing and includes excellent illustrations.

Current Bibliography

Begelman, Mitchell, and Martin Rees. *Gravity's Fatal Attraction: Black Holes in the Universe.* New York: Scientific American Library, 1995. This book is number 58 of the Scientific American Library series. It deals with gravity, stellar evolution, black holes, galaxies, quasars, and cosmic jets. Excellent graphics enhance the text.

Kaufmann, William J., III. *Universe.* New York: W. H. Freeman, 1994. This is a slightly more advanced introductory astronomy text. It covers the basic topics in astronomy with more emphasis on cosmology. It is accompanied by a CD.

Space Telescope Science Institute. *http://oposite.stsci.edu/pubinfo/.* The Internet offers a wealth of information about gravitational lenses, including one site with a bibliography of current papers on the subject. Although many of these sites are fairly technical in nature, one of the best sources of information about gravitational lenses is the site for the Hubble Space Telescope (under this website). This site includes several spectacular colorized images of distant galaxies and quasars formed by gravitational lensing. The site includes captions explaining each picture. It is updated frequently.

Cross-References

Black Holes, 48; General Relativity, 302; Gravitational Singularities, 323; Quantum Cosmology, 767; Space-Time, 926; Space-Time Distortion by Gravity, 933; The Universe: Evolution, 999; The Universe: Expansion, 1007.

Gravitational Singularities

Various solutions to the field equations of Albert Einstein's general theory of relativity describe an infinite distortion of space and time, which is known as a black hole. The heart of a black hole is a singularity—a point with zero volume and infinite mass.

Overview

To discuss the concept of a gravitational singularity, it is first necessary to gain some understanding of Albert Einstein's general theory of relativity. Unlike Sir Isaac Newton's universal law of gravitation, which holds that gravity is an attractive force, general relativity shows that a gravitational field is a consequence of the shape of the universe. A large mass, such as the Sun, distorts the fabric of space-time around it.

Consider four people tightly holding a sheet by each of its corners. If a heavy ball is then placed in the center of the sheet, the sheet is stretched or distorted. A smaller ball placed on an edge of the sheet would then move according to the curvature of the sheet. This example illustrates the concept of warped space-time. The smaller ball is moving toward the larger ball, not because of any force acting between the two balls, but because of the shape of the sheet.

When it was first proposed in 1916, the general theory of relativity was thought to be beyond comprehension. In fact, it was often stated that only a few scientists fully understood its complexities. To more fully appreciate the problem, consider that the theory contains sixteen nonlinear, partial differential equations. Each of these equations contains sixteen unknown factors. In his original paper, Einstein had worked out only an approximate solution to the equations.

The first exact solution was accomplished by the German astronomer, Karl Schwarzschild (1873-1916). In a 1916 paper, Schwarzschild investigated the consequences of infinite gravity around a spherical, nonrotating body. Schwarzschild's solution describes a bizarre object: a gravitational singularity, or what is commonly called a black hole. Schwarzschild concluded that, if a star were to collapse within a certain radius, then the escape velocity at its surface would exceed the speed of light. In other words, light would not be able to escape from this body and, in effect, it would disappear from the universe. The radius that Schwarzschild identified is the event horizon or, as it is often called, the Schwarzschild radius. The event horizon or Schwarzschild radius is a boundary in the geometry of space-time beyond which events cannot be detected. Anything inside of an event horizon is totally disconnected from the universe.

The size of this radius depends on the mass that formed the singularity and is equal to 2.95 kilometers multiplied by the mass of the black hole in solar mass units. For example, a 10-solar-mass black hole has a radius of 29.5 kilometers.

The effects on matter encountering an event horizon can be predicted. Only matter on the outside moving inward can cross the event horizon; matter on the inside is forever trapped. Consider two spacecraft, A and B, in the vicinity of an event horizon. As ship A approaches the event horizon, B will observe that A's clocks are running more slowly. The crew of spaceship A will, however, find that everything is normal. As A crosses the event horizon, B will observe that A is frozen in time at the event horizon boundary. The instant that A crosses the event horizon, it will appear to A's crew members that they are about to strike the collapsed star. This image, however, is only the fossil remains of the light that was emitted as the star collapsed through the event horizon, probably millions of years earlier. The image quickly vanishes as A is pulled inward at increasing velocities toward the singularity. As the spacecraft nears the singularity, immense tidal forces will distort its shape, stretching it along its axis of motion. As the ship is stretched, its volume is being reduced. Eventually, the ship and its crew would be crushed out of existence. The crew of spaceship B, however, would observe A suspended at the end of the event horizon forever.

Since the Schwarzschild solution was published in 1916, several other physicists have proposed solutions to the equations of general relativity. Shortly after the publication of Schwarzschild's paper, the German physicist Heinrich Reissner and the Finnish physicist Gunnar Nordström solved the equations for a body with both mass and electrical charge. The electrically charged black hole would have two event horizons that separate it from the rest of the universe. One event horizon would be caused by the mass of the black hole, the other would be attributable to its charge. Most scientists believe that the chances of such an object as a Reissner-Nordström black hole actually existing are highly unlikely. Because such a massive object with a charge would project a huge electric field, particles of the opposite charge would quickly be attracted to it. The overall charge on the black hole would soon be neutralized.

In the early 1960's, Roy Kerr solved the equations of general relativity for a rotating mass. The singularity predicted by Kerr's solution is in the shape of a ring. This conclusion is significantly different from the solutions of Schwarzschild or Reissner and Nordström in which the singularity is a point. It would, in theory, be possible to travel through the center of a ring singularity without experiencing the infinite distortion of space-time. On the other side of the singularity would lie the bizarre world of negative space-time. Exactly what this world might be like is a matter of conjecture, but it is suspected, based on current models, that time flows in a reverse direction and gravity exists as a repulsive force.

A few years after the publication of the Kerr solution, Ezra Newman and his colleagues expanded that solution to include charged, rotating bodies. Shortly after this development, still another solution predicted the possibility of a singularity being exposed, with no surrounding event horizon. In this "super extreme Kerr object" (SEKO), the event horizon does not exist.

A Kerr black hole consists of two event horizons, one for mass and the other for spin. The gravitational attraction is the dominating force as long as the event horizon for mass is larger than that for angular momentum. As the angular momentum becomes larger, its event horizon expands toward the event horizon for mass. If the angular momentum event horizon continues to expand, then it will eventually meet and fuse with the event horizon for mass. According to theory, any further expansion in angular momentum will cause the fused event horizons to vanish and, subsequently, will expose the ring singularity. Physicists refer to such an object as a "naked singularity." In principle, a naked singularity could be visited by astronauts without the danger of becoming entangled in the infinite space-time warp that is caused by an event horizon.

According to the general theory of relativity, infinite forces exist at a singularity. The theory also indicates that termination at the singularity is the fate of all particles that become trapped within the event horizon. Further models developed by physicists, however, indicate the possibility of a somewhat different fate for those particles.

In the 1930's, Einstein and Anders Rosén developed mathematical models of the gravitational fields around static black holes. They found that, as the singularity is approached, the field becomes increasingly strong and the distortion in space-time becomes more pronounced. The tool that they used in their investigation is called an embedding diagram or a gravity well diagram. Embedding diagrams were first used to explain the general theory of relativity in its early days. A large mass produces a distortion in space-time, and an embedding diagram is simply a drawing of this phenomenon. The more massive is the body, the deeper is the well or depression in the embedding diagram. As the depression becomes deeper, the energy needed to escape or climb out of the well becomes greater as well. A singularity should produce a gravity well of infinite depth, according to theory, but the equations of Einstein and Rosén produced a model in which the embedding diagram suddenly opens up again. Exactly what is connected to the other end of this so-called Einstein-Rosén bridge is not known. It may connect to another remote part of the universe or, perhaps, another universe altogether.

In the 1960's, British theoretical physicists Stephen W. Hawking and Roger Penrose proposed that infinite spacewarps or "wormholes," if they exist, must lead to other universes; it would be impossible for them to terminate in this universe. Other universes, however, are beyond the domain of experimental science.

Applications

According to gravitational theory, singularities are formed when massive stars go through their evolutionary stages and eventually die out. During the lifetime of a star, two major forces work in opposition to each other. Within the core of a star, the process of nuclear fusion occurs, and a vast quantity of heat flows from the core toward the outer layers of the star. Because of this outward flow of heat, the tendency would be for the star to expand. This result would occur if it were not for the crushing force of gravity. During the main portion of a star's lifetime, these two forces are balanced and the star is in equilibrium.

When a star that is larger than 3.1 times the mass of the Sun exhausts the supply of nuclear fuel in its core, nuclear burning begins in the layers surrounding the core. This burning causes an expansion of the outer layers of the star against the force of gravity. In the case of a massive star, the core may have been entirely converted into iron and, at this stage, iron atoms are degenerate; that is, the iron atoms cannot be compressed any further and are supporting the entire weight of the star. New iron, which is being made in the shell around the core, now begins to fall inward upon the core. This tremendous buildup in mass causes core temperatures to skyrocket, perhaps exceeding 5 billion degrees Celsius. At this temperature, energetic photons break up the iron atoms into elementary particles. Protons and electrons are combined in a process called neutronization to form a core of pure neutrons. The mass of the core is so great that not even the degenerate pressure of neutrons can stop the collapse. The collapse continues until the matter that made up the core is crushed down to a point, the singularity.

For each gravitational body in the universe, there exists a Schwarzschild radius. If the body in question collapses within that radius, according to theory, a singularity must exist. Consider the Sun as an example. The velocity that it takes to escape from the surface of the Sun is about 625 kilometers per second. If the Sun were collapsing, then the escape velocity would increase as the Sun became smaller. At about one-tenth of the Sun's current radius, the escape velocity would be nearly 2,000 kilometers per second. As the collapse continued, light leaving the surface of the Sun would be distorted in its path and would be strongly redshifted (the spectrum would be displaced toward longer wavelengths). When the Sun's radius became 2.95 kilometers, the escape velocity from its surface would exactly equal the speed of light; the Schwarzschild radius will have been reached. If the Sun were to continue its collapse, then a singularity would be formed.

It is believed that only massive stars can undergo such a process as a gravitational collapse to the Schwarzschild radius and beyond. It is the high mass of the core that prevents electron or neutron degenerate pressure from stopping the collapse and forming a white dwarf or a neutron star.

Advances in technology have taken the world of singularities beyond the exercise in mathematics stage. Scientists have gathered data which, perhaps, may prove the existence of these bizarre objects.

Although black holes cannot be optically observed, they may be detected by the gravitational influence that they have on a neighboring star. For example, gases falling into a black hole might be detected, or physicists may discover strong gravitational perturbations in the movement of a star in binary linkup with a black hole. Another effect of black holes may be "gravitational lensing," in which a massive body such as a black hole distorts the light heading toward Earth from a distant galaxy. As the light bends around either side of the black hole and is recorded on Earth, it may appear that there are two galaxies instead of one.

An additional method of black-hole detection may be in the location of X-ray emitting objects. One model for X-ray emission suggests that, as the black hole attracts gas and dust into its gravitational field, the matter spreads out and forms a thin accretion disk. Because the belts of matter that are nearest to the black hole are orbiting faster, friction between the belts causes the generation of tremendous amounts of heat. As the heat builds up, radiation in X-ray frequencies is released. Astronomers have speculated that many black holes may be identified from the dozens of known X-ray sources in the universe.

Context

The idea of a gravitational singularity is not a twentieth century concept. In fact, it was first suggested in 1796 by the French astronomer and mathematician Pierre-Simon Laplace. At that time, light was thought to consist of tiny little particles or corpuscles. Laplace considered the possibility that a massive body might have enough gravitational attraction to keep these particles from escaping. He speculated on the possibility that space may contain an infinite number of massive gravitational bodies. Since there was no way to substantiate his hypothesis, however, it was soon discarded.

The idea was revived again after the Schwarzschild solution was published. Although he had described a static black hole, Schwarzschild had no idea whether such an object could actually exist. His paper was purely theoretical mathematics.

In 1939, Einstein published a paper in which he attempted to demonstrate that it was impossible for matter to be so highly compressed that it could collapse within its Schwarzschild radius. At that time, it was generally believed that, when a star decayed, it would lose most of its mass during the supernova stage. It was assumed that the small remnant of the core would decay into a white dwarf.

Later that same year, physicist J. Robert Oppenheimer, of the University of California, Berkeley, and his colleagues proposed that, if a star exceeded the Sun's mass by a small amount, then it would be massive enough to collapse through its Schwarzschild radius. Oppenheimer discussed various types of condensed states of matter and proposed laws that would apply to matter in the ultradense state. He found that, with a massive hypothetical body, there was no opposing force that could stop the collapse into a singularity.

Interest in the possibility of black holes in space was rekindled in the early 1960's with the discovery of quasi-stellar radio sources (Quasars). The mass of these objects was believed to be far in excess of the mass that Oppenheimer had predicted as being capable of infinite collapse.

Calculations completed by John Wheeler at Princeton University regarding spherical, static bodies indicate that such a body, if massive enough, will collapse indefinitely. Eventually, an event horizon would form around such an object, effectively shielding it from observation from any other part of the universe.

Since an object such as a black hole is theorized to exist, the next task is to find observational evidence. There are bodies in space that are strongly suspected to be black holes, such as the X-ray source Cygnus X-1. Only further research and observation will determine the accuracy of these speculations.

David W. Maguire

Basic Bibliography

Asimov, Isaac. *The Collapsing Universe.* New York: Walker, 1977. A very readable volume describing such topics as the forces of nature, planets and planetary formation, and the stages of stellar evolution. Geared for the layperson.

Bergmann, Peter G. *The Riddle of Gravitation.* New York: Charles Scribner's Sons, 1968. This fairly technical volume covers the historical development of Newtonian mechanics and special relativity in the introductory units. Bergmann also presents a detailed discussion of general relativity and its implications. Recommended for the general reader.

Greenstein, George. *Frozen Star.* New York: Freundlich Books, 1983. This volume is concerned with such topics as pulsars, black holes, and stellar evolution. The reader should have some general physics and astronomy background.

Herbert, Nick. *Faster than Light.* New York: New American Library, 1988. This volume considers topics in relativistic physics, such as black holes and time travel. Excellent descriptions of the types of black holes proposed by modern theory are included. Suitable for the lay reader.

Kaufmann, William J. *Black Holes and Warped Spacetime.* New York: W. H. Freeman, 1979. This well-illustrated volume deals with stellar evolution and the warped space-time of general relativity. The study of the structure and properties of black holes is well presented. Written for the layperson.

Shipman, Harry L. *Black Holes, Quasars, and the Universe.* Boston: Houghton Mifflin, 1976. Covers such topics as stellar evolution, galaxies, active galaxies, cosmology, and topics in astrophysics. The reader should have some background in elementary physics and astronomy.

Taylor, John G. *Black Holes.* New York: Avon Books, 1973. An excellent look at black holes, their formation, and some interesting speculations on what a trip into a black hole might be like. Suitable for the general reader.

Current Bibliography

Begelman, Mitchell C., and Martin Rees. *Gravity's Fatal Attraction: Black Holes in the Universe.* New York: Scientific American Library, 1996.

D'Eath, P. D. *Black Holes: Gravitational Interactions.* New York: Oxford University Press, 1996.

Thorne, Kip S. *Black Holes and Time Warps: Einstein's Outrageous Legacy.* New York: W. W. Norton, 1994.

Wald, Robert M. *Space, Time, and Gravity: The Theory of the Big Bang and Black Holes.* 2d ed. Chicago: University of Chicago Press, 1992.

Cross-References

Black Holes, 48; General Relativity, 302; Gravitational Lensing and Einstein Rings, 317; Quantum Cosmology, 767; Space-Time, 926; Space-Time Distortion by Gravity, 933; The Universe: Evolution, 999; The Universe: Expansion, 1007.

Gravity
Measurement

Gravity, the most dominant universal force, attractive in nature, affects all forms of matter and even energy in spite of its extreme weakness. Traditional Newtonian gravitational theory, adequate for navigation and general astronomical purposes, requires modification when great precision in measurement is necessary.

Overview

Gravity is the natural tendency of objects to move downward toward the Earth, and such objects are said to have weight. Gravity has been traditionally described as a field with every particle of matter as a source of a gravitational field. The intensity of this field is affected by the distance from and position on the Earth's surface and the local mass distribution in relation to the total mass of the Earth.

The gravitational field produces an attractive force between bodies, which is directly proportional to the product of their masses and inversely proportional to the square of the distance between their centers. This statement summarizes the law of universal gravitation, as formulated by Sir Isaac Newton in 1687. This law assumes that the masses are distributed symmetrically about a sphere of constant radius and uniform density. Actual gravity surveys, however, demonstrate that no mathematical formula has been found that describes exactly the gravitational field of the Earth, which is complicated by irregularities in the topography and mass distribution, combined with a pronounced flattening of the Earth at its poles, caused by rotation.

The force of gravity varies with position on the Earth's surface. The acceleration of free-falling bodies caused by the force of gravity is determined experimentally as greatest at the poles and smallest at the equator. The value for the acceleration of gravity, g, for example, is only 9.782 meters per second per second (m/s^2) in the Canal Zone of Panama, but is 9.825 meters per second per second in Greenland, which is closer to the North Pole. This value of g near the equator is lessened by a factor, which is the square of the velocity of a point on the Earth's surface divided by the radius of the Earth (V^2/R). Since points closer to the equator move with a greater velocity, the value of g will be smaller at the equator.

Gravitational acceleration diminishes with altitude, an object at the Earth's surface and near the equator that would have a value of g equal to 9.83 meters per second per second would have that value drop to 8.70 meters per second per second at an altitude of 400 kilometers. This decrease is observed because the effect of the gravitational force on acceleration follows an inverse square law; that is, the farther the object is from the center of Earth, the less the acceleration. At twice the distance, for example, the force and resulting acceleration would be only one-fourth of the original amount.

The equation for the law of universal gravitation has a constant G, the gravitational constant that was not known at the time Newton formulated the law. The constant G is assumed equal for all conditions and locations on the Earth and in the universe. The weight of an object W is equivalent to its mass m multiplied by the acceleration g ($W = mg$). If the weight is equated to the pull of gravity from the law of universal gravitation, then the gravitational constant G may be calculated directly. The value of G is found by squaring the radius of the Earth, R, then multiplying the result by g and dividing by the mass of the Earth, M ($G = R^2 g/M$). This result is a constant for a given location, which implies that g should be the same also for any location.

The technical problems of the measurement of G were solved by Henry Cavendish in 1798. Cavendish devised a sensitive torsion balance composed of a light rod supported at its center by a thin wire approximately 1 meter long, with lead balls about 5 centimeters in diameter placed at the ends of the rod. If a force were applied to each lead ball in opposing directions and at right angles to both the wire and rod, the wire is subjected to a rotation that may be measured as an angular displacement. Cavendish initially applied small forces, measuring the amount of twisting that resulted. Carefully shielding the experimental equipment from air currents, Cavendish placed two large lead balls about 20 centimeters in diameter nearly in contact with the small lead balls but on opposing sides. Gravitational force between both sets of balls caused a twist in the wire, and from the angle displaced by the wire, Cavendish was able to measure the forces between the large and small balls. The force turned out, as expected, to be very small, only one two-millionth of a newton. The value of G could then be calculated directly, since Cavendish now knew the force involved as well as the masses of the lead balls and their distance of separation. The results of Cavendish, as well as later determinations, have established that G has the same value, whatever the composition of the masses or the location; the constant is truly universal in nature.

The gravity pendulum has been used to measure the differences in gravitational force on Earth. Modern gravity pendulums are governed by the principle relating to the period of oscillation discovered by the Dutch scientist Christiaan Huygens. The period of the pendulum, as he noted, varies directly with the square root of the length and inversely with the square root of the local value for the acceleration of gravity *g*. Gravity pendulums are built nearly friction-free, supported on knife-edge jewel bearings, and swing in chambers from which air has been evacuated. The period of oscillation is timed with precise chronometers enabling determinations to within a few parts per million. Unfortunately, gravity pendulums are unwieldy and difficult to transport; consequently, now most gravity measurements are made with portable instruments called gravimeters.

Gravimeters make use of the principle of a spring balance—that the distortion or strain is directly proportional to the applied stress or force, provided that the measurements are made within the elastic limits of the material. A small quartz fiber is distorted in the local gravitational field at an observed station with results compared to a measured pendulum station. The readings are generally so precise that distortions to one part in 10 million can be recorded. Through development of such instruments, variations in gravity over large areas can now be measured. Some instruments have been adapted to operate from aircraft in flight for aerial surveys of the Earth and for use on surface vessels at sea in regions not suitable for gravity pendulums because of wave disturbances and motions.

A torsion balance employs an arrangement similar to a Cavendish balance, but as opposed to measuring the deflection produced by large masses, the period of oscillation is measured when the large masses are placed perpendicular to the equilibrium positions of the small masses and next when the large masses are rotated another 90 degrees. When the large masses are located at the first position, the period is less as a result of the additional restoring force. In the second position, the period is increased by the large masses, pulling the small ones away from the equilibrium position. The difference in the periods from both of these measurements gives the value of *G*. The advantage of this method is that the period may be measured more precisely than a corresponding deflection; the precision in error is estimated as 0.5 percent with this technique.

Although measurement of the gravitational constant *G* has improved, the value is not known with nearly the precision of other physical constants; the value itself is given to only four places of accuracy. The laboratory measurement of *G* is difficult because of the extremely small forces between the masses. Planetary sized objects are much larger, but the problem is not resolved because the product of *G* and the mass of the attracting planet both appear in the equation. Planetary observations alone cannot determine the individual values of *G* or mass.

A torsion balance may also be used for ascertaining the equivalence between inertial mass and gravitational mass, known also as the principle of equivalence. For these experiments, one body called the inertial mass is defined with respect to a standard mass of 1 kilogram. The body and the standard will either accelerate toward or away from each other. The gravitational mass of the body is defined in terms of this acceleration and the distance between the objects. Experiments have tested a variety of materials, obtaining a ratio between the masses. Results indicate that various types of energy contribute to the inertial mass of a system to the same degree that they would contribute to the gravitational mass.

A gravity gradiometer is an instrument designed to measure local tidal fields. The instrument is portable and designed for use on an airplane or satellite and permits precise mapping of anomalies in the Earth's gravitational field. The instrument, in the shape of a Greek cross, has four masses at the ends of each arm, which are held together at the center by a torsional spring. When pressed together, the arms oscillate with a frequency of 32 hertz (oscillations per second). If placed in a tidal field at right angles, the cross will be deformed. Rotated with an angular frequency of 16 hertz in the reference frame of the cross, a tidal driving force would appear at 32 hertz. Since the oscillation frequency matches the natural vibration frequency of the arms, a resonance condition is established, producing large amplitudes. Very small tidal fields have been detected with this instrument.

Detectors of gravitational radiation, or waves, were first built in 1966 at the University of Maryland by Joseph Weber. This type of detector consists of a large aluminum cylinder placed inside a vacuum tank and suspended on a wire. The cylinder is supported on rubber blocks as an insulation to external mechanical vibrations. Any oscillations of the cylinder in the fundamental or longitudinal mode are detected by piezoelectric strain transducers bonded to the outside middle section. The ability of the device to detect radiation at resonance is termed its cross section, which turned out to be quite small. Limiting the ability to detect this type of radiation is the thermal motion of the individual molecules and oscillations of the cylinder that interfere with observations. Experimental results obtained by Weber and his group have not been duplicated elsewhere, casting doubt on the reliability of this technique.

More sensitive detectors are now under construction and involve strains in solid bodies employing resonance; they are more sensitive to radiation of a given frequency and reject all other frequencies.

Applications

Measurement of the gravitational field over Earth demonstrates that the field is not uniform. The Earth departs from being a perfect spheroid because of rotational effects and topographic variations. Regions that are topographically higher than a datum surface are located farther from the Earth's center and experience a smaller gravitational force. Other regions located below the surface, although closer to the Earth's center, may experience compensating effects from mass concentrations, thereby increasing the strength of the field over its expected value.

Gravity data indicate that the field is increased near mountain ranges because of the greater concentration of rock. Closer observations show that mountain masses do not deflect the field as much as expected if the mountain were a load resting on top of a uniform crust. If the mountain were merely a load on the rigid crust, the force of gravity (corrected for the effect of additional altitude) should be larger on top of the mountain than on the surrounding plains as a result of the increased gravitational pull of the mountain mass beneath the crust. Such observations led geophysicists to conclude that a rigid crust is not responsible for supporting the load of the mountains but is instead buoyed up by floating on a denser deformable interior. The interior of the Earth must yield and be subject to lateral flow to compensate for loads on equal-size regions. Areas of depression in the crust, as oceanic trenches, show lower values of the gravitational field, as there is less mass near the surface.

Newtonian mechanics, traditionally used to describe the behavior of bodies at the surface of the Earth, tend to break down outside the range of normal observable motion. The theory fails when gravitational fields become very intense near collapsed objects such as neutron stars or black holes.

In 1915, Albert Einstein completely changed the understanding of gravitation with his general theory of relativity. According to theory, gravity is not a force in the usual sense but is the result of the curvature of space-time. Bodies then follow the easiest course through space-time, which is manifested in the shape of their orbits. Einstein theorized that gravity may be explained by geometry. Mercury's orbit could not be explained adequately by ordinary mechanics but only by the warping of space near the Sun. Time warps at the Earth's surface may be detected by using very precise clocks.

Gravitational time dilation—the slowing down of clocks in a gravitational field—may be used as a direct test of the curvature of space-time. For these experiments, cesium-beam atomic clocks are used. Small frequency shifts are measured in the clocks placed in a potential and are calibrated against clocks at rest in a stationary gravitational field. The pulses of the clocks are monitored to rule out the possibility of a frequency loss during the light beam propagation. The clock tick rate is found to depend upon the strength of the gravitational field and, therefore, space-time geometry is dependent upon the gravitational field. The possibilities that strong tidal forces would have an effect on the clock may be ruled out because it is known that the atomic forces are stronger and resist tidal distortions.

Gravitational redshifts have been measured on light emitted from the atoms on stellar surfaces. It has been difficult to obtain reliable results for these measurements because of strong convection currents in the stellar photosphere masking the spectral lines, which are Doppler shifted by gaseous motion. Measurements made above the photosphere of the Sun have given more definitive results. Gravitational redshifts should be very prominent in light emitted by white dwarf stars because these stars have about 1 solar mass contained in a much smaller radius than the Sun and would consequently have very intense gravitational fields. Past observations on white dwarf stars have been difficult because these stars are so small that many of them cannot be observed.

Context

All of nature's events and activities can be explained in terms of four fundamental forces. In the historical context, gravity was the first of these four forces that was investigated scientifically. Although scientists have had an awareness of gravity and the direction in which it acts, the role of gravity as a force was not appreciated fully until Newton's law of universal gravitation was published. The importance of gravity is its universal nature—everything in the cosmos is affected by it and every particle of matter is a source of gravity. The force of gravity as observed is always attractive, tending to pull matter together.

One of the surprising facts concerning gravity as the dominant universal force is its extreme weakness. Gravity is so weak that physicists generally ignore its effects completely when dealing with masses on the level of the subatomic particle. Gravity's strength on the atomic scale is vastly overwhelmed by the nuclear and electrical forces at that distance.

The law of universal gravitation, which was adequate for more than two hundred years, was not effective in the twentieth century in explaining discrepancies in observations near very massive objects. In this respect, the law of universal gravitation conflicted with the relativity theory. In Newton's theory, gravitational force between two bodies should be transmitted instantaneously across space, but Einstein's theory rejects physical effects that travel faster than the speed of light. Gravitational fields around objects as massive as the Sun appear to distort space and time to a degree that is detectable. Observing stars near the Sun during solar eclipses indicates that they are not observed in their true positions; that is, the light from these stars has been bent or deflected noticeably toward the Sun by its gravitational field. Black holes appear to distort severely the space and time surrounding them to unimaginable degrees. They are the final state of very massive stars that have collapsed into nothing with a gravity so overpowering that not even light can escape.

For all of its success, the theory of general relativity is at odds with the quantum theory, which describes subatomic particles on a statistical basis, and is at odds with the theory of superstrings, which treats subatomic particles as very tiny vibrating loops. Physicists are now searching for a more comprehensive theory of quantum gravity that perhaps will be more useful in mapping out the very early history of the universe very near the moment of creation.

Some physicists now postulate the existence of a fifth force in nature that may diminish the effectiveness of the gravitational force out to a limited range. Experiments performed in mines, for example, seem to show that the measured gravitational force does not agree with predicted values from theory. These observations as well as others, however, have not established conclusively the existence of a previously unknown repulsive force.

The nature of just how gravitation is transmitted at a distance has not been resolved as to whether it has a wave or particle nature, or both. If gravity has a particle nature, then this particle must be extremely tiny because gravity as a force is very weak.

Michael L. Broyles

Basic Bibliography

Asimov, Isaac. *The History of Physics.* New York: Walker and Company, 1985. Gravitation is presented in a format and style comprehensible to the lay reader of physics. The chapter on the gravitational constant discusses Cavendish's experiment, the method, and its significance.

Davies, Paul. *Superforce.* New York: Simon & Schuster, 1984. Written in a style that the average reader will appreciate, this book presents the symmetry and beauty of the universe in terms of gravity, electromagnetism, and the weak and strong forces. The existence of a superforce is speculated upon and the possibility of a universe of eleven dimensions is discussed.

Hawking, Stephen W., and William Israel. *Three Hundred Years of Gravitation.* New York: Cambridge University Press, 1987. A comprehensive treatise spanning the development of gravitation from Newton to concepts of quantum gravity and time asymmetry. Additional chapters discuss gravitational radiation, gravitational interaction of cosmic strings, inflationary cosmology, quantum cosmology, and superstring unification. An important reference in gravitational physics.

Holton, Gerald. *Introduction to Concepts and Theories in Physical Science.* Princeton, N.J.: Princeton University Press, 1985. A unique perspective on the historical development of physical theories with emphasis on the geometric derivation of Newton's law of universal gravitation. A section is also included on the discovery of planets using this law. Photographs, diagrams, and tables abound with minimal use of mathematics.

Ohanian, Hans C. *Gravitation and Spacetime.* New York: W. W. Norton, 1976. Intended for the student with a background in physics. Discusses the emission and detection of gravitational waves, gravity in and around rotating and nonrotating black holes, curved space-time, gravitational time dilation, and tidal forces associated with gravitation.

Parker, Sybil P., ed. *McGraw-Hill Encyclopedia of Physics.* New York: McGraw-Hill, 1983. An excellent reference for the nontechnical as well as for the technical reader. Topics under gravitation include Newton's law of universal gravitation, gravitational constant, mass and weight, gravity, gravitational potential energy, application and accuracy of Newtonian gravitation, relativistic theories, supergravity, and gravitational waves.

Current Bibliography

Bursa, Milan, and Karel Pec. *Gravity Field and Dynamics of the Earth.* Translated by Jaroslav Tauer. New York: Springer-Verlag, 1993.

Chen, Y. T., and Alan Cook. *Gravitational Experiments in the Laboratory.* New York: Cambridge University Press, 1993.

Gambini, Rodolfo, and Jorge Pullin. *Loops, Knots, Gauge Theories, and Quantum Gravity.* New York: Cambridge University Press, 1996.

Cross-References

The Greenhouse Effect

"Greenhouse" gases absorb or trap infrared, or heat, energy emitted by the Earth's surface. The absorbed or trapped heat energy is then released or reemitted by the greenhouse gases, resulting in an additional heating of the Earth's surface. Atmospheric greenhouse gases include water vapor, carbon dioxide, methane, nitrous oxide, ozone, and a class of man-made molecules called chlorofluorocarbons. There is serious national and international concern that increasing atmospheric levels of these gases will lead to a global warming.

Overview

The Earth and the other planets receive almost all their energy in the form of electromagnetic radiation from the Sun. While the Sun emits radiation over the entire electromagnetic spectrum, from shortwave X rays to longwave radio waves, the bulk of the solar radiation is in the visible part of the electromagnetic spectrum, from about 0.15 to about 4 microns. The Sun radiates energy primarily in the visible part of the spectrum, as that is the spectral region of maximum emission for an object at a temperature of about 6,000 Kelvins, or about 5,727 degrees Celsius, which is the temperature of the Sun's surface, or "photosphere." According to the laws of physics governing the emission of electromagnetic radiation, an object at a temperature of 6,000 Kelvins emits most of its radiation at a wavelength of about 0.55 micron, which corresponds to visible radiation with a yellowish-white color. Hence, the Sun appears as a yellowish-white object in the sky.

The amount of solar radiation intercepted by the Earth and available for heating the planet depends on the product of the amount of solar radiation reaching the top of the planet and the area of the disk of the Earth as seen from the Sun. At the Earth's distance from the Sun (about 150 million kilometers), the amount of solar radiation hitting the top of Earth's atmosphere is about 1.4 million ergs per square centimeter per second. Not all this incoming solar radiation, however, is available for heating of the Earth's surface. A fraction of the incoming solar radiation is reflected back to space by clouds and by the surface itself. The fraction of incoming solar radiation reflected back to space is called the albedo of the planet. The albedo of the Earth is about 33 percent. Therefore, about 67 percent of the incoming solar radiation is available for heating the surface of the Earth. This incoming solar radiation is absorbed at the Earth's surface and heats the surface. The Earth's surface in turn emits its own radiation to balance the incoming solar radiation, which heats the surface. If the total amount of earth-emitted radiation were greater than the incoming solar radiation, the Earth would cool off; however, if the total amount of earth-emitted radiation were less than the incoming solar radiation, the Earth would heat up. Over a period of several years, the earth-emitted radiation just balances the incoming solar radiation. By equating the earth-emitted radiation, which depends on the temperature to which the surface is heated, to the incoming solar radiation, one can find the "effective" temperature of the Earth.

The Earth's effective temperature is about 253 Kelvins, or about −20 degrees Celsius. At this temperature, the earth-emitted radiation falls in the infrared part of the electromagnetic spectrum, between about 4 and 80 microns. Unlike the incoming solar radiation, however, which travels through the atmosphere without significant attenuation or loss from absorption by atmospheric gases, the earth-emitted infrared, or heat, energy is absorbed by several atmospheric gases, called greenhouse gases. Greenhouse gases absorb the earth-emitted infrared, or heat, energy; however, these gases cannot continuously absorb infrared radiation. After a fraction of a second, the greenhouse gases release or reemit the absorbed or trapped infrared radiation in all directions. About 50 percent of the reemitted infrared radiation is directed in the upward direction, and about 50 percent is directed in the downward direction. The downward component of the reemitted infrared radiation is absorbed by the surface, with an additional heating effect. Hence, the surface of the planet is heated not only by incident solar radiation (0.3-5 microns) but also by earth-emitted infrared radiation (4-80 microns) that was absorbed and then reemitted by atmospheric greenhouse gases. The additional heating of the Earth's surface by the reemitted infrared radiation heats the surface an additional 35 Kelvins, from the effective temperature of about 253 Kelvins to 288 Kelvins, or about 15 degrees Celsius—the average temperature of the Earth. The 35-Kelvin temperature enhancement is termed the greenhouse effect. It is this temperature enhancement that makes the Earth habitable for life.

While the greenhouse gases are only very minor constituents of the Earth's atmosphere, carbon dioxide is the major constituent of the atmosphere of Venus. Carbon dioxide comprises about 96 percent by volume of Venus' atmosphere, with nitrogen accounting for the remaining 4 percent. The surface pressure of the atmosphere of Venus is about 90 atmospheres, compared with 1 atmosphere for the Earth. As a result of the high percentage of carbon dioxide and the high surface pressure of the atmosphere, there is a very efficient and significant greenhouse effect on Venus. The greenhouse effect increases the temperature of Venus by about 450 Kelvins (177 degrees Celsius), from its effective temperature of about 244 Kelvins (−29 degrees Celsius)—close to the effective temperature of the earth—to the measured surface temperature of Venus of about 700 Kelvins (427 degrees Celsius)—close to the melting point of lead.

There is national and international concern that the buildup of greenhouse gases in the Earth's atmosphere will lead to an enhanced greenhouse effect and a global warming resulting in record-high temperatures in many regions and severe droughts in other regions. Such a global warming may lead to thermal expansion of the oceans, as ocean water expands in volume when heated. In addition, warming may result in a significant melting of the ice and snow at the Earth's poles, producing an even greater volume of water in the world's oceans. An increase in the world's oceans could result in the flooding of many low-lying land areas.

The most important atmospheric greenhouse gases are water vapor, carbon dioxide, methane, nitrous oxide, tropospheric ozone, and a man-made family of gases termed "chlorofluorocarbons," of which CFC-11 and CFC-12 are the most abundant species. All the greenhouse gases are very minor constituents of the atmosphere, which is composed primarily of nitrogen (78.08 percent by volume), oxygen (20.95 percent), and argon (0.93 percent). Water vapor is a variable constituent of the atmosphere and ranges from a small fraction of a percent to several percent. The concentration of

The Greenhouse Effect

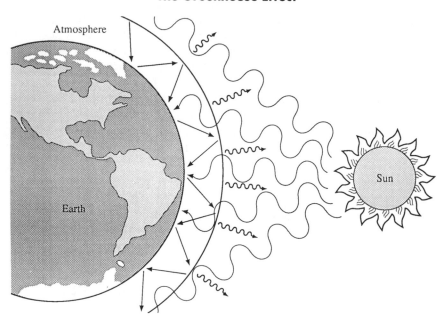

With the increase in Earth's atmosphere of "greenhouse gases" such as carbon monoxide, the Sun's heat becomes trapped (straight arrows), permitting less heat to escape back into space (wavy arrows). As a result, the overall temperature of the planet rises.

carbon dioxide is about 0.035 percent, or 350 parts per million by volume. The concentration of methane is about 1.7 parts per million by volume. The nitrous oxide concentration is about 0.31 part per million by volume. Ozone is a variable constituent of the troposphere and ranges from about 0.02 to 10 parts per million by volume. The atmospheric concentrations of CFC-12 and CFC-11 are only 0.00038 and 0.00023 part per million by volume, respectively. All these greenhouse gases, with the exception of water vapor, are produced by human activities, such as the burning of fossil fuels and biomass (trees, vegetation, and agricultural stubble), the use of nitrogen fertilization on agricultural areas, and various industrial activities. Each of the greenhouse gases produced by human activities is increasing in concentration in the atmosphere with time. Carbon dioxide is increasing at a rate of about 0.3 percent per year; methane is increasing at a rate of about 1.1 percent per year; nitrous oxide is increasing at a rate of about 0.3 percent per year; and CFC-11 and CFC-12 are each increasing at a rate of about 5 percent per year. Estimates suggest that tropospheric ozone is also increasing with time, with increases of between 1 and 2 percent per year over North America and Europe during the 1970's and 1980's. Collectively, methane, nitrous oxide, tropospheric ozone, and chlorofluorocarbons are now estimated to trap about as much infrared radiation as does carbon dioxide alone. These gases absorb infrared radiation in the spectral region, from about 7 to 13 microns, known as the atmospheric window, where water vapor and carbon dioxide do not absorb. Water vapor is a strong absorber below about 7 microns, and carbon dioxide is a strong absorber above about 13 microns. If the rates of increase of the greenhouse gases persist with time, the greenhouse effect of the other gases, when added to that of carbon dioxide, will amount to an effective doubling of carbon dioxide levels by the year 2030, some fifty years sooner than the level of carbon dioxide alone is likely to double.

A doubling of carbon dioxide in the atmosphere would lead to a global temperature increase of about 1.2 Kelvins if there were no other changes in the climate system. A warming caused by the doubling of carbon dioxide would lead to more evaporation of water vapor from the ocean. In addition, a warming would permit the atmosphere to hold more water vapor, as the capacity for air to hold water vapor increases with increasing temperature. Because water vapor is itself a greenhouse gas, as its concentration increases in the atmosphere, the Earth would warm even further. The net result of these different feedback processes would be that for a doubling of atmospheric carbon dioxide, the surface temperature would increase about 4 Kelvins. It is estimated that the average surface temperature has increased globally by about 0.5 Kelvin over the twentieth century, although this temperature increase cannot unambiguously be attributed to the buildup of greenhouse gases over this period. Temperature records also indicate that the 1980's have been the warmest decade on record.

The sources of the greenhouse gases, with the exception of water vapor, are mostly human-initiated. Carbon dioxide results from the burning of fossil fuels and of living and dead biomass, such as deforestation burning in the tropics and the burning of agricultural stubble after the harvest. Methane is produced as a combustion product of biomass burning, natural gas leakage, and by the action of anaerobic bacteria in wetlands (such as rice paddies), in landfills, and in the stomachs of ruminants (such as cattle and sheep). Nitrous oxide is produced as a combustion product of biomass burning and by the action of nitrifying and denitrifying bacteria (which add and remove nitrogen) in natural, fertilized, and burned soils. Ozone results from atmospheric reactions involving methane, carbon monoxide, and oxides of nitrogen, which are produced by the burning of fossil fuel and by biomass burning. Chlorofluorocarbons (CFC-11 and CFC-12) are released into the atmosphere when they are used as propellants in aerosol spray cans, as blowing agents for foam insulation, and as refrigerants.

There are a number of other important players in the climate scenario whose roles must be more fully understood before scientists can completely assess the impact of increasing concentrations of greenhouse gases on the future climate. Other climate factors that must be studied in more detail include the role of clouds and, especially, their impact on a warmer Earth; the role of the ocean, its heat capacity and circulation; and the variability of the incoming solar radiation. The Earth's climate is a complex system affected by many processes and parameters. Experts need to learn more about the interplay of atmospheric greenhouse gases, clouds, the ocean, and solar variability before they may accurately assess the future climate.

Methods of Study

Studies of the greenhouse effect and its impact on the climate of the Earth are multidisciplinary in nature and involve theoretical computer modeling, laboratory studies of the spectroscopic parameters and properties of greenhouse gases, atmospheric measurements of greenhouse gases, and aircraft and satellite measurements of parameters that control climate. Theoretical computer models of climate include zero-dimensional, one-dimensional, two-dimensional, and three-dimensional models. Zero-dimensional models give climate parameters that represent an average for the entire system, such as the mean temperature of the Earth's surface. One dimensional models are used to study climate in either a horizontal (latitude) or vertical (altitude) direction. In these models, a latitude-dependent surface temperature is the climate parameter of major interest. The vertical one-dimensional model is known as a radiative-convective model and is used to study the effects of changes in concentrations of greenhouse gases on the surface temperature. Two-dimensional models involve characterizing the temperature variation as a function of latitude and altitude. The most complex climate model is the three-dimensional model, or the general circulation model (GCM). This model gives a complete description of climate as a function of latitude, longitude, and altitude.

Major uncertainties exist in the understanding of several key parameters in the theoretical modeling of climate. A major uncertainty in these models is the role of cloud feedback, particularly as the Earth heats up. Calculations indicate that as the temperature of the Earth increases, clouds will appear in greater quantity. Clouds both reflect incoming solar radiation and trap Earth-emitted thermal infrared radiation. Hence, clouds can enhance or decrease global warming. The radiative properties of clouds and how they will vary with a warmer Earth are poorly understood and therefore are not included in most theoretical climate models.

To understand the greenhouse effect of gases, the spectroscopic parameters and properties of greenhouse gases are measured in laboratory experiments. These studies provide information on the spectral location of the absorption of infrared radiation by these gases and the intensity of the absorption. These laboratory spectroscopic studies involve filling an absorption cell with a known concentration of a greenhouse gas and measuring the absorption of infrared radiation as a function of spectral wavelength using a scanning spectrometer.

To assess the impact of atmospheric greenhouse gases on the Earth's climate, scientists must obtain accurate measurements of those gases that are found at trace levels in the atmosphere—for example, at atmospheric concentrations of parts per million by volume, parts per billion by volume, and parts per trillion by volume. Measuring atmospheric greenhouse gases at these very low atmospheric levels involves a series of different analytical chemistry instruments. Carbon dioxide may be measured with a gas chromatograph equipped with a thermal conductivity detector or using nondispersive infrared instrumentation. Methane is measured with a gas chromatograph equipped with a flame ionization detector or using nondispersive infrared instrumentation. Nitrous oxide, CFC-11, and CFC-12 are measured using a gas chromatograph equipped with an electron capture detector. Ozone may be measured using various ultraviolet and infrared absorption techniques. Water vapor is measured using a hygrometer. Aircraft and satellite measurements have provided very important data on several of the parameters that control climate, including the flux of incoming solar radiation, the flux of outgoing Earth-emitted thermal infrared radiation, the flux of solar radiation reflected by clouds, and the geographical and temporal variability of clouds and surface temperature. Earth-orbiting satellites have provided important information on these important climate parameters.

Context

The buildup of greenhouse gases in the atmosphere, such as carbon dioxide, methane, nitrous oxide, tropospheric ozone, CFC-11, and CFC-12, will result in a global warming of the Earth. Atmospheric greenhouse gases are increasing with time. These greenhouse gases result from a variety of human activities, including the burning of fossil fuels (carbon dioxide), the burning of living and dead biomass (carbon dioxide, methane, and nitrous oxide), and the application of nitrogen fertilizers and the burning of agricultural and grasslands (nitrous oxide). Greenhouse gases are also produced from rice paddies, cattle, and sheep (methane) and from several industrial applications (CFC-11 and CFC-12).

A global warming of the Earth from the buildup of greenhouse gases in the atmosphere would have a significant impact on people's daily lives. Most areas would experience more 90-degree-plus days per year, the growing seasons in most regions would change, and patterns of rainfall would change. One of the most important effects would be a predicted increase in the height of the world's oceans. The increased height of the oceans would result from the thermal expansion of seawater because of the Earth's high temperature (water is a compressible fluid and expands in volume when heated) and because of the melting of polar ice and snow as the Earth becomes warmer. An increase in the height of the oceans would result in the flooding of the world's low-lying land areas. It has been estimated that a global temperature increase of about 4 degrees Celsius might result in a 2-meter increase in the height of the world's oceans. This increase in water level would cause the flooding of low-lying land areas presently occupied by more than 40 million people worldwide. Higher temperatures resulting from the buildup of atmospheric greenhouse gases would tax the world's air-conditioning facilities, which require the burning of fossil fuels for their operation. Ironically, the burning of fossil fuels is a major source of atmospheric greenhouse gases.

It must be emphasized that there are fundamental uncertainties and deficiencies in scientists' understanding of climate and the processes and parameters that control it. More must be learned about the effect of clouds and oceans on climate and how these phenomena would affect the climate as the Earth begins to warm. Theoretical computer models of climate are not complete; more research is needed before the future climate of the Earth can be assessed with greater certainty.

Joel S. Levine

Basic Bibliography

Environmental Protection Agency. "The Greenhouse Effect: How It Can Change Our Lives." *EPA Journal* 15 (January/February, 1989). Popular, nontechnical accounts of the impact of climate change on agriculture, forests, energy demand, and other areas in a special issue devoted to the greenhouse effect. The principles that control and regulate global climate, including the greenhouse effect, are presented in a simple and readable manner for a general audience. Well illustrated with photographs and charts.

Goody, R. M., and J. C. G. Walker. *Atmospheres.* Englewood Cliffs, N.J.: Prentice-Hall, 1972. A good nontechnical description of solar and infrared radiation in planetary atmospheres and how the radiation balance controls the temperature of a planet. The chapters of the book include sections on the Sun and the planets, solar radiation and chemical change, atmospheric temperatures, winds of global scale, condensation and clouds, and the evolution of atmospheres.

Hansen, Joel E., and T. Takahashi, eds. *Climate Processes and Climate Sensitivity.* Geophysical Monograph 29. Washington, D.C.: American Geophysical Union, 1984. A collection of papers dealing with various aspects of the climate system, including atmosphere and ocean dynamics, the hydrologic cycle and clouds, albedo and radiation processes, polar ice, and ocean chemistry. Each paper was written by an expert in that particular area of climate research. The papers summarize what is known, along with the major uncertainties and deficiencies in understanding of the processes and parameters that control climate.

Henderson-Sellers, A., ed. *Satellite Sensing of a Cloudy Atmosphere: Observing the Third Planet.* London: Taylor and Francis, 1984. The subtitle refers to the Earth being third planet from the Sun. The subjects of the chapters in this volume, each written by an active researcher in the area, cover radiation and satellite sensors, the Earth's radiation budget and clouds, water and the photochemistry of the troposphere, vertical temperature sounding of the atmosphere, cloud identification and characterization from satellites, and the remote sensing of land, ocean, and ice from space.

Levine, Joel S., ed. *The Photochemistry of Atmospheres: Earth, the Other Planets, and Comets.* Orlando, Fla.: Academic Press, 1985. A comprehensive textbook covering atmospheric composition, chemistry, and climate, the sources and sinks of greenhouse gases, and the climate modeling of the Earth. The chapter on climate includes discussions on zero-dimensional, one-dimensional, and three-dimensional (global circulation model) climate models and the underlying physical, radiative, and dynamic processes and parameters in each model.

National Research Council. *Changing Climate: Report of the Carbon Dioxide Assessment Committee.* Washington, D.C.: National Academy Press, 1983. Technical report that addresses the possible impacts of climate change on sea level, agriculture, plant growth, and society in general. Considers future carbon dioxide emissions from fossil fuels, the dissolution of carbon dioxide into the oceans, the biosphere storage of carbon dioxide, and the impact of increased carbon dioxide on climate, agriculture, and sea level.

Current Bibliography

Ahrens, C. Donald. *Essentials of Meteorology: An Invitation to the Atmosphere.* Minneapolis/St. Paul, Minn.: West, 1993.

Barry, Roger Graham. *Atmosphere, Weather, and Climate.* 6th ed. New York: Routledge, 1992.

Kraljic, Matthew A., ed. *The Greenhouse Effect.* New York: H.W. Wilson Co., 1992.

McIlveen, J. F. R. *Fundamentals of Weather and Climate.* 2d ed. London: Chapman and Hall, 1992.

Singh, Hanwant B., ed. *Composition, Chemistry, and Climate of the Atmosphere.* New York: Van Nostrand Reinhold, 1995.

Swanson, Eric. *The Greenhouse Effect.* Boston: Little, Brown, 1990.

Cross-References

Halley's Comet

Halley's comet is the brightest, most famous and conspicuous of the periodic comets, and definite records of sightings go back more than two thousand years. The comet travels around the Sun once every seventy-six years or so in a highly eccentric and retrograde orbit that is inclined at almost 20 degrees to the main plane of the solar system. Its orbital period has enabled many observers to see Halley's comet twice during their lifetimes.

Overview

For many years, the idea that comets were "dirty snowballs" had generally been accepted by astronomers. First proposed by Fred L. Whipple in 1950, that was one of a number of different ideas about the makeup of comets. By far the most popular idea was that they were "flying sandbanks," or collections of interstellar dust and gas accreted as the Sun and planets periodically passed through vast clouds of interstellar matter in their journey through the galaxy; the Sun's gravity drew in the material that eventually collected to form individual bodies. This idea was popular during the first half of the twentieth century and was championed by the British astronomers R. A. Lyttleton and Fred Hoyle. Since the middle of the nineteenth century, meteor streams have been associated with comets, and supporters of the flying sandbank model of cometary nuclei suggested that the particles within meteor streams arose from the escape of material from comets as they moved through the solar system.

It is now widely believed that cometary nuclei are composed of material that condensed from the solar nebula at the same time as did the Sun and planets. The armada of space probes that intercepted Halley's comet in March, 1986, and the European Giotto probe in particular, taught scientists much about these objects and revealed copious amounts of carbon, nitrogen, and oxygen. The materials given out by the comet signify that these objects were formed in the outer regions of the solar system, where the extremely low temperatures necessary for them to solidify from the solar nebula were to be found. Giotto showed that the nucleus of Halley's comet is a tiny and irregularly shaped chunk of ice, measuring some 15 kilometers long by 8 kilometers wide, coated by a layer of very dark material. This layer is thought to be composed of carbon-rich compounds and has a very low albedo, reflecting merely 4 percent of the light it receives from the Sun. This low reflectivity makes the nucleus of Halley's comet one of the darkest

Halley's Comet. *(National Aeronautics and Space Administration)*

objects known. Various bright spots were seen on the nucleus, as were a hill-type feature seen near the terminator and a feature resembling a crater located near a line of vents. The vents seen on the nucleus appear to be fairly long-lived features. Dust jets detected by the Vega 1 and Vega 2 probes appear to have emanated from the same vents, two of which were identified by Giotto several days later. It may even be that some of the larger vents have survived successive perihelion passages.

The gas and dust that give rise to all the cometary activity seen, including the coma and tail, emanate from the nucleus via localized vents or fissures in the outer dust layer. These vents cover approximately 10 percent of the total surface area of the nucleus and become active when exposed to the Sun, ceasing to expel material when plunged into darkness as the nucleus rotates. The force of the jets of material escaping from the nucleus plays an important role in the comet's motion around the Sun, affecting the speed of travel in its orbit. Halley's comet was several days late in reaching perihelion during the last apparition in 1986, a result of the jetlike effects of the matter being expelled. The late arrival of Halley's comet that time around was one of the factors examined by the Swedish astronomer Hans Rickman, who attempted to calculate the mass of the nucleus from the amount of material being given off. Linking the rate of ejection to the delay in perihelion, he judged the volume of the nucleus to be somewhere between 50 and 130 cubic kilometers. The measurements obtained through spacecraft imagery, however, revealed a true volume nearer 500 cubic kilometers. The only conclusion was that the nucleus is markedly porous and far less dense than at first anticipated, with an average density of no more than a quarter that of ice. This porosity ties in with the belief that comets formed in the outer regions of the solar nebula, where material coming together would remain loosely bound rather than compacting, as did other objects elsewhere in the solar system.

The fact that the nucleus of Halley's comet rotates is not in doubt. What does remain unresolved is the period of rotation. Using photographs of the comet taken during its apparition in 1910, astronomers calculated the rotation period to be 2.2 days, this rotation being around an axis that was fairly well aligned with the pole of the comet's orbit around the Sun. Results obtained by the Giotto, Vega, and Suisei probes appeared to support this value. Ground-based observations carried out during 1986, however, indicated a rotation period of 7.4 days, a value supported by other ground-based observations together with results from the Pioneer Venus Orbiter that examined Halley's comet when near perihelion. Controversy ensued over these differing values, although a possible explanation has been suggested. The nucleus of Halley's comet could actually display both periods of rotation, one being a spinning around its axis and the other a precession of the axis of rotation. Precession is not a newly discovered phenomenon. The Earth's axis precesses, as does that of a spinning top. The combination of rotation and precession, however, is still contested by some astronomers, to some extent because of the porosity of the nucleus. Any precessional properties would quickly disappear unless the nucleus were fairly rigid.

Comets give off copious amounts of gas and dust that spread out as tails across large areas of space. Investigation of this material can reveal much about the composition of cometary interiors. Many of the investigations carried out by the European, Japanese, and Soviet space probes were directed toward a survey of the material ejected by Halley's comet. These investigations were supplemented by observations both from ground-based astronomers and the Pioneer-Venus, International Cometary Explorer (ICE), and International Ultraviolet Explorer (IUE) spacecraft. As is the case with the surface of Halley's nucleus, the dust thrown off by the comet was found to be very dark and may have emanated from the surface itself rather than the interior. The Giotto and Vega craft carried out analyses of the dust and found a mixture of different material, including the lighter elements oxygen, hydrogen, nitrogen, and carbon and the heavier elements silicon, iron, and magnesium. The amount of carbon found during the investigations ties in quite well with the observed abundance of this material elsewhere in the galaxy, indicative that comets are made up of interstellar material.

More than three-quarters of the gas ejected from the nucleus was found to be water vapor, which appears to constitute more than 80 percent of the nucleus. The rate of production varied during the interval the comet was examined by the space probes. Vega 2 found somewhere in the region of 16 tons of water coming away from the nucleus during its flyby, while Vega 1 detected double this rate. These large changes are reflected in the fact that Halley's comet was sometimes seen to vary by a factor of two or three from night to night. The velocity at which the vapor was ejected was found to be between 0.8 and 1.4 kilometers per second. This was the first time that water had been positively identified in a comet, in spite of the fact that cometary nuclei were widely thought to consist of a mixture of dust and water ice. Carbon monoxide and carbon dioxide were also detected, although methane was not found at all. This is strange, in that either any methane which existed in the comet may have been changed chemically during the period since the formation of the comet or methane was lacking in the cloud of material from which the comet formed. If there is methane in Halley's nucleus, it must constitute a very tiny percentage of the total makeup.

The processes involved in the release of gas from the nucleus may have played a prominent role in the evolution of its surface. It has been suggested that, as a comet approaches the Sun after spending its time in the temperatures of approximately 40 Kelvins in the outer regions of the Sun's influence, the warming effects of the star can cause the ice within the nucleus to expand. This would result in the generation of heat and the release of trapped gas. Some of this gas may collect in pockets, which eventually explode, producing craterlike features similar to that imaged by Giotto.

Methods of Study

Halley's comet is unusual (though not unique) in that it is named for the astronomer who first calculated its orbital path rather than the person who discovered it. Edmond Halley observed a bright comet in 1682, the impression of this sighting staying with him and eventually expanding into a deeper interest in comets. In 1705, Halley began a study of a number of bright comets seen between 1337 and 1698. Using methods developed by Sir Isaac Newton, he carried out work on the orbital motions of some twenty-four comets seen during this period. He noticed from his results that there were many similarities between the orbits of the comets observed in 1531 and 1607 and the bright comet he had seen in 1682. The intervals between the sightings were also roughly identical at around seventy-six years. This led Halley to predict that these sightings were of the same comet and that it would reappear in 1758.

Halley died in 1743, although astronomers began a search for the returning comet as the date forecast by Halley drew near. The French astronomer and mathematician Alexis-Claude Clairaut, with the help of Joseph-Jérome de Lalande and Madame Nicole Lepaute, attempted to calculate its orbital path in more detail. Taking into account the gravitational effects of Jupiter and Saturn, they calculated that the comet would reach perihelion on April 13, 1759, and published ephemerides to help astronomers with their search. Many famous astronomers joined in the search, although it was the Dresden amateur astronomer Johann Georg Palitzsh, who first spotted the comet on Christmas Day, 1758. The recovery was quickly confirmed, and the comet was named for Halley in honor of the fact that he had correctly predicted its return. Once a number of observations had been obtained, a revised orbit was calculated and it was found that Clairaut's calculated perihelion date was in error by thirty-two days. Scientists were at a loss to explain this error, although they did not know about the existence of the two giant planets, Uranus and Neptune, which were not to be discovered until 1781 and 1846, respectively.

Since the 1759 appearance, Halley's comet has been seen on three occasions: in 1835, 1910, and 1985-1986. Times of previous visits of the comet have been calculated by taking into account the gravitational effects of other solar system bodies and plotting its orbital course back in time. The dates calculated for previous apparitions have been substantiated by checking against ancient astronomical records, primarily those of Chinese astronomers. The first definite appearance of Halley's comet took place in 240 B.C., although the 12 B.C. appearance is the first about which detailed information is available. The most famous return was that of 1066, which was taken as a bad omen by the Saxons and, in particular, by Harold, the last of the Saxon kings. William of Normandy, who took the apparition as a good sign, invaded England, following which Harold died at the Battle of Hastings in October of that year. The Bayeux Tapestry shows the comet suspended above Harold, who is seen tottering on his throne as his courtiers look on in awe and terror.

The 1531 appearance is important as being one of two apparitions studied by Halley (the other being that of 1607) prior to his deduction that these sightings were of one and the same object and that the comet that now bears his name was a regular visitor to this region of the solar system. A comprehensive set of observations of the 1531 appearance was made by the astronomer Peter Apian, who published his results in 1540. The 1607 appearance was observed and recorded by many astronomers, including Johannes Kepler. This was the last apparition of Halley's comet before the introduction of the telescope.

After the comet's reappearance in 1759 and the discovery of Uranus in 1781, astronomers were able to plot its orbit with accuracy. Long before its scheduled return in 1835, many attempts were made to calculate the expected date of perihelion passage. The consensus of opinion was that Halley's comet would pass closest to the Sun in November, 1835. The search for the returning comet started as early as December, 1834, almost a year before it was due to sweep through the inner solar system. The first sighting was not made, however, until August 6, 1835, by Father Dumouchel and Francisco di Vico at the Collegio Romano Observatory. Confirmation came via Friedrich Georg Wilhelm von Struve, who saw the comet on August 21. Perihelion took place on November 16.

Prominent among the astronomers who studied the comet during the 1835 apparition was Sir John Frederick Herschel, who was then based at a temporary observatory near Cape Town, South Africa. He was in the process of completing the sky survey started by his father, Sir William Herschel, and had moved to South Africa in order to survey the southern stars that were visually inaccessible from England. John Herschel made his first attempt to locate the comet in late January, 1835, although he did not see it until October 28. The 1835 apparition was remarkable in that much activity was seen to occur in the comet. Prior to its temporary disappearance in the Sun's rays as it rounded the Sun, a number of changes were observed in the tail, these disturbances continuing after its reappearance. The tail was seen to vary noticeably in length. The head also altered in appearance, at times appearing almost as a point of light, while at others taking on a nebulous form. It was noticed that the coma expanded while undergoing a reduction in brightness, eventually becoming so dim that it merged into the surrounding darkness. Herschel's last observation of Halley's comet in mid-May, 1836, was the last that any astronomer saw of it until the 1910 return. All the information scientists have about the 1835 apparition is in the form of sketches and visual descriptions. Photography was yet to make its impact on astronomy, although the appearance in 1910 of the comet was, through the use of the camera, to provide the most comprehensive and detailed study up to that time.

The 1910 apparition was the third predicted return and was awaited eagerly by astronomers all over the world. The interval between the 1835 and 1910 visits had been littered with numerous bright comets, notable among which were the Great Comet of 1843, Donati's comet of 1858, and the Great September Comet of 1882. This latter was particularly significant in that it was the subject of the first successful attempt at photographing a comet, a good image being obtained by Sir David Gill in South Africa. Observation of Comet Morehouse in 1908 demonstrated that a series of photographs were an ideal way of monitoring cometary structural changes. Comet Morehouse itself underwent a number of prominent changes which, coupled with the fact that Halley's comet had suffered in a similar fashion three-quarters of a century before, whetted the appetites of the astronomers who were geared up for the forthcoming apparition. The prolonged period of cometary activity following its last visit had allowed astronomers to perfect their observing techniques and paved the way for the return of Halley's comet.

The comet had passed aphelion in 1872, after which it once more began its long journey toward the inner solar system. The first astronomer to detect the returning visitor was astrophysics professor Max Wolf at Heidelberg, Germany, on a photographic plate taken on the night of September 11-12, 1909. The comet was close to its expected position, calculated from past observations and the known positions of the major planets. It did not become visible to the naked eye until well into 1910. Prior to this, another bright comet made an unexpected appearance. The Great Daylight Comet was first spotted by diamond miners in Transvaal, South Africa, during the early morning sky of January 13, 1910. Confirmation of the discovery was made four days later, and news of this spectacular discovery was sent to the world's observatories. Unlike Halley's comet, which was to appear later on in the year, the Great Daylight Comet became a brilliant evening object for observers in the Northern Hemisphere, its tail attaining a maximum length of 30 degrees or more by the end of January. This object became so bright that it was visible to the naked eye even in broad daylight, hence its name.

The Great Daylight Comet was widely mistaken for Halley's comet by many people who had been expecting its return at about this time, although Halley's comet did not put on as grand a show. A mixture of bad weather in the Northern Hemisphere together with the fact that a full moon occurred at what should have been the best time for observation for northern observers meant that astronomers above the equator were disappointed.

Yet, even working against these odds, they did obtain many useful photographs and were able to study the comet spectroscopically. The best results, however, were obtained from observatories in the Southern Hemisphere, notably in Santiago in Chile. From mid-April to mid-May, 1910, Halley's comet was in the same area of the morning sky as the planet Venus, the two objects together forming a marvelous visual spectacle in the constellation of Pisces. Much activity was noted both in the head and the tail of the comet. Sequences of photographs showed marked changes in the head, including material being ejected from the nucleus and halos expanding out from the nucleus. The tail was also undergoing violent changes, with material being seen to condense in various regions. On April 21, the day following perihelion, the previously smooth northern edge of the tail became irregular and distorted. Material seemed to be thrown out in various directions, and parts of the tail seemed to be ejected into space, an event clearly visible on photographs obtained at the time. For some days following perihelion, a jet of material from the nucleus seemed to be refueling the northern section of the tail. Once this activity ceased, the tail's southern section increased in brightness. A few weeks after perihelion, the two types of cometary tail appeared, a straight and distinct gas tail contrasting with the fainter, more diffuse and curved dust tail. Halley's comet passed between the Sun and Earth on May 18, although in spite of many attempted observations, no trace of the nucleus could be seen as the comet transited the solar disc. This proved that the nucleus must be tiny and the gas around it very tenuous. During this time, it was thought that the Earth may pass through the tail, although there is no evidence that this actually occurred. The pronounced curve of the tail seems to have taken it away from the Earth, preventing a passage of the planet through it. The closest approach of the comet to Earth was on May 20, when the distance between the two bodies was 21 million kilometers. For a time afterward, the comet became a prominent evening object for American observers, and many useful results were obtained by astronomers at Lick Observatory and Mount Wilson Observatory in California. A number of changes in the comet's structure were seen, and many spectroscopic observations were taken. These showed the presence of a large number of different molecules in the comet and helped astronomers to understand more clearly its chemical constitution.

As the comet started on its journey back to the outer regions of the solar system, it grew steadily fainter and fainter. It was last seen when beyond the orbit of Jupiter on a photograph taken on June 15, 1915, on its way toward aphelion in 1948. The next return would be accompanied by an unprecedented campaign by astronomers and scientists to expand their understanding of comets in general, and Halley's comet in particular.

The return of 1985-1986, the most recent to date, provided astronomers with their best ever chance of exploring a comet. Unlike other bright comets, many of which appear suddenly, the orbital path of Halley's comet is known with great precision, and the route of the comet around the Sun is known to a high degree of accuracy. Therefore, it was possible to plan missions by unmanned space probes to rendezvous with the comet during its last return. For a comet rendezvous mission, the position of the comet at time of interception must be known well in advance, as was the case with Halley's comet. In all, five space probes were sent to examine the comet. Two of these were the Soviet Vega probes, launched in December, 1984, to release balloons into the Venusian atmosphere on the way to encountering the comet on March 6 and March 9, 1986, at distances of 8,890 kilometers and 8,030 kilometers, respectively. Among the equipment they carried were cameras, infrared spectrometers, and dust-impact detectors. The two Japanese probes carried out their investigations from greater distances. Sakigake, launched in January, 1985, flew by the comet on March 11, 1986, at a distance of 6.9 million kilometers, its primary purpose being to investigate the interaction between the solar wind and the comet at a large distance from the comet. One of the main aims of Suisei, launched in August, 1985, was to investigate the growth and decay of the hydrogen corona. Suisei flew past the comet on March 8, 1986, at a distance of 151,000 kilometers.

By far the most ambitious, and most successful, of the probes to Halley's comet was the European Giotto, named in honor of the Italian painter Giotto di Bondone and launched toward the comet on July 2, 1985. Giotto was cylindrical in shape, with a length of 2.85 meters and a diameter of 1.86 meters. Its payload included numerous dust-impact detectors, a camera for imaging the nucleus and inner coma of Halley's comet, and a photopolarimeter for measuring the brightness of the coma. Giotto flew within 610 kilometers of the nucleus on March 14, 1986, at a speed of more than 65 kilometers per second. The data collected by Giotto were immediately transmitted back to Earth via a special high-gain antenna mounted on the end of the space probe, facing away from the comet. This information was received back on Earth by the 64-meter antenna at the Parkes ground station in Australia. At the opposite end, Giotto was equipped with a special shield to protect it from impacts by dust particles during its passage through the comet's head.

The exploration of Halley's comet by space probes was a truly international effort, the images and measurements obtained by the Soviet Vega craft helping scientists to target Giotto precisely. From Earth, the nucleus of a comet is hidden from view by the material surrounding it, and it was not until the Vega images were received that its position was established and the subsequent trajectory of Giotto determined. During the encounter, all the instruments performed well, although disaster struck immediately before closest approach to the nucleus. A dust particle, weighing an estimated 1 gram, impacted Giotto. This had the effect of temporarily knocking the spacecraft and, hence, the antenna out of alignment with Earth, and for thirty minutes contact was lost. This, however, was rectified and contact reestablished. After the encounter, it was found that approximately half of the scientific experiments had suffered damage, although scientists were able to redirect the craft and put it on a course back to Earth. Tests carried out by the European Space Agency in 1989 paved the way for the reactivation of Giotto, which was expected to pass within 22,000 kilometers of the Earth and be placed into a new orbit that would allow it to intercept another comet, probably Comet Grigg-Skjellerup, by July, 1992.

Context

Although study of Halley's comet has taught scientists much about comets in general, there is still much to learn about these ghostly visitors. Halley's comet has provided a chance to investigate the origins of the solar system. Future exploration by space probe of comets will include rendezvous missions, during which a probe will position itself close to a cometary nucleus for a prolonged period and perhaps send a lander to the surface of the nucleus. The possibilities of such a mission are already being examined by the National Aeronautics and Space Administration (NASA). Known as Comet Rendezvous and Asteroid Flyby (CRAF), it would enable scientists to undertake close-up exploration of both asteroids and comets. Sample return missions, by which scientists will be able to examine at firsthand material plucked from the heart of a comet, are also a possibility. The hopes of astronomers and scientists include a manned mission to Halley's comet during its next apparition in 2061.

Brian Jones

Basic Bibliography

Berry, Richard. "Giotto Encounters Comet Halley." *Astronomy* 14 (June, 1986): 6-22. A summary of the Giotto mission, describing in detail the Giotto craft and its experiments, its launch and route to the comet, and its passage through the coma. The article, although concentrating primarily on Giotto, also contains details of the other probes sent to the comet. Suitable for the general reader.

Berry, Richard, and Richard Talcott. "What Have We Learned from Comet Halley?" *Astronomy* 14 (September, 1986): 6-22. A summary of the information gleaned from probes sent to intercept Halley's comet. Each of the main parts of the comet—the nucleus, coma, and tail—is covered individually, and the article is supplemented by photographs taken both by earth-based astronomers and passing spacecraft. Suitable for the general reader.

Gingerich, Owen. "Newton, Halley, and the Comet." *Sky and Telescope* 71 (March, 1986): 230-232. This article provides background information on Sir Isaac Newton and Edmond Halley and describes how Halley used the information gained from Newton's work with gravitation to draw comparisons between the orbital motions of comets seen in 1531, 1607, and 1682 to conclude that they were all sightings of the same object and to predict its return in 1758. Suitable for the general reader.

Harpur, Brian, and Laurence Anslow. *The Official Halley's Comet Project Book.* London: Hodder and Stoughton, 1985. A comprehensive guide to knowledge of Halley's comet prior to its exploration by space probe. As well as a general description of comets, the book contains details of Edmond Halley and his work, many facts relating to Halley's comet and its previous appearances, and a detailed description of the 1910 apparition of the comet. Includes a discussion on the pronunciation of Halley's name and a collection of poems written about the comet in 1910. A useful book for the general reader, containing many items not printed elsewhere.

Meadows, Jack. *Space Garbage.* London: George Philip, 1985. Chapter 6, "Unusual Garbage," is devoted mainly to an account of Halley's comet, including past apparitions, meteor streams related to the comet, and orbital details. Suitable for the general reader.

Whipple, Fred L. "The Black Heart of Comet Halley." *Sky and Telescope* 73 (March, 1987): 242-245. An examination of the information received regarding the nucleus of Halley's comet and what it tells scientists. Comparisons are drawn between previous models of the structure of cometary nuclei and current knowledge. Suitable for the general reader.

_____. *The Mystery of Comets.* Washington, D.C.: Smithsonian Institution Press, 1985. Chapter 4, "Halley and His Comet," outlines the life and work of Edmond Halley and his involvement with cometary orbits. Chapter 5, "The Returns of Halley's Comet," describes the apparitions of Halley's comet from the earliest sightings to 1910; chapter 24, "Space Missions to Comets," is a description of the various space probes that intercepted Halley's comet during its return in 1985-1986. Suitable for the general reader.

Current Bibliography

Grewing, M., M. Grewing, F. Praderie, and R. Reinhard, eds. *Exploration of Halley's Comet.* New York: Springer-Verlag, 1988.

Mason, J. W., ed. *Comet Halley: Investigations, Results, Interpretations.* New York: E. Horwood, 1990.

Moore, Abd al-Hayy. *Halley's Comet.* Santa Barbara, Calif.: Zilzal Press, 1988, 1986.

Sekanina, Zdenek, ed. *The Comet Halley Archive Summary Volume.* Pasadena, Calif.: Jet Propulsion Laboratory, California Institute of Technology, 1991.

Cross-References

Asteroids, 9; Comets, 70; Meteorites: Achondrites, 539; Meteorites: Carbonaceous Chondrites, 548; Meteorites: Chondrites, 556; Meteorites: Nickel-Irons, 563; Meteorites: Stony Irons, 569; Meteors and Meteor Showers, 576.

Helioseismology

Helioseismology is the study of the oscillations that take place within the Sun. These periodic vibrations are caused by sound waves, which originate within the convective zone of the Sun. By analyzing the motion of these waves, scientists can image the interior of the Sun and develop a more accurate model of the Sun.

Overview

It was discovered in the early 1960's that areas of the Sun's surface are periodically oscillating up and down. This discovery, like many other scientific discoveries, was made somewhat by accident. The evidence for solar quakes was obtained while astronomers were attempting to measure the oblateness of the Sun to verify another theory.

It was known for quite some time that the orbit of the planet Mercury did not follow the precise path predicted by the solution to Sir Isaac Newton's laws of gravity and motion. In fact, as Mercury orbited the Sun, its orbit would also revolve around the Sun. Although some precession was predicted, a precession in Mercury's orbit of 43 arc seconds per century was not predicted. It was proposed by some scientists that there was another planet within the orbit of Mercury. Others suggested that, after so many accurate predictions, Newton's law of gravity needed some alteration. In 1916, Albert Einstein proposed that a massive object, such as the Sun, warps the space-time around itself. Mercury's orbit would then follow the curvature in space-time caused by the Sun. Einstein's general theory of relativity accurately accounted for the motion of Mercury. According to an opposing theory of gravity, the scalar-tensor theory of Carl Brans and Robert H. Dicke, the Sun is not a perfect sphere but has a slight equatorial bulge caused by the rotation of its core. Dicke proposed that a distortion of 0.05 percent of the Sun's surface would explain the observed behavior of Mercury's orbit.

At the University of Arizona, astronomer Henry Hill built a telescope that was designed specifically to detect a distortion in the shape of the Sun. When the telescope became operational and the Sun's surface was studied, no evidence of a distortion was observed. Upon further observation and an additional series of measurements, Hill and his colleagues discovered the periodic oscillations of the Sun's surface.

Light from the Sun is analyzed by the use of a spectrometer. This device, similar to a glass prism, breaks up sunlight into its component colors. Since the cooler gases of the Sun's atmosphere absorb some wavelengths of light, a spectrum, which contains several dark lines, is produced. These dark lines in the Sun's spectrum form the chemical signature of the various elements that compose the Sun.

The discovery of surface oscillations was made by observing the Doppler shift of various spectral lines in the light from the Sun. By analyzing light, astronomers can determine whether the source is moving toward or away from the observer. If the spectral lines have been shifted to the blue (or short-wavelength) end of the spectrum, the source of the light is moving toward the observer. If the shift is toward the red (or long-wavelength) end of the spectrum, the source is moving away from the observer. By observing various points on the surface of the Sun, astronomers were able to show the periodic oscillation of those points, as spectral lines would be alternatively redshifted and then blueshifted.

It was first observed that these periods of oscillation were about five minutes in duration. Since then, it has been determined that the entire surface of the Sun is in a state of constant oscillation, with periods varying between minutes and hours. It might be said that the Sun is ringing like a bell. In this case, however, the bell is being struck continuously.

Astronomers believe that the origin of these waves is the convective zone beneath the photosphere or "surface" of the Sun. These huge boiling columns of gas carry heat from the Sun's interior to the surface. The tops of these convecting cells produce the granulation seen in solar photographs. These granules may each be hundreds of kilometers across. The gas rises toward the surface accompanied by a tremendous roar. These sound waves oscillate through the Sun and cause its surface to rise and fall periodically.

As sound waves travel downward into the Sun, they encounter higher temperatures and pressures. These changing physical conditions result in the wave's velocity being increased. Eventually, the waves begin to bend upward toward the surface of the Sun. When they reach the bottom of the photosphere, they are reflected back into the interior of the Sun. The depth that the wave travels depends upon its length. The wavelength also determines how far a wave will travel around the Sun before it hits the surface.

The Sun's interior is conducting waves with virtually millions of different wavelengths and frequencies. Some waves have the exact length necessary to make an even number of bounces before they return to where they began. Astronomers categorize these waves by the number of times that they strike the surface in one complete cycle of the Sun. For example, a wave with the designation I-4 strikes the surface in three places before it bounces back to its starting position. Once it returns to its origin, it has struck the surface of the Sun four times. Scientists have found that waves with low I numbers travel deep within the Sun and may be a key to revealing physical characteristics there, while waves with higher I numbers may be used to probe the shallow zones of the Sun's interior.

Applications

During an earthquake, various types of seismic waves are generated. These waves are received at seismic stations around the world and their arrival times are noted. By determining the path and velocity of these waves, scientists learn much about the interior of the Earth. Similar methods are used by exploration geophysicists to study the subsurface when searching for mineral deposits or potential oil traps. In this case, the seismic waves are generated by explosive charges or other artificial means. The waves then travel into the Earth and are reflected as they strike various rock layers. Scientists can then determine the depth of these layers.

Scientists hope to be able to use solar seismic waves to image the interior of the Sun, just as geophysicists use seismic waves to study the interior of the Earth. Prior to this new development in solar physics, the processes that occur within the Sun and the locations of various boundaries within the Sun were theoretical. It is hoped that future helioseismic studies will continue to increase human knowledge of the Sun.

Theorists believe that the Sun is a giant ball of gas that is sustained by a thermonuclear fire burning within its core. Because of the great pressure and high temperature within this region of the Sun, the nuclei of hydrogen are fused together to form helium. During this process, which is known as the proton-proton cycle, 600 million tons of hydrogen are consumed each second and turned into some 590 million tons of helium. The tonnage that is not converted into helium is transformed into energy. Most of the energy leaves the core in the form of high-intensity radiation called gamma rays. The remainder is in the form of chargeless, massless, subatomic particles called neutrinos.

By studying the rate at which neutrinos are emitted from the core, scientists can gain some insight into the processes that are occurring within the core. In the late 1960's, an experiment was set up deep within an abandoned gold mine in Lead, South Dakota. Conducted by Raymond Davis of the Brookhaven National Laboratory, this ongoing experiment uses a 378,000-liter tank of a chlorine solution to detect the solar neutrinos. As the neutrinos pass through the solution and strike individual atoms of chlorine, argon nuclei are formed. Since these argon nuclei are radioactive, they can be detected easily and the neutrino flux can be calculated. The results of the Davis experiment have touched off one of the major debates in modern astrophysics. The experiment is detecting only about one-third as many neutrinos as the theory indicates should be detected. Astrophysicists are wondering what is happening to the missing neutrinos. Several theories have been proposed to solve the problem. It has been suggested that perhaps the Davis experiment has flaws. This possibility has been examined thoroughly; the high-technology equipment involved in this experiment has been checked several times and the data have been interpreted and reinterpreted. The problem of the missing neutrinos remains.

There is a possibility that the model of the solar interior is incorrect. The

359

possibility exists that the core of the Sun is not as hot as current theory indicates. If the core is cooler, then the number of neutrinos emitted from the Sun would be less, and this would account for the missing neutrinos. A particle known as WIMP, or weakly interacting massive particle, has been proposed as a possible solution. According to modern theory, WIMPs were formed in the early universe, when matter was in a very dense state and temperatures were extremely hot. These particles migrated toward the center of newly forming stars, where they remain today. It is believed that WIMPs may circulate within the interior of the Sun, carrying heat away from the core. As a result of this process of carrying away heat, the fuel cycle would be slowed somewhat, thus reducing the number of neutrinos emitted.

There are still other possibilities to be considered. One interesting possibility is that the Sun's core is rotating much faster than its outer layers. If this is true, the core temperature would be lower and, thus, the rate of neutrino emission from the core would be lower. A potential problem with this solution is that a rapidly rotating core would cause an equatorial bulge, and no such bulge has been detected.

It is obvious that the only way to determine precisely the cause of the missing neutrinos and whether the core is rotating is to have images of the interior of the Sun. Helioseismic waves may provide the answer. It has already been determined by studying solar seismic patterns that the Sun's convection zone is deeper than previously believed. Apparently, it composes about 30 percent of the solar radius. New information has been found that links the rate of rotation of the interior of the Sun to the formation of sunspots.

More extensive studies using helioseismology have been planned. The Global Oscillation Network Group (GONG) at the National Solar Observatory in Tucson, Arizona, was founded to begin such studies. Also, the European Space Agency (ESA) plans to install helioseismology instrumentation on its Solar and Heliospheric Observatory (SOHO), which will be able to take relevant data for years to come.

The GONG program has outlined several specific goals for their solar studies program. The first goal is to determine the internal temperature, pressure, and composition of the Sun from the surface down to the core. A second goal is to determine the rotational rates of internal layers of the Sun. In addition to determining rotation rates, scientists will again attempt to detect any solar oblateness. This test will allow the accuracy of the general theory of relativity to be checked again and quite possibly, between the oblateness and rotation tests, the problem of the missing neutrinos can be solved. Scientists also hope to use helioseismic studies to investigate how energy is transferred from the solar surface to the chromosphere and corona. It is currently believed that intense magnetic fields, along with acoustic shock waves from the tops of convecting cells, are responsible for temperatures of 400,000 Kelvins in the chromosphere and temperatures of 2 million Kelvins in the corona.

GONG's plans include building a chain of 50-millimeter refracting telescopes to be stationed at various locations on the Earth. These locations will ensure that at least two telescopes will be gathering data from the Sun at all times. The network will observe the Sun continually for a three-year period. This large amount of data is necessary if astronomers are to determine the path of sound waves through the Sun and convert that information into a model of the solar interior. Each of the telescopes that will be deployed by the GONG project contains an instrument called a Fourier tachometer. This device is capable of measuring extremely small Doppler shifts at more than sixty-five thousand different points on the surface of the Sun. By observing these shifts, astronomers can determine oscillation periods of these various points and form a detailed model of the solar disk.

Context

The discovery that the surface of the Sun is oscillating was made in the early 1960's. At the time, scientists were gathering data on the oblateness of the Sun in an attempt to determine which theory—the scalar-tensor theory of Dicke and Brans or Einstein's general theory of relativity—could best explain the motion of the planet Mercury. As it turned out, there was no noticeable oblateness of the Sun, but subsequent observations revealed a Doppler shift in the solar spectra taken from various points on the Sun. This Doppler shift provided evidence for periodic oscillations. Further investigations have revealed that the Sun is ringing as if it were a large bell that is continuously being struck.

The millions of different wavelengths and frequency combinations of waves are believed to originate within the Sun's convective zone. In this area, the tremendous heat from the core is flowing outward toward the surface. This method of heat flow, convection, is found only in a gas or a liquid. Here, the material toward the base of the zone is extremely hot. Hot liquids and gases are also less dense than cooler liquids or gases. As a result, the less dense material rises toward the surface, carrying the heat. At the base of the zone, cooler material flows in to fill the void. This material will be heated subsequently and will begin to move toward the surface. The sound waves given off by this movement of huge amounts of hot gases are the waves that cause the Sun to vibrate.

The discovery of helioseismic waves and, therefore, the science of helioseismology will enable solar scientists to map the interior of the Sun and perhaps solve some of the perplexing problems in solar physics. For example, if it can be determined whether the core is rotating or if the Sun has an equatorial bulge, it may be possible to solve the problem of the missing neutrinos. Helioseismic imaging will also make it possible for astronomers to determine the boundaries for such zones as the convective zone, radiative zone, and the core itself. In addition, the accumulation of data from the GONG program will, over a period of years, enable astronomers to form an accurate model of the solar surface and interior.

David W. Maguire

Basic Bibliography

Gamow, George. *A Star Called the Sun.* New York: Viking Press, 1964. This very readable volume describes the Sun, solar processes, and energy generation within the Sun. Stellar evolution is also discussed. Some basic algebra is used in illustrations. Well suited for the layperson.

Lopresto, James Charles. "Looking Inside the Sun." *Astronomy* 17 (March, 1989): 20-28. A somewhat technical article discussing the origin of the study of helioseismology and its possibilities in solar research. Although very little mathematics is used, the article contains an abundance of technical terms. The reader should have a background in basic physics and astronomy.

Mitton, Simon. *Daytime Star: The Story of Our Sun.* New York: Charles Scribner's Sons, 1981. A nontechnical volume accessible to the general reader. Mitton discusses the Sun, its structure, its processes, and its future.

Pasachoff, Jay M. *Astronomy: From the Earth to the Universe.* Philadelphia: Saunders College Publishing, 1991. A fairly technical volume covering topics in stellar and solar system astronomy. This volume is used as a text for college freshman-level astronomy courses but would be accessible to the informed reader. Contains an excellent unit on the Sun.

Seeds, Michael A. *Foundations of Astronomy.* Belmont, Calif.: Wadsworth, 1990. This general astronomy textbook contains a section on the Sun. Suitable for the general reader.

Seeds, Michael A. *Horizons: Exploring the Universe.* Belmont, Calif.: Wadsworth, 1991. Although this volume is intended for use as a college-level general astronomy text, it is accessible to the general reader. Contains an excellent discussion on the Sun.

Current Bibliography

Cox, A. N., W. C. Livingston, and M. S. Matthews, eds. *Solar Interior and Atmosphere.* Tucson: University of Arizona Press, 1991.

Gough, D. O., A. G. Kosovichev, J. Toomre, E. Anderson, et al. "The Seismic Structure of the Sun." *Science* 272, no. 5266 (May, 1996): 1296-1301.

Gribbin, John R. *Blinded by the Light: The Secret Life of the Sun.* New York: Harmony Books, 1991.

Harvey, J. W., F. Hill, R. P. Hubbard, J. R. Kennedy, et al. "The Global Oscillation Network Group (GONG) Project." *Science* 272, no. 5266 (May, 1996): 1284-1287.

Hellemans, Alexander. "SOHO Probes Sun's Interior by Tuning in to Its Vibrations." *Science* 272, no. 5266 (May, 1996): 1264-1266.

Levenson, Thomas. "The Sounds of Sunlight." *Sciences* 31, no. 1 (January/February, 1991): 12-16.

Cross-References

Heliospheric Physics, 363; Solar Geodetics, 855.

Heliospheric Physics

Advances in both theoretical physics and astronomical observing capability have provided a detailed description of the Sun. Since most stars have many things in common with the Sun, these insights can be applied throughout the universe.

Overview

The Sun is a typical star. Many stars are cooler than the Sun, many are hotter; many stars are brighter, and many are not as bright. All stars, however, are much farther away from Earth than the Sun, which is a mere 150 million kilometers away. The next closest star is Proxima Centauri, which is about 25 trillion kilometers away. Light from the Sun takes only eight minutes to reach Earth, while light from Proxima Centauri takes about four years.

The Sun thus provides a "laboratory" where normal stellar processes can be observed and studied without the complications of light-years of separation in space. (A light-year is the distance that light travels in one year.)

The superficial appearance of the Sun is deceptively simple, because one can normally see only one of the many layers of the Sun. This layer is called the photosphere, which means "sphere from which the light comes." When one looks at the Sun with the naked eye or through a light-absorbing filter, one is seeing the photosphere. If one photographs the Sun, the picture will show the photosphere.

The photosphere is the lowest level of the atmosphere of the Sun. It has a temperature of about 5,800 degrees Celsius and consists primarily of hydrogen (94 percent) and helium (6 percent), the two simplest elements. Minute quantities of several other elements are also present, most notably oxygen, carbon, nitrogen, silicon, magnesium, neon, iron, and sulfur.

When examined with high-resolution equipment, such as that aboard Spacelab 2, the photosphere reveals a wealth of structure and detail not visible to the naked eye. Most pronounced is the presence of granulation, an alternation of dark and light spots resembling a mixture of salt and pepper. Each granule is a region of gas about 1,000 kilometers in diameter, larger than the state of Texas. The bright part at the center of the granule is believed to be matter rising rapidly from the convection zone, located just below the photosphere. (Convection is the tendency of hot gases to rise and cool gases to fall.) The dark border regions of a granule are cooler gases falling to the convection zone.

The convection zone on the Sun is a source of very intense heat and produces waves of thermal energy that shoot up through the photosphere. These waves make the photosphere appear to oscillate, with periods ranging from minutes to hours.

Above the photosphere is another layer of the solar atmosphere that is normally completely invisible. This layer is called the chromosphere, meaning "sphere of color." Under normal conditions the photosphere is so bright that it overwhelms the other layers of the Sun, making them impossible to detect. During an eclipse, however, the Moon can block the photosphere and the chromosphere will be visible, extending out around the shadowed edges of the Moon.

Unlike the photosphere, the chromosphere is not a spherically symmetrical layer of solar atmosphere. It is actually composed of innumerable small spikes that rise dramatically and then fall, creating a dynamic appearance, like the dance of a thousand small candle flames. These spikes are known as spicules. These spicules are about 700 kilometers across and 7,000 kilometers tall. The height of a spicule is thus greater than the diameter of the

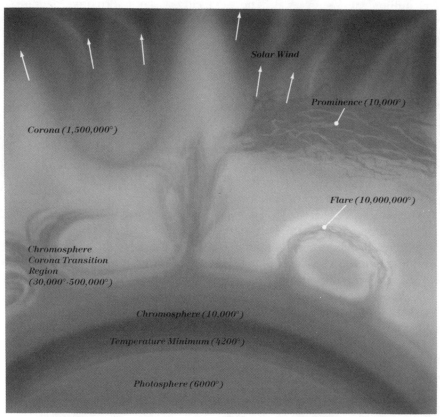

A diagram illustrating the regions and temperatures above the Sun's photosphere. *(National Aeronautics and Space Administration)*

Moon. Although spicules are very hard to study, astronomers have been able to determine that there are probably a half million spicules on the Sun at any given time and that each spicule has a lifetime of several minutes.

Like the photosphere, the chromosphere has a granulated structure. This structure cannot be directly observed, but has been inferred from studies of the motion of particles on the Sun. The motion of a distant light-emitting particle can frequently be determined from the electromagnetic Doppler effect, which is the change in the frequency, or color, of the radiation emitted by an atom as a result of its motion. If an atom is moving toward the viewer, any light that it might emit will have a higher frequency and thus be bluer than if it were stationary. Conversely, if the atom were moving away from the viewer, the emitted light will have a lower frequency and thus appear redder.

Analyzing the motion of particles on the Sun has revealed that the chromosphere contains large, organized cells of matter that move in unison under the influence of convective forces. These supergranules are 30,000 kilometers in diameter and contain hundreds of normal granulation regions. The spicules are located at the boundaries of the supergranules.

The temperature of the chromosphere is about 6,000 to 10,000 degrees Celsius, somewhat higher than the temperature of the photosphere. These high temperatures produce a strong ultraviolet spectrum. A satellite known as the International Ultraviolet Explorer (IUE) has detected similar ultraviolet spectra in other stars. The chromosphere of the Sun is thus a good laboratory for studying processes common to many stars in different parts of the universe.

During a total solar eclipse, both the photosphere and the chromosphere can be blocked by the Moon. When this happens, the flarelike outer region of the solar atmosphere known as the corona of the Sun is visible. The corona is an extremely thin gas with a temperature of about 2 million degrees Celsius.

The extremely high temperatures and intense thermal activity in the Sun raise the ancient question of where the Sun gets its enormous energy. Ever since Anaxagoras in the fifth century B.C. suggested that the Sun was not a god but simply a big ball of fire, the question of solar fuel has been a point of contention. What has kept the Sun shining so intensely for billions of years? Simple calculations show that the Sun cannot get its energy from any familiar source, such as fossil fuels, for they are incapable of such longevity. Energy released during a slow gravitational collapse was proposed for a time as the source of the Sun's energy but then found to be inadequate.

The answer to this important question emerged out of the theory of relativity, developed by Albert Einstein at the beginning of the twentieth century. In studying the relationship between matter and energy, Einstein discovered that it was possible to change matter into energy. This conversion of matter into energy can take place only under unusual circumstances, but the amount of energy obtained from a very small quantity of matter is enormous. This relationship is described mathematically in Einstein's famous formula $E = mc^2$. In this equation, E represents the energy released when a quantity of matter, m, is destroyed. The exact energy is determined by multiplying the mass, m, by c^2, where c is the speed of light (30 billion meters per second). Since the speed of light is so great, a very small quantity of mass can produce a huge amount of energy.

The conversion of mass into energy involves either fusion or fission. Fusion occurs when two atoms combine to form a heavier atom, but the heavier atom does not weigh quite as much as its lighter components. Fission is just the reverse—a heavier atom splits into separate pieces, but the separate pieces do not weigh as much as the original atom. In both of these reactions—fusion and fission—some mass is lost by being converted into energy.

The nuclear reaction in the Sun is fusion, specifically the fusion of light hydrogen atoms into heavier atoms, primarily helium. In order for fusion to occur, the dense central regions of atoms, the nuclei, must be packed very tightly together. Under normal conditions, the electrical forces of the positively charged nuclei resist such compression, and the nuclei remain too far apart for fusion to occur. Because the Sun, or any star, is so large, the strong gravitational forces can overwhelm the nuclear repulsion and compress the nuclei to the point at which fusion can occur.

Ongoing nuclear fusion reactions occur in the core of a normal star. These fusion reactions convert nuclear matter into energy in the form of photons, which are bundles of light. These photons then migrate from the core of the star, through the main body of the star, through the photosphere and chromosphere, and eventually leave the star and travel through space, perhaps ending up at a beach on Earth.

Knowledge Gained

A thorough understanding of the physics of the Sun has been obtained in two ways: through careful observation, especially by some of the solar observers that have been launched from Earth, and through advances in the understanding of physics, especially the development of the concept of nuclear fusion in the early decades of the twentieth century and the development of the field of particle physics. Advances in theoretical physics have provided explanations for many of the observed solar phenomena. The development of comprehensive star catalogs has further helped to establish that the Sun is a typical star and that the processes that take place in the Sun are representative of stellar processes throughout the universe.

Through a combination of observation and theoretical analysis it has been determined that the Sun is not a uniform sphere of fire as was once believed; rather, it has a complex series of layers, each with fundamentally different properties.

At the center of the Sun is the core, where the gravitational pressure from the huge mass of the Sun is so great that normally repulsive hydrogen nuclei are forced together into states of high compression. These nuclei then undergo nuclear fusion reactions that liberate tremendous amounts of electromagnetic energy in the form of photons, producing temperatures in excess of 15 million degrees Celsius. The photons are initially very high-energy gamma rays. As they migrate from the core to the outer layers of the Sun, the energy of the photons diminishes through numerous collisions with other atoms, thus heating up the entire mass of the Sun.

The brightest of the many layers of the Sun is the photosphere, with a temperature of almost 6,000 degrees Celsius. The photosphere is located roughly 700,000 kilometers from the center of the Sun and is about 500 kilometers thick. Above the photosphere is the chromosphere, which is about 2,500 kilometers thick. The temperature of the chromosphere ranges from about 6,000 degrees Celsius along the boundary where it overlaps the photosphere to 50,000 degrees at the top. The chromosphere is so dim compared to the photosphere that it is only visible when the photosphere is obscured. The atmosphere of the Sun gradually diminishes beyond the chromosphere in the corona, an extremely low-density region of the solar atmosphere that gradually merges into the emptiness of outer space. The hottest part of the corona has a temperature above one million degrees.

The dramatic thermal activity on the Sun is responsible for a variety of effects: granulation in the photosphere, supergranulation in the chromosphere, oscillation of the photosphere, and prominences and spicules in the chromosphere.

Detailed observation of other stars has revealed that they have many properties in common with the Sun. Research into solar activity thus sheds light on stellar properties throughout the universe.

Context

Unraveling the timeless mystery of how the Sun shines is one of the great achievements of science in the twentieth century. Not only is the Sun the source of life and energy on this planet, but the ongoing shining of the Sun affects Earth in a variety of ways, including weather patterns, radio transmission activity, and all biological activity on the planet.

The earliest explanations for the Sun's behavior were crude and, by the standards of modern science, very unscientific: The Sun was a flaming chariot, the Sun was a god, the Sun was a hole in the sky through which light shone. About five hundred years before Jesus Christ, a Greek named Anaxagoras suggested that perhaps the Sun was simply a huge ball of fire. This notion was quickly discarded as absurd, however, and the Sun once again became a revered entity.

In the centuries following Christ, the Sun continued to generate controversy, not because of its composition but because of its location. As astronomers, inspired by Nicolaus Copernicus, began to develop the modern view of the solar system, the Sun was given a privileged location in what everyone thought was the center of the universe. Astronomers were accused of worshiping the Sun.

With the great contribution of Isaac Newton, the Sun was shown to be merely one of many stars in a corner of an incomprehensibly vast universe. The important question became "How does the Sun shine?" Calculations showed that the Sun could not possibly be burning in any conventional sense; certainly, if the solar fuel were wood or coal or any known fuel, it would have burned out long ago.

One interesting explanation proposed in the nineteenth century was that the source of the Sun's radiance was the slow release of gravitational energy as the Sun contracted under the force of its own gravity. This explanation became inadequate, though, as evidence began to accumulate that the Sun was billions of years old, not thousands as had previously been thought. Gravitational collapse could not have lasted for billions of years.

When Albert Einstein first predicted that mass could be converted into energy and that even a tiny amount of mass could produce vast quantities of energy, it was clear that at last there was a mechanism that could explain the phenomenal energy output of the Sun. The only problem remaining was the determination of the details of the process. These details were provided by Hans Bethe when he suggested that the nuclear fusion reaction of the Sun involved the formation of helium from hydrogen atoms. The centuries-old riddle had been solved.

In the last few decades of the twentieth century, the rest of the details have been filled in. The full explanation of the various solar processes now stands as a remarkable testament to the ingenuity and determination of the scientific community. When consideration is given to the fact that the object under investigation is more than 175 million kilometers away, the accomplishment becomes all the more remarkable.

Karl Giberson

Basic Bibliography

Braun, Wernher von, Frederick Ordway, and Dave Dooling. *Space Travel: A History.* Rev. ed. New York: Harper and Row, Publishers, 1985. This is the fourth edition of the popular book *History of Rocketry and Space Travel.* The lead author, Wernher von Braun, is one of the greatest American rocket engineers. The book, written for the general reader, contains extensive information on all aspects of space travel, including those missions that studied the Sun.

Emiliani, Cesare. *The Scientific Companion.* New York: John Wiley and Sons, 1988. A somewhat more technical book than others listed here, yet accessible to the general reader with a limited science background. Contains a full chapter dedicated to the physics of the Sun and related chapters on nuclear physics and stellar evolution. This book is recommended for the reader who may be interested in some of the more technical aspects of the material in this article.

Gamow, George. *A Star Called the Sun.* New York: Viking Press, 1970. An updated version of the classic *The Birth and Death of the Sun,* first published in 1940. Highly accessible to the general reader and written in a charming style by one of the great scientists of the twentieth century. Contains thorough discussions of most of the material presented in this article.

Goldsmith, Donald. *The Evolving Universe.* 2d ed. Menlo Park, Calif.: Benjamin-Cummings Publishing Co., 1985. A standard astronomy text with a good discussion of all aspects of the Sun. Contains numerous illustrations. Suitable for general audiences.

Kaufmann, William J. *Discovering the Universe.* New York: W. H. Freeman and Co., 1987. A well-written astronomy text with excellent nontechnical discussions. This book is one of the most readable general astronomy texts available. A full chapter is devoted to the physics of the Sun, with several excellent illustrations.

Noyes, Robert W. *The Sun, Our Star.* Cambridge, Mass.: Harvard University Press, 1982. A thorough treatment of all aspects of the Sun. Contains hundreds of black-and-white photographs of solar phenomena. Nontechnical and accessible to the general reader. Comprehensive and detailed.

Pasachoff, Jay M. *Astronomy: From the Earth to the Universe.* 3d ed. New York: Saunders College Publishing, 1987. A popular astronomy text, with thorough discussion of the Sun. Includes several excellent color photographs of solar phenomenon. More detailed than Goldsmith's text (see above).

Current Bibliography

Cox, A. N., W. C. Livingston, and M. S. Matthews, eds. *Solar Interior and Atmosphere.* Tucson: University of Arizona Press, 1991.

Gribbin, John R. *Blinded By the Light: The Secret Life of the Sun.* New York: Harmony Books, 1991.

Schaefer, Bradley E. "Sunspots That Changed the World." *Sky and Telescope* 93, no. 4 (April, 1997): 34-39.

Cross-References

Helioseismology, 357; Solar Geodetics, 855.

The Hertzsprung-Russell Diagram

From 1904 to 1915, two astronomers, Ejnar Hertzsprung and Henry Norris Russell, independently discovered a consistent relationship between stars' luminosity and their temperature.

Overview

The Hertzsprung-Russell diagram (H-R diagram) is named to honor two men who discovered a fundamental relationship between a star's brightness and its spectral class: Ejnar Hertzsprung (1873-1967) and Henry Norris Russell (1877-1957).

Typically, in an H-R diagram (see figure), the ordinate (vertical axis) is the axis used to describe a star's brightness. The intrinsic brightness of a star can be described by several terms: apparent magnitude, absolute magnitude, absolute bolometric magnitude, or simply luminosity. The abscissa (horizontal axis) is calibrated to indicate a star's spectral class. The spectral class is indicative of a star's color index and surface temperature. All variations of the H-R diagram describe the same basic relationship; the different nomenclature refer to qualitative and/or quantitative parameters.

Stars depicted near the top of the H-R diagram represent very hot, luminous stars, while those at the bottom indicate cooler, dimmer stars. Stars falling on the left of the diagram are the hottest, and those plotted on the right are the coolest. A star plotted on an H-R diagram describes not only the relationship between its luminosity and surface temperature but also its stage of development within the stellar life cycle.

About 90 percent of all known stars fall along the main sequence of the H-R diagram. This broad region extends diagonally across the graph in a lazy "S" shape. Stars in this region represent those in the most stable chapter of their lives. Earth's sun is a main sequence star of spectral type G2, with an absolute magnitude of +5. Not all stars, however, have luminosities and temperatures that allow them to be placed within the main sequence. Stars falling outside the main sequence represent the extremes of the stellar life cycle.

Hertzsprung-Russell Diagram

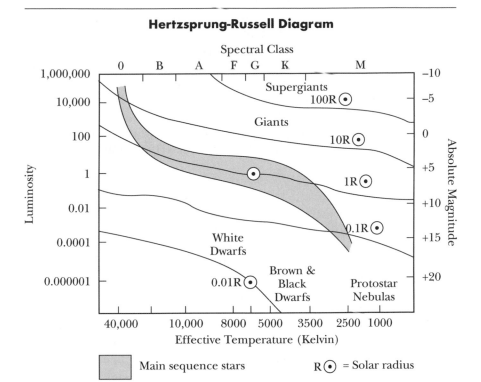

Approximately 1 percent of the stars are plotted higher and to the right of the main sequence. These are the red giants and supergiants. Characteristically, they are not only bright, in comparison to Earth's own Sun, but also cool by star standards. The Stefan-Boltzmann law, which describes the characteristics of radiating bodies, allows astronomers to determine that red giants have roughly one hundred times the surface area and luminosity of Earth's sun and about the same surface temperature. A red giant placed in Earth's solar system would occupy an area about the size of Earth's orbit. The name is derived from its reddish appearance in the night sky. Two easily observed red giants are the stars Aldebaran (alpha) in the constellation Taurus, and Arcturus in the constellation Boötes. The biggest and most luminous of all stars are the supergiants. They range in size from ten to a thousand times the diameter of Earth's sun. These stars would barely fit within Earth's solar system. Examples of supergiants include Betelgeuse in the constellation Orion and Antares in the constellation Scorpius. The other extreme of the stellar family, representing about 10 percent of all stars, is found in the lower left portion of the H-R diagram. These are the white dwarfs, which are characteristically small (about the size of Earth), very faint, and hot. Dwarfs are seen only with the aid of telescopes.

The distribution of stars along the H-R diagram demonstrates several interesting relationships within the evolution of stars. Using Earth's sun as a reference, most of the stellar population is fainter, smaller, and lower on the main sequence. Stars plotted on the H-R diagram are typically distributed in the following proportions: About 90 percent are associated with the main sequence, about 10 percent are white dwarfs, and some 1 percent are the red giants and supergiants. This distribution suggests that a star evolves through at least three very different stages in its life: from main sequence to giant to white dwarf; each stage has its own characteristic luminosity/surface temperature range.

The H-R diagram assists astronomers in the reconstruction of a star's life cycle. The process is similar to taking a picture of a crowded football stadium and trying to reconstruct the life cycle of the human species from the people in the stands. The photograph would reveal a diversity; some people would be small, others large, some old, others young. Correlating a few basic parameters would reveal a progression in the human life cycle. As one can hypothesize about the various stages of human development from the stadium picture, astronomers can construct a diagram of the lives and evolutionary paths of stars from a picture of their spectra.

The evolutionary development of a star like Earth's sun might take the following path on the H-R diagram. As interstellar dust and gas contract gravitationally into a protostar, the core increases in temperature. Upon reaching several million degrees, the nuclear fire ignites, converting hydrogen to helium, and the star's luminosity and surface temperature qualify it for a place along the main sequence. This begins the most stable period for a star. Earth's sun, about halfway through its 10-billion-year life, will spend most of its life on the main sequence.

When most of the hydrogen in the core is converted to helium, the core contracts, while the hydrogen in its atmosphere continues to burn and expand. The star enters the red giant phase. This phase is brief on the stellar evolutionary path. Most red giants consume the hydrogen of their bloated atmospheres and blow off as much as half of their mass, producing planetary nebula (gas clouds), recycling their outer shells into space to become the substance of future stars and planets. The remaining core contracts, collapses, and enters the white dwarf stage. When the fuel of the white dwarf is consumed, its final phase is a low or nonluminous core described as a brown or black dwarf. It is in the dwarf phase that most stars end their lives. Yet, a very massive star (more than three times the mass of Earth's sun) can end its life with an explosion (supernova) in which the outer shells are blown away, leaving a collapsed core (known as a neutron star or a black hole). Neutron stars and black holes are not detected in the visible wavelengths and therefore are not part of the traditional H-R diagram. As the stellar cycle is also a function of time, the H-R diagram provides information about the relative ages of stars and approximates the length of time a star may spend in each stage of stellar evolution.

Applications

The Hertzsprung-Russell diagram and its many variations illustrate the evolutionary stages of a star's life and have played a central role in astrophysics and cosmology.

As a star consumes its fuel, its color, luminosity, and size change. By utilizing the H-R diagram, astronomers can describe these changes. The forces governing these fluctuations are in a constant tug-of-war between a star's tendency to collapse under its own gravity and the outward push of the nuclear fire. A star's position along the H-R diagram is a reflection of the balance or imbalance of these forces.

The evolutionary path of a star along the H-R diagram is dependent upon the mass it collects as a protostar. The more mass a star collects in this early stage, the faster it consumes its nuclear fuel (hydrogen), thereby shortening its stay among the main sequence stars. In contrast, less massive stars burn fuel at a slower rate and remain longer on the main sequence.

Earth's sun "appeared" on the main sequence from the red, cool side of the H-R diagram (lower right) during its protostar contraction phase. The gas and dust of space, the interstellar medium, is chemically dominated by hydrogen (75 percent) and helium (25 percent), with traces of heavier elements: carbon, calcium, sodium, iron, and silicates. These molecules congregate as density centers forming nebulas. If these nebulas are not disturbed by thermal motion and turbulence, they may contract. Shock waves from supernova explosions or an encounter with a galactic arm may compress the density center further into a nucleus. As this nucleus gravitationally collects mass, its density and temperature increase until the gas becomes ionized. As its temperature rises, the nuclear fires (conversion of hydrogen to helium) begin; it then becomes luminous and finds a place as a spectral type "G" star with a magnitude of +5.

A star's location along the H-R diagram is also determined by its chemistry. A protostar may collect material gravitationally from previous supernova events (nebulas) that may be rich in metals (those elements heavier than helium). With each stellar cycle, the percentage of metals increases. This addition of metals to younger stars effectively shifts the main sequence further to the right as the universe ages.

A star's position along the main sequence represents the conditions in which it will spend most of its life. While the Sun, or any star, maintains a balance between the contraction of its core and rate of nuclear burning, it remains within the main sequence. This is the Sun's most stable stage and, fortunately, one astronomers expect to continue for about another 5 billion years. In old age, the Sun will become brighter and hotter, and it will appear slightly larger. On the H-R diagram, its position will rise slowly to the left along the main sequence. Approximately 5 billion years in the future, when most of the Sun's hydrogen will be consumed, the gravitational and nuclear forces will no longer be balanced, the core will collapse, the nuclear reactions that converted hydrogen to helium will release energy, and it will move into the outer shells, where the remaining hydrogen will be burned. As the shells expand, the surface will cool and become redder. Life on Earth will be extinguished as the Sun's outer shells expand into the solar system, consuming the inner planets; the gaseous shells of the outer planets will boil away, exposing their rocky cores. The Sun will then be a red giant.

In the red giant phase, the hydrogen shell expands and burns, while the helium core, whose nuclear fire is extinguished, contracts. The energy from gravitational contraction is converted into thermal energy, raising the temperature of the core until the helium is ignited. The life of its helium burning is short, perhaps a billion years, compared to the previous hydrogen burning time of almost 10 billion years. The helium is converted into carbon, which becomes the next generation of nuclear fuel. Again, a thermal pulse ignites the hydrogen shell. The core contracts and ignites the carbon, which is converted into oxygen. Another thermal pulse ignites and so on, in a complex chain of contractions and nuclear ignitions. After each fuel is exhausted, the star tries to maintain itself by further contraction of its core and burning the next available fuel. The process does not continue indefinitely, and the star eventually dies. A star's own solar wind, along with the thermal pulses, can drive the outer shells of a star away in a gradual explosion, leaving an exposed hot core. In this final stage, the ejected outer layers, unfortunately identified as planetary nebulas, effectively recycle heavier elements into space. These nebulas become the genesis material for future stars and planets. (The term "planetary nebula" is confusing and inaccurate. It developed in the nineteenth century, when these expanding gaseous disks were thought to be distant planets. Nevertheless, later research demonstrated that planetary nebulas have no relationship with planets.) These nebulas are the products of stars, such as Earth's sun, expelling their outer shells near the end of their red giant phase. Ultraviolet radiation from the hot core often ionizes these gases, illuminating the nebula. Examples of these nebulas are the Helix in the constellation Aquarius and the Ring nebula in the constellation Lyra.

Stars similar to Earth's sun do not get hot enough in the red giant stage to ignite carbon, their remaining source of fuel in the core. Their fate is a gravitational collapse into a small but still luminous body, a white dwarf. At the white dwarf stage, Earth's sun would not have enough internal energy to oppose the gravitational collapse of its core, crushing the matter into "degenerate matter" (matter so compressed it cannot be squeezed further). Since white dwarfs are unlike stars, which generate nuclear energy, they are referred to as compact objects rather than stars. These compact objects eventually lose their heat and luminosity to become cold and dark, ultimately becoming black dwarfs. The fate of stars many times more massive than Earth's sun, in the compact object stage, is to be compressed into either neutron stars or black holes.

The H-R diagram is a versatile astronomical tool. The recognition of a correlation between magnitude and spectral type resulted in a domino effect for astronomical research. The basic parameters of magnitude and spectral type have been redefined to finer and more discriminating levels. The distribution of stars along the H-R diagram suggests an evolutionary time-sequence among stars. The many variations of the diagram are useful in comparing theory to observations. A plot of a star's surface gravity to spectral type is one such application. Stars with the same surface temperature and surface gravity decrease with an increase in luminosity. Therefore, a super-giant has a lower surface gravity than a dwarf of the same spectral type.

While much attention is focused on stars, galaxies may also be plotted in H-R fashion, using their total luminosity and color. The brightness of a galaxy in the short wavelengths is an index of the rate of star formation, and the long wavelengths suggest the total number of stars in the galaxy. Utilizing the H-R diagram in this manner furthers an understanding not only of the evolutionary steps of stars and galaxies but also of the cosmos.

Context

Ejnar Hertzsprung's interest in astronomy was fostered by his father, who, although educated as an astronomer at the University of Copenhagen, worked for the Danish Department of Finance. He encouraged his son's interest in astronomy as an avocation, not a vocation, believing that it was not possible to make a living staring at the stars. Hertzsprung was graduated with a degree in chemical engineering in 1898 from the Polytechnical Institute in Copenhagen and began work in St. Petersburg (Leningrad). In 1901, Hertzsprung went to Leipzig and spent a year studying photochemistry in Friedrich Wilhelm Ostwald's laboratory. Photography's technology was developing as a serious scientific tool, and Hertzsprung realized its inherent advantages in the study of astronomy, particularly of a star's spectra. In 1902, Hertzsprung returned to Denmark, where he corresponded regularly with astronomer Karl Schwarzschild. In 1905 and 1907, he published two papers on stellar spectra. Hertzsprung realized that stars with very sharp and intense absorption lines were more luminous than others; this discovery was the basis for the measurement of luminosity by means of spectra. In these papers, he alludes to the existence of stars beyond the main sequence: the giants. Hertzsprung noted in his observations of apparent magnitude and color that stars could be divided into two groups: the larger one, later known as the main sequence on the H-R diagram, and a smaller group currently recognized as red giants and supergiants. It is interesting to note that Hertzsprung did not include a diagram with either the 1905 or the 1907 paper. The first published graphical representation of the magnitude-spectral type relationship came in 1913 with Henry Norris Russell.

An American astronomer, Russell began to study stellar parallaxes through photographic techniques in 1903 in Cambridge. By 1910, he had accumulated hundreds of photographic plates. Russell's analysis revealed an interesting correlation between the spectral type and absolute magnitude of different stars. The stars were not scattered randomly over the graph but demonstrated a correlation between spectral type and absolute magnitudes. As the absolute magnitude decreased, so did the surface temperature (spectral type). This seemed contrary to the current paradigm, which held that stars evolved continuously from high temperature to low temperature. In December of 1913, Russell presented a graphical representation of the relationship (later the H-R diagram) to the American Astronomical Society. In his address, he also identified giant and dwarf stars for which he laid the theoretical foundations in his papers of 1910 and 1912; he was unaware of Hertzsprung's work.

Through the filter of history, the priority of the idea goes to Hertzsprung. Although he did not initially present a graph of the relationship in his papers of 1905 or 1907, in 1911 Hertzsprung published a graph of the relationship of color to magnitude based on the few stars of the Pleiades cluster. Meanwhile, Russell published his diagram, based on hundreds of stars studied from 1903 to 1910, and correlated the relationship to stellar evolution.

The origin of identifying the relationship as the "Hertzsprung-Russell diagram" is not clear but seems to have evolved gradually with the help of astronomer Sir Arthur Stanley Eddington, who in 1924 formulated the mass-luminosity law of stars. The H-R diagram is also included in the articles and lectures of Bengt Strömgren during the 1930's. Hertzsprung often remarked that it should be called a color-magnitude diagram for clarification purposes.

Richard C. Jones

Basic Bibliography

Korn, Katherine G. "Henry Norris Russell (1877-1957)." *Vistas in Astronomy* 12 (1970): 3-6. A general biography of the man with insights.

Leuschner, A. O. "The Award of the Bruce Gold Medal to Professor Ejnar Hertzsprung." *Publications of the Astronomical Society of the Pacific* 49 (1937): 65-81. A very readable summary of his astronomical career with an emphasis on the significance of the H-R diagram.

Nielsen, Axel V. "Ejnar Hertzsprung: Measurer of Stars." *Sky and Telescope* 35 (January, 1968): 4-6. This obituary notice explores the work and life of Hertzsprung. A good introduction to the man and how his contribution influenced the astronomical paradigm.

Philip, D. A. G., and L. C. Green. "The H-R Diagram as an Astronomical Tool." *Sky and Telescope* (May, 1978): 395-400. Contains summaries of the International Astronomical Union's symposium No. 80 of 1977, in which the H-R diagram was examined from various points of view. Identified a more precise construction of the diagram, how the data should be presented to illuminate particular problems, such as the distribution of stars and their chemical composition, and age, variations from one star cluster to another, and galaxy to galaxy.

Russell, Henry Norris. "Relations Between the Spectra and Other Characteristics of the Stars." *Nature* 93 (1914): 227-230, 252-258, 281-286. This is the paper in which Russell illustrates the relationship between absolute magnitudes and spectral types.

Sitterly, Bancroft W. "Changing Interpretations of the Hertzsprung-Russell Diagram, 1910-1940: A Historical Note." *Vistas in Astronomy* 12 (1970): 357-366. A historical perspective addressing the evolving nature of this astronomical tool.

Struve, Otto. "The Two Fundamental Relations of Stellar Astronomy." *Sky and Telescope* (August, 1949): 250-252, 262. This is a fine introductory article on the mass luminosity relationship described by Hertzsprung and Russell. Includes discussions of other possible relationships and/or correlations and that the priority for the idea is credited to Russell (December 30, 1913).

Current Bibliography

Bergeat, J., and A. Knapik. "The Barium Stars in the Hertzsprung-Russell Diagram." *Astronomy and Astrophysics* 321, no. 1 (May, 1997): L9.

Perryman, M. A. C., L. Lindegren, and H. Walter. "Parallaxes and the Hertzsprung-Russell Diagram from the Preliminary Hipparcos Solution H3O." *Astronomy and Astrophysics* 304, no. 1 (December, 1995): 69.

Schonberner, D., and R. Tylenda. "The Observed Hertzsprung-Russell Diagram for Planetary Nebula Nuclei." *Astronomy and Astrophysics* 234, no. 1/2 (August, 1990): 439.

Strothers, Richard B., and Chao-wen Chin. "Luminous Blue Variables at Quiescence: The Zone of Avoidance in the Hertzsprung-Russell Diagram." *The Astrophysical Journal* 426, no. 1 (May, 1994): L43-45.

Cross-References

Cosmology, 97; Galactic Structures, 279; Galaxies and Galactic Clusters, 287; Stellar Evolution, 942; The Universe: Evolution, 999; The Universe: Structure, 1015.

Infrared Astronomy

Infrared astronomy explores the universe by focusing on wavelengths of the electromagnetic spectrum that are longer than those of visible light. This area of the spectrum is very useful for studying the process of star formation, for studying objects that are obscured by clouds of interstellar material, and for studying lower-temperature objects that do not radiate in the visible portion of the spectrum.

Overview

Infrared astronomy focuses its study on wavelengths of electromagnetic radiation that are a little longer than those of visible light. The infrared region of the spectrum covers a wide range of wavelengths from waves slightly longer than those of visible light (0.7 micron) up to 1,000 microns. (A micron is a millionth of a meter.) The longest infrared wavelengths are about one millimeter in length and mark the boundary with the radio spectrum.

Infrared radiation is very difficult to detect from distant sources. The Sun is so close that the infrared radiation it emits can be detected in the form of heat. The Moon also emits easily detected infrared radiation. Yet, to detect emissions from other stars, planets, nebulas, or galaxies, very sensitive detectors are needed.

The shortest infrared waves are known to astronomers as the "photographic infrared" because they are very similar to visible light and can be detected with certain types of photographic emulsions and other types of optical detectors. At longer wavelengths of infrared radiation, objects can be detected that are not visible at optical wavelengths. Nevertheless, at these wavelengths, the detectors used for the photographic infrared are no longer useful.

Modern infrared detectors use a substance called indium antimonide, which changes its electrical conductivity when exposed to infrared radiation. In order to be effective, however, it must be kept very cold. Solid nitrogen or liquid helium is used to surround the material to bring its temperature from –223 degrees Celsius (50 Kelvins) to within a few degrees of absolute zero. Another long-wavelength infrared detector uses a crystal of the semiconducting material germanium that contains traces of the rare metal gallium. This detector must be kept to a temperature only 2 degrees above absolute zero.

Earth's atmosphere provides advantages as well as disadvantages to infrared astronomy. Some infrared observations can be done during the day as well as at night, allowing infrared detectors to be mounted on large optical telescopes for daytime use. The disadvantage posed by the atmosphere is that water vapor and carbon dioxide absorb certain wavelengths of infrared radiation, making them invisible to astronomers. Infrared astronomers therefore have to choose particular wave bands at which the atmosphere allows a clear window. To see through these windows is often a challenge, as common objects—such as telescopes and even the sky—can radiate at these same wavelengths if they are at the appropriate temperature.

Infrared astronomers have designed ways of partially overcoming the problems posed by the atmosphere. Infrared instruments are designed so that no stray radiation from the instrument itself can enter the detectors. To overcome sky brightness in the infrared, astronomers take measurements of the observational target. The measurements include the infrared brightness of both the object and the sky. The telescope is then moved slightly so that it is no longer pointing at the source, where it takes an infrared measurement from the background sky only. When the second measurement is subtracted from the first, it is possible to determine the brightness of the object itself. This technique works well for stars, but works less well for objects such as nebulas, which cover a wider field of view. The technique can be modified to scan a wider portion of the sky, making images of larger areas possible. Detectors have been developed that can record such images in a single exposure.

The ideal earthbound infrared observatories are at very high altitudes, and in arid atmospheric conditions. The best site is on Mauna Kea in Hawaii, 4,200 meters above sea level, where two of the world's largest infrared telescopes reside: the National Aeronautics and Space Administration's 3-meter-diameter telescope and the United Kingdom Infrared Telescope (UKIRT), with a 3.8-meter-diameter mirror.

At wavelengths longer than about 30 microns, the atmosphere begins to absorb so much of the infrared radiation that ground-based observation is impossible. To observe these longer wavelengths, or far infrared, observa-

The Colors in the Electromagnetic Spectrum

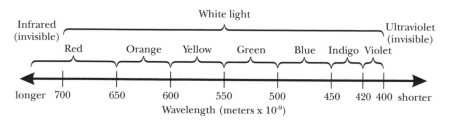

The human eye perceives discrete bands of the electromagnetic spectrum as particular colors. Radiation of longer or shorter wavelengths is invisible, whereas white light contains all visible wavelengths. Wavelength is measured here in meters $\times 10^{-9}$.

tions have been made remotely. In the 1970's, ten rocket flights carrying infrared detectors performed a survey of nine-tenths of the sky. During these early flights, it was discovered that the center of the Milky Way and other galaxies were strong sources of far infrared radiation. High-altitude balloons have also been used to make observations, and NASA has converted a C-141 transporter plane into a flying infrared observatory complete with a 0.9-meter telescope (the Kuiper Airborne Observatory). The Observatory carries scientists to altitudes of about 12,500 meters, where they can make observations free of about 99 percent of the atmosphere's water vapor. Although these types of observations are valuable, the best way to solve the observational problems posed by the atmosphere is to observe outside the atmosphere completely.

Although astronomers have flown many satellites to measure other types of radiation from space, the infrared band has presented difficulties because of the necessity of keeping the detectors at extremely low temperatures. In 1983, an infrared satellite was finally launched. The Infrared Astronomical Satellite (IRAS) was a joint project by the United States, The Netherlands, and England. IRAS investigated the sky from an orbital altitude of 900 kilometers. Throughout its development, it proved to be one of the most difficult missions ever attempted. The infrared detectors had to be designed so that even in orbit, they were cooled to within a few degrees of absolute zero with nearly 200 pounds of liquid helium. The lifetime of the satellites was limited because the liquid helium slowly boils away. IRAS was able to function efficiently for a total of ten months. The principal instrument aboard IRAS was an array of sixty-two semiconductors that were sensitive to the majority of the infrared spectrum. The satellite was roughly the size of a small automobile and weighed 1,076 kilograms.

In spite of the complexity of keeping the instruments cold, the mission was highly successful. IRAS scanned 95 percent of the sky a total of four times at the middle and far infrared wavelengths. It was able to detect about 250,000 celestial sources of infrared radiation. In 1995 the European Infrared Space Observatory (ISO) was launched and began observing in the 7.5- to 15-micron range.

Applications

The infrared spectrum is a wide band of radiation, containing a range of wavelengths ten times larger than the range of visible wavelengths. Objects having temperatures from about 2,000 degrees Celsius down to about 20 degrees above absolute zero (−253 degrees Celsius) radiate most of their energy in the infrared. This wide range of temperatures includes all kinds of objects, both celestial and terrestrial, from cool stars to people, planets, and automobiles. To screen out earthly sources of infrared radiation, astronomers have had to develop special techniques and instruments. In space, any object that does not have its own source of energy or a nearby source will cool eventually and radiate energy in the infrared. Many astronomers believe that a large part of the mass of the universe is composed of this type of material, which is invisible to optical telescopes.

An important aspect of infrared radiation is that it penetrates clouds of interstellar dust and gas. The particles in dust clouds are about the same size as wavelengths of visible light, making it difficult or impossible for visible light to penetrate them. Longer wavelengths, however, penetrate the dust clouds quite readily. Thus, objects that are hidden from the view of optical telescopes can be detected by the infrared radiation they emit.

Infrared radiation can give astronomers very valuable information about the formation of stars. Stars are believed to be formed from large clouds of rotating dust and gas that condense under their own gravity. Energy released in the collapse causes the forming star, or "protostar," to increase in temperature until nuclear reactions begin. It is not until the star "turns on" in this way that it begins to emit radiation in visible wavelengths. As a result, the process of star formation is difficult to study optically. As the star begins to shine, the newly created energy warms the surrounding dust, which radiates the energy away as infrared waves. The process is still not understood completely, and astronomers have learned much by the study of infrared and radio wavelengths.

Many infrared sources are clouds of dust that are heated by a nearby star. Infrared stars generally are either very young or very old stars, those that are associated with dust clouds. One of the early infrared discoveries was of a giant cloud of gas and dust in the constellation of Orion: the Kleinmann-Low nebula, named for its discoverers. It was found to have a mass greater than two hundred times that of the Sun, yet it is invisible at optical wavelengths. In the infrared, it outshines the Sun more than 100,000 times. It was determined to be a relatively close area of active star formation (within sixteen hundred light-years). Detailed studies of the Kleinmann-Low nebula in the infrared and radio bands indicate that it contains a number of young stars and clouds of dust and gas, which may be in the process of collapsing to form new stars. By studying this nebula, astronomers are learning more about the process of star formation. ISO detected such "stellar nurseries" in the Milky Way and other galaxies, where, its data suggest, star formation occurs at a higher rate than astronomers expected.

One of the most exciting discoveries made by IRAS was a disk of dust grains around the star Vega. Scientists believe this disk of material may be remnants of the dust cloud from which the star formed. The theory in 1990 of planet formation suggests that a similar but smaller disk of material around the Sun provided the raw material from which Earth and other planets were formed. If the disk of material around Vega follows the same pattern, it could eventually form asteroid or planet-sized bodies. The IRAS findings suggest that such material is common around other stars as well.

A year after the disk of material was found around Vega, a small companion object was found orbiting a faint star. The object was between thirty and eighty times the mass of Jupiter. It was too small to sustain nuclear reactions as a star would, and some astronomers suggested initially that this was the discovery of the first planet outside our solar system. It is theorized that the object is a brown dwarf, an object that is somewhere in between a star and a planet. It was an important discovery, as astronomers are finding there may be many more brown dwarf-type objects than expected. It is thought they may actually outnumber visible stars by a large factor. If this is the case, astronomers' theories regarding the amount of matter in the universe (and its eventual fate) would be revised dramatically.

IRAS examined many peculiar galaxies, one of which is a galaxy known as Arp 220. IRAS found that the galaxy was emitting eighty times more energy in the infrared than in all other wavelengths. Although the object is not excessively bright at optical wavelengths, its infrared brightness would make it about as energetic as some quasars. (Quasars are extremely powerful, bright sources of energy located in a very small area at the center of a galaxy that outshine the entire galaxy around them.) Although it is not known what the source of the energy is, many astronomers believe that Arp 220 is actually two galaxies that are colliding. While the individual stars of the galaxies are not likely to collide, huge clouds of dust and gas would collide, generating shock waves and heat by compression. This energy would be radiated in the infrared.

Researchers using IRAS employed a very rigorous observational screening process to weed out any stray infrared detections caused by charged particles. They screened out all but the sources that remained stationary over time and were repeatable. This method of observation lent itself to the discovery of some fast-moving objects that were eliminated because they moved too quickly from one observation to the next. In studying the rejected observations, scientists discovered a comet in 1983—the IRAS-Araki-Alcock—named for the satellite and for G. Iraki and E. Alcock, the independent discoverers. The comet passed closer to the Sun than any other comet in the last two hundred years, and IRAS was able to study it in detail, along with other ground-based observations. In total, six comets were discovered by the satellite, and five other known comets were studied.

Although the results from IRAS have been spectacular, ground-based telescopes are useful for observing many infrared phenomena. Infrared observations from NASA's Infrared Telescope Facility on Mauna Kea have revealed volcanic eruptions on Jupiter's moon Io. A volcano that had been erupting at the time of the Voyager flybys in 1979 was found to be erupting still, and a new volcano was detected. Observations such as these help to gather valuable information over time that can elaborate on the findings of other missions.

Context

Infrared astronomy is part of the revolution that has been called the "New Astronomy." The instruments of modern astronomers give them access to information from the entire range of the electromagnetic spectrum. This revolution has occurred mostly since the early 1960's, when it became possible to place remote detectors above Earth's atmosphere. Before this time, astronomers relied for the most part on the optical range of wavelengths for their information about the universe.

It was not until 1800 that the first sign of another way to look at the universe was discovered. While analyzing sunlight by separating the white light into a spectrum, the English astronomer Sir William Herschel noticed that a thermometer he placed in the dark area just outside the red limit of the spectrum registered an increase in temperature. In 1881, the American astronomer Samuel Pierpont Langley developed the bolometer, an electrical detector that measures heat over a broad range of wavelengths. In measuring the Sun's energy from a high altitude, Langley found that the radiant energy of the Sun extended far past the visible portion of the spectrum and far past the region that Herschel had discovered previously. Herschel had discovered the near infrared, whereas Langley was detecting the longer-wavelength middle infrared band.

Infrared radiation from the Sun was fairly simple to detect, but new, more sensitive instruments had to be developed before it was possible to detect the infrared from far distant sources. In 1856, near-infrared radiation was detected from the Moon, but it was not until the 1920's that it began to be detected from the other planets and bright stars. Available instruments were still unable to see into the far infrared. While working on superconductivity experiments in the late 1950's, a physicist named Frank Low began the development of new, more sensitive instruments. By the early 1970's, Low was among the first to attempt observations of the far infrared by leading observations aboard high-flying jets.

An infrared satellite was first proposed in the mid-1970's. NASA was facing troubled times with budget cuts, inflation, and cost overruns in other projects. It might have scrapped the project entirely except for the interest of the Dutch space agency. The Dutch had completed several successful satellite programs and were interested in collaborating on an infrared satellite. England then joined the project and it became known as the Infrared Astronomical Satellite program. The project was a difficult one, but the diplomatic aspects of an international collaboration helped to give the program stability, and the satellite was launched successfully in 1983.

NASA's Space Infrared Telescope Facility was planned for launch near the end of the millennium, its goal being to study the formation of stars, galaxies, and planets, and to search for comets and brown dwarf stars in the outer part of the solar system.

Divonna Ogier

Basic Bibliography

Disney, Michael. *The Hidden Universe.* New York: Macmillan, 1984. Discusses the underlying goals of modern astronomy. Gives an overview of the study of the universe in all wavelengths; highlights gravitation, the question of dark matter, cosmology, and the future of astronomy. Written for the general reader with some background in astronomy.

Editors of Time-Life Books. *The New Astronomy.* Alexandria, Va.: Time-Life Books, 1989. One volume of a series that examines different aspects of the universe and its study. Comprehensively covers all invisible astronomies, including high-energy astronomy and imaging techniques. Illustrated, suitable for the general reader with an interest in astronomy.

Henbest, Nigel. *Mysteries of the Universe.* New York: Van Nostrand Reinhold, 1981. Explores the limits of what is known about the universe. Ranges from theories about the origin of the solar system and the universe, exotic astronomy, and astronomy at invisible wavelengths.

Henbest, Nigel, and Michael Marten. *The New Astronomy.* New York: Cambridge University Press, 1983. Compares optical, infrared, ultraviolet, radio, and X-ray observations of well-known astronomical objects. For general readers.

Marten, Michael, and John Chesterman. *The Radiant Universe.* New York: Macmillan, 1980. An overview of imaging that is not accessible in visible wavelengths. Includes electronic processing as well as infrared and ultraviolet wavelength imaging. Beautiful pictures, with easy-to-read and informative text.

Tucker, Wallace, and Karen Tucker. *The Cosmic Enquirers.* Cambridge, Mass.: Harvard University Press, 1986. Gives a good picture of the state of modern astronomy in the context of its development and history. Introduces readers, through interviews, to the astronomers who make the science. Covers radio astronomy, high-energy astronomy, and infrared astronomy and ends with a chapter on the Hubble Space Telescope. Easy-to-read, biographically styled text.

Current Bibliography

Canary Islands Winter School on Astrophysics. *Infrared Astronomy: IV Canary Islands Winter School of Astrophysics.* Edited by A. Mampaso, M. Prieto, and F. Sanchez. Cambridge, England: Cambridge University Press, 1993.

McLean, Ian S., ed. *Infrared Astronomy with Arrays: The Next Generation.* Astrophysics and Space Science Library 190. Boston: Kluwer, 1994.

Predoctoral Astrophysics School. *Star Formation and Techniques in Infrared and Mm-Wave Astronomy: Lectures Held at the Predoctoral Astrophysics School V, Organized by the European Astrophysics Doctoral Network (EADN) in Berlin, Germany, 21 September-2 October 1992.* Edited by T. P. Ray and S. V. W. Beckwith. Lecture Notes in Physics 431. New York: Springer-Verlag, 1994.

Cross-References

Cosmic Microwave Background Radiation, 84; Cosmic Rays, 91; Cosmology, 97; New Astronomy, 621; Novas, Bursters, and X-ray Sources, 628; Quantum Cosmology, 767; X-ray and Gamma-ray Astronomy, 1068.